POSTMODERNISM AND PERFORMANCE

Postmodernism and Performance

NICK KAYE

St. Martin's Press   New York

First published in the United States of America in 1994 .

Printed in Hong Kong

ISBN 0–312–12023–0 (cloth)
ISBN 0–312–12024–9 (paper)

Library of Congress Cataloging-in-Publication Data
Kaye, Nick.
Postmodernism and performance / Nick Kaye.
p.   cm.
Includes bibliographical references and index.
ISBN 0–312–12023–0 (cloth). — ISBN 0–312–12024–9 (pbk.)
1. Theater.   2. Performing arts.   3. Postmodernism.   I. Title.
PN2037.K35   1994
792—dc20
                                              93–32470
                                                CIP

Contents

General Editor's Preface   vi
Acknowledgements   vii

Introduction: Limiting the Postmodern   1

1 From Postmodern Style to Performance   5

2 Theatricality and the Corruption of the Modernist Work 24

3 Looking Beyond Form: Foreman, Kirby, Wilson   46

4 Modern Dance and the Modernist Work   71

5 The Collapse of Hierarchies and a Postmodern Dance   90

6 Telling Stories: Narrative Against Itself   118

Conclusion: Postmodernism and Performance   144

Notes   147
Select Bibliography   163
Index   173

General Editor's Preface

In the past ten years, Theatre Studies has experienced remarkable international growth, students seeing in its marriage of the practical and the intellectual a creative and rewarding discipline. Some countries are now opening school and degree programmes in Theatre Studies for the first time; others are having to accommodate to the fact that a popular subject attracting large numbers of highly motivated students has to be given greater attention than hitherto. The professional theatre itself is changing, as graduates of degree and diploma programmes make their way through the 'fringe' into established theatre companies, film and television.

Two changes in attitudes have occurred as a result: first, that the relationship between teachers and practitioners has significantly improved, not least because many more people now have experience of both; secondly, that the widespread academic suspicion about theatre as a subject for study has at least been squarely faced, if not fully discredited, Yet there is still much to be done to translate the practical and educational achievements of the past decade into coherent theory, and this series is intended as a contribution to that task. Its contributors are chosen for their combination of professional and didactic skills, and are drawn from a wide range of countries, languages and styles in order to give some impression of the subject in its international perspective.

This series offers no single programme or ideology; yet all its authors have in common the sense of being in a period of transition and debate out of which the theory and practice of theatre cannot but emerge in a new form.

JULIAN HILTON

Acknowledgements

In the course of completing this book, many people have been generous with their time and interest and I have received invaluable support from institutions and funding bodies. The University of Warwick granted me a period of study leave which allowed the project to be completed. An important part of my research would not have been possible without financial support from the British Academy, the University of Warwick and the Joint School of Theatre Studies of the University of Warwick, which allowed me to undertake a period of study in New York. Here I was greatly assisted by the staff of the Museum of Modern Art, the Performing Arts Research Center, the Dance Collection and the Jerome Robbins Archive of the Recorded Moving Image of the New York Public Library at Lincoln Center. I should also like to thank those artists and other individuals whose generosity with their time, and help with source material, has been much appreciated. In particular, I should like to thank Michael Kirby, Joan Jonas, Richard Foreman, Ping Chong, Elsa Jacobson of the Brooklyn Academy of Music, Richard Schechner, George Ashley, and Bruce Allardyce of the Ping Chong Company. Finally, I should like to express my gratitude to the late John Cage for an interview of special value to this book, but which was conducted before this project was conceived.

The author and publishers wish to thank Peters Edition Ltd, London, for permission to reproduce *4'33"* and *0'00" (4'33" No. 2)* by John Cage.

Every effort has been made to trace all copyright holders, but if any have been inadvertently overlooked the publishers will be pleased to make the necessary arrangements at the first opportunity.

N. K.

To Diane

Introduction

Limiting the Postmodern

It would seem only reasonable to begin a book entitled *Postmodernism and Performance* by defining the term 'postmodern' and, in turn, the characteristics of 'postmodern theatre'. Any attempt to provide such an explanation, however, must consider first of all the difficulties that intrude upon any categorical definition of what the 'postmodern' actually *is*.

In *The End of Modernity* (Oxford, 1988) the philosopher Gianni Vattimo introduces the term 'postmodernity' by considering the significance of the prefix 'post-'. The condition of modernity, he argues, is dominated by the idea that the history of thought is a progressive 'enlightenment' which develops toward an ever more complete appropriation and reappropriation of its own 'foundations'.[1] Modernity, in this sense, is characterised by a consciousness of an 'overcoming' of past understandings and a striving toward future 'overcomings' in the name of a deeper recognition of that which is fundamentally legitimating and 'true', whether this is within science, the arts, morality or any other realm of thought or practice. In this context, however, the term 'postmodernity' finds itself in a peculiar position. In 'taking leave' of modernity, Vattimo argues, postmodernity is marked by a departure from the very process of overcoming that the prefix 'post-' would seem to suggest. Indeed, to use the term 'postmodernity' to indicate a literal overcoming of modernity would be to perpetuate, through a description of the postmodern, precisely that which one would define a departure from. It follows that if postmodernity indicates a 'taking leave' of this process of overcoming, then it must call into question the modernist projection forward, and so the striving toward foundation. Postmodernity, in this

1

sense, is a turning against modernity in a questioning of legitimacy which refuses to supplant that which is called into question with the *newly legitimate*.

In this context, the tensions in the term 'post-*modern*' are more easily seen. If 'postmodernity' indicates a calling into question of the modernist faith in legitimacy, then it marks modernity at its *end* rather than a true *surpassing* of modernity. It follows that one might understand 'postmodern' art and discourse as unravellings of modernist claims to legitimacy. Here the postmodern becomes complicated and multiple, occurring as phenomena which define, limit and subvert the cultural products, attitudes and assumptions of modernity. In this case the post-modern cannot be said to be properly 'free' of the modern, for the modern is the ground on which the postmodern stands, a ground with which it is in dispute and on which it is able to enter into dispute with itself. From this perspective, the problem of defining the features of a 'postmodern art' become clearer. First, in order to come to the post-modern, it seems, one must look toward the modern and the modernist.

Set against the 'critical overcoming' Vattimo describes, the various 'overturnings' of modern art can be read as struggling, through competing claim and counter-claim, towards a revelation of art's fundamental terms and values. The 'modernist work', in this sense, is one that is anxious to define itself, that overcomes the work of the recent past in a projection towards 'foundation', towards a revelation of its own unique and legitimating terms as art. It is to this process that those critics whose writing has tended to define the terms of the debate over the modernist work have looked. On precisely this basis, the American art critics Clement Greenberg and Michael Fried set out a clear and instrumental reading of the modernist work in painting and sculpture, a reading that has provided a model for influential descriptions of modern, modernist and postmodern forms of dance by the critic Sally Banes. As proponents of the modernist project, Greenberg and Fried's writing also provides a ground on which the idea of the self-legitimating work of art can be traced through the work of an earlier generation of writers on art and dance, including John Martin and Curt Sachs, as well as Suzanne Langer whose writing still shapes and influences dance theory and criticism.[2] Here, too, it becomes apparent that self-consciously 'modernist' criticism pursues the very ends that it ascribes to the 'modernist' work of art, seeking, in its address to particular works, to participate in an uncovering of the fundamental terms by which art operates.

For the critic whose sympathies lie with an unravelling of this notion of a legitimating foundation, however, a description of the postmodern in art presents a very different kind of problem. In so far as it critiques and upsets a 'modernist' striving toward foundation, the postmodern must occur as an anti-foundational disruption of precisely the move towards category and definition that a general or prescriptive account of the 'forms' and 'meanings' of postmodern art would produce. Ironically, it follows, in seeking to describe the 'postmodern' in art and performance the critic attempts to characterise that which is disruptive of categories and categorisations and which finds its identity through an evasion or disruption of conventions.

One cannot, from this perspective and with consistency, it follows, begin a study of the postmodern in performance by setting out a prescriptive view of what 'postmodern theatre' *is*. One might much more appropriately say what postmodern theatre *is not*. Evidently, this notion of the postmodern cannot readily be identified with 'conventional' theatre and drama. The forms of 'performance' considered here are 'wilfully' unconventional and 'experimental', acting, in one way or another, to upset or challenge the idea of what a painting, sculpture, dance or drama is. This 'postmodern' evasion of definition and category draws the critic, too, across disciplines and categories. Just as the idea of the modernist work and the notion of a 'postmodern style' emerge first of all in art criticism, so that 'performance' which occurs as a disruption of the projection towards the self-contained and self-supporting work of art emerges from the visual arts. Here, in addresses to exchanges, events and occurrences which disrupt the idea of the autonomous, 'auratic' work, various artists have sought to make visible 'events', occurrences and exchanges which can be considered in terms of the theatrical or the performative. In this respect, and after the modernist critic Michael Fried, this book supposes that the very idea of 'theatre' is disruptive of the 'modernist' attempt to entrench the work of art within a set of unique and exclusive terms, and that the 'postmodern' occurs as unstable, 'theatrical' and, in certain senses, 'interdisciplinary' evasions of definition and foundation.

This understanding of the postmodern also has consequences for criticism. If one accepts a 'postmodern' rejection of a final or stable foundation in art, then the 'foundation' the modernist project seeks to realise cannot be thought of as some independent thing toward which art and criticism strive. If the work of art cannot be legitimated *in its own terms*, then the very idea of the self-legitimating and self-supporting work which is in possession of its own value cannot be separated from the 'modernist' discourses of which, properly speaking, it is an effect. For the critic, this sites the 'problem' of the postmodern within criticism itself. Like the 'modernist work', the postmodern, here, is not something 'in' art and so 'out there' as an object to which criticism responds, but *is* an unravelling of the narrative of the modernist work, wherever and however this occurs. The postmodern, it follows, is inseparable from the texts and events which effect this unravelling; there is no 'authentic' or 'original' postmodernism around which various texts and events position themselves.

In this context, and rather than attempt to survey or 'sum up' the features of a postmodern theatre or performance, this study responds to the 'problem of definition' which might be said to constitute the postmodern. To this end, *Postmodernism and Performance* does not offer a definition of 'postmodern' forms and tropes, nor does it attempt a 'comprehensive' address to 'postmodern' theory or practice. Instead, the book seeks to act in a deliberately partial way, setting out and taking issue with readings of the postmodern in art, and of the modernist in art and dance, in order to trace out a series of *postmodern* disruptions. Taking as its point of departure the conflicts and exclusions produced by the model of the 'postmodern style', which, although first formulated in architectural criticism, has formed the basis of wide-ranging descriptions of 'postmodern' departures in painting, sculpture, literature, photography, television, film and aspects of dance and theatre, the study seeks to identify 'postmodern' instabilities with a specific notion of theatre and the theatrical. It is in this context that the study focuses on recent and contemporary North American performance, setting limits that allow a more effective deployment of the debts, influences and points of reference that can be read as lying between performances, against prescriptive readings of 'postmodern' tropes and figures. To this end the study deliberately sets historical readings against each other so as to challenge the limits of certain critical readings of the modern and postmodern. Finally, in engaging with the postmodernism debate in this way, *Postmodernism and Performance* seeks to fashion, through its own qualification and limitation of the postmodern, an appropriate address to the interdisciplinary sources and modes of a formally diverse range of performances, an address which could readily reach across a much broader range of work than can possibly be considered within the confines of this book alone.

Chapter 1

From Postmodern Style to Performance

In his account of the *Strada Novissima*, an exhibition of façades designed by some 30 architects and first shown in 1980 at the Venice Biennale under the title 'The Presence of the Past', Paolo Portoghesi describes a turning against the values and stylisations of modern architecture. Including the work of Robert Stern, Ricardo Bofill, Charles Moore, Robert Venturi, John Rauch and Denise Scott Brown, Aldo Rossi, the TAU Group, Hans Hollein and Portoghesi himself, among other European and American architects, the *Strada Novissima* marked a crystallisation of a rejection of modern design which can be traced back to the late 1960s.[1] In a flat opposition to modern architecture's valorisation of uncluttered geometrical form and its casting off of reference, symbol and the traditional grammar of architecture, Portoghesi describes a new '*architecture of communication*', an 'architecture of the image',[2] characterised by ironic plays with conventions and styles from the past. Observing the loss of faith in the modernist tenets of 'useful = beautiful', 'structural truth = aesthetic prestige', ' "form follows function" ... "ornament is crime," and so on',[3] Portoghesi argues that the *Strada Novissima* speaks of a widespread attack on the modernist aspiration to a 'pure language' of form. Significantly, too, Portoghesi takes such 'postmodern' design to be more than an 'overcoming' of modernist stylisations, more than 'a simple change of direction', but 'a refusal, a rupture, a renouncement'[4] of the fundamental assumptions legitimating the modernist rejection of the past.

For Portoghesi this disruption of the modern has two inter-related sources; at once a loss of faith in the 'narratives' of modernity and so in the legitimacy of the 'rationalist statute' of the modernist movement and, bound up with this, the practical verification of modern buildings by their users. In his declaration of the arrival of postmodern design, *Postmodern: The Architecture of Postindustrial Society* (New York, 1982), Portoghesi suggests that modern architecture has come to be judged by its natural product:

> the modern city, the suburbs without qualities, the urban environment devoid of collective values that has become an asphalt jungle and a dormitory; the loss of local character, of connection with the place: the terrible homogulation that has made the outskirts of the cities of the whole world similar to one another, and whose inhabitants have a hard time recognizing an identity of their own.[5]

In his detailed account of *The History of Postmodern Architecture* (London, 1988), Heinrich Klotz elaborates this process, tracing, in particular, the influence of Ludwig Mies van der Rohe's rejection of 'aesthetic speculation' in favour of function through the postwar proliferation of buildings based upon his early designs. Citing Mies's sketch for an office building of 1923 as a key prototype, Klotz describes the period from the early 1950s as one in which Mies's influential dictum that architectural design should achieve 'the maximum effect with the minimum expenditure of means'[6] gained a new importance as earlier aesthetics gave way to new priorities. As a consequence, Klotz concludes, and as commercial expediency overrode many of the solutions proposed by 'classical modernism' in favour of a narrow vocabulary of cost-efficient designs, the postmodern occurs as a break with an increasingly limited and limiting vocabulary in favour of a self-conscious play with fiction, representation, symbolisation and meaning.

In his lengthy survey, *Post-modernism: The New Classicism in Art and Architecture* (London, 1987), Charles Jencks, on whom Portoghesi draws and who participated as juror and exhibitor in the *Strada Novissima*, extends this stylistic model in a consideration of the 'emergent rules' of a postmodern art. Against the overriding unity, simplicity and functionalism of modernist architecture, Jencks reads a 'postmodern' fragmentation and discord, a mode of design which abandons the ideal of the 'finished totality "where no part can be added or subtracted except for the worse" (Alberti)' in favour of a ' "difficult whole" or "fragmented unity" '.[7] In opposition to the 'modern' aspiration to simplicity and a 'universally valid geometrical form',[8] Jencks sets a postmodern play with familiar languages and conventions which serves to disarm and disrupt particular readings of style, figure and form.

Jencks's formulation of the postmodern and the importance of his analysis becomes clearer in his description of particular pieces of work. In his account of James Stirling, Michael Wilford and Associates' *Neue Staatsgalerie, Stuttgart* (1977–84), which, he argues, is one of the 'high points' of postmodernism, and which he has presented in a number of forms,[9] Jencks sets out key aspects of the new mode of work. In a clear opposition to the modernist aspiration towards an overriding unification through style, the *Neue Staatsgalerie* is comprised not so much of a single building as 'a series of fragments placed on an acropolis (or car park)'.[10] The gallery complex embraces a variety of styles and conventions and openly sets conflicting architectural languages against each other. In this way the building fosters radically different interpretations amongst its visitors. According to Jencks:

> The young I talked to compared the building to the Pompidou Centre – a valid comparison only if one subtracts all the classical masonry ... The older people – a group of 'plein air' painters and some business-men – also liked the building but gave completely different readings. One group saw the complex as a Greco-Roman ruin, another as a typical German institution in the tradition of Schinkel's *Altes Museum.*[11]

This 'pluralism' is produced not simply by Stirling's readiness to take up aspects of both traditional and modern styles but by his refusal to synthesise the various languages he employs or offer any uniform set of conventions. In turn the various readings which may be made of the building tend themselves be qualified and declared as 'games', for none of them can effectively resolve those conflicts Stirling has sought to heighten. It is precisely this 'pluralism' that Jencks sees as the underlying perspective of the postmodern style. Stirling's presentation of a clear, strong and unresolved dichotomy between traditionalism and modernism leads Jencks to suggest that:

> if one conclusion is drawn throughout this site it is that both positions are legitimate and partial. Neither can win, nor can there be a transcendent Hegelian synthesis. There is simply the juxtaposition of two world views with the ironic reversal of both: the Modernist high-tech mode has been used for symbolic ornament, while the traditional rustication functions to clothe the volumes.[12]

Stirling's use of irony and paradox further qualifies this eclecticism. Jencks points to the gallery parking garage, where, having removed several blocks of masonry, Stirling allows them to fall on the ground before the building 'like ruins set in an eighteenth century landscape'.[13] The holes in the wall that these blocks reveal are, however, functional, acting as vents for the garage, while 'the fallen blocks are a sham. The sandstone and travertine of the building are only an inch thick and are suspended from a steel frame – the reality of construction today.'[14] Rather than fully take up the implications of the conventions he appropriates, Stirling transforms them through irony and juxtaposition, creating a work in which conventions are displaced, undercut and made ambiguous.

Extending his description of these 'emergent rules' through a consideration of the overlapping qualities and practices that surround this central style, Jencks goes on to catalogue the 'outbreak of parody, nostalgia and pastiche' as well as more complex means in painting and sculpture such as 'anamnesis, or suggested recollection', 'enigmatic allegory' and 'suggested narrative'[15] in work which has found a new 'complex relation to the past'.[16] Most prevalent, he argues, is a *double-coding*, use of irony, ambiguity and contradiction'[17] and he goes on to list a variety of related techniques and rhetorical figures that are important to the style, amongst them 'paradox, oxymoron, ambiguity ... disharmonious harmony, amplification, complexity and contradiction, irony, eclectic quotation, anamnesis, anastrophe, chiasmus, ellipsis, elision and erosion'.[18]

Such departures from the vocabulary and aesthetic of the dominant modes of modern architecture speak not simply of a shift of 'style' but of a new attitude towards the nature and purpose of stylisation. Evidently, for many modern architects, the move towards economy, simplicity and functionalism was underwritten by political and moral imperatives. In his 'Principles of Bauhaus Production' of 1926 Walter Gropius set the making of art against the industrial production process, calling for an architecture that, defined in strictly functional terms, would give up 'romantic gloss and wasteful frivolity'[19] in favour of a limited vocabulary of primary forms and colours. For Frank Lloyd Wright, and despite his own deviations from the modernist ideal,[20] this question of legitimacy could be addressed in purely aesthetic terms. Wright's influential call for an 'Organic Architecture' of 1911 epitomised the modernist desire for an overarching unification through style. Here, all aspects of the building, including chairs, tables, cabinets 'even musical instruments' would be 'of the building, never fixtures upon it'.[21] In the writing of Le Corbusier, in particular, the connection between this straining towards function, simplicity, a vocabulary of basic geometrical forms and a revelation of the essential and so legit-imating terms of architecture becomes explicit. In *Towards a New Architecture* (London, 1927) he presents the first of three reminders to architects, in which he asserts that:

> Architecture is the masterly, correct and magnificent play of masses brought together in light. Our eyes are made to see forms in light; light and shade reveal these forms; cubes, cones, spheres, cylinders or pyramids are the great primary forms which light reveals to advan-tage; the image of these is distinct and tangible within us. It is for that reason that these are *beautiful forms, the most beautiful forms.*[22]

In this context, Portoghesi, Klotz and, particularly, Jencks's con-sideration of 'postmodern style' may be understood in terms of a falling away of the idea of a fundamental core or legitimating essence which might privilege one vocabulary over another. This loss of faith is evident in the rubrics Jencks himself compiles. Whereas modernist architecture, in striving towards its own foundation, is concerned with its own unique properties, with a purpose and presence to be, literally, imposed upon the landscape, the vocabulary of 'postmodern' architecture is concerned to put its own purpose and presence into question. The tropes Jencks lists engage in seemingly self-effacing and playful or quizzical denials of the forms and figures which they bring before the user or viewer. In these respects, this postmodernism is constituted by a playing of languages and figures against each other and through this a disarming of the very ele-ments of which it consists.

This idea of the postmodern clearly has a resonance that goes beyond the realm of architectural practice. Extending Portoghesi and Jencks's analyses of architecture, Linda Hutcheon, in *A Poetics of Postmodern-ism* (London, 1988), and while privileging literature, suggests that anal-ogous work has appeared in painting, sculpture, film, video, dance, television and music. Beginning with the notion that postmodernism is a phenomenon that at once 'uses and abuses, installs and then subverts, the very concepts it challenges',[23] Hutcheon argues that recent popular 'paradoxical' fiction has given rise to work which is specifically post-modern. In her discussion of such novels as Gabriel Garcia Marquez's *One Hundred Years of Solitude*, Gunther Grass's *The Tin Drum*, John Fowles's *A Maggot*, Nigel Williams's *Star Turn* and Salman Rushdie's *Shame*, Hutcheon focuses upon an ironic and self-conscious use of tech-nique married to an acute awareness of historical context and process.

Here, she suggests, a genre of work arises which, in addressing the writing of history, not only considers its own 'constructing, ordering and selecting processes'[24] but in doing so offers self-reflexive narratives which address their own implication and participation in the historical processes they critique.

In Rushdie's *Shame*, for example, Hutcheon cites the narrator's open address to his own position as 'insider/outsider' writing about the events of Pakistan:

> *Outsider! Trespasser! You have no right to this subject!* ... I know: nobody ever arrested me. Nor are they ever likely to. *Poacher! Pirate! We reject your authority. We know you, with your foreign language wrapped around you like a flag: speaking about us in your forked tongue, what can you tell but lies?* I reply with more questions: is history to be considered the property of the participants solely? In what courts are such claims staked, what boundary commissions map out the territories?[25]

Writing in English, Rushdie addresses the process by which, in the wake of its formation, Pakistani history was written, and so *rewritten*, in imported tongues. In doing so, however, Rushdie implicitly acknowledges the implication of his own writing in the processes he critiques, forced, as he is, by the very history he recounts, to write in England and in English. In this respect, Rushdie offers a text that brings its own position into question, and that draws the reader towards an awareness that its subject-matter is to be found in part through the way it reveals itself to be enmeshed within and compromised by the very conflicts it considers.

Other work uses a variety of analogous techniques to a similar end. In *Foe*, J. M. Coetzee addresses the question of 'the relation of "story" and "history" writing to "truth" and exclusion'[26] in a play on Defoe's *Robinson Crusoe*. Here Coetzee supposes that Defoe derived his story from a subsequently silenced woman and in doing so allows himself to explore the creation of interpenetrating perspectives and fictions that come to surround the event, including, by implication, his own. In contrast Marquez's *One Hundred Years of Solitude* and Grass's *Tin Drum* use parodic reference to other texts in order to put their own authority and, by implication, the authority of any act of writing into question, so undermining, through their own overt construction of historical discourses, the distinctions between history and fiction.

From the early 1980s various theatre performances have emerged which can be read against these models of the postmodern. The work of Ping Chong, who collaborated closely with Meredith Monk until the late 1970s, has been read in terms analogous to the 'fragmented unity' or 'difficult whole' Jencks outlines. Jonathan Kalb describes Ping Chong's use of a 'fragmented narrative' in pieces which 'contained story elements, but [whose] purpose was not mainly to tell a story'.[27] Noel Carroll, in an article for *The Drama Review*, goes further, noting that in this multi-media work:

> each constituent medium, each channel of address is usually discreet: Chong shifts rather than mixes media. Each new medium introduces a separate issue rather than building toward a unified effect or theme ... Only gradually does one become aware of who the characters are; since only selected bits of events are represented, one grasps the outline of the underlying story slowly, while many details remain obscure.[28]

Under the direction of Elizabeth LeCompte, and beginning with the third play of their *Rhode Island Trilogy*, *Nyatt School* (1978), the Wooster Group have combined excerpts from plays with images, actions, film and sound drawn from a variety of sources to produce often disruptive and alarming performance collages. *Nyatt School* is structured around six 'examinations' of *The Cocktail Party*, each of which is set against material ranging from a recording of the play featuring Alec Guinness to reconstructions of popular comedy-horror sequences. *Point Judith* (1979) is structured around a 13 minute-long rendering of *Long Day's Journey Into Night* pared down to its most famous lines and played at high speed. *Route 1 & 9 (The Last Act)* (1981) sets extracts from Thornton Wilder's *Our Town* against reconstructed blackface routines by Pigmeat Markham as well as video and film. *L.S.D. (... Just the High Points ...)* (1984) combines a 30-minute performance of *The Crucible* with reconstructions of the performers' experiences of taking LSD and the reproduction through performance of a film record of a public debate between Dr Timothy Leary and Gordon Liddy. *Frank Dell's Temptation of St Anthony* (1987) collages, among other things, rehearsals of a stand-up routine, after Lenny Bruce, and televised interviews with naked respondents in the manner of New York's 'Channel J' with images and narrative lines drawn from Flaubert's *La Tentation de Saint Antoine*, while *Brace Up!* (1990) appropriates Chekhov's *Three Sisters*. Not only do the Wooster Group draw their material from a wide variety of sources, but in their juxtaposition of 'found' elements they resist integrating the various aspects of their presentations into a unified whole. Frequently, these conflicts are amplified by corresponding contrasts in style, heightening a sense of quotation, where texts, sequences and images are set against each other in such a way that they come to stand on uncertain and unstable ground.

In the later work of Joan Jonas, who trained as a sculptor in the early 1960s and participated in the 'post-modern' American dance of the 1960s and early 1970s, familiar narratives, genres and styles are treated in ways which seem calculated to disrupt their ability to unify a performance. *Upside Down and Backwards* (1979) is structured around a collage of retold and invented narrative lines. Beginning with recordings of her own versions of two Grimm Brothers' fairy tales, *The Frog Prince* and *The Boy Who Went Out to Learn Fear*, Jonas presents a literal paragraph-by-paragraph montage of the stories read in reverse with actions, images and descriptions that disrupt and digress from the sequence. As the piece progresses so the narratives collapse into each other, finally merging into a new, dense and fractured story. Rather than offer its audience a clear way through the piece, a central line and sequence through which meaning and significance can be clarified, Jonas's narratives are incorporated into the performance in such a way that they undercut and subvert one another.

Under the terms of this model, one might go on to consider Karen Finley's use of 'pornographic' language and imagery in monologue performances such as *The Constant State of Desire* (1986) and *We Keep Our Victims Ready* (1992) which have been accused both of subverting and confirming the abuses she would vilify as she replays them before her audiences. Finley's work might be contrasted with Laurie Anderson's appropriations and displacements of popular imagery and her telling of paradoxical stories in pieces such as *United States* (1983)[29] as well as her breaching of the conventional distinctions between fine art, video art, music video, performance art and rock performance. Both Anderson and the Wooster Group's multi-media performances can be related to Yvonne Rainer's multi-media work of the early 1970s in which a self-conscious manipulation of narrative elements serves to invite readings of character and plot while pointedly resisting any final or single coherence. Emerging out of her work with the Judson Dance Theater and The Grand Union, such pieces as *Rose Fractions* (1969) and *This is the story of a woman who ...* (1972) employ a form of 'bricolage' in which narrative development is displaced and undermined as the audience's attention is drawn from one narrative element to another, or between conflicting narrative promises. Alternatively, the Mabou Mines' *Red Horse Animation* (1972) employs a single narrative which self-consciously traces its own animation, observing and drawing attention to the coherences it variously offers and withdraws, in a subversion of narrative stability and transparency. One might go on to address Spalding Gray's treatment of monologue and persona,[30] Richard Schechner's deconstruction of texts such as *Don Juan* through game-structures and antithetical narratives and events,[31] Meredith Monk's use of imagery and story in such pieces as *Vessel* and *Education of a Girl Child* of the early 1970s or Kathy Acker's overtly intertextual texts for the theatre such as *Lulu* (1987) and *Birth of the Poet* (1985).

Against postmodern style

Despite its prolific nature, however, and especially where it is extended across the arts in this manner, the model of a 'postmodern style' raises questions concerning how one acts critically in dealing with the 'postmodern'. In drawing on an even expanded list of self-effacing or paradoxical tropes which are taken as characterising a 'postmodern art', one risks moving unself-consciously away from that which one would identify. Despite the fact that these 'postmodern' figures exemplify an attitude towards their own presence and value which seems quite opposed to the 'modernist' reaching towards foundation, the very fact of this opposition tends to effect the surpassing of one 'style' with another. Ironically, this model even sets out a stylistic paradigm of a 'postmodern' pluralism and fragmentation for which there is no 'modern' correlate precisely because of the contradictory and fragmentary nature of modernism in the arts. It follows that, despite its declaration of a new 'complex' relation to the past, this model of the postmodern risks a characteristically 'modern' shrugging off of past and present alternatives.

This exclusivity becomes particularly evident in an address to theatre and performance. The work of the Wooster Group, Ping Chong, Joan Jonas, Yvonne Rainer and others who employ a 'fragmented' style in presentations which might be read as incorporating that which they challenge in a 'postmodern' parody,[32] are closely bound to other very different kinds of presentation. The productions of Richard Foreman and Robert Wilson are evidently important to the Wooster Group's work, and can be read as elaborating distinctly 'postmodern' contingencies and fragmentations, yet neither Foreman nor Wilson's pieces exemplify a postmodern 'quotation' or 'double-coding'. In turn, both Foreman and Wilson's work can be set against various departures of performance art and dance which attack self-consciously *modernist* practices yet whose 'style', where the idea of a style can be sustained, is quite removed from the characteristics of a 'post-modern style'. As if to compound these complexities, both Joan Jonas and Yvonne Rainer's multi-media performance, and their address to narrative, developed from presentations which, in drawing explicitly on minimal art, overtly rejected a play with conventional form and figure.

In response to this, and instead of looking toward an elaboration of a 'postmodern style' through a separating out of contrasting figures and tropes or even of differing postmodern 'genres', one might more usefully acknowledge criticism's implication in the construction of the postmodern and ask questions of this model itself. Thus the tendency of this account of a 'postmodern practice' towards exclusion and prescription might be challenged through a reconsideration of two of its principal aspects; first, its dispute with the modernist claim to the work's possession of its own identity and, in this context, the 'postmodern' claim to a new and 'newly complex' relation to the past. In this way, one might set the ground for a reading of the postmodern across a more diverse range of work before returning, finally, to performances that can be linked with this attitude to 'style'.

Meaning and the postmodern

In exploring contradictions and weaknesses within Ferdinand de Saussure's account of the functioning of language, Jacques Derrida sets out an understanding of language, and of the functioning of the sign, in which meaning is never fully *present*. Set against the method and import of Derrida's analysis, the 'postmodern' dispute with foundation can be qualified both in terms of a departure from the modern and a self-reflexive turning of what would become the 'work' against the forms and figures upon which it ostensibly depends.

Saussure's structural linguistics rests upon the idea that language operates as a self-contained, self-regulating system upon which the identity and functioning of its individual elements depend. Against the understanding of language as an historically determined phenomenon consisting of an aggregate of elements and rules which have 'acquired' meanings, Saussure sets out a description of language as a system always complete in itself and which functions independently of its historical aspect. Key to this is his distinction between the two aspects of any linguistic system; between *parole* and *langue*. Language, Saussure argues, is always manifested as parole, as a specific use of particular elements, and yet this use is always dependent upon the langue, the set of rules and relationships which constitute the system of language and whose existence is implicit in any use of any of its elements. Through this relationship, Saussure re-reads an earlier understanding of the constitution of the sign. Conventionally, a sign can be understood to consist of two aspects: a signifier (a sound, mark, movement and so on) and a signified (a concept or unit of meaning). It is through the joining of signifier and signified that the sign comes into being and presents itself as meaningful. By drawing this reading into the context of the functioning of parole and langue Saussure is able to argue that the relationship between a particular signifier and signified is not determined by any 'fitness' of one to the other, but is purely a function of the self-contained structure of language itself.

Saussure's argument leads to two radical conclusions concerning the operation of language. In the first place, if the joining of a signifier to a signified is purely a function of a conventional and self-contained structure, it follows that the referent, or that to which the sign refers, does not play a part in the production of meaning. As a self-contained system, the functioning of language is not dependent upon anything beyond its own terms. Indeed, Saussure takes language itself to be the pre-condition to thought and so to any knowledge of that to which language may refer. In this context, the full implication of the conventional nature of language for the functioning of the signifier becomes clearer. If the joining of a particular signifier to a particular signified is determined only by the arbitrary relationships which make up the language system, then the ability of a signifier to join with a signified is at each moment dependent upon the signifier's relationship to all the other elements of which the system consists. In practice, as Saussure points out, this means that the reading of a signifier literally involves, at the moment of reading, the elimination of all other possibilities which the structure holds. It follows that meaning, in the shape of the signified, is not brought into play by what the signifier *is*, not by any positive value or quality it *possesses*, but only by the set of differences and so oppositions out of which the particular structure is made up.

One can, however, and after Derrida, set the very self-contained nature of this system against itself. By supposing that the signifier functions through its difference from other signifiers, and yet that through this difference the signifier is able to join with a signified, Saussure can be accused of supposing that there is a realm of the signified, and so of meaning, somehow existing beyond the functioning of the signifier.

Only by gaining access to such a realm can the play of *difference*, by which the signifier functions, result in the *presence* of meaning. Plainly, though, any such realm would both precede and exist beyond language as Saussure describes it, for neither the signifier nor the signified can have an independent existence. It would follow from this that the very set of oppositions which serve, in Saussure's system, to make the sign meaningful, cannot in themselves allow meaning to become *present*.

To put this system into question in this way, however, is to doubt the very 'decidability' of meaning. Within Saussure's conception of language, the ability of the signifier to make a relationship with the signified is dependent not upon what the signifier *is* but upon what it *is not*. Signification, then, is a function not of presence but of absence and difference, for the signifier functions only with reference to all those possibilities the system holds and which it is differentiated from. It follows that where the signifier is cut off from the anchor of an independent signified, where the unit of meaning becomes inseparable from the functioning of the signifier, then, paradoxically, meaning becomes subject to the same processes of differentiation which permit the functioning of the signifier. Thus, meaning is always being defined not simply in terms of what it *is* but in terms of *what it is not*. Here, it follows, where 'the signified always already functions as signifier',[33] the sign can never be self-identical, never fully in possession of 'meaning', for the move toward the signified finds itself caught in the endless reference between signifiers, and so a reading which is beyond closure.

This disjoining not only of the sign from the referent but of the signifier from the independent signified has profound consequences. In deconstructing the 'transcendental signified', Derrida acts on the assumption that, as an effect of the uncertain and undecidable play of signifiers, the signified is always subject to the play of difference and deferral within any linguistic system, always subject to a 'differance'.[34] Importantly, too, Derrida does not 'overcome' Saussure in the name of another foundational account of the operation of language and the functioning of meaning, but acts in such a way as to inhabit Saussure's terms while calling them into question. Through such criticism, Derrida challenges by his very means fundamental assumptions of criticism and philosophy, acting to subvert claims to the transparency of language and the possibility of uncontested meaning by deploying the contradictions texts suppress, and which are the result of this very slippage, against themselves.

After Derrida's proposition, then, and in terms of the work of art, the modernist projection towards foundation can be read as an attempt to overcome the arbitrariness and instability of the sign.[35] In striving toward 'essence' the modernist work seeks to realise qualities and values which are legitimate *in their own terms*, and so to transcend the play of difference Derrida reveals in an appeal to the 'transcendental signified' and so the *presence* of meaning. The postmodern disruption of this modernism, it follows, would occur as a disruption of the illusion of the self-identical and unitary sign, and so as an uncovering of the uncertain and indefinite play between elements the modernist projection towards foundation attempts to suppress. Consistently with this, however, one must conclude that the figures or terms out of which the 'postmodern work' is constituted cannot properly be said to be in *possession* of its 'meanings', for here the postmodern occurs as a disruption of this very claim to meaning.

Equally, and on this basis, one might go on to extend a reading of the postmodern through the disjoining of the signifier from the signified and in doing so question the idea that the postmodern rests upon or defines itself in relation to the modern. Here, the postmodern would entail a giving over of the modernist concern for singularity, depth and the stability of meaning to a free play of signifiers, to exhibitions of fragmentation and multiplicity, where meaning is shifting and undecidable. For Jean Baudrillard, this reconsideration of the functioning of the sign leads to a conflation of the signifier and the referent through which the operation of contemporary signifying systems may be read. In an echo of the postmodern style's play with codes, Baudrillard takes the contemporary condition to be that of the simulacrum, the material imitation, the copy without an original, the 'hyperreal'; a condition without 'transcendence or depth'[36] and marked by an endless parade and exchange of equivalences.

In both these cases, the corollary of the postmodern disruption of the modernist claim to foundation is that the postmodern cannot, with consistency, be defined in terms of a given set of formal elements without a reversion to the modernist claim that meaning (and so the signified) resides 'within' and so is 'present to' the work of art *in its own terms*. One can conclude here, then, that the postmodern cannot be identified with particular figures or forms precisely because the 'postmodern' occurs as a displacement and subversion of the very terms of which it would seem to consist.

While such a reconsideration of the functioning of the sign permits a thinking of the postmodern in terms of a declaration of the undecidability of meaning, Jean-François Lyotard's understanding of the contingent nature of language-systems allows an extension of this formulation in terms of narrative and narrativity. In *The Postmodern Condition: A Report on Knowledge* (Manchester, 1984), Lyotard reads the 'critical overcoming' through which the 'modern' reaches toward foundation in terms of the conflict between differing systems of knowledge. The modern, here, involves an act of 'totalization', an appeal to 'metanarrative', to a story that can explain the true meaning of all other stories. Conversely, the postmodern occurs as an awareness of the contingent nature of systems of knowledge. Thus, Lyotard suggests:

> I will use the term *modern* to designate any science that legitimates itself with reference to a metadiscourse ... making an explicit appeal to some grand narrative, such as the dialectics of the Spirit, the hermeneutics of meaning, the emancipation of the rational or working subject, or the creation of wealth.[37]

While:

> Simplifying to the extreme, I define *postmodern* as incredulity toward metanarratives.[38]

Lyotard's distinction rests upon the idea that all knowledge, including scientific knowledge, ultimately draws its legitimacy from agreements made by participants in a language-game, agreements constructed and perpetuated through the process by which knowledge is imparted and received. In this sense all knowledge is narrative knowledge, for all knowledge depends for its legitimacy upon values and beliefs constructed and confirmed by a process of telling, and so an active relationship between addressor and addressee. In this context, Lyotard takes narrative to have two aspects: *figure*, the event of narrativity, or the telling, and *discourse*, the process by which narrative represents and gives meaning. The modern, in its appeal to metanarrative, it follows, suppresses the event of its own narrativity, emphasising *discourse* over *figure*. Conversely, the postmodern is marked by an awareness of the event of narrativity; the contingent aspect of narrative that is so completely *other* to discourse that it cannot be incorporated, accounted for or 'totalized' by it. Here the 'postmodern' indicates a moment of struggle between narratives, or systems of knowledge, in which the awareness of *figure* disrupts the claim of *discourse* to universality. The postmodern occurs as a moment in which 'no single instance of narrative can exert a claim to dominate narratives by standing beyond it';[39] where the 'grand narrative' is given over to the 'little narrative' and the telling of *the* story is displaced by the telling of *a* story that looks toward its own displacement.

Lyotard's account of 'postmodern art' extends these terms. Here the postmodern cannot be described as a stable category for it occurs as a breaking down or evasion of categories, a radical scepticism towards and transgression of that which is *known*. For Lyotard, this idea of the postmodern as an instability undermines the commonsense view that the postmodern is that which follows the modern. In 'Answering the Question: What is Postmodernism?', he asserts that 'a work can become modern only if it is first postmodern. Postmodernism ... is not modernism at its end but in its nascent state, and this state is constant.'[40] Taken as a moment in which the terms in play are disrupted, as a profoundly disruptive breaking of rules, the postmodern in art becomes deeply implicated within the formulation of the modern as 'a tradition against itself'.[41] On being asked what art might be considered postmodern, Lyotard responds:

> All that has been received, if only yesterday ... must be suspected. What space does Cezanne challenge? The Impressionists'. What object do Picasso and Braque attack? Cezanne's. What presupposition does Duchamp break with in 1912? That which says one must make a painting, be it cubist. And Buren questions that other presupposition which he believes had survived untouched by the work of Duchamp: the place of presentation in the work.[42]

In this sense, the term 'postmodern art' is a contradictory formulation, describing an occurrence which at once refers to and escapes from the languages by which it is recognised. Postmodern art is, ironically from the critic's point of view, an occurrence beyond categories; it is that which, in Bill Readings reading of Lyotard, 'both is and is not art at the same time'.[43] Such notions exemplify the postmodern as an instability, as an evasion, a making visible of uncertainties or contingencies. In making such an equation, these readings implicate the postmodern 'event' in that which it precedes and surrounds, looking towards the possibility of its future transformation, and so of the recurrence of the modern.

Here, again, the postmodern is resistant to prescription and exclusivity. Occurring as a crisis forced into being by a breaking of rules or a reversal of terms, the 'postmodern' indicates a calling into question of the languages, styles and figures through which it is seen. Against this, one could set Jencks's and Hutcheon's accounts of treatments of styles and discourses, such as 'traditionalism and modernism', 'history and fiction', in such a way that the conventional oppositions through which they secure their identity and efficacy are called into question. In this way, the very ground on which the 'work' depends is rendered unstable, as the languages by which it is constituted are deployed in such a way as to make visible problems and limitations which cannot be resolved or transcended. This 'postmodernism' is synonymous with a kind of *excess*; an event or events produced by a clash or subversion of the rules, terms and conventions out of which the work would be constituted. It follows that the postmodern in art is subversive and transgressive, that it occurs as a critical and sceptical stepping beyond bounds, a disruption that purposefully upsets the terms by which the 'work of art' would constitute itself.

History and the postmodern

This qualification of the postmodern also puts into question the nature of the new and 'newly complex' address to the past with which the 'postmodern style' is often identified. If language is a site of conflict between discourses which act to construct values and perspectives without *a priori* claim to truth, then the writing of history must be subject to the struggle between narratives. It follows from this that the past cannot simply be considered to be 'out there', as a thing which is somehow 'available', but must be read as an effect of the very narratives that would seek to describe it. Here, language itself must be seen as limiting and shaping any view of history, while the historical narrative must be understood as rooted in and acting to legitimate contemporary forms, assumptions and ideas.

It follows from this, though, that the 'postmodern' address to 'historical' material should be identified with a loss of faith in the efficacy of the very historical and theoretical models that legitimate the modern 'overcoming' of the past. Perversely, while the 'modernist' project rejects the past precisely *because* it can be read, understood and so transcended, the postmodern self-consciously 'replays' images of a past that cannot be known, but that can only be constructed and reconstructed through a play of entirely contemporary references to the *idea* of the past.

This upsetting of the writing of history not only has consequences for an understanding of the 'postmodern' 'presence of the past' but to a reading of the history of the postmodern itself. Here, where the distinctions between history, theory, criticism and fiction become blurred as each is seen to be a discourse which creates the 'object' it would address, the perspicacity of all theory and discourse is threatened. In this context, Baudrillard understands the very idea of the 'object' of criticism to be a product of the desire for the definitively *meaningful*; a desire, it would follow, that is played out most fully through the modernist projection toward foundation. In *The Ecstasy of Communication* he argues:

> The critique of objects was based on signs saturated with meaning, along with their phantasies and unconscious logic as well as their prestigious differential logic. Behind this dual logic lies the anthro-pological dream: the realm of the object existing beyond and above exchange and use, above and beyond equivalence ... [44]

It follows from this that a history of the development of a 'postmod-ern style' cannot be accepted as a 'true' explanation of how a store of figures and styles from the past became newly available to contemporary artists, for such a history effects a 'backward glance'[45] which acts to construct the very notion of the postmodern style it seeks to describe.

With these qualifications in mind, and instead of attempting to con-struct a single history, one might come to consider the postmodern in terms of the interaction of different histories and the various descriptions of the modern and the postmodern which they construct. Thus Jencks's account of a 'progression' of styles toward a 'full-blown' postmodern-ism might be set against Umberto Eco's description of the avant-garde's destruction of itself through its attempt to 'deface the past'. Eco's account is, in fact, analogous to Jencks's, reading the postmodern in terms of an ironic quotation of familiar elements. Yet in using the figure of a self-destruction rather than a progression forward, Eco draws dif-ferent meanings around these tropes. Rather than suppose that the post-modern's 'return to the past' promises a 'new classicism', Eco traces a process by which the impossibility of its erasure leads to an ironic atti-tude towards the act of remembering. Since the past cannot be destroyed, he suggests, 'because its destruction leads to silence', it 'must be revisited: but with irony, not innocently'.[46]

Alternatively, that work which would seem to undermine the legitimacy of the self-contained work of art might be set against the modernist projection towards an autonomous aesthetic sphere and an absolute distinction between the respective arts. In *Sociology of Post-modernism* (London, 1990), Scott Lash, associating non-realist and anti-realist modernist painting with the differentiation of the aesthetic sphere from the political and the social, describes the postmodern in terms of a de-differentiation, a 'transgression of the boundaries that separates the aesthetic from other cultural spheres'.[47] In the work of art this de-differentiation takes the form of an explicit transgression and confusion of category, a 'postmodernist refusal to separate the author from his or her work or the audience from the performance'.[48]

More radically, but reflecting the same process in an extension of Lyotard's description of the postmodern, Thomas Docherty, in *After Theory: Post-modernism/Post-Marxism* (London, 1990), offers an account of art and criticism in the 'wake' of theory. In this context, the 'postmodern work' emerges as an evasion of categories, occurring not so much as a 'thing', as a 'rootless movement'; a work or act of writing existing in paradoxical or transgressive forms and in a perpetual and anti-foundational flight from itself. Here, ironically, postmodern strategies share the modern preoccupation with the rules and forms of art, yet in the event of the postmodern these rules are sought out not in the name of an essence but in an attempt to evade the realisation of a self-legitimating narrative. The postmodern in art, then, takes on the nascent state Lyotard ascribes to the postmodern condition, seeking always to postpone the possibility of the 'modern' and so its own final definition.

Performance and the postmodern

If the postmodern occurs as a disruption of a striving toward foundation, as an unravelling of the *meaningful*, then one cannot prescribe the features of a 'postmodern art' either according to its 'meanings' or the features which might 'best' represent it. Similarly, if one cannot have access to a history of the postmodern, one cannot impartially limit the forms of the postmodern through a definition of the history and purposes of the modern. Indeed, here and in both these respects, the postmodern occurs as an unravelling of precisely such definitions and limits through its own dispute with foundation. At the same time, though, this notion of what one *cannot* say looks toward a certain kind of circumscription of the postmodern in art.

If, as Linda Hutcheon suggests, parody might be considered 'a perfect postmodern form', then perhaps performance may be thought of as a primary postmodern mode. Where the postmodern in art, literature and performance is identified with a disruption, with instabilities precipitated by a challenge to the 'totalising' capacity of the terms in play, then the postmodern might be best conceived of as something that *happens*. Here, Hutcheon's 'parody' may itself be understood as giving rise to an 'event', an instability forced into being by a strategy or figure which challenges and upsets its own definition.

Critically, too, this idea of an 'occurrence', of the postmodern as something that 'happens', allows a formulation of the 'postmodern event' which breaks free from specific forms and figures. Such a postmodern 'theatricality' does not supersede Hutcheon's notion of a postmodern parody, or Jencks's 'double-coding', but coexists with it, as a moment *produced* by it. 'Theatricality', in this sense, is not some*thing*, but is an effect, and an ephemeral one at that. It is in terms of this instability, of this *excess* produced by the figures in play, that one might then speak of a moment which is both 'theatrical' or 'performative' and properly *postmodern*.

In this context, the condition of 'performance' may be read, in itself, as tending to foster or look towards postmodern contingencies and instabilities. More than any other mode of work, one might argue, a 'performance' vacillates between presence and absence, between displacement and reinstatement. It is for precisely these reasons that both theatre and the condition of theatricality have been read as peculiarly resistant to the modernist project and even as necessarily effecting a corruption of the modernist ideal.[49]

At the same time, though, this very reading of the postmodern throws into question the oppositions such a privileging of medium and form would rest upon. Plainly, this 'postmodern' moment is not the property of any particular discipline. The work addressed within the parameters of this study, alone, emerges variously in a reconceiving of the 'object' in art, in the extension of this conception of the 'object' into theatre-presentations, in an unravelling, through dance, of a modernist projection beyond performance's ephemerality and contingency, and, finally, and after the postmodern style, in subversions of and clashes between narrative elements. In so far as they 'are' postmodern, these presentations are disruptive and evasive, occurring as questionings of limits and boundaries, as threats, even, to the terms by which they themselves invite definition. The postmodern in art and performance, here, occurs as a making visible of contingencies or instabilities, as a fostering of differences and disagreements, as transgressions of that upon which the promise of the work itself depends and so a disruption of the move toward containment and stability.

Chapter 2

Theatricality and the Corruption of the Modernist Work

In identifying the postmodern in art with a disruption of the move toward self-containment and self-sufficiency, one can readily set a 'postmodern' play with appropriated figures and forms against very different kinds of presentation.

Despite what would seem to be a complete removal from the 'conventional' vocabulary of theatre and a 'postmodern' eclecticism, the minimal art of the late 1960s was not only a touchstone for Michael Fried's seminal defence of the modernist project, but also for a wide variety of entries into theatre and performance. For Richard Foreman, Michael Kirby and Robert Wilson, as well as the Body Artist Vito Acconci and performance artists such as Joan Jonas, minimalism and minimal art would seem to have offered a direct intersection between art and theatre. The critical and aesthetic vocabulary of minimalism also provided a means by which dancers such as Yvonne Rainer could more effectively define their rejection of the dominant modes of American modern dance, while artists such as Robert Morris, whose work was influential in defining a minimalist aesthetic, readily stepped into dance and performance.[1] In this context, minimalism provides a meeting between a critical defence of the modernist work which explicitly opposes 'theatricality' in art, and a range of performance practices and interactions between art and theatre which challenge the ideal of the self-contained and self-determining work of art.

Theatricality and the modernist work

For Clement Greenberg, the influential theorist and proponent of American modernism, the emergence of American abstract painting after the war continued the self-critical development of a specifically modernist art. Arguing that major art 'is impossible, or almost so, without a thorough assimilation of the major preceding period or periods',[2] Greenberg stressed the inheritance from European painters and understood both Abstract Expressionism and the formalist painting that followed it to be firmly located within a clearly defined and progressive artistic modernism. In his seminal essay of 1962, 'After Abstract Expressionism', in which he traced this process at work, he suggests:

> The aim of the self-criticism, which is entirely empirical and not at all an affair of theory, is to determine the irreducible working essence of art and the separate arts. Under the testing of modernism more and more of the conventions of the art of painting have shown themselves to be dispensable, unessential.[3]

For Greenberg, while the work of painters such as Ashille Gorky, Willem de Kooning and Jackson Pollock of the 1940s and 1950s had continued the move toward the discovery of painting's 'viable essence',[4] making 'explicit certain constant factors of pictorial art that the past left implicit',[5] the 'cooler' formalist abstractions of the late 1950s and 1960s extended this process again and in especially significant ways. In rejecting Abstract Expressionism, painters such as Kenneth Noland, Clyfford Still, Mark Rothko, Barnett Newman, Morris Louis and Jules Olitski had, he suggested, 'established ... that the irreducible essence of pictorial art consists in but two constitutive conventions or norms: flatness and the delimitation of flatness'.[6]

Greenberg's notion of modernism in art as the culmination of an historical development with its roots in the Enlightenment not only defines an autonomy as essential to the modernist work but sees a separation between the arts as fundamental to each discipline's realisation of itself. In response to the loss of purpose that the Enlightenment secularisation brought with it, Greenberg argued, the arts could either become a mere entertainment or attempt to demonstrate and clarify the uniqueness of each art and the experience it could offer. It follows, he suggested in his article on 'Modernist Painting' of 1965, that the 'task of self-criticism became to eliminate from the effects of each art any and every effect that might conceivably be borrowed from or by the medium of any other art'.[7]

In modernist art, then, this pursuit of the essential properties of each form becomes self-conscious and as such it is the culmination of this process. Rather than subordinate their own properties to any re-presentational end, the modernist arts attempt to address explicitly the nature of their own condition, using 'the characteristic methods of a dis-cipline to criticise the discipline itself – not in order to subvert it, but to entrench it more firmly in its area of competence'.[8] Thus modernist painting progresses toward a self-conscious focus on 'flatness, two-dimensionality'.[9] In this way each art projects itself toward its own formal essence, the discovery of those unique terms which define it as what it is. In an earlier and signal essay, 'Avant-Garde and Kitsch' of 1939, Greenberg explicitly described this process of purification as a projection toward the absolute:

> It has been in search of the absolute that the avant-garde has arrived at 'abstract' or 'nonobjective' art – and poetry, too. The avant-garde poet or artist tries in effect to imitate God by creating something valid solely on its own terms ... something *given*, increate, independent of meanings, similars or originals. Content is to be dissolved so com-pletely into form that the work of art or literature cannot be reduced in whole or in part to anything not itself.[10]

It follows that for Greenberg modernist art only makes explicit what has been the real project of art since the Enlightenment and what are the actual terms by which art has always operated. In revealing what is essential to the making and experiencing of art, he concludes, modern-ism does not lower the standing of Leonardo, Raphael, Titian, Rubens, Rembrandt or Watteau, but rather, 'What Modernism has made clear is that, though the past did appreciate masters like these justly, it often gave wrong or irrelevant reasons for doing so.'[11]

In his celebrated article 'Art and Objecthood' of 1967, the American critic Michael Fried extended the terms of Greenberg's argument in an opposition to those forms of work which would undermine or corrupt this reaching towards foundation. Attacking the minimalist sculpture, which by the mid-1960s was offering its own particular response to the 'cool' abstractions of the non-objective painters, Fried set the self-contained purity of modernist work against that which looked beyond its own terms and towards the 'literal' conditions in which an object stands. For Fried, such conditions were the most banal aspects of the object's life, and facts that any work of art must necessarily strive to suspend or defeat.

Typically, the 'minimalist' objects presented by artists such as Robert Morris, Frank Stella and Donald Judd from around 1965 and 1966 rejected not only representation, reference and symbol, but the very idea that the art-object should be composed of inter-related parts. These forms are minimal firstly in the sense that they consist of simple self-sufficient, geometrical shapes, often rectangles or cubes presented singly or in series. Placed flatly within the gallery space, such objects seem to offer themselves as irreducible 'facts', asserting nothing more than their own sheer physical presence. Yet despite their apparent pursuit of the absolute, self-supporting and self-contained work, the very 'blankness' of such objects may force a reconsideration of their actual subject-matter. For the Body Artist Vito Acconci, far from asserting their autonomy, the refusal of such sculpture to allow itself to be 'read' served to reveal to the viewer the circumstances and relationships upon which the work of art is dependent. Minimalism, he notes:

was the art that made it necessary to recognise the space you were in. Up until that time I had probably assumed the notion of a frame. I would look at what was inside the frame, I would ignore the wall around it. Finally, then, with minimal art, I had to recognise I was in a certain floor ... I was in a certain condition, I had a headache, for example. I had a certain history, I had a certain bias ... what minimal art did for me was to confirm for myself the fact that art obviously had to be this relation between whatever it was that started off the art and the viewer.[12]

To Fried, far from revealing what is of inherent value within sculptural form, such work forces the viewer to look towards extraneous terms and relationships. While modernist composition attempts to suspend its own, literal 'objecthood' in favour of that which is essential to the interior life of the work, such objects emphasise the terms and relationships that constitute this very sense of objecthood. In resisting a reading of internal relationships between parts, in echoing the geometry of the rooms in which they are placed, and so in forcing the viewer's attention back on itself, Fried argued, the work becomes 'theatrical' and so fundamentally flawed:

Literalist sensibility is theatrical because, to begin with, it is concerned with the actual circumstances in which the beholder encounters literalist work ... Whereas in previous art 'what is to be had from the work is located strictly within (it),' the experience of literalist art is of an object *in a situation* – one that, virtually by definition, *includes the beholder ...* .[13]

Like theatre, too, and unlike the modernist work of art, the experience the literalist object has to offer necessarily emphasises duration. Dependent upon the developing self-consciousness of the viewer as she is drawn toward her own presence and condition before the object, the minimalist object provokes a heightened awareness of the time spent before it, the time given to it. The self-contained modernist work, however, attempts to lift itself out of even this aspect of its literal condition by offering a work which is fixed and whole, which is 'at every moment ... wholly manifest'[14] and so which may offer an experience which is complete even in the briefest of moments.

It follows that for Fried, literalist art does not represent simply a new and less-worthy departure within abstract art but an attack upon the fundamental values that legitimise art and which the modernist work seeks to make explicit. Where, after Greenberg, the arts must look to their respective essences in order to establish their uniqueness and so value, that work which insists on looking beyond these terms to a relationship with the viewer in space and time must be antithetical to the very development of art. So, Fried argues, 'there is a war going on between theatre and modernist painting, between the theatrical and the pictorial'[15] and he states categorically that '*Art degenerates as it approaches the condition of theatre*'.[16]

Nor does this theatricality emerge simply through an attention to the literal conditions in which the art-object stands. Again, following Greenberg, Fried sees the exploration of connections between the arts as a dangerous and corrupting distraction from the search for values inherent within the respective arts. He concludes:

The concepts of quality and value – and to the extent that these are central to art, the concept of art itself – are meaningful, or wholly meaningful, only *within* the individual arts. What lies *between* the arts is theatre.[17]

Against the modernist object

In retrospect, Fried's attack upon the theatrical in art provides a framework through which earlier departures from the 'self-contained' artwork may be clearly seen. In the 1950s work by Robert Rauschenberg and Jasper Johns, who drew self-consciously on the prewar European avant-garde, signalled a rapid proliferation of forms and practices that drew attention to the presence and activity of the viewer before the painting or sculpture. In certain forms these presentations even pursued the dissolution of the physical object and a direct step into performance.

In his *White Paintings* of 1951 and 1952, Robert Rauschenberg placed the formal parameters and integrity of the work of art directly into question. Consisting of apparently 'blank' single and tryptich canvases, these presentations invite a confusion between the self-contained abstraction of a white painting and a frame which will admit elements entirely contingent upon the circumstances of their exhibition. The early showing of the pieces, lit so that the viewers' shadows were cast on to the canvas, made this explicit, while Rauschenberg has described such work as a form of 'open composition' which he sees as 'responding to the activity within their reach'.[18] Rauschenberg's later 'combines', a radical form of collage made up of disjointed and profuse collections of personal bric-a-brac, found objects and blank reproductions of familiar images and fragments of newspaper, reflect this concern to draw attention to the viewer's presence and condition before the object, threatening, by their resistance to thematic closure, to provoke an awareness of the dependency of the work upon the choices of the viewer. In this context, Rauschenberg also incorporated entirely direct references to the conditions within which the object stands. In commenting on his inclusion of working radios in combine pieces he emphasises that 'listening happens in time – looking also has to happen in time'.[19]

Like Rauschenberg, Jasper Johns's early work sought a ground on which the terms of the self-contained work might be put into question. Pursuing a deliberately limited vocabulary, in which numbers, flags and targets predominate, Johns's paintings set out formal and thematic ironies by presenting figures that resist being transformed by their incorporation into a painting. Such figures, Clement Greenberg suggests in 'After Abstract Expressionism', introduce a play between the image and its representation, offering 'the literary irony that results from *representing* flat and artificial configurations that can only be *reproduced*'.[20] Johns's appropriations are of elements that pointedly retain an aspect of their own identity, that, in one way or another, stand independently of the 'work' despite their incorporation within it. Such elements live a double life, putting the integrity of the painting into question by resisting a final closure, a complete assimilation into its formal strictures and coherences. Here Johns works to place the language and status of the painting into question and looks towards an uncertain relationship between viewer and object. In this context, the work also makes explicit addresses to the viewer's presence and activity. In *Tango* (1955), a small music box is incorporated into a large blue canvas. While in the top left hand corner the word TANGO is printed, at the bottom of the painting, on the right, a small key protrudes through the canvas which when wound plays a hidden music box. Through these means the piece provokes an awareness of the viewer's active presence over time before the object:

> I wanted to suggest a physical relationship to the pictures that was active ... In 'Tango,' to wind the key and hear the sound, you had to stand relatively close to the painting, too close to see the outside shape of the picture.[21]

Like Rauschenberg's combines, such 'paintings' proceed on the basis that it is not simply the formal integrity of the painted surface that legitimates the work. In provoking and naming an active response, a 'dancing', *Tango* challenges the conventional terms and parameters of painting, revealing the painting's 'objecthood' in order to force a reconsideration of the terms by which it is defined.

In his seminal essay, *Assemblages, Environments and Happenings* (New York, 1966), Allan Kaprow traces connections between 'combine' and 'assemblage' and his own 'Happenings'. Observing the consequences of the extension of collage-sculpture, such as Rauschenberg's, into 'environmental' presentations, Kaprow suggested that where the compositional principle underlying assemblage was allowed a free development, the very idea of a compositional whole would be put into question. Not only were such environments by Claes Oldenburg, Robert Whitman, Jim Dine, Kaprow and others created without regard to the formal unities of an 'organic whole', but they refused to offer the viewer even a perceivable whole. In the generation of such work, Kaprow argues:

> Molecule-like, the material (including paint) at one's disposal grow in any desired direction and take on any shape whatsoever. In the freest of these works the field, therefore, is created as one goes along, rather than being there *a priori*, as in the case of a canvas of certain dimensions. It is a process, and one that works from the inside-out, though this should be considered merely metaphorical, rather than descriptive, since there actually exists no inside, a bounded area being necesssary to establish a field.[22]

The viewer's experience of such a 'work' is by a literal entry into its form, an entry which, while eminently theatrical in Fried's sense, also looks toward a further contingency and ephemerality. Here, Kaprow notes, the very movement and interaction of visitors within the environment sets the ground for an increasing intersection between the viewer's presence and that which the environment offers. As a result of this intersection and the contingencies it reveals, Kaprow observes:

> mechanical moving parts could be added, and parts of the created surroundings could then be rearranged like furniture at the artist's and visitor's discretion. And, logically, since the visitor could and did speak, sound and speech, mechanical and recorded, were also soon to be in order. Odours followed.[23]

The fact of many environments' impermanence, built as temporary transformations of gallery rooms, also permitted the entry of a new range of materials which escaped the conventional values and hierarchies of sculptural form. So Kaprow points to the use of debris, waste products and materials which will rapidly decay such as toilet paper and bread. Such materials, by their very presence, introduce a process of change, of 'event' into the environment. That such processes of change should be incorporated into what would be the work, Kaprow argues, 'suggests a form principle for an art which is never finished, whose parts are detachable, alterable, and rearrangeable in theoretically large numbers of ways without in the least harming the work. Indeed, such changes actually fulfil the arts' function.'[24] Such means and materials explicitly put the parameters of the work into question, divorcing a definition of what is and is not proper to the 'work of art' not only from the bounded field but even the physical integrity of the object and its elements.

While Kaprow's work takes the form of an extended and expanded collage, George Brecht, whose activities were closely bound up with the concerts, publications and events presented by the Fluxus[25] group of artists from 1961, offered games and loose assemblages of often rearrangeable objects or even unsigned objects presented variously within and outside of the formal circumstances of the gallery. His first exhibition, *toward EVENTS: an arrangement* at the Reuben Gallery, New York, in 1959, included *The Case*, a collection of small and ordinary 'found' objects whose presentation is described by Brecht in the invitation to the exhibition. Brecht's statement typifies his attitude toward his work and its containment:

THE CASE is found on a table. It is approached by one to several people and opened. The contents are removed and used in various ways
appropriate to their nature. The case is repacked and closed. The
event (which lasts possibly 10–30 minutes) comprises all sensible
occurrences between approach and abandonment of the case.[26]

The Case, like so many of the later Fluxus objects and editions, deliberately confuses the 'art-object' with its use, breaking down the conventional distinctions between the 'work' and the occasion of the viewer's
meeting with it. Here, as with so many of Brecht's presentations, the
simple re-presentation of familiar, everyday objects with little or no
transformation places the meaning, formal identity and parameters of
what would be 'the work' into question.

Prefiguring Pop Art's appropriation of the commercial image and
object and extending the environment's conflation of object and place,
Claes Oldenburg's *Store* of 1961 consisted of a real store at 107 East
2nd Street, New York. Here he kept a stock of approximately 120
everyday objects of all kinds recast in a variety of materials and offered
for sale. Oldenburg's treatment of ' "real" place' as if it were 'itself an
object'[27] threatens to collapse the boundaries between the work and its
literal context, and so between the environment and the activities within
it. In turn, the particular choice of a store also moves to conflate the
viewer with the consumer, artist with salesman, and 'art-work' with
commercial product. *The Store* might be best considered as an 'event'
not simply because of the 'performances' it might embrace, but in its
setting of conflicting meanings against each other, as objects and roles
are torn between the two aspects of the place Oldenburg directs attention toward. Here, the formal distinction between what is and is not
'proper' to the work becomes, like the meanings of the objects and
interactions Oldenburg calls attention towards, slippery and evasive of a
final determination. Indeed, the point of *The Store* seems to lie not so
much in what it *is*, but in its blocking together of conflicting readings
and possibilities.

In these contexts the emergence of strategies which look specifically
toward *performance* can be read as a final move towards an unravelling
of the discrete or bounded 'work of art'. In October 1959 Allan Kaprow
presented *18 Happenings in 6 Parts* at the Reuben Gallery in New
York,[28] in which he drew on John Cage's Black Mountain College
'event' of 1952 which had brought together a radical rethinking of
musical composition with dance by Merce Cunningham, paintings by
Rauschenberg and poetry by Charles Olsen and Mary Caroline

Richards.[29] Within a week of *18 Happenings in 6 Parts*, the Reuben Gallery showed Brecht's *toward Events: an arrangement* and, in January 1960, followed this with four days of performances by Allan Kaprow, Robert Whitman and Red Grooms. During February and March 1960, the Gallery at the Judson Church on Washington Square hosted *The Ray Gun Specs*, which presented live work by Claes Oldenburg, Jim Dine, Al Hansen, Allan Kaprow, Robert Whitman, Red Grooms and Dick Higgins.

Minimalism and the event of the work

Set against this history, both minimalism and Fried's defence of the modernist work need to be reconsidered.

Evidently, Fried's concern with minimalism is not simply that it toys with theatricality in the manner of much painting and sculpture that precedes it, but that it does so by siting itself in relation to the modernist reduction of the work to its formal essence. Read as the pursuit of a self-enclosed sculptural form, minimalism ostensibly acts in a way which is consistent with the self-critical progression Greenberg describes. Here, though, the very reduction of the sculptural work to a simple geometrical shape threatens to turn this progression against itself. Ironically, in this reading, it is the minimalist presentation of an 'irreducible' form that precipitates the theatrical, forcing attention away from what might be *interior* and so 'proper' and 'necessary' to the work of art.

In response to this threat to the modernist ideal, Fried reconsiders both Greenberg's account of the modernist project and his own earlier view of modernism.[30] It is in this very reformulation of the modernist work, however, that one can trace out contradictions that put into question the very idea of the work of art's legitimation of itself *in its own terms*.

In order to distinguish between the 'literalist' nature of the minimalist object and the modernist projection toward autonomy, Fried now makes a distinction between the formal integrity of the work of art and the physical integrity of the object. Arguing that painting's 'timeless conditions', that is 'the *minimal conditions for something being seen as a painting*', should be seen as distinct from 'what, at a given moment, is capable of compelling conviction, of succeeding as painting', Fried questions Greenberg's account of the modernist projection toward an 'absolute'. Yet, he argues:

> This is not to say that painting *has no* essence; it *is* to claim that
> essence – i.e., that which compels conviction – is largely determined
> by, and therefore changes continually in response to, the vital work of
> the recent past. The essence of painting is not something irreducible.
> Rather, the task of the modernist painter is to discover those conven-
> tions that, at a given moment, *alone* are capable of establishing his
> work's identity as painting.[31]

In other words, the modernist work is not a projection toward that which
ultimately legitimates the medium but is a search for *quality* and *value*
in the context of a particular set of historical conditions. Yet this particular re-reading, which not only Fried but more recent proponents of modernism and the modernist work have advanced,[32] puts into question the
very possibility of the 'essence' and so the 'foundation' which the idea
of the work of art's self-legitimation assumes.

If the modernist project within painting is understood to be one
which seeks to establish the identity of the medium in a *particular* historical and cultural context, then its teleological aspect, its projection
toward the 'viable essence' of all painting, is lost. Yet without such a
teleology, the very notion of the modernist work as a work that reveals
the interior terms by which an art-form legitimates itself is thrown into
question. In these circumstances, the history of modern painting can no
longer be regarded as a progression towards that which underlies and
legitimates the medium, but must be read as the construction and reconstruction of 'essence'. Yet to describe an 'essence' that is 'constructed',
is to enter into a contradiction, for it is to describe an 'essence' penetrated and legitimated by terms beyond its own. Indeed, a work which
exemplifies a particular understanding of what painting *can be*, rather
than what it has *always been*, can only offer itself as one possibility
among others, and in this way declare its own departure from the very
idea of an 'essence'. It follows that Fried's yardstick for modernist art,
that 'painting of the past whose quality is not in doubt'[33] must also
come into question. If there is no constant, no trans-historical *fact* to be
revealed from within painting, then the reading of the history of painting becomes a site of dispute over value rather than the discovery of
value. If the very qualities that determine the *identity* of painting are
themselves subject to historical and, by implication, cultural context,
then the criterion for 'success' becomes as much a matter of *who looks*
as *what is seen*.

In such circumstances, the modernist project becomes multiple and
contingent as its appeal to metanarrative is lost to an awareness of the

contingent nature of the legitimacy of the work. The legitimating core of the work of art as Fried describes it here is inseparable from the circumstances, histories and assumptions that have produced its particular aesthetic terms. In fact, here, the modernist work finally loses its meaning, its *possession* of its own definition.

Performance: Allan Kaprow's *Self-Service* (1967) and George Brecht's *Water Yam* (1962)

After these reconsiderations of the object, and in the context of Fried's identification of the 'theatrical' with an 'anti-modernist' corruption of art, one can readily identify a 'postmodern' evasion of stable parameters, meanings and identities with 'performance' emerging from the visual arts in the early 1960s. The 'theatricality' which defines the work of Allan Kaprow and George Brecht, in particular, emerges from a radical reconceiving of the 'object' through an attention to the contingencies the specifically modernist work, in Fried's terms, would transcend or suppress. In the development of these presentations and activities, the very idea of a 'performance' would seem to be bound up with a giving of voice to occurrences that surround, penetrate and disrupt the boundaries of what would be the 'work of art'. Kaprow's 'Happenings for performers only' and Brecht's 'event-scores', in particular, exemplify such strategies, as they invite a questioning of the very realisations they look toward, even at the risk of undermining the final coming into being of a distinct 'thing', of a recognisable and bounded 'work'.

In *Self-Service* of 1967, which, like his earlier 'Happenings', emerges and develops directly out of his work with assemblage and environment, Kaprow pursues an acute fragmentation, dispersing individuals and events in space and time. According to Kaprow's published score, *Self-Service* is to be comprised of a possible 45 events; nine may take place in Boston, ten in New York and 26 in Los Angeles. Each of these events is to be quite isolated in its realisation, the whole pattern of activities emerging across three different states and over a total possible period of four months. Although no one action is directly dependent upon another for its realisation, Kaprow's score allows events to take place simultaneously across the three states. More frequently, activities will simply overlap or remain quite separate. Just as events are separated in place and time so there is little connection between activities through any 'subject', theme or obvious imagery. In his documentation Kaprow notes that in New York, for example:

People stand on empty bridges, on street corners, watch cars pass. After two hundred red ones, they leave.

While at another time:

An empty house. Nails are hammered halfway into all surfaces of rooms, house is locked, hammerers go away.

In Boston:

People tie tar paper around many cars in a supermarket lot.
On another day, twenty or more flash-gun cameras shoot off at the same time all over the supermarket; shopping resumed.

While in Los Angeles:

Cars drive into filling stations, erupt with white foam pouring from windows.
Couples kiss in the midst of the world, go on.[34]

Kaprow's method of working, as well as the strictures surrounding an engagement with the project, serve to further disrupt the physical and conceptual integrity of this set of activities. For the participants there will be no single activity involving the entire group, no set of activities completed by everybody, nor any particular focus serving to define a group experience. Kaprow goes on to specify that the piece is to be 'for performers only', as if to counter any focus that may be defined by the gathering of spectators. Furthermore, while those who would be an audience to *Self-Service* must engage in prescribed activities, Kaprow avoids both rehearsal and repetition. In a conversation with the critic Richard Kostalanetz, published in Kostalanetz's book *The Theatre of Mixed Means* (New York, 1968), Kaprow remarks, 'if you're interested in playing my game, then come and talk it over, and we'll decide who's going to do what at that time. After that, we'll do it.'[35] Once ended, he is quite reluctant to repeat any realisation or to have any person engage in it again. In *Assemblages, Environments and Happenings* he states categorically that, however detailed the preparations or predetermined its rules or strictures, '*Happenings should be performed once only.*'[36]
   While Kaprow's rules for performance seemed designed to resist any actual or easily perceivable sense of an organised 'whole', the nature and identity of the individual activities of which the piece is to consist

would seem themselves to be rendered unsteady or uncertain in their realisation. In prescribing each activity in the way he does Kaprow usurps their functions, and looks toward a catching of the elements of this 'performance' in a double-bind. Without their usual purposes and sense these largely functional activities might become arbitrary, no longer belonging to the 'everyday' though they are taken directly from it and sometimes remain embedded within it. In the frame of Kaprow's prescription, the identity and value of each action is called into question, just as close attention is called to their enactment or performance. In his essay 'Participation Performance' Kaprow draws attention to the effect of this prescription:

> Intentionally performing everyday life is bound to create some curious kinds of awareness. Life's subject matter is almost too familiar to grasp, and life's formats (if they can be called that) are not familiar enough.[37]

The 'performance' of such activities by those who would be spectators to the 'Happening' also serves to put into question their framing as part of a 'work'. To engage in an activity in a supermarket, for example, is not to discover a single or clear focus but to rehearse a simple action embedded within a flow of 'everyday' events and distractions. Again, Kaprow envisages just such a questioning of the parameters of these elements. In a Happening, he argues:

> the very materials, the environment, the activity of the people in that environment, are the primary images, not the secondary ones. The environment is not a setting for a play ... which is more important than the people ... there is an absolute flow between event and environment.[38]

Displaced from their usual purposes, these activities offer points from which occurrences beyond the artist's control or determination may become a focus of attention. In doing so, the boundaries, even the possibility of drawing parameters around the elements of a 'work', come into question.

Such strategies, however, do not mean that *Self-Service* is simply antithetical to the idea of the 'work of art'. Indeed, the promise these strategies make, their reference to a 'whole', despite the dispersal of elements and focuses, looks toward a negotiation, a testing of identities and meanings, and a catching of events *between* possibilities. Of *Self-Service* Kaprow notes:

> So many things had just that quality of dropping things in the world and then going about your business. The whole thing teetered on the edge of not-quite-art, not-quite-life.[39]

Despite the deliberate confusion of *Self-Service* as a distinct entity, Kaprow's strictures look toward another kind of coherence, one rooted in a shared function or purpose and so in the character of the participant's active engagement. First, then, and through each of the activities the participant engages in, a *self-service* is in some way brought into play. Amongst the 'available activities', Kaprow describes:

> People shout in a subway just before getting off, leaving immediately.
>   Many shoppers begin to whistle in aisles of supermarkets. After a few minutes they go back to their shopping.
>   In glass booths, people listen to records. They look at each other and dance.
>   Some people whistle a tune in the crowded elavator of an office building.
>   People enter phone booths, eat sandwiches and drink sodas, look out at the world.[40]

In each of these places of self-service the participant is to make the piece for herself. It is not a single pattern of actions, but a service by oneself to oneself, a common manner of behaviour defined by place, intention and means. At other times the participant is to serve herself in her choice from prescribed activities:

> Everyone watches for either
>   a signal from someone
>   a light to go on in a window
>   a plane to pass directly overhead
>   an insect to land nearby
>   three motorcycles to barrel past.[41]

Kaprow's rules take up and amplify this play of association. In describing the rules of the event to Richard Schechner, Kaprow notes:

all of the events were 'self-service' – a person could choose to participate in as many as he wished down to one; if anything came up – as it will during the summer – a person had the right to cancel out and substitute something else later on.[42]

Although Kaprow specifies the total sum of different events for each state, he does not shape the frequency of these events, their repetition or their timing. At the same time, and while the totality of events remains disjointed and fractured, Kaprow notes that *Self-Service* 'was programmed so that everybody participating knew exactly what else was going on'.[43] In this way, Kaprow's rules promise a balance between a physical involvement with the piece, a direct initiation of activities, and a knowledge of other activities to be initiated elsewhere. As the participant executes her actions so this structure seeks to draw attention between that execution and her knowledge of that in the process of execution or which has or will be executed. In *Assemblages, Environments and Happenings*, Kaprow emphasises that:

> Although the participant is unable to do everything and be in all places at once, he knows the overall pattern if not the details. And like the agent in an international spy ring, he knows, too, that what he does devotedly will echo and give character to what others do elsewhere.[44]

Kaprow's strategies would seem designed to draw a participant's attention in two directions at once. What is offered here is the dissolution of what would be a work, as any sense of 'whole', of material or conceptual integrity is broken down, put into question. Paradoxically, though, and at the moment of this dissolution, the viewer-participant's activity is one of building, of a movement toward realisation. Indeed, in taking up the invitations of *Self-Service*, the 'viewer-participant' becomes instrumental not only to the production but also to the reception of the 'Happening' and so to the possibility of its very existence. Kaprow's conception of the participant's experience echoes this point, as he suggests that 'by knowing the scenario and one's particular duties beforehand, a person becomes a real and necessary part of the work. It cannot exist without him.'[45] To play such a game would be to engage once and once only in an activity of building, in the making of a game which is a game of making a 'work of art'. In *Self-Service*, and in these respects, Kaprow's strictures repeatedly provoke a move towards and yet a postponement of a determination of what is or is not a part of that with which the viewer-participant should be concerned. In this sense, *Self-Service* might be best read as the provocation and shaping of moves toward a 'work', and yet, simultaneously, a set of strategies which serve to stave off a closure and so identification of what this work might be. As it is presented by Kaprow, *Self-Service* consists simply of a set of rules that, in their activation by the participant, at once look towards a realisation, and yet seek to stave off any final closure of what would be 'the work', of any end to the process of realisation.

While through his rules Kaprow takes a direct control over the formal operation of *Self-Service* and so aspects of the participant's choices and activities, George Brecht, through his *Water Yam* and other 'event-cards', steps back from even this determining frame. As a result, these 'scores' seem less concerned with the disruption or breaking down of a 'work' than with a catching of attention at a point at which the promise of a work, and the move toward closure, is first encountered.

Through their very slightness, many of the cards presented as part of the *Water Yam*, a boxed edition by Brecht and published first of all by Fluxus in 1962,[46] imply identities of various kinds. *Three Aqueous Events*, a card measuring five by five-and-a-half centimetres, might be taken to be a poem or simple statement. At the same time, it may appear more like a list or a description of a process of change. Then again, it has the qualities of a score, and could be taken as looking towards the performance of three activities in response to 'ice', 'water' and 'steam', or as an invitation to take three events or occurrences as a focus for attention. Considered as a score, the card seems to be even more open and unclear, as it becomes an ambiguous stimulus to something or other that is yet to be made or occur. In doing so, it places its own self-sufficiency into question and explicitly looks towards a decision yet to be made.

In this way, instead of asserting itself as any 'thing' in particular, *Three Aqueous Events* remains pointedly open to suggestion, as if it might embrace any and all of the characteristics a reader, observer or performer may care to assign to it. It may even be that such an 'open-ness' serves to qualify the various responses it invites, provoking an awareness of the contingent nature of any particular determination of the score. Such a level of ambiguity may well disarm the possibility of any single or simple response, perhaps leaving the reader to wonder how one might effectively react to such a lack of definition.

Brecht's own comments only serve to heighten these ambiguities. In an interview with the critic Henry Martin, Brecht argued that through such cards 'I don't demand anything. I'd leave the maximum of freedom

TWO SIGNS

● SILENCE

● NO VACANCY

THREE AQUEOUS EVENTS

● ice

● water

● steam

Summer, 1961

THREE YELLOW EVENTS

I ● yellow
   ● yellow
   ● yellow

II ● yellow
   ● loud

III ● red

to Rrose
Spring, 1961
G. Brecht

WORD EVENT

● EXIT

G.Brecht
Spring, 1961

George Brecht, cards from the *Water Yam*,
originally published by Fluxus (New York, 1962)

to everybody.'[47] Yet while dismissing the notion that there might be any particular way to respond, Brecht also suggests that these games are not self-sufficient. He refers to the *Water Yam* cards as 'scores' or 'event-cards'[48] and has stated categorically, and of all his work, be it event-card or object, that 'an event is always intended, or implied'.[49] Henry Martin, who has documented Brecht's work in his book *An Introduction to George Brecht's Book of the Tumbler on Fire* (Milan, 1978), argues that it is necessary to find something to 'do' with what Brecht offers in order to make sense of it:

> Brecht's work is concerned with moments in which mind is active, creative and autonomous. The work resists being appreciated on the basis of a passive perception of what it is; it finds its sense and its function on the basis of some things one can do with it, on the basis, that is, of a possible relationship one can create with it. The work remains opaque and meaningless until one decides actively to collaborate with it.[50]

Such descriptions of the formal nature of this card, however, only seem to make the 'work' towards which it might point further out of reach. A 'collaboration' with the card may involve or look toward an 'event', yet an event is not, particularly, an example of theatre or 'non-theatrical' activity or music or even a private act. According to Brecht, 'event simply has the meaning it has in the dictionary',[51] indicating perhaps 'a thing that happens' and as such could imply any or all of these things. It would seem that in seeking to collaborate actively with that which Brecht offers, the reader or viewer must define not only the particular terms of any card but the formal identity or identities of the 'event' it may provoke.

Brecht's realisations of *Three Aqueous Events* reflect such a process. Henry Martin notes that Brecht has made a film in which he performed the piece,[52] while Michael Kirby in his anthology *Happenings* (New York, 1965) describes a theatre performance of *Three Aqueous Events* in which Brecht poured water into three glasses.[53] Brecht himself has recalled using the event-card as the basis for another object, score and event:

> A canvas with the word 'Glace' in the upper left corner and the word 'Buee' on the bottom at the right and a glass in the middle half filled with water. It's a score, it's a realisation, and what's more it's an event as the water is evaporating.[54]

In contrast to Brecht, Allan Kaprow was prompted to make himself a drink in response to the flexibility of the score. In his article on 'Non-theatrical Performance' he notes that he 'once made a delicious iced tea on the stimulation of the piece and thought about it while drinking'.[55] Henry Martin goes on to suggest that a realisation of *Three Aqueous Events* could take almost any form, all of which would be equally appropriate:

A work such as this ... is in constant existence no matter what the modality of forms of human consciousness directed to it. Simply reading the work is a performance of the work, and the same can be said of simply thinking it, and one can think of it as three words, or three sounds, or three physical entities. It can be oral, aural, tactile, visual, taste or any other kind of experience; it can be of any duration and of any order of dimension.[56]

In presenting a score which is so ambiguous, Brecht at once stimulates a move towards closure and intervenes to stave off its possibility. Clearly, in this reading no individual choice can provide a final resolution to *Three Aqueous Events*, despite the fact that it offers itself as a 'work' yet to be realised. Whatever the reader 'does' or chooses, the possibility of another choice threatens to displace the move toward 'realisation' at the moment in which it is made. In his article, 'George Brecht: An Art of Multiple Implications', the critic Jan Van der Marck sets this aspect of Brecht's work against Marcel Duchamp's earlier consideration of the observer. Here, he argues:

Duchamp's notion that it is the observer who completes the work of art becomes in Brecht's interpretation the notion of the observer forever trying, like Sisyphus, but never able to finish the work – or dispose of the idea.[57]

Such invitations to the reader or viewer to discover her own implication in the meaning and identity of things permeate Brecht's work. Among many kinds of objects, Brecht exhibits signs which exemplify the status he wishes to lend to the various aspects of his work. He notes:

To me, all the various parts of my work amount to the same thing. I think of my works as events, and the signs exist to create the possibility of an event. When you go into a room and find a sign that says 'No

Smoking' you have to make a decision. And to make a decision is an event.[58]

Such an object cannot be separated from the event of its being read. Although different in their mechanism from *Three Aqueous Events*, the signs remain parallel to it. To discover the 'object' is to have made a relationship, to have made, in Brecht's terms, an 'arrangement'. Furthermore, just as the 'object' has no independent identity so, by implication, the viewer can never be neutral, can never attend to a thing that somehow remains apart from her. In pursuing this notion of an arrangement Brecht attempts to shift the focus of his work entirely from the 'object' as a thing in which properties reside and to a shifting set of relationships operating through stimulus and response. In this way, Brecht's activities proceed on the notion that to perceive is to constitute and so be responsible for that which is perceived. In conversation with Henry Martin, he concludes:

> for me, an object does not exist outside of people's contact with it. There is no 'real' object as opposed to out idea of the object. The only object that exists is the object there and me here. You with the object at a different moment is a different object.[59]

Here there can be no separation of the 'work' from the viewer, nor can 'art' be considered a special case, something self-contained and self-justifying, but is itself an effect of an 'arrangement', a point defined by and subject to shifting processes of negotiation. Art and the work of art are not 'things' but occurrences, which the artist's making can no more be said to give an identity to than the viewer's act of seeing. Consistently with this, Brecht's focus falls not so much upon the 'work of art' as upon the relationships within which this very notion of 'a work' is bound. In an early interview of 1965 with the artists Marcel Alocco and Ben Vautier, he suggested that 'Everyone's a creator ... I never think of what I do as art or not art. It's an activity, that's all.'[60]

In declaring their incompletion and attempting to stave off closure, Brecht's 'scores' endanger the idea that they may present, make or look towards a 'work' in any tangible sense. Yet this very evasion of a final realisation is pursued in an address to a process of 'arrangement' on which the 'work of art' is contingent. It follows that these 'scores' are not an attempt to provoke a particular end, but to make visible that which the work depends upon but which it cannot contain, to trip up and make apparent the move towards the 'event' of its definition. Such activities exemplify a reaching towards instabilities and contingencies which evade the 'self-legitimating' work of art, and engage instead with events, transactions and negotiations which might look, literally, towards a 'borderline art'. For Brecht, it seems such fragile contents are entirely at the centre of his concerns:

Sounds barely heard; sights barely distinguished – borderline art. See which way it goes (it should be possible to miss it).[61]

Chapter 3

Looking Beyond Form: Foreman, Kirby, Wilson

While the debates surrounding the minimalist object provide positions from which a 'postmodern' corruption of the boundaries of the work can be set against various steps from the object and into theatre, the forms and methods of minimal and serial sculpture also offer points from which developments in theatre practice can be read against the postmodern.

In the work of Richard Foreman, Robert Wilson and Michael Kirby, a concern for structural and formal pattern is evident in presentations offered in the more conventional surroundings of a theatre. Read in relation to familiar models of representational drama, such performance can be seen as a retreat from 'content' in the name of a 'New Formalism',[1] an increasingly self-absorbed focus upon form and structure in its own right. Set against minimal art, however, this refutation of 'content' seems not so much a sign of a faith in the self-supporting nature of form as an attempt to throw the viewer's effort to read the performance sharply back upon itself. Such strategies put into question not only the very possibility of an 'autonomous' form, but take their place in a more elaborate questioning of the very means through which these performances constitute themselves and the readings they seem, variously, to invite.

At the most immediate level, connections between the work of Kirby, Wilson and Foreman, and the practices and vocabulary of minimal art are apparent. Michael Kirby's later work in theatre and performance is clearly shaped by his work as a visual artist. Following an engagement with 'Happenings' in the early 1960s and a realisation, through contact with the composer John Cage's use of chance method, of the validity of 'a giving up of the aesthetic decision',[2] Kirby was involved as a visual artist with minimal and serial painting and sculpture. In his work with the Structuralist Workshop, founded in 1975 with his production of *Eight People*, Kirby brought these 'systematic' methods of composition to bear directly on to performance. Subsequently, in pieces such as *First Signs of Decadence* (1985), Kirby applied strict and often complex rules to the generation of plays in an otherwise 'realistic' style in order to overcome aspects of his own intention while foregrounding form and structure. For Richard Foreman both the practices of systematic art and the implications of the minimalist object provided a clarification of work rooted in a variety of sources. Under the influence of film-makers such as Jonas Mekas and Jack Smith, notions of performance developed by Yvonne Rainer[3] and the work of various 'poets and non-theatrical people',[4] Foreman's early work systematically inverted the 'good practice' he had acquired through his training as a playwright. In this context, Foreman suggests, at the time of his first *Ontological-Hysteric Theatre* production, *Angelface* of 1968:

> minimalism and a very superficial encounter with some of the ideas of Alchemy ... were really at the centre of the way I began ... how the stuff was mixed and remixed or boiled and reboiled. And the repetition of that activity, again and again and again.[5]

Unlike Kirby and Foreman, Robert Wilson's work has important roots in entirely non-artistic sources. While he studied painting in Paris in 1962 and then trained as an architect in New York, Wilson's experience of being cured of a speech impediment in his late teens by a dancer, Mrs Bird Hoffman, proved as formative as his involvement with the visual arts. During his college studies he worked with children, teaching theatre and working on performance projects designed by his students.[6] After 1965 Wilson came to work with brain-damaged and handicapped children, applying 'movement exercises to release tension'[7] which often involved extreme slow-motion and were drawn directly from his memory of Bird Hoffman's work.

In developing his early operas, and while pursuing a distinctly architectural concern for space, Wilson drew directly on the experiences, behaviour and writing of the children with whom he worked. *The King of Spain* (1969), *The Life and Times of Sigmund Freud* (1969) and, particularly, *Deafman Glance* (1970) called on Wilson's work with Raymond Andrews, a deaf and mute teenager he had met in 1968. From 1973 Wilson collaborated with Christopher Knowles who, although

born with severe brain damage, played a prominent part in the develop-
ment and performances of *The Life and Times of Joseph Stalin* (1973),
A Letter for Queen Victoria (1974), *The $ Value of Man* (1975) and
Einstein on the Beach (1976).

At the same time, Wilson's first presentations in New York, around
1967 and 1968, came to be strongly related to a prevailing minimalist
aesthetic as his concern 'to go back to the simplest thing I could do ...
how do I walk ... how do I sit in the chair and walk off'[8] emerged in performance. To some of his collaborators the influence of minimal art and
music seemed evident, even where Wilson's later and often visually
extravagant presentations appeared to move in quite another direction.
Franny Brooks, who participated in Wilson's earliest work, notes that:

> Those early pieces were very sparse – I think he was influenced a lot
> by John Cage around this time ... the concert he played with one note
> ... he was very influenced by this minimalist thinking. I don't know
> what happened when he went into *King of Spain*, but somehow he
> became much more baroque, a sort of combination of baroque and the
> minimal.[9]

For Kirby and Foreman, in particular, and in a recognition of the 'theatricality' of the minimalist object, 'minimalism' is associated not with
self-sufficiency and an exclusion of the viewer, but a recognition of
relation and contingency. Foreman observes that 'structure is always a
combination of the THING and the PERCEIVING of it',[10] while Kirby, similarly, does not understand either the work or its structures to exist in
any way independently of a process of negotiation with the viewer.
Stressing the paramount importance of the address to the nature and
effect of structure to his Structuralist Theatre, Kirby qualifies this
emphasis, writing that:

> 'Structure' is being used to refer to the way the parts of a work relate
> to each other, how they 'fit together' in the mind to form a particular
> configuration. This fitting together does not happen 'out there' in the
> objective work; it happens in the mind of the spectator.[11]

Rather than move towards an exclusion of the viewer from the terms
by which the work is defined, in this work 'structure' is foregrounded in
order to address the viewer's act of reading. Indeed, Foreman understands the self-referentiality of the minimalist object in precisely this
way. By excluding any relationship between its parts, he assumes, this

sculpture does not turn inward, but reflects back outward, forcing the viewer's attention away from what might be 'interior' to the work and back on to the act of reading. In referring directly to minimal and systematic work in his *Ontological-Hysteric Manifesto I* (1972) he notes:

> as Stella, Judd, *et al.* realised several years ago ... one must reject composition in favour of shape (or something else) ... Why? Because the resonance must be between the head and the object. The resonance between the elements of the object is now a DEAD THING.[12]

Richard Foreman: *Pandering to the Masses: A Misrepresentation* (1975)

In *Pandering to the Masses: A Misrepresentation*,[13] Richard Foreman offers a stream of elements that repeatedly refer to one or more plays or narratives but which remain a flow of fragments, incompletions, new beginnings and shifts in logic. Employing references to character, narrative, symbol and discourse, the performance rapidly and overtly collages conflicting elements and categories one upon the other in such a way as to defeat any sense of unity. Not only the structure, but the design, set construction, performance style, as well as the self-reflexive nature of the moment-to-moment progression of the piece, all serve to put the conventional function of its elements into question.

Shortly after its beginning, the performance is announced to be only the prologue to *Pandering to the Masses: A Misrepresentation*, at the centre of which will be a play within a play, *Fear*. Yet *Fear* offers only the reported entry of the personification of fear, whose invisibility provides a cue for the 'characters' of *Pandering to the Masses* to discuss their lack of fear. Shortly afterwards, Foreman's own taped voice announces a 'return to the central narrative of the play entitled *Pandering to the Masses: A Misrepresentation*'.[14] Like the title itself, which pointedly leaves open the question of precisely where the misrepresentation lies, the performance pursues uncertainties, repeatedly shifting its ground in order to put itself into question.

As the lights come up the audience faces a space only 16 feet wide and some 20 feet deep. 'Max' sits centre, looking directly at the spectators. A man sits at a bicycle down-centre; he pedals rapidly but the bicycle does not move. Foreman's taped voice announces that the play concerns Rhoda's introduction to a secret society concerned with a very particular kind of knowledge. The performer playing Max exclaims: 'You ...

understand ... NOTHING!' Foreman's voice informs the audience that they
will not understand. A buzzer. The voice announces a recapitulation. Yet
the recapitulation signals a new action; Rhoda enters, downstage, discovering a letter. The voice reflects, in a contradictory manner, on the
audience's mode of thought, supposing that they think through 'the
associative method ... Each thought is accompanied by overtones which
are images but may not be pictures but are, certainly.'[15] This in turn cues
what might be a play on such association:

> A buzzer. Music overlaps. RHODA, SOPHIA and ELEANOR revealed
> naked at the top of a hill. Three men run down the hill with giant
> pencils and wave them threateningly at MAX. Then the women start
> down the hill, and when the music stops, turn sideways in provoc-
> ative poses.[16]

The walls at the rear have opened to reveal a 30-foot raked stage. Max
looks at the women through the wrong end of the telescope. A buzzer.
Music. Max dances as a wall slides in, blocking his view of the women
as the voice considers what would be the nature of Max's motivation for
dancing in the conventional theatre. Max stops dancing. The prologue is
announced, the play itself 'will begin in, perhaps, five minutes'. Then:

> MAX: (Holding out his hand) Now I want some water.
> VOICE: Now, he reaches out his hand. What could go into his hand.
> MAX: Another hand.
>   (RHODA enters, puts her hand in his.)[17]

The dialogue, like the commentaries and actions, prove unpredictable
and open to more than one logic. Max and Rhoda talk to each other, but
might both be the voice's own reflections, and yet Max shares in this
control and is, in any case, physically at the centre. Rather than manifest
any single familiar or conventional logic the play self-consciously
reflects on the processes which underlie its own construction and reception. Yet even this does not provide concrete ground, as the demonstration of any particular process seems to disappear under the weight of
repeated interruptions, ironic digressions, slapstick exchanges or simple
contradictions and changes of sense. Instead of attending to each other
through the play, the performers present themselves directly to the audience, who are brightly lit. Speaking unemotionally and with a variety of
inflections,[18] the performers drain their behaviour of the emotional

contents to which scenes and dialogue refer, throwing suggestions of character and fictional interaction starkly into relief.

Just as the organisation of the sequence of elements and the distribution of elements in space serves to frustrate the building of a unified picture, so the presentation of the theatre-space reveals Foreman's choices. Props and furniture are placed in order to show and emphasise the basic design of the space. Strings which run across its width, rather like lines in a diagram, demonstrate its division and are manipulated by the performers to accentuate and create frames and focuses. The peculiar nature of Foreman's Ontological-Hysteric theatre also allows a continual remaking of the performance space involving, in *Pandering to the Masses*, a transformation of depth from 12 to as much as 75 feet.

As if such means were not enough to ensure the audience's self-conscious remove from the sequence of actions and images, *Pandering to the Masses* employs a system which serves to fragment the dialogue in the most arbitrary of ways. The exchanges of the four principal performers are taped, 'each separate word being spoken by a different one of those four performers in sequence, no matter who was listed in the script'.[19] In turn, the voice of each performer is isolated on one of four speakers, placed one at each of the four corners of the audience. As the dialogue proceeds, each performer speaks key words over the taped dialogue, while certain lines remain unrecorded, to be spoken live for emphasis. Foreman's own voice is heard in deep, measured tones from the furthest rear speaker, as if to counterbalance the focus offered by the physical presence of the performers.

Like each of his Ontological-Hysteric productions, *Pandering to the Masses* is shaped through Foreman's concern to attend to his act of writing at each successive moment in which he writes. His scripts evidence, first of all, a continually renewed attention to the present moment, and are a product of an attempt to resist a projection toward continuity and unity through the material he commits to the page. In practice, Foreman's process involves a literal and continual 'beginning again' through which he arrives at a structure of repeated 'false starts'.[20] Key to his method, he suggests, is:

Sleep. I take naps during the day. To 'clear' my mind, so that I can 'begin again' – start a new day, as it were, whose writing comes from a new place ... I 'fire' bursts of writing ... then, to avoid being dragged into the river of that 'discourse which has just gotten under way,' I need to move back to the firing area. I SLEEP, I NEGATE THE DRIFT of the writing burst I've just fired, its tendency to 'ive its own life and write its own development. I wake up cleansed, and fire again![21]

Such processes result in work which is not only acutely self-referential but in certain respects paradoxical. In particular, Foreman's method involves a continual attempt to observe and defeat his writing's coming into being as a 'play' and so to escape the formal and thematic implications of whatever elements he introduces. In his *Ontological Hysteric Manifesto I* (1972) Foreman emphasises that one must 'write by thinking *against* the material ... don't sustain anything'.[22] Yet at the same time the very elements that occur to Foreman, or which he chooses, invite precisely the kind of attention he apparently wishes to deny himself and his audience. Just as *Pandering to the Masses* begins with the promise of an explanation which, we are told, will not be realised, so signs of plot or narrative are evident, yet no plot emerges. In his staging, too, Foreman extends precisely this same mode of self-consciousness, looking back towards the fragmentation of his writing rather than forward towards any kind of final coherence. He notes:

> the staging ... is not an attempt to CONVINCE the audience of the play's reality or verisimilitude ... but rather an effort to rewrite the text back into manuscript ... It is a CONTINUATION of my writing process.[23]

While indications of individual roles are clear, the dispersal and fragmentation of dialogue, the performers' attention to the audience rather than each other, as well as the self-reflexive nature of the text, work against a coherent reading of these indications and frustrate the coming into being of any particular 'characterisation'. Instead Foreman continually returns to the various promises such elements may make in the belief that 'the gesture, the impulse which comes to nothing (which doesn't fulfil itself) ... fulfils that other thing which is truthfully operating through me'.[24] In other words, the 'false start' returns him (and, by implication, the viewer) to an awakening to his own act of construction, either at the point of writing, directing or reading.

Such attacks on sense and continuity, which typify Foreman's Ontological-Hysteric productions, clearly go further than a disruption of the conventional unities of a play or representational piece of theatre. At each successive moment Foreman would seem to direct his strategies towards a wrong-footing of the viewer's move towards closure, towards interpretation and understanding. Such a resistance to a reading of the elements of what would be the 'play' through the construction of a sensible or organised pattern, serves to stave off the emergence of the 'object', a sense of 'whole' to which meaning and purpose might be attributed. For Foreman, it seems, the emergence of this 'object' is synonymous with the viewer's escape from responsibility. In his *Ontological Hysteric: Manifesto II* (1974) he remarks that 'if each moment is new, if we die to each moment as it arises, we are alive. Development (sequential) is death. Is objectification.'[25]

Such objectification, Foreman argues, is brought into play by habit, by a desire for security and, ultimately, perceptual and intellectual sleep. He concludes that 'we are taught to see objects (rather than perceptual acts) and we are by those objects, enslaved'.[26] It follows that rather than celebrating and reinforcing this inheritance art might 'begin the process of freeing men by calling into doubt the solidity of objects – and laying bare the fact that it is a web of relations that exists, only ... '[27]

Yet although the systematic fragmentation of Foreman's productions and his self-conscious address to the process of looking involve a rejection of the illusion of the 'object', this work pointedly retains its trappings. In contrast to the work of John Cage, in particular, but also a wide range of departures in art, performance and dance that have employed chance method in composition and performance,[28] Foreman pursues what he sees as a route that evades both conventional representational schemes and aleatory processes. Foreman associates the attempt to 'give up' meaning through chance operations with another kind of 'objectification' and understands his own approach not as an escape from such 'distortions' but an awakening to them. In his first manifesto he lists three principal distortions:

1) logic – as in realism, which we reject because the mind already 'knows' the next move and so is not alive to that next move.
2) chance & accident & the arbitrary – which we reject because in too short a time each choice so determined becomes equally predictable as 'item produced by chance, accident, etc.'
3) the new possibility (what distorts with its weight) – a subtle insertion between logic and accident, which keeps the mind alive as it evades over quick integration into the mental system. CHOOSE THIS ALWAYS![29]

Consistently with this, *Pandering to the Masses* continually returns to indications of representation and signification in order to wrong-foot the expectations such indications may bring into play. Instead of inviting a reading of the 'object' or attempting to escape its terms altogether,

Pandering to the Masses repeatedly renews a promise of the object's coming into being yet always seeks to frustrate the continuities and coherences on which it depends. Thus the performance undercuts itself as it traces out, at each successive moment, expectations that are systematically let down. This leads, Foreman suggests, to a critique that 'is the body and flesh of the play', and that, because it is the very substance of the performance, becomes, paradoxically, 'the critique of a play that isn't there'.[30] It is a 'play' whose elements seem continually to come into view but which never finally appears, a play whose realisation and so closure is perpetually staved off.

It follows that while Foreman is concerned to disrupt the 'object', it is the process of disruption, rather than the presence or otherwise of the object itself, that is his primary concern. In this way, the object, or at least its possibility, remains in play at the moment at which it is dissolved. Foreman emphasises:

> I do think that some sort of *dissolving* of the object – which is invariably dishonest in its need to convince, is desirable. But what seems most interesting to me is to dissolve the art-work as self-consciously as possible ... I'd like to build it into the object ... in such a way that my actual making of the work is a *being-there* with the dissolving process.[31]

Such a tension is fundamental not only to the notion of the 'object' in Foreman's work, but also to his treatment of particular elements. Operating through what can be read as a systematic distraction from possible points of view or continuities, Foreman frequently disrupts any sense of centre by the presentation of simultaneous and unreconcilable focuses. Rather than simply present contradictory events, he offers a collage of competing points of attention bound to one another through a single structure or pattern. Thus Foreman will add whistles to the dominant beat of music.[32] He will frequently frame, punctuate or counterpoint dialogue with 'foghorns, thuds, pings, boings, glass shatterings, drum rolls, bells, whistles and screams',[33] disrupting the rhythm and meaning of the exchange. The actor's manipulation of the strings running across the space may at once reveal Foreman's design of a scene and bring 'material that has less than official status within the scene'[34] to the attention of the audience by framing parts of the body or objects. In this way, while many of the elements Foreman introduces play on the spectator's expectations, and even imply some future continuity, each element is placed in such a way as to disarm another, as different expectations are played against each other. Here, Foreman suggests, 'the field of the play is distorted by the objects within the play, so that each object distorts each other object and the mental pre-set is excluded'.[35] Similarly, the performance style Foreman has fostered can be understood as another means of disarming that which would, at face value, seem to be offered in the text. Working within a precise scenographic design into which performers are placed without regard to psychological continuities, Foreman chose in his early work to use non-actors; performers free of a vocabulary through which they might attempt to draw a continuity from the text. Such a lack of technique allows a draining of psychological depth and the disarming of what might be, by implication, an emotional content.

In her work with Foreman since 1971, Kate Manheim, who remained Foreman's principal performer until the late 1980s, sought to extend these qualities into a more specific vocabulary. Her physical work, Manheim notes, is marked by a breaking up of the continuities of movement and an effort to always work 'against what comes naturally to the body'.[36] Similarly, she focuses upon her own presence as a performer rather than any notion of role or developing mood, alternating in performance between attending to her own sense of presence, which the physical difficulty she pursues serves to heighten, and allowing her mind to dissociate from the text and wander.[37] Through such techniques, she suggests, 'I try to keep myself off-balance ... to keep myself in a state when I'm always surprised by what I'm doing or what's happening.'[38] Thus while the play offers signs of character, Manheim does not pursue any coherent characterisation, and while Manheim looks out towards the audience, considering her own presence, the text provides no direct voice with which she can articulate this focus.

In this way, Foreman's work can be understood as an attempt to place elements in such a manner as to provoke reverberations between the expectations or possibilities each brings into play and a context which diffuses or distracts from the realisation of any particular set of expectations. This is not simply a matter of the disruption of a projection forwards, but rather involves indications of character, emotion, plot and significance being confounded at the moment of their appearance by their framing and manner of presentation. Such a pattern does not look directly toward a plurality of 'interpretations', but towards a 'suspension' of interpretation, toward the moment before a decision is made, in order that the fact of the decision rather than its consequences might be revealed. In his first manifesto Foreman argues:

Only one theatrical problem exists now: How to create a stage performance in which the spectator experiences the danger of art not as
involvement or risk or excitement ... but rather the danger as a
possible *decision* he (spectator) may make upon the occasion of confronting the work of art.[39]

In these respects, Foreman's work points towards the contingent
nature of its own means and seeks to expose this contingency by tripping
up and revealing the audience's bringing of the 'object' into play. In
doing so, the work looks toward the provocation of a self-reflexive
attention in the audience analogous to that self-awareness Foreman pursues in his generation of the text:

The result of being awake (seeing): You are in two places at once (and
ecstatic). Duo-consciousness: 1. You see 2. You see yourself seeing.[40]

It follows from this that form, here, is not to be understood as something within which meaning or significance inheres, but is literally performative, a strategy or set of moves which serve to reveal the fact of its
own conventional nature. In this work, where 'the subject is not anything that you can see',[41] form and subject are understood to be arbitrary
and conventional in their significance, serving as means to address the
negotiation towards meaning rather than anything they can concretely
embody. Hence:

form isn't a container (of content) but rather a rule for generating a
possible 'next move.' That's where the subject is (in that next move,
dictated or made possible by the form). The commonly-thought-of
content or subject is the pretext to set a process in operation, and that
process is the real subject.[42]

Michael Kirby: *First Signs of Decadence* (1985)

In contrast to Foreman's Ontological-Hysteric Theatre Michael Kirby's
plays and productions with the Structuralist Workshop have been characterised by the incorporation of conventional forms and styles. *First Signs
of Decadence* (1985), which Kirby describes as a 'drawing room play',[43]
is set in a wealthy apartment in Berlin in 1931, where five characters
meet to present the first reading of a new play to potential backers. As the
piece unfolds the audience is introduced to Beatrice Walden, the author

of a new play, Dr Gottfried Schernchen, the author of a popular book of psychology, Señora Rosella San Cristofa, the wife of a wealthy industrialist, and Elfriede Elpner and John Charles Fort, both actors. Typically, the reference to genre is immediately apparent and so a stable context through which the play may be read implicit. Consistently with this, and as always, Kirby writes toward a realistic performance style, arguing that 'theatre to me is realistic' and 'we all understand realism'.[44]

A concern for structure, however, operates through this play without regard for the conventional unities and transparencies of realistic drama. Rather than directly support the realism itself, the structure of *First Signs of Decadence* is determined by a complex array of rules to which the interaction of characters as well as entrances, exits, lighting, music, and even patterns of emotional response, are subject. In the first act, as the characters meet in anticipation of the reading, actors may stand or sit in only nine places, each of which 'is related to the classical stage directions of "up" and "down," of "left," "centre" and "right" found in those books on directing'.[45] Only three of the five actors may be on stage at any one time, one performer leaving as another enters. Every 25 seconds all three actors move to new positions. In this context 'every combination of three, out of the nine, positions is used once; none is used more than once'.[46] By the end of the act, each actor will have been on stage for the same amount of time. In the short second act the characters address the audience as if they were the backers awaiting the reading, while their dialogue is structured around repeated words and phrases. Once each character has addressed the audience directly the act ends. Finally, in the third act, the characters move between eight positions closely related but not identical to those of the first and may only speak while moving. Made up of 31 units, each character is alone for 30 seconds, appears once with every other character for one minute, while every combination of three and four characters appears, respectively, for 90 seconds and two minutes. Finally, all five characters appear simultaneously for two-and-a-half minutes. As the act progresses, various characters are seen in recurring stage-pictures. These rules, Kirby suggests, 'give their activity an entirely different perceptual quality than that of the first act, even if the spectator does not consciously understand the patterning'.[47]

In setting a realistic style against such arbitrary patterns, Kirby sets up conflicts and tensions that cannot readily be resolved by the actor or the audience. Kirby himself stresses the importance of this difficulty, seeing a 'tension between the representational and non-representational aspects' through which the performance is always being 'torn apart'[48] as fundamental to the piece. For the actor in *First Signs of Decadence* this tension is evident in the necessity to justify behaviour which may seem unjustifiable, as actions generated by a formal logic fall into an ostensibly realistic scheme. For the audience, the interdependence of these two schemes serves to bring apparently irreconcilable readings into the same space. Kirby himself suggests that this tension is a key to the piece, observing that 'the structuring works against the traditional dramatic material ... involving and juxtaposing two modes of thought'.[49]

Such juxtaposition does not constitute an attack on realism or formalism as such. Indeed, the structures of *First Signs of Decadence* are not simply set against a realism but invite the audience to read a realism through, and despite, an obvious formal patterning. The structures themselves are manifested through a self-conscious display of the conventions realism has fostered but which are normally rendered transparent. Here, then, the 'rules' of realism are effectively deployed against themselves as the piece attempts not so much to defeat realism as to qualify its reception, working at once 'with and against common expectations and conventions'.[50] In this way the performance can be seen as declaring the conventional nature of realism despite its efficacy, inviting an engagement which may observe at once the nature and effect of the 'realistic' style. Kirby emphasises that 'realistic acting has nothing to do, for me, with suspension of disbelief', arguing that:

> it's a marvellous thing in the theatre if an actor acts realistically and you don't say, 'Wow, how realistic!' You say, 'Wow, what an actor!' I want the second one ... we realise it's acting and yet it's so real.[51]

Just as *First Signs of Decadence* resists an unselfconscious reading of style and structure, so its apparent subject-matter reflects on these tensions and disrupts any straightforward reading of meaning. Here the characters' own discussions may frequently be read both as dialogue in a realistic drama and as self-reflexive commentaries on the formal nature and significance of *First Signs of Decadence*. Caught between opposing possibilities, meaning becomes subject to dispute despite the clarity of the play's elements.

Ostensibly concerned with the reading of Beatrice Walden's new play to potential backers, the nature and significance of the dramatic presentation around which *First Signs of Decadence* is shaped remains elusive. While the characters prepare themselves for the reading in act one and preface the reading to the audience in act two, neither the play nor its title or subject-matter are ever presented. Act three offers only the aftermath of the reading, while the response of the backers and the future of the play are left a matter for speculation. Instead we discover simply that the play may lack a centre. In response, Elfriede, an actress, offers to play the male role of Moreau, so following the advice of Dr Schernchen's popular book, *Dreams, Symbols and the Rational Mind,* which takes the androgenous figure of Mephistopheles as 'a perfect balance of sexual dynamics. A centre from which all experiences radiate.'[52] Read through her possible motivations, Elfriede's suggestion is clearly self-serving. In the formal context of the piece as a whole, though, it is ironic, as her suggestion implies that Beatrice's play, and so *First Signs of Decadence,* might best be centred around an ambiguity. As if to compound this the ambiguity has been drawn from Dr Schernchen who intermittently presents himself as interpreter and interpolater of the new play.

Here, too, another aspect of *First Signs of Decadence* is brought into play through the reference to an ambiguous sexuality. While Dr Schernchen implies that John Charles is homosexual and, in doing so, associates homosexuality with a moral degeneration, he too comes to be implicated in a decadence. *Dreams, Symbols and the Rational Mind,* it seems, might not only be the product of a corrupt scientism but may also serve to legitimate Nazi persecution. More generally, as evidence of anti-Jewish violence in the streets sporadically filters through to the apartment, the characters' own attitudes to the rise of Nazi power remain ambivalent. It appears, too, that government figures, presumably Nazis, may be present in the audience and at various times there is excitement at the possibility that the state itself might support their production.

Beatrice's play, too, it seems, may exemplify another decadence. Rosella associates the play with late nineteenth-century aestheticism, observing that it is 'quite symbolist ... a neo-symbolist play'.[53] Later, Beatrice is accused in her absence of producing a pornography which feeds off a moral and aesthetic decadence. It is a pornography for 'collectors, aesthetes' produced by 'people with taste'.[54] The evidence of this work, however, seems far from pornographic, consisting merely of photographs promoting the benefits of nudism. In turn, Beatrice addresses her potential backers in a way that suggests either a desire for her art to be free of social and moral responsibility or that her audience should decry art without moral direction. She declares:

> We believe that theatre is an art that should be produced by people with taste. We're looking for those who would like to counteract the systematic degradation of art in our society today.[55]

Such ambiguities are reproduced by *First Signs of Decadence* at a formal level too. Indeed, the application of formal patterns 'conceived separately from the subject matter' and 'completely unrelated to characters and events'[56] to material referring to the rise of the Nazis, the persecution of the Jews and the moral responsibilities of art might be understood as a pre-eminent example of aesthetic and moral decadence. Here *First Signs of Decadence* is itself implicated in the various notions of moral and aesthetic degeneration it brings into play. At the same time, such a conflict may also serve to put the possibility of an actual decadence into question, as the play's self-reflexive and shifting commentaries on its own formal nature takes this issue into its possible subject-matter. Finally, while the meaning of decadence remains ambiguous, the attitude of the play itself becomes deeply ambivalent. Here, it seems, if the play itself can be accused of being decadent, this is because of its calculated demonstration of the very slipperiness of the meaning of decadence, and so the fact that this 'slipperiness' has become not simply a 'theme' but the key to its formal construction. Kirby himself argues that the play will tend to disrupt the attempt to read its 'meanings', particularly if one seeks to discover coherent readings rooted in theme or content. He remarks:

> I don't want to do something that has one answer ... I would like to do something that's completely open to many contradictory experiences all of which are equally 'correct' ... the way to try and do it is to build in contradictions and not to tack everything down, building openings where it can escape.[57]

As if to draw attention to this dilemma, the characters themselves periodically consider the meanings of their own actions and the events they find themselves caught up in. In doing so, however, each of them seems only to put particular meanings further out of reach. In act one, following a moment of silence, Elfriede asks after Schernchen's consideration of the symbolic nature of silence in his book. Schernchen, however, seems able only to consider the formal function and character of a symbol rather than its meaning, noting that 'I'm sure if we thought about it, we'd find it symbolic.'[58] Later, he announces that when he speaks to the potential backers he will point out the archetypes within the play in order to 'help comprehension'.[59] Faced with the audience in act two, though, this evades him and he stands silently, re-enacting the silence he suggested we might find symbolic. Finally he reveals the silence to be merely a ploy, declaring 'I thought that would be a good way of getting everyone's attention.' Yet the repetition is immediately followed by a slip of the tongue by John Charles, who is then given to expand, unself-consciously, on Schernchen's earlier conclusion:

SCHERNCHEN: Was it symbolic?
JOHN CHARLES: I'm sure if we thought about it we'd find it symbolic. (TO AUDIENCE) That kind of thing is only serious if it recurs.[60]

As the piece progresses such formal repetitions and symmetries repeatedly pose the question of where the meaning lies, while confusing what seemed to be the particular meanings of actions, costume, objects and photographs. In turn, what would appear, at one moment or another, to be safe assumptions about the five roles are quickly thrown into question as clues to attitudes and relationships are read differently at different times by different characters. During this process, individual characters even comment on the way in which such repetition itself invites consideration of the nature and meaning of events, so pushing the play towards a more and more open reflexivity. Faced with yet another coincidence, Beatrice comments on the compelling nature of the patterns which, while sublimated by realistic circumstance and relationship, are nevertheless making their presence felt:

Earlier someone made a mistake about the address. Now, someone is lost. Neither by itself would be unusual. Together, they are very unusual. Together they make one question the very order and balance and symmetry of everyday occurrences.[61]

Rather than support the articulation or invite the reading of coherent themes or points of view, form and structure in this 'Structuralist' play serve to provoke an awareness of the contingency of meaning. Such work might be considered formalist, yet these formal strategies are, in themselves, no more the 'subject-matter' or centre of the work than the realistic elements they organise and frame. Here form is not an end in itself, nor is it allowed to remain transparent. Like Foreman's Ontological-Hysteric theatre, the concerns of this mode of performance is not embodied within a form or content but are to be found at the moment at which one acts upon the other and meanings are destabilised. In *First Signs of Decadence* the possibility of meaning is always present but particular meanings are subject to shifting, ambiguous and self-reflexive relationships and points of view. Here, the viewer is presented with a

form and style of work which, through its very familiarity, invites readings which are then displaced and confounded, a set of moves which
repeatedly demonstrate the instability of any particular meaning and so
which stave off and frustrate the move toward a final closure.

Robert Wilson: *Deafman Glance* (1970)

Robert Wilson's *Deafman Glance* (1970) begins before a high prison
wall. On a white platform stands a tall, black woman in a dark, high-
collared dress, her back to the audience. To her right is a table, covered
with a white cloth, on which is placed a pitcher of milk, two glasses and
a knife. To her left is a child, who sits on a low white stool. Near him is
another child, apparently sleeping under a sheet. Moving extremely
slowly, the woman pours milk into a glass and takes it to the boy, who
drinks. She returns to the table, picks up the knife in her right hand,
wipes it, and moves to the boy again. She leans over him. He pays no
attention. Slowly, she stabs him. At this moment, Stefan Brecht observes
in his meticulous documentation of the piece:

> he collapses, she guides him down to the floor ... stabs him again,
> again very deliberately, carefully, in the back, withdraws the knife,
> walks back to the table, wipes off the knife again. Her action has been
> entirely unemotional.[62]

As she performs this act an older boy, Raymond Andrews, enters. He
stands and watches. At the same slow pace the woman pours another
glass of milk. She reveals a girl under the sheet and, waking her,
watches her drink. Replacing the glass on the table she collects the knife
and returns to the girl. As the girl sleeps the woman stabs her in the
same manner as the boy. This time, though, and when she stabs a second
time, Andrews makes the only sound he is capable of, 'a discontinuous
almost neuter scream, emotionally colourless jabs at utterance'.[63] The
woman returns to the table, wiping the knife. Finally, at the same pace,
she approaches the watching boy, whose scream becomes louder. Rather
than stabbing him the woman touches first his forehead, then his open
mouth, smothering his cry with a gesture of reassurance. The boy is
silent. The sequence takes up to a full hour to complete.

Presented at a pace she describes as approaching 'true slow motion ...
near-photographic time',[64] Sheryl Sutton's actions are such as to put into

question the nature and significance of the events she plays out. According to Stefan Brecht in *The Theatre of Visions: Robert Wilson* (Frankfurt am Main, 1978), such a mode of performance draws attention to itself as a possible source of meaning, and one which is in conflict with the expectations the events which it presents might normally raise. In his detailed record of the piece Brecht suggests that such acute slow-motion serves to make 'our experience ... pervasively dual: we are watching images and performers creating images.'[65]

For Wilson it would seem that the nature and pace of the performance serves to reveal complexities that normally remain unseen. In response to Ossia Trilling's enquiry as to the source or subject-matter of *KA MOUNTAIN AND GUARDenia TERRACE* (1972), Wilson recounted an experience evidently of great importance to him. Working for an anthropologist in New York in the 1960s, he made more than 300 films of mothers picking up and comforting their crying babies. Slowed down these films revealed that:

> when the baby's crying, in eight out of ten cases ... the initial reaction ... [is that] ... the mother is ... (a long, loud, low-pitched screech through the teeth) lunging at her baby. And the baby's responding with the body by (short screech, and grimace) fear, or many emotions simultaneously. Now, when we showed this film to the mother, she didn't believe it ... You see, we're not conscious. It's happening at another level, but with the body communicating in ways that sometimes we don't comprehend.[66]

Wilson's account offers a point from which the prologue to *Deafman Glance* may be read, and the scene has even been attributed directly to this experience. In *Robert Wilson and His Collaborators* (New York, 1989) Lawrence Shyer notes 'the maternal presence as the power of comfort (milk) and terror (knife)'.[67] Brecht observes that Sutton's gestures 'indicate a complete imbuement with a sense of maternal duty'.[68] Andrews's witnessing of the event can be read as a further play on these ambiguities. Here it is the witness to the event rather than the victim who is distressed, while his cry, which could speak for the children, the woman or the audience, is met by a gesture of reassurance.

Such a combination of elements, however, can also be related to the more complex implications of Wilson's anecdote. Wilson has suggested that the film demonstrates that 'the body doesn't lie ... we can trust the body'.[69] In this context, Wilson's story may suggest that when such actions are seen fully what they reveal is a great deal of complexity underlying apparently simple exchanges. It follows that the pace of Sutton's performance may be understood as an attempt to reveal ambiguities and raise questions that complicate a reading of her actions. Thus, the scene might not be so much a thematic exploration of 'motherhood' as a bringing into play of unexpected and multiple possibilities. The result is a performance which, in its development and despite its emotional power and resonance, resists the attempt to resolve images and sequences of images in terms of a particular meaning or meanings. It is from this point of view, of a resistance to a single resolution, that Sutton understands the effect of the figure she presents:

> the character crosses so many cultural lines and periods. It's hard to say who it is. It's hard to say it's even a mother sometimes. She's a ritual figure. She might also be a priest – the black dress, the severe lines and the little white collar. Because the staging is so ritualistic, the murders seem almost religious. There are so many paradoxes, it's hard to define or delineate what you see. That's what makes it rich.[70]

The attempt to generate and sustain conflicting possibilities is evident too in the manner in which Wilson's large-scale performances unfold. In *Deafman Glance*, this first scene over, Andrews walks towards the wall which rises revealing 'a musical garden party on the old plantation'.[71] Music plays. A 'Black Mammy' dressed in white mimes playing a piano several inches above the keyboard. A dozen or so women sit listening to music, birds perched on the right hand of each. Nearby are an 'elegant waiting couple',[72] a young girl and an elderly gentleman. As the wall rises a 'pink angel' retreats and a stage-magician, dressed in top hat, tails and a cape, advances to the sound of piano chords. The murderess stops near the group of women. Andrews sits unobtrusively to one side of the stage. Now:

> A grotesque outsider enters, destroying the reality of the plantation scene, a vulgar woman in a short, tight, cheap, worn, ill-fitting black dress, ankle boots and red socks, ridiculous black hat, with an awkwardly practical hand-bag attached to her stiffly sticking out arm.[73]

The newcomer writes in the air as if on an invisible surface. Another woman enters leading a live goat. Once the writing is complete the two make some kind of contact, then exit in different directions. The curtain gradually begins to fall. The murderess walks slowly towards the audience, then exits, followed by the waiting couple. The magician trails behind. The curtain down, the magician's motif announces the entry of a tall woman in a black dress. She is blindfolded. As she stands facing the wall, with one arm raised, the magician and his assistant remove the table, chairs and, finally, the corpses of the children. This done, the magician's assistant moves forward into a spotlight and announces the beginning of *Deafman Glance* which, he tells us, will last three hours. This he does 'in phoney, stage, ironic, demanding, weird tones, as though the play we are about to see was a play within some other play in which he was acting, a put-on: or a trick!'[74]

Here, while the parameters of the play are put into question, a process of extending and disrupting the various implications arising out of the murders has begun. The murderess has been followed out by the couple, who might take the place of the children, yet who never reappear as victims. The stance of the blindfolded woman echoes that of the murderess, yet she has entered to the magician's motif as if to take his place. The magician, in turn, gathers up the corpses and later, faintly in the distance, performs a wake for the dead children. As these sequences offer puzzling correspondences, individual images and actions are again put into question. Brecht, who performed in *The Life and Times of Sigmund Freud* (1969), *Overture to Ka Mountain* (1972) and *A Letter for Queen Victoria* (1974), suggests that 'the timing that holds a gesture the precise amount of time needed to make it sink in *and* make its mark is wrong in the Wilsonian performance: the Wilsonian performer either withdraws it as soon as it is being noticed ... or *holds* it until the spectator feels *exposed* to it.'[75]

As the piece proceeds, the juxtaposition of different kinds of performance also serves to fragment a sense of a formal coherence. While Raymond Andrews sits quietly and unself-consciously, the striking figure of the Black Mammy presents a deliberately exaggerated and self-conscious image, one which, Wilson suggests, is 'theatrical' and 'articulated as such'.[76] The awkward announcement of the play's beginning is strongly related to Wilson's own mode of performance, which Brecht describes as falling between a display of the difficulties of performing and bad acting.[77] Periodically, too, Wilson introduces actions and performers that seem out of place, presenting live animals or entirely inexperienced performers[78] who offer arbitrary and awkward presences which resist any easy incorporation into the developing actions and images.

Ironically, though, and despite such fragmentation, *Deafman Glance* continually alludes to the possibility of thematic and formal centres. As the piece progresses references to the child and murder are woven through the transforming and interlacing images. Andrews's continuous presence and the title itself may invite the idea that the piece is somehow the dream of the deaf boy or a meditation upon his mode of experiencing. The pattern into which these elements fall, however, serves only to stave off or complicate any particular thematic reading, as images and actions are placed in relationships which imply many possible and often competing significances.

This fragmentation and confusion of readings is fostered by Wilson's mode of composition. In his introduction to *The Life and Times of Sigmund Freud* (1969), originally presented as a prologue to its performance, Wilson set out his working method, which, despite any apparent subject-matter, involves an attention first of all to the formal and visual aspects of the presentation:

> the stage is divided into zones – stratified zones one behind the other ... in each of these zones there's a different 'reality' – a different activity defining the space so that from the audience's point of view one sees through these different layers, and as each occurs it appears as if there's been no realisation that anything other than itself is happening outside that particular designated area.[79]

In this way, elements are combined through an organising principle which, whatever correspondences it comes to imply between images and actions, has in its operation taken very little account of the thematic implication of any particular set or sequence of images. The resulting sense of dislocation is extended, too, in the repetition and variation of images through this process. Each image 'has a full register', meaning that 'at any point one element may be in full focus with all its parts together and later less or more of the parts are together'.[80] As a consequence not only thematic development but also the reading of role and conventional distinctions between performers tend to become confused. Observing his construction of *the CIVIL warS* (1984), Janny Donker notes the effect of Wilson's subordination of the actor to a developing formal logic:

> A role may ... be distributed among various actors, like a melody that is passed from one instrument to another. Conversely an actor may be playing various roles in succession – or even, from the viewpoint of the audience – simultaneously.[81]

In this context, the suggestion of a thematic key or centre, which in *Deafman Glance* has tended to be associated with Andrews's presence, is

typical of Wilson's work. Far from rejecting the possibility of such significances, Wilson builds his variations and sequences around highly
charged emotional, social and historical images. His performances have
embraced figures such as the King of Spain, Stalin, Queen Victoria, Einstein, Hess, Edison and Lincoln.[82] In each case, though, Wilson's mode of
composition has served to counter any simple articulation of the 'subject'
apparently at hand, while individual productions have had little to 'say' or
develop in connection with these figures. Wilson has also combined these
'historical' images and subject-matters in apparently arbitrary ways, and
certainly without regard to historical necessity. *The King of Spain* (1969)
was incorporated into *The Life and Times of Sigmund Freud* (1969),
becoming its second act, while in 1971 *Freud* was combined with
Deafman Glance to create a single 12-hour piece.

Wilson's use of language, too, follows a similar pattern, implying by
its presence logic and discourse while in its organisation confusing logical or discursive readings. Although in *Deafman Glance* language is
sparse, mostly conversational and constituted largely of *non sequiturs*, in
later productions such as *A Letter for Queen Victoria* (1974) and *The
Golden Windows* (1982), language is used extensively and Wilson has
published scripts.[83] Here, though, language seems to be organised
according to criteria that have little to do with its semantic properties. In
developing *A Letter for Queen Victoria* Wilson collaborated closely with
Christopher Knowles, who, like Wilson, was fascinated with pattern and
rhythm. According to Wilson, Knowles 'uses language as much for its
geometric structure as for its meaning. Sometimes he will take a word or
a phrase and build a structure out of it. He'll extend it to a pyramid or
some other shape and then reduce it back to a single phrase or letter ...
His constructions are very beautiful to look at. It's structured language.'[84]

A Letter for Queen Victoria is constructed out of such patterns in
which snatches of conversations are subjected to continual construction
and reconstruction according to rhythmic and visual schemes. The performers, of which Brecht was one, accepted this fragmentation, seeking
in performance to give their lines 'meanings independent of their literal
meanings'.[85] The result, Brecht argues, is a play which is primarily
visual and which offers 'the image of conversation, of different ways of
talking to each other'.[86]

Such paradoxes are fundamental to the effect of Wilson's work, where
formal correspondences between events and images draw attention and
give weight to juxtapositions and sequences that, thematically, have only
the most tendentious of connections. Through this Wilson offers a performance that repeatedly appears to articulate something in particular,

but which in fact presents images in ambiguous and ambivalent relation-ships to one another. Repeatedly, these performances invite readings of connections and parallels whose actual significances remain obscure. Consistently with this the performances are not generated out of any sin-gle scheme, while the subsequent sense of fragmentation is amplified by the independence of light and sound, including dialogue, which is often separated from its source and projected variously around the space.

In the context of such fragmentation, Wilson's choice of subject-matter is of great importance and takes its place alongside the work's more overtly formal strategies. Rather than articulating an historical subject-matter, Wilson's social and historical imagery can be read as serving an overtly formal function. Such images as these, by their very familiarity and emotional resonance, and so their formal weight as sub-ject-matter, promise significance and invite readings. It is this 'formal weight' that Wilson exploits in his drawing of formal correspondences and equivalences across unlike and, seemingly, unrelated events and figures. It follows that the more socially significant or resonant the theme, the more effectively an audience might be drawn into the ten-sions that define the effect of the performance. Consistently with this, for Wilson the importance of figures such as Freud or Einstein would seem to lie not so much with the issues their presence might raise as their immediate resonance for an audience. Wilson has suggested that a research into the figures he uses would be counter productive to his work. In using the image of Einstein in *Einstein on the Beach* (1976), he stresses that 'I don't want to know any more about Einstein than what everyone knows about Einstein. I just want to know what the man in the street knows because that's what they'll bring to the work.'[87] Wil-son's account of his treatment of the theme of *the CIVIL warS* (1984) similarly reflects not so much a concern with social, historical or politi-cal import as formal function, an elaboration of images which serves to set one thing against another while staving off particular conclusions. In *the CIVIL warS*, then, the way Frederick the Great relates to his father:

> could be a civil war. How the soldier puts his sock on before march-ing off into battle is a civil war; even a child learning to tie his shoe could be a civil war. It can be a situation like we have in Beirut today where there is no difference between civilians and soldiers.[88]

Such a gradual transformation and development of images which reflect and fold into each other as the piece progresses continually

invites and at the same time seeks to displace particular readings. At a
formal level, Wilson seems to understand his work as inviting or provoking a mode of seeing which might accept such conflicting and separate elements, each of which may be seen through or against each other.
So, Wilson suggests, in its performance, *Freud* offers:

> a collage of different realities occurring simultaneous[ly] like being
> aware of several visual factors and how they combine into a picture
> before your eyes at any given moment. Awareness in that way occurs
> mostly through the course of experience of each layer rendering the
> others transparent.[89]

Such a process serves to put into question familiar objects, actions
and events, where the attempt to read meaning and significance into
emerging correspondences and patterns is deflected by multiple possibilities and implications. Here the act of reading itself becomes part of
the subject-matter of the work, as meaning becomes multiple and elusive, constantly a possibility but always seeming out of reach. In his
influential review of *Freud*, Richard Foreman emphasised the importance to Wilson's work of multiplicity and uncertainty. Fundamental to
this work and its importance, he argues, is 'a sweet and powerful
"placing" of various found and invented stage objects and actions – so
placed and interwoven as to "show" at each moment as many of the
implications and multi-level relations between objects and effects as
possible.'[90]

At one level, this work seems impervious to 'reading'. Yet Wilson's
presentations continually call attention to a developing play and parallel
of resonant and familiar images, and so to a promise of purpose and significance. In this way, the work negotiates with the *act* of reading, but
does so in order to stave off or deflect the attempt to close any particular
reading and so arrive at any final, single or unself-conscious conclusion.

Against depth

Like the minimalist object, such performances resist the effort to penetrate
the surface of the work, frustrating the reading of structure, sequence, pattern and image. In doing so, they mark out a fundamental opposition to
the desire for *depth*, for the discovery of a 'centre' from whose vantage
point the various elements which are presented may be understood. For
Foreman such 'depth' is, unequivocally, 'the ultimate fantasy':

The ultimate evasion. Linked, of course, to a concept of centre. So de-
centre. Displace. Allow thought to float up from the depths and rest
on the surface.[91]

Not only Foreman but also Kirby and Wilson bring strategies into
play which move to reflect the viewer's attention back from a surface or
which displaces attention from one surface to another. While *Pandering
to the Masses* persistently and immediately denies its elements those
functions and purposes they promise to bring into play, *First Signs of
Decadence* offers 'realism' as a self-conscious construction, one whose
conventions are made visible through their arbitrary repetition and patterning. *Deafman Glance* presents a series of transforming surfaces
which would displace the attention from one image to another both
simultaneously and in sequence. While Foreman's presentations undermine the attempt to read meaning from moment to moment, Kirby and
Wilson's work invites multiple and conflicting readings. Even the promise of meaning, here, is shifting and unstable, while the desire to discover meanings, the promise of which these pieces invariably play with,
is always frustrated. What remains is a play of prompts, of indications or
traces which displace one other, a de-centring which continually staves
off a final closure.

In this way, all three of these pieces exemplify a resistance to that
totality which would be definitively *meaningful*. Through shifting and
self-reflexive strategies the notion that meaning can somehow *belong* to
the 'work', that its elements can be understood as *possessing* its meaning, is directly challenged. These performances, one can argue, look
above all towards the 'event' which occurs between the spectator and the
presentation, an 'event' made visible both by the resistance to depth and
the deflection between and across surfaces and signifying elements. Such
a refutation of the properly meaningful amounts to an attack not only on
the autonomy of the work of art but the specularity of the sign, as the
attempt to read, to discover depth, is persistently deflected, de-centred,
thrown back upon itself, in an exposure of the contingency of the 'work'
and that which the viewer discovers in the moment of its presentation.

Chapter 4

Modern Dance and the Modernist Work

In performance theory and criticism the use of the term 'postmodern' has had its longest history in association with the changes in American dance of the early 1960s. Like the modern architectural styles against which Charles Jencks sets his description of the postmodern in art, the rejection of a self-consciously modern and stylised American dance by the dancers and artists associated with the Judson Dance Theater in New York has been taken to mark a radical departure from 'modern' modes of work. After Clement Greenberg's account of the modernist project, influential readings of the modern, the modernist and, consequently, the postmodern in performance have been constructed around the Judson Dance Theater's rejection of the expressionism characteristic of modern choreographies. In the context of Michael Fried's unequivocal condemnation of the 'theatrical' in art, however, one might challenge the very possibility of a properly 'modernist' performance, and, in turn, these readings of the move from a modern and to a postmodern dance.

From modern to postmodern dance

As it came to be defined in the work of Martha Graham, Doris Humphrey, her partner Charles Wiedman and the German-born dancer Hanya Holm, American modern dance had its roots in the rejection of the conventional languages of classical dance and an exploration of the

71

expressive properties of movement and compositional pattern. In his book with Carroll Russell, *Modern Dance Forms* (San Francisco, 1961), which drew on Graham's method and recorded his own influential teaching, Graham's partner and musical director, Louis Horst, stressed the importance of the modern dance's rejection not only of the formal strictures of the classical tradition but also the 'free dance' inspired by Isadora Duncan. Arguing that modern dance had turned away from both 'the dry technicalities of ballet and the vague formlessness of "interpretative" dance',[1] Horst saw Graham and her contemporaries as rediscovering the expressive function of dance through an address to the essentials of choreographic form.

Yet despite Horst's injunction against Duncan's romanticism and Graham's own dismissal of the 'weakling exoticism'[2] of Ruth St Denis and Ted Shawn, the work of this second generation of modern dancers had its roots firmly within that which it ostensibly rejected. Most obviously, the work of Graham, Humphrey and Wiedman was born directly out of a reaction against the Denishawn Company, with whom they had been associated until as late as 1923. Evidently, too, the formal innovations of St Denis and Shawn, among others including Loie Fuller and Maud Allen,[3] acted as a spur to this second generation of dancers' revitalised concern with form. At the same time, and despite Horst's rejection of her pursuit of the spontaneous, Isadora Duncan's understanding of the unity of choreographic and musical composition, her desire to discover languages natural to the body and so direct in their communication, and her notion of the dance's unique embodiment of feeling, find themselves echoed in the new generation's assumption of the expressive function of dance.

Building on these earlier departures, this second wave of modern dance was characterised not only by a concern for form but an assumption that the identity of dance as an art must be bound up with the expressive power and significance of dance-movement. So while Doris Humphrey grounded her compositional method in what she saw as the fundamental properties of dance-movement and pattern,[4] for her the key to the modern remained that of 'working from the inside out ... it's the dominant expression of our generation, if not of the age'.[5] Graham, similarly, understood dance to be an externalisation in which the acting out of an 'interior landscape' was bound up with the formal properties of dance as a medium. The expressive function of dance was not simply something marked out by style or intent, but was to be discovered within its very form, as an inherent property of movement. Graham notes:

Dance is another way of putting things. It isn't a literal or literary thing, but everything that a dancer does, even in the most lyrical thing, has a definite and prescribed meaning. If it could be said in words, it would be; but outside of words, outside of painting, outside of sculpture, *inside* the body is an interior landscape which is revealed in movement.[6]

For Susan Foster, in her book *Reading Dancing* (Berkeley, Cal., 1986), this understanding of dance as the externalisation of inner, subjective but universal truths defines an expressionism which embraces the work of modern dancers from Duncan through to Graham and a subsequent third and fourth generation of choreographers. At the same time, and as a part of this expressionism, Foster understands the continuity of modern dance to lie in the very process of rejection and re-invention of movement vocabularies. Rather than build upon prevailing languages of dance, she suggests, the second generation of modern dancers rejected the work of their teachers, and often their contemporaries, as a testimony to the validity and seriousness of their own artistic impulses. Thus, the very fact that 'one person chose the subject-matter of the dance, invented the vocabulary to express that subject, and then danced the final composition' served only to heighten its 'immediacy and authenticity'.[7]

In the consolidation of American modern dance after the war, however, the emphasis upon the fundamental properties of form and the techniques and compositional methods understood to reveal those properties came to the fore. Both Horst's *Modern Dance Forms* and Doris Humphrey's *The Art of Making Dances* (New York, 1959) emphasise formal compositional problems and look towards the essentials of choreographic method and so the parameters of movement vocabulary. Horst, aligning the Graham technique to the modern styles of art, even stresses the absolute nature and continuity of the laws of composition. Drawing attention to the 'fundamental rules' of form he states categorically that 'composition is based on only two things: a conception of a theme and the manipulation of that theme, whatever the chosen theme may be, it cannot be manipulated, developed, shaped, without knowledge of the rules of composition'.[8] Such a manipulation, he argues, should also follow certain basic patterns which underlie all artistic composition and which include 'theme and variation', the 'Rondo' and 'the most deeply instinctual aesthetic form ... the ABA'.[9] Here art even takes up:

the universal pattern of life itself: we are born, we live, we return to the unknown. It is the *three part form* which is the rhythm of the natural drumbeat, the pattern of the common limerick verse, and also the usual basis of serious musical composition, from a single song to a complex symphony.[10]

In Horst's work, particularly, but also through the pervasive influence of the Graham and Humphrey schools on the teaching of dance, this consolidation came to look towards the circumscription of a vocabulary of means. It is as a rejection of this prevailing understanding of dance in terms of a particular expressive function, of appropriate styles and materials, and so of a limited range of methods and patterns of composition, that Sally Banes defines a specifically 'post-modern' performance in her influential book *Terpsichore in Sneakers: Post-modern Dance* (Boston, Mass., 1980). In the work of the Judson Dance Theater presented between 1962 and 1964, in particular, Banes identifies a break away from the work of modern choreographers and the emergence of new attitudes and styles of work that define a range of specifically postmodern departures.

Defining postmodern dance

Although Merce Cunningham had introduced chance into his compositional method as early as 1951, and had worked with the composer John Cage since 1942, by the late 1950s the assumptions and practices of expressionist dance still prevailed in non-classical teaching and practice. Cunningham himself had been a principal dancer in Graham's company, while many of Cunningham's own company had trained in the modern dance methods defined by Humphrey, Graham and Horst. Of the 15 dancers and artists who showed work in the first concert of dance presented at the Judson Church in June 1962, Steve Paxton, Ruth Emerson, William Davis, Judith Dunn and David Gordon, each of whom had been associated with the Cunningham company, had all trained in the Graham technique or taken classes with Louis Horst. Robert Dunn, whose classes in choreography at the Cunningham studio between 1960 and 1962 had given rise to the Judson Dance Theater's first concerts, went so far as to set his interest in chance method against Horst's concern for the expressive function of music and the close correspondence of musical and choreographic composition. In a similar vein, Dunn set the openness of his classes against the 'oppressive' nature of Horst's teaching, suggesting, in an interview with Sally Banes, that 'if indeed I helped liberate people from Louis [Horst] and Doris

[Humphrey] (who was a great woman, but still) ... that was well worth doing'.[11] In fact, the eclecticism of Dunn's teaching served to challenge the very notion of 'appropriate' function and form. Rather than pursue any particular idea of the nature or purpose of dance, Dunn looked towards other disciplines, using his classes as a 'clearinghouse for structures derived from various sources of contemporary action: dance, music, painting, sculpture, Happenings, literature'.[12] In her detailed record of the Judson concerts, *Democracy's Body: Judson Dance Theater, 1962–1964* (Ann Arbor, Mich., 1983), Banes identifies just such an exchange between disciplines with a sensibility underlying the Judson work as a whole:

> Perhaps even more important than the individual dances given at a Judson concert was the attitude that anything might be called a dance and looked at as a dance; the work of a visual artist, a filmmaker, a musician might be considered a dance, just as activities done by a dancer, although not recognizable as theatrical dance, might be re-examined and 'made strange' because they were framed as art.[13]

Such an eclecticism and sense of a liberation from prevailing assumptions is evident, too, in the sheer variety of departures that characterised the Judson concerts. Banes observes that the work of the Judson Dance Theater embraced the 'baroque style' of David Gordon, Fred Herko and Aileen Rothlein, a form of multi-media performance exemplified in aspects of Elaine Summers's and Judith Dunn's work as well as the 'analytic, reductive' performances with which it is often associated. Even here Banes sees distinct and contrasting styles:

> Yvonne Rainer's dialectical work, mixing ordinary or grotesque movement with traditional dance techniques ... Steve Paxton's fusion of nature and culture, his framing of mundane actions like eating and walking ... Robert Morris' task dances, using objects to focus the attention of both performer and audience and his references within works to other artworks ... Lucinda Childs' cool performance style, rooted first in the handling of objects and later in pure movement structures; Trisha Brown's improvisations and flyaway movements.[14]

For Banes, though, while the Judson Dance Theater defines itself as 'historically post-modern' in its break from expressionist modes of choreography, its work represents a phase of dance in which fundamental aspects of *modernism* come to the fore, as the theatrical style and emotional content of expressionist choreographies are rejected in favour of a more exclusive focus upon form. Suggesting that the term 'postmodern' 'means something different in every art form', Banes argues in her introduction to the second edition of *Terpsichore in Sneakers* (Middleton, Conn., 1987) that 'in dance, the confusion the term "postmodern" creates is further complicated by the fact that historical modern dance never really was *modernist*'.[15] In seeking to strip movement of 'expression', in doing away with choreography's tie to music and narrative, the dancers and artists associated with the Judson concerts are understood by Banes to have pursued a modernist aesthetic analogous to that which Greenberg proposes for modernist painting. It follows that the resultant pared-down or 'minimal' dance might properly be considered at once 'post-modern', in the sense of an open reaction against a self-styled modern American dance, and yet *modernist* in its stripping away of that which is 'unessential' to dance as a medium.

Important as it is, however, Banes's reading raises both historical and theoretical questions concerning the possible relationships between modern, modernist and a postmodern dance. Historically, one can argue that a description of 'post-modern' dance as modernist involves a separating out of certain Judson presentations from work with which it seems to interpenetrate and yet which is not consistent with Greenberg's project. Robert Rauschenberg, for example, extended his work directly into the realm of performance through a participation in nine of the sixteen Judson concerts. Robert Morris, whose minimal sculptures Michael Fried later pronounced to be antithetical to the modernist work, regularly presented performances with the Judson group and, later, under the aegis of Fluxus. The dancer Simone Forti and the artist Carolee Schneemann performed both within the Judson Dance Theater and as members of the Fluxus group.[16] Yvonne Rainer and Aileen Rothlein of the Judson group both performed in Schneemann's *Environment for Sound and Motions* in a concert organised by Philip Corner and Dick Higgins in May 1962, shortly before the first of the Fluxus and Judson Church concerts. In this way, the participation of many of the Judson Church dancers in the YAM festival of May 1963, which brought together Happenings, Fluxus, new music and dance, and which was organised by George Brecht and Robert Watts, can be read as part of a wider exchange of ideas, practices and presentations.[17]

More fundamentally, though, the very notion that, after Greenberg, a 'reduction' of dance to movement without regard to representation or expression, or even to the presence of the dancer alone, constitutes a projection toward a legitimating essence needs to be put into question.

After Greenberg, Fried emphasises the difficulty theatre has in so far as it aspires to the modernist ideal. Like music, he argues, theatre is durational and, like any performance, 'theatre *has* an audience – it *exists for* one – in a way the other arts do not'.[18] For Fried, then, 'this more than anything else is what modernist sensibility finds intolerable in theatre generally'.[19] Fried's charge challenges not simply the analogy between modernist painting and 'post-modern' dance, but the very prospect of a properly modernist programme within performance.

Modern dance and the modernist work

In considering a modernist dance after Greenberg, one can begin either by addressing, as Banes does, coincidences with non-objective art and so between a 'post-modern' dance and that abstract painting Greenberg privileges, or critical and theoretical readings of dance as an autonomous aspect of art. In the first instance one begins with the morphology and development of the work, in the second one might look towards a theoretical ground and a reading of dance animated by assumptions close to Greenberg's own. Yet in addressing readings of dance as a formally unique and self-legitimating medium, one not only returns to criticism and theory bound up with modernism, but to assumptions and ideas which are coincident in various ways with the practice of 'modern' rather than 'post-modern' choreographers. Indeed, and ironically, in taking this route through theory and criticism, one can return to presentations that have little to do with non-objective art; in fact, to 'historical modern dance' itself.

In *Reading Dancing* Susan Foster observes that the three most influential theories of dance composition, formulated by the ethnologist Curt Sachs, the critic John Martin and the philosopher Suzanne K. Langer, all 'locate the origins of dance in early human gestural attempts at communication'.[20] In doing so, she notes, 'they oppose these primal yearnings to express human feeling to the subsequent artificiality of civilised movement, and they look to dance as a medium that can return us to a vital energy and an unalienated sense of wholeness'.[21] For Sachs and Martin modern dance, specifically, is characterised by an attempt to rediscover this vitality, and so implicitly obtains a special place and purpose with regard to the nature and function of dance, as it projects itself toward the foundations of the medium.

Writing in his *World History of the Dance* (New York, 1937), Sachs argues that both Duncan's break from classical convention and the popularity of 'American Negro and Creole dances' signalled a rediscovery of the body and a desire to return to the fundamental sources of dance. In doing so, he suggests, modern dance sought a new authenticity:

> Our generation does not find what it seeks in ballet ... It cries out, as Noverre once did, for nature and passion; again it desires, as he did, though perhaps too strongly, to exchange stereotyped movement for something genuinely of the soul.[22]

Martin, who, unlike Sachs, specifically sought to theorise the moderns' practice, argues similarly in his *Introduction to the Dance* (New York, 1939) that Duncan's work should be understood as 'a profound overturning, clearing away ages of accumulation of intellectual restraints and yielding the power of motion to the inner man'.[23] In doing so, Martin supposes, modern dance seeks not only its own origins but that of art itself, for 'the medium in which the art impulse first expresses itself is that of movement'.[24]

This primitivism, which Robert Goldwater traces widely throughout European modernism in *Primitivism in Modern Art* (London, 1938), was self-conscious in the work of modern dancers themselves. In 1931 Graham's celebrated *Primitive Mysteries* employed Christian imagery and ritual forms drawn from her studies of North American Indians, while Humphrey's *Shakers* of the same year incorporated studies of ecstatic religious worship. Similarly, and drawing on Graham's practice, Horst points toward the 'elemental nature' of the impulse to dance and the 'deep responsiveness between body and mind'[25] out of which he believed the art of dance was formed. Dance, in Horst's view, carries within it this aspect of the primitive and the essential, as if to remind us that '[t]housands of years of civilisation have endowed us moderns with only a veneer of refinement to separate us from our crude and naive ancestors'.[26]

Importantly, too, in their association of the sources of dance with pre-verbal, non-intellectual impulses, these ideas speak not only of the special significance of dance as a medium but of the difficulty of discussing the actual significances of any particular dance. In this way, again, Sachs, Martin and Langer participate in a critical modernism, finding themselves on common ground with self-consciously modern practitioners in their assumptions about the dance's special and defining qualities. For these critics, Foster suggests, 'as for the majority of early twentieth century choreographers ... the dance functions as a luminous symbol of unspeakable human truths, which, because they are un-speakable, leave us with little to say about the dance's organisation'.[27]

The notion that dance reveals a 'special' significance, however, serves not only to set it apart from a criticism which is unable to re-present that which the 'art-dance' articulates, but also from other genres of art. Indeed, in considering the nature and importance of such 'signifi-cance' these accounts of dance look toward those qualities which make dance 'distinct', which, in fact, embody what is unique to it as an artistic medium. In this respect, what emerges from a close reading of Langer and Martin's theorising of dance, as opposed to Sachs more broadly historical approach, is an understanding of the 'art-dance' as a self-determining work of art, existing in its own aesthetic realm, and a cor-responding conception of how the medium of dance legitimates itself *as a fine art*. In elaborating these ideas, one might first address Langer's comprehensive theory of art and performance and, in this context, Martin's detailed address to the nature of modern dance.

Suzanne Langer begins her address to the fundamental characteris-tics of art by reviewing the body of ideas upon which she builds. In the work that precedes her own, Langer argues, the key concerns and ques-tions of aesthetic theory 'all converge on the same problem: what is significant in art? What, in other words, is meant by "Significant Form"?'[28] As this question implies, Langer assumes at her point of departure that 'significance' is a property of artistic form; that the vital import and so the qualities by which the work of art is defined reside, definitively, *within* it. In *Feeling and Form: A Theory of Art* (London, 1953), Langer emphasises the necessity of looking 'upon the art object as something in its own right, with properties independent of our pre-pared reactions – properties which command our reactions, and make it the autonomous and essential factor it is in every human culture'.[29] It is on this basis, too, that Langer understands art and critical discourse to be entirely separate and distinct. Indeed, Langer defines 'significance' in art by opposing it to the nature of meaning in language, producing, through this opposition, an account of the function and effect of the work of art.

Accepting the transparency of language, Langer argues that the ele-mentary unit of language exists on the basis of a simple and convention-ally fixed correlation between a word or combination of words and a given object or idea. So far as such 'associative symbols' are concerned, meaning is fixed and straightforward. In the operation of language, how-ever, and where such symbols are used in combination, meaning, and so the symbol itself, become more complex. In a sentence, she notes, meaning is expressed through the organisation of associative symbols rather than through the value of the symbols alone. Here, 'one may say that the elements of propositions are *named* by words, but propositions themselves are *articulated* by sentences'.[30] It follows that a sentence, which is a 'complex symbol', can properly be described as an 'articulate form', where meaning is found through the perception of its internal structure rather than simply through the presence and value of its constituent elements.

It is after this model that Langer characterises the symbolic nature of art, a nature which she first sets out in *Philosophy in a New Key* (Cambridge, Mass., 1942) in her special theory of music. Like a complex symbol in language, Langer observes, a musical composition is an 'articulate form':

> Its parts not only fuse together to yield a greater entity, but in so doing they maintain some degree of separate existence, and the sensuous character of each element is affected by its function in the complex whole. This means that the greater entity we call a composition is not merely produced by mixture, like a new colour made by mixing paints, but is *articulated* ... .[31]

Yet music is fundamentally different from language, for its constituent elements, what would be the associative symbols, do not make fixed and specific reference to any idea or object. Thus while language is pre-eminently logical and intellectual, music, which presents itself as pattern without conventional reference, cannot possess rational significance and is an analogue of experience as it is felt rather than understood. The corollary of this is not simply that art and criticism lie in separate and distinct realms, but that the formal terms by which the work of art is constituted and the nature of the significance art has to offer are bound one within the other. Thus, one can say definitively that the work of art *is* an analogue of sensual and emotional experience. In elaborating this model of art as an 'articulate but non-discursive form', Langer not only defines an opposition between art and language, but, in describing the self-determination of the work of art, oppositions between the 'significant form' that announces the work and its literal contexts as well as the various genres of art.

Within Langer's conception of art as an 'articulate form', the identity of the work of art cannot be understood simply in terms of the individual elements of which it is constituted. Instead, it is 'significant form', arising through the *articulation* of physical elements, that announces the work of art. It follows from this that, in the most fundamental sense, the work of art comes into being at the point at which it separates itself from the material elements upon which it is reliant, at the point at which it establishes itself as an 'illusion', a 'virtual object'. Langer empha- sises the importance of this distinction, observing that the 'illusion, which constitutes the work of art, is not a mere arrangement of given materials in an aesthetically pleasing pattern; it is what results from the arrangement, and is literally something the artist makes, not something he finds'.[32] It follows that at the very heart of the work of art is an abstraction, a separateness from the material environment that sur- rounds it, even a separateness from the physical object without which it could not exist. Langer emphasises the importance of the 'air of illu- sion, of being a sheer image' that she associates with the work of art, noting:

> Every real work of art has a tendency to appear thus dissociated from its mundane environment. The most immediate impression it creates is one of 'otherness' from reality – the impression of an illusion enfolding the thing, action, statement, or flow of sound that consti- tutes the work.[33]

Nor is this effect produced by the way in which the work is seen or understood by the viewer. Arguing that the work of art constitutes itself by this very 'detachment from reality',[34] Langer emphasises that 'it is not the percipient who discovers the surroundings, but the work of art which, if it is successful, detaches itself from the rest of the world; he merely sees it as it is presented to him'.[35] In these terms, and coinciden- tally with Fried, the successful work of art can be said, by its very nature, to effect not only a separation of itself from its mundane en- vironment but a transcendence of its own objecthood.

It is in the context of this autonomy, this separation of the definition and qualities of the work from the 'literal' materials and circumstances upon which it is dependent, that Langer makes her distinctions between the various modes of art. If the fundamental condition of art is one of abstraction, it follows that the identities of the various forms of art may lie in the particular nature of the abstraction of which they consist. Thus, Langer argues, each 'art gender' is defined by its own 'primary illu- sion', its own 'virtual realm' consisting of 'the basic creation wherein all its elements exist' and which, in turn, its elements 'produce and sup- port'.[36] By their very natures, each of these realms is separated both from the material contexts in which the work of art is found and any other virtual realm. The absolute nature of this distinction, and of the work's separation of itself from its mundane environment, is demonstrated in Langer's account of the primary illusion of the plastic arts. Langer begins by setting out what she takes to be the formal function of this particular mode of art:

> The purpose of all plastic art is to articulate visual form, and to present that form ... as the sole or at least paramount, object of perception. This means that for the beholder the work of art must be not only a shape in space, but a shaping *of* space – of all the space that he is given.[37]

For Langer this means that the treatment of space within the plastic arts is quite removed from our experience of space in life. While we perceive objects in relation to one another in space, 'space' as we experience it over time and through our various senses, Langer suggests, cannot be said to have 'shape' for it has no 'concrete totality'.[38] It follows that the 'picture space' which is defined in the plastic arts is not an articulation of space as we experience it in life at all, but of a created virtual space, an illusory space 'that exists for vision alone'.[39] Not only this, but by its very nature as an illusion, virtual space has a discontinuous relationship with practical space and so with the literal contexts in which the work of art presents itself. Langer observes:

> Being visual this space has no continuity with the space in which we live; it is limited by the frame or by the surrounding blanks, or incongruous things that cut it off. Yet its limits cannot even be said to *divide* it from practical space; for a boundary that divides things always connects things as well, and between a picture space and any other space there is no connection. The created virtual space is entirely self-contained and independent.[40]

The autonomous nature of this primary illusion also establishes a fundamental distinction between any work that articulates virtual space and any work whose primary illusion lies in another virtual realm. Just as 'everything that is relevant and artistically valid in a picture must be visual',[41] so whatever elements enter into a piece of music must find a place and a function within its primary illusion of 'virtual time'. In turn, Langer notes, the primary illusion of poetry is that of 'virtual life'; of drama, 'virtual future'. Dance, similarly, establishes itself through its own unique abstraction; that of gesture, drawn out of its practical contexts so that it may enter into the symbolic realm of art. Langer observes that 'dance gesture is not real gesture, but virtual ... it is *actual movement*, but *virtual self-expression*'.[42] On this basis Langer's understanding of the symbol in art allows her to reveal dance's basic abstraction and its primary illusion, that of the 'virtual realm of Power':

> Every being that makes natural gestures is a centre of a vital force, and its expressive movements are seen by others as signals of its will. The spontaneously gestic character of dance motions is illusory, and the vital force they express is illusory; the powers (ie: centres of vital force) in dance are created beings – created by the semblance gesture.[43]

In this way, each art is necessarily defined by that virtual realm which is its primary illusion and in which it, alone, exists. It is a realm that is entirely self-contained and self-supporting, a realm that, like the work itself, is autonomous. So, Langer concludes, 'a work never belongs to more than one realm, and it always establishes that one completely and immediately as its very substance'.[44]

It follows that not only does Langer's theory assert the autonomy of the work of art, its transcendence of its material conditions and even its own objecthood, but it also proposes an absolute distinction between the various forms of art and what is proper to them. Therefore, Langer concludes, a recognition of the virtual realm of dance finally allows a proper consideration of what is unique to dance, and offers a solution to common confusions in both dance criticism and practice over what is and is not truly appropriate to the medium. Thus:

> The recognition of a true artistic illusion, a realm of 'Powers' ... lifts the concept of dance out of all its theoretical entanglements with music, painting, comedy and carnival or serious drama, and lets one ask *what belongs to dancing*, and what does not.[45]

Clearly, Langer's theory does not specifically look towards the legitimation of the modernist programme Greenberg elaborates. Indeed, Langer explicitly rejects such a programme for art and sees no necessary connection between the abstraction she takes to be the fundamental condition of art and a modernist projection towards the formal essence of the work of art. Langer states categorically that 'abstract form as such is not an artistic ideal. To carry abstraction as far as possible, and achieve pure form in only the barest conceptual medium, is a logician's business, not a painter's or poet's.'[46]

At the same time, though, this theorising of the work's possession of its own meaning and identity and of the necessary and unbridgeable separation of 'art-genders' enters into a concept of the work of art with which Greenberg's modernist project participates. Like Langer, both Greenberg and Fried argue for the immanence of the work; its inherent significance, its necessary separation from its material conditions, its transcendence of its own objecthood. Indeed, unless the work of art is understood as imbued with qualities entirely its own, unless it can be seen as standing apart from its 'mundane environment', self-possessed and self-sufficient in an autonomous realm, then a projection towards those qualities which lie definitively *within* the work cannot make sense. It follows that while Langer's theory does not seek to define a modernist art or dance, it nevertheless rehearses assumptions essential to the modernist programme.

While it is on this ground that Langer's understanding of art intersects with Greenberg's notion of the modernist work, it is here, too, that her conception of art crosses with John Martin's analysis of the function and character of modern dance. This is not to imply that these theories and practices should be collapsed one into the other, but simply that their coincident assumptions mark out a ground which this idea of the modernist work assumes and depends upon. It is on this ground, then, that one can look towards ways in which Greenberg's understanding of modernist painting crosses with a reading of historical modern dance.

In defining dance as 'the expression, by means of bodily movement arranged in significant form, of concepts which transcend the individual's power to express by rational and intellectual means',[47] John Martin accords in general with Langer's assumptions about the character and function of art. More specifically, in this context, Martin understands the emergence of modern dance to signal a return to the proper purpose and nature of 'dance as a fine art';[48] that is, the expression through appropriately 'significant', rather than conventional or codified, forms, of 'extra-intellectual' and so ineffable meaning.

In his account of the history and development of modern dance, Martin points first to its fulfilment of romantic ideals; its rejection of the 'artifice' of the inherited languages of classical ballet and its chief aim, which it shares with romanticism, of 'the expression of an inner compulsion'.[49] Yet it is precisely here, too, that for Martin modern dance departs from the more problematic assumptions of romanticism and, in particular, from romantic attitudes toward composition in a distinct and defining 'realisation of the aesthetic value of form'.[50] Where romantic or 'free dance', with its emphasis upon spontaneous expression, Martin supposes, threatens to confuse artistic significance with 'self-expression', the modern dance concerns itself directly with the creation of compositional forms which possess and articulate 'significance'. In this way, Martin argues, modern dance defines itself in opposition to the 'decadence' of classical ballet while transcending the naive aspects of the romantic movement and, in doing so, looks toward the fundamental character of dance as an art-form. Indeed, Martin understands the projection toward a marriage of expressive function and significant form as a projection toward a realisation of the defining principles underlying the medium itself. Here modern dance not only takes up the proper function of dance as a fine art but, in an explicitly modernist mode, looks towards its fundamental and legitimating characteristics as a discipline.

Clarifying this critical aspect of modern dance in *The Modern Dance* (New York, 1933), Martin considers its four principal discoveries. The first of these emerges at the point at which modern dance defines itself as distinct from romanticism and where movement itself, as an independent entity, is understood to lie at the core of dance as an artistic medium. Here, Martin argues, rather than employing movement as a means of animating and unifying a highly conventional vocabulary of attitudes and poses, or allowing movement to arise spontaneously from an intense focus upon the dancer and the inspirational effect of music, modern dance takes movement itself to be the essence of dance and the key to its significance. This is not simply to say that all dance consists of movement, but rather that movement is what is significant in dance; that movement is the very substance of dance and literally the site of its meaning.

Out of this arises the second discovery. Asserting that as 'the most elementary physical experience of human life'[51] no movement of the body can ever be entirely non-representational or meaningless, Martin argues that the kinaesthetic response to movement, the sympathetic muscular response of the spectator to the impulse of the dancer, is inevitably complimented by a psychical response of some kind; an image, idea or a feeling. This being the case, Martin concludes, movement, as such, is by its nature *significant*. It follows that, just as it is only with the advent of modern dance that movement is understood to be the substance of dance, it is only with the emergence of modern dance that this 'metakinesis' can come fully into play as a compositional element. This is not to say that this process has not always been important to the nature and effect of theatrical dance, but rather that in modern dance, through its isolation of movement, this essential property becomes fully available to the artist. So Martin states categorically that 'no conscious artistic use was made of metakinesis until the modern dance arose'.[52]

Having concluded that movement itself is the substance of dance and that all movement is inherently significant, it follows that the 'substance' or 'material' properly appropriate to dance is 'continuous or sustained movement', movement that 'contains no static elements, no attitudes however decorative which might be considered points of rest'.[53] Hence the characteristic 'dynamism' of modern dance, in which 'there is never a moment in which the dancer lapses into natural physical rest'[54] represents an exclusion of elements unessential and so corruptive to dance as an art form.

Finally, Martin's assumption that movement is the site of meaning and that all movement has significance leads him to conclude that while 'compositional form' is inherently significant, no one form, or set of conventional forms, can circumscribe the possible vocabulary of dance. In fact it is the very freedom from conventional vocabularies that allows the modern dancer to employ the various properties of movement in an entirely appropriate way and, through this, to create compositional forms free of ornamentation and distraction which are appropriately expressive and significant. Martin emphasises that in modern dance 'each dance makes its own form'[55] and that in making its own form each successful dance will come to a unique 'significant form'. Here, again, Martin's understanding coincides with Langer's:

> Form ... is capable of operating of itself. It may, indeed, be the result of unifying diverse elements whereby they achieve collectively an aesthetic vitality which except by this association they would not possess. The whole thus becomes greater than the sum of its parts. This unifying process by which form is attained is known as composition.[56]

Although in *The Modern Dance* Martin does not use the term 'modernist', what he describes here is the self-conscious realisation within the work of art of the essential terms underlying the medium. In dance, he asserts, 'the leaders of the modern movement ... have succeeded in performing the greatest service to their art in discovering its essential substance and the dimension in which it exists'.[57] For Martin, and because rather than in spite of its expressionism, historical modern dance is taken to be a projection toward the 'essence' of dance as a medium which, at its height, promises to reveal the absolute dance, 'that pure essence of dancing which contains no element of anything else'.[58]

The object of dance

Martin's position does not simply reveal theoretical and critical coincidences between a reading of the modernist project in art and dance, but demonstrates the very difficulty of extending the model of a modernist autonomy into a reading of performance. Indeed, the juxtaposition of Langer, Martin and Banes's readings of dance against Greenberg's ideal of the self-legitimating work, reveals not simply a debate over the terms of a modernist performance, but the very resistance of 'theatre' to a realisation of a properly modernist programme.

Despite his assertion that movement is the substance of dance and that all movement has significance, Martin does not suppose that all movement is possible or suitable material for the 'art dance'. Indeed, he takes the modern dance's realisation of the essential properties of the medium to involve an exclusion of elements inappropriate to it as a fine art. Martin states categorically:

> All movement ... is not suitable material for the creation of the dance. All dance is made of movement, but all movement is not dance; just as all music is sound, but all sound is not music; or all poetry is words, but all words are not poetry.[59]

In seeking to create 'significant form', Martin argues, the dancer must discard that movement which 'is the stuff of daily, routine physical living' and 'select the kind of movement that is not subordinate and subsidiary to physical necessity, but is the product of a mental, an emotional, or non-physical demand'.[60] In Martin's view such a distinction is essential to dance's definition of itself as an art-form. Martin even concludes that 'art and nature are irreconcilable opposites. For this reason natural movements and natural rhythms are impossible materials for the art dance'.[61]

Langer makes an analogous distinction. Here the 'work of art' is never something the artist finds or to which the spectator gives identity by the act of looking, but is something that has been *made* and which asserts *its own* identity as art. It follows that a dance is never simply 'movement', but is always movement that has been transformed, movement that has been 'imagined', remade and made 'articulate'. With regard to dance, Langer argues:

> Gesticulation, as part of our actual behaviour, is not art. It is simply movement. A squirrel, startled, sitting up with its paws against its

heart, makes a gesture, and a very expressive one at that. But there is no art in its behaviour. It is not dancing. Only when the movement that was a genuine gesture in the squirrel is *imagined*, so it may be performed apart from the squirrel's momentary situation and mentality, can it become an artistic element, a possible dance gesture.[62]

The autonomous work of art makes its nature clear by an absolute differentiation of itself, by properties which are its own, from the mundane circumstances in which it presents itself. For the 'art dance', this self-determination necessarily involves a differentiation of 'the dance' from 'movement-in-general'. Hence Martin's antipathy toward 'everyday' movement and 'natural' rhythms. For Martin, as for Langer, dance cannot be merely 'movement', but is necessarily a movement or pattern of movement which has set itself apart from movement-in-general by what it *is*. Such movement is not defined as 'art' by a contingent set of circumstances or contexts, for it creates its own context, differentiating itself from that which is around it. Here there can be no confusion between the 'art dance' and everyday movement, because the art dance is in possession of its own identity as art. Indeed, Greenberg's reading of the projection of the modernist work toward those terms which are definitively *within* it, is a reading of the work of art as an uncovering of precisely such a self-determination.

The significance of this becomes clearer when it is set against the model of historical postmodern dance. For Sally Banes it is the reduction of dance to simply the presentation of 'movement', even taking the form of a simple functional task, that defines historical postmodern dance as *modernist*. Yet where 'dance' is understood to be differentiated from 'movement-in-general' only by the fact of its presentation to an audience, then the very notion of a self-determination is threatened. Movement defined as dance by how it is *framed* and, therefore, by how it is *seen*, is not self-determining in the way Langer, Martin and Greenberg suppose that the work of art must be. In fact, in Fried's terms, such a challenge to the differentiation of the work of art from its mundane circumstances, including the circumstances of its presentation, can only bring dance to a point where it is antithetical to the very idea of the work of art.

In this context, then, and in opposition to Banes's reading, one might understand historical modern dance to be properly modernist in so far as, in the name of such a self-determination, it is shaped by an attempt to overcome its own contingent nature as a *performance*. In this way, the definition by modern theorists and practitioners alike of dance as an art whose elements are, as Langer emphasises, 'made' rather than 'found', which are 'composed' rather than 'framed', and whose significances inhere within a fixed and unified form, describes the 'art dance' as that which would overcome its ephemerality as theatre. In *Modern Dance Forms* Horst emphasises that 'it should never be forgotten that there must be a form into which the qualities and style can be arranged if the dance is to have choreographic validity'.[63] Similarly, he calls on Langer for authority, who states simply that 'Nothing has an aesthetic existence without form. No dance can be called a work of art unless it has been deliberately planned and can be repeated.'[64] Such statements flatly suppose that as a performance aspires to the condition of art, so it attempts to defeat its own ephemeral and contingent nature and acquire the condition of an object.

Consistently with this, and after Fried, one can readily argue that, however much it strives toward the ideal, no *performance* can be modernist after the manner of Greenberg's project. Such a conclusion does not attempt to resolve the question of whether modern or postmodern dance is modernist, but rather looks toward the way in which assumptions inherent within Greenberg's notion of the modernist work begin to unravel once they are brought into the realm of performance. In turn, this unravelling sets the ground for a reading of historical postmodern dance not simply in the terms of a rejection of modern dance styles, but as a questioning of the assumptions which animate this whole idea of the modernist project. Far from rehearsing Greenberg's programme through dance, the historical postmodern dance's reduction of dance to simply 'movement', or even the presence of the dancer alone, attacks the very notion of the autonomous work of art, revealing a contingency, and so an instability, in place of the centre the modernist project would seek to realise.

Chapter 5

The Collapse of Hierarchies and a Postmodern Dance

The character and development of the early Judson Dance Theater reflected, first of all, the nature of Robert Dunn's classes in choreography from which the Judson group emerged. Held initially in the autumn of 1960 and culminating in the earliest of the dance concerts at the Judson Memorial Church in Greenwich Village in 1962, Dunn began his classes at the Merce Cunningham studio at the invitation of John Cage.[1] Cage himself, following the start of his series of influential courses on 'Composition in Experimental Music' at the New School of 1956–60 which were attended by Allan Kaprow and George Brecht among other artists engaged with Happenings, Fluxus and the new dance, had taught an analogous course on modern dance composition at the request of members of the Cunningham company.[2] Although he was neither a dancer nor a choreographer, Dunn had studied music and dance before attending Cage's classes at the New School and shared both Cage's eclectic interests and his enthusiasm for chance procedures. In his own teaching, Dunn not only drew upon his experience of Cage as a teacher, but sought to make clear methods and principles of composition close to Cage's own. In her detailed account of the history of the Judson Dance Theater, Sally Banes emphasises the variety of influences acting upon Dunn's work and sensibility which, quite apart from his enthusiasm for the contemporary arts, ranged from the Bauhaus to Heidegger, Sartre and Taoism. Nevertheless, Banes concludes, 'for all the diversity of models, the unifying and paradigmatic form of choreography in Dunn's class was the aleatory process.'[3]

The nature and extent of this concern for chance procedure and its implications are evident in the composition of the first of the Judson Dance Theater concerts. Comprised primarily of pieces developed within the composition class, *A Concert of Dance*, presented on 6 July 1962, included work by Judith and Robert Dunn, Bill Davis, Ruth Emerson, Deborah Hay, Fred Herko, David Gordon, Steve Paxton, Yvonne Rainer and Elaine Summers. In their publicity, the group stressed the importance of choreographic process, suggesting that the work would include such means as 'indeterminacy, rules specifying situations, improvisations, spontaneous determination'.[4] While these approaches directly echoed Cage's methods, the pattern of the concert itself introduced another element of chance and drew further on Cage's aesthetic.

Organised so that the identity of individual choreographies might become confused, the programme to *A Concert of Dance* lists 15 items incorporating a total of 23 originally discrete presentations. In this way, dances were presented simultaneously or were at times allowed to run on from one to the next without clear demarcation. In the same spirit, the framing of the concert served to confuse conventional categories. 'Dance number one' was a film, *Overture*, compiled from chance edited footage shot by Elaine Summers and John Herbert McDowell and played as the audience entered the space. The interval, itself listed as the eighth item on the programme, included a performance of Rainer's *Divertissement*, while the concert as a whole ended in darkness as the dancing continued. For *Rafladan*, in which Deborah Hay danced while Alex Hay manipulated a light and Charles Rotmil played a Japanese flute, Banes notes:

> the dancing happened in the dark, suggesting that the movements of a person not directly visible might still fall within the realm of dance. One could see Alex Hay's movements indirectly by watching the lights as he manipulated them. But Deborah Hay's movements were present only by implication.[5]

Within this framework, dances utilising chance procedures were combined with work embracing a variety of styles and methods. While Fred Herko chose to perform a 'barefoot Suzi-Q'[6] to music by Erik Satie in *Once or Twice a Week I Put on Sneakers to Go Uptown*, Ruth Emerson's solo *Timepiece* was created by applying chance procedures to a gamut of predetermined actions, movement qualities, timings and positionings in space. In contrast, David Gordon's *Helen's Dance* had been devised as a rejection of a rigid adherence to chance method and an attempt to circumvent an exercise from one of Dunn's classes, while Rainer's *Divertissement*, Banes recounts, satirised partnered dances in a spoof of the traditional ballet entr'acte of European opera. In other work, chance procedure was combined with alternative means. In *Narrative*, Emerson introduced an element of indeterminacy into performance, giving each of her dancers a score of actions including movements triggered by the activities of other performers. In *The Daily Wake*, Elaine Summers based her selection of movement elements on the photographs and text of newspapers, while the layout of individual pages provided a floorplan for the dance. In yet other pieces connections with Cage were clearly stated. Item number twelve consisted of dances by Ruth Emerson and Carol Scothorn devised by cutting up and reassembling Labanotation and performed as Cage's *Cartridge Music* was played. Extending these kinds of concerns, Summers's *Instant Chance* introduced chance processes into performance. Here individual dancers determined the type, speed and rhythm of their successive movements within parameters defined by repeatedly throwing large styrofoam blocks as if they were giant dice. For Summers the piece evidenced the process of its own making while engendering a spontaneity and sense of play.

For Yvonne Rainer and Steve Paxton, as for many of the others, chance procedure provided an important method amongst a variety of means. While in *Ordinary Dance*, Rainer combined her own choice and organisation of movement with autobiographic text, in *Dance for 3 People and 6 Arms* she allowed her performers free and improvised choices from a gamut of previously determined movements. Punctuated by certain actions which would trigger a given sequence for all three performers, the 15-minute piece looked towards the dancers' remaking of Rainer's choreography through its very complexity, which itself introduced an indeterminacy into performance. Similarly, while in *Transit* Paxton 'presented a spectrum of movement styles, from classical dance (ballet) to "marked dance" ... to pedestrian movement' in a procedure he describes as 'just taking items and playing their scales',[7] in *Proxy* he sought to give up aspects of his own authority as choreographer. In response to work with Cage's scores, Paxton sought to use chance procedure to select as well as organise movement. Rather than communicating his movement choices directly, Paxton employed a photo-score made up from sports photographs to mediate between choreography and performer. While he was involved in a selection process, decisions affecting fundamental aspects of the presentation were left open to each participant. In this way:

I made the score and handed it over to the performers, and they could take a linear or circular path through the score. You could start any place you wanted to, but then you went all the way through it. You did as many repeats as were indicated. But how long it took and what you did between postures was not set at all.[8]

As these various departures suggest, Cage's practice provides a point from which the early Judson presentations at once drew and against which they defined themselves. Such an equivocal relationship with Cage's means and purposes make his work an important point of reference from which to consider the underlying logic of these strategies.

Chance method and the object of art

Through the concert-hall performance of the first of his 'silent pieces' in 1952, Cage sought to clarify the principles underlying his work as a whole. In his closing of the piano lid for the duration of each of its three movements, David Tudor's original presentation of *4'33"* made absolutely clear Cage's denial of conventional musical vocabularies. In pointedly refusing to fill the 'silence' of what was evidently presented as a musical piece while insisting on a playing out of three timed movements, Cage sought to invite an attention to the 'noise' of the environment, to whatever sounds happened to fall within a durational frame. For Cage, the piece, which he had conceived of as early as 1941,[9] made clear the discovery in which his work was rooted, that:

> nothing takes place but sounds: those that are notated and those that are not. Those that are not notated appear in the written music as silences, opening the doors of the music to the sounds that happen to be in the environment ... There is no such thing as an empty space or an empty time. There is always something to see, something to hear .... [10]

Such a conception of 'music' explicitly attacks the notion of the autonomy of the work of art; its separation of itself from its mundane environment. In its performance, *4'33"* strips the musical work of everything but a context and the listener's experience of her own presence. In doing so, the piece explicitly rejects the notion of the self-contained, self-sustaining 'object' and redraws the work of art as an occasion or event marked out by a self-reflexive attention or receptivity. In Cage's own terms *4'33"* offers each viewer 'a discipline which, accepted, in

4' 33"

FOR ANY INSTRUMENT OR COMBINATION OF INSTRUMENTS

John Cage

NOTE: THE TITLE OF THIS WORK IS THE TOTAL LENGTH IN MINUTES AND
SECONDS OF ITS PERFORMANCE. AT WOODSTOCK, N.Y., AUGUST 29. 1952,
THE TITLE WAS 4'33" AND THE THREE PARTS WERE 33", 2'40", AND
1'20". IT WAS PERFORMED BY DAVID TUDOR, PIANIST, WHO INDI-
CATED THE BEGINNINGS OF PARTS BY CLOSING, THE ENDINGS BY OPEN-
ING, THE KEYBOARD LID. AFTER THE WOODSTOCK PERFORMANCE, A
COPY IN PROPORTIONAL NOTATION WAS MADE FOR IRWIN KREMEN.
IN IT THE TIMELENGTHS OF THE MOVEMENTS WERE 30", 2'23", AND 1'
40". HOWEVER, THE WORK MAY BE PERFORMED BY ANY INSTRUMEN-
TALIST(S) AND THE MOVEMENTS MAY LAST ANY LENGTHS OF TIME.

FOR IRWIN KREMEN

I

TACET

II

TACET

III

TACET

0'00"
SOLO TO BE PERFORMED IN ANY WAY BY ANYONE

FOR YOKO ONO AND TOSHI ICHIYANAGI
TOKYO, OCT. 24, 1962
John Cage

IN A SITUATION PROVIDED WITH MAXIMUM AMPLIFICATION (NO FEEDBACK), PERFORM
A DISCIPLINED ACTION.

    WITH ANY INTERRUPTIONS.
    FULFILLING IN WHOLE OR PART AN OBLIGATION TO OTHERS.
    NO TWO PERFORMANCES TO BE OF THE SAME ACTION, NOR MAY THAT ACTION BE
       THE PERFORMANCE OF A 'MUSICAL' COMPOSITION.
    NO ATTENTION TO BE GIVEN THE SITUATION (ELECTRONIC, MUSICAL, THEATRICAL).
                                    10·25·62

    THE FIRST PERFORMANCE WAS THE WRITING OF THIS MANUSCRIPT (FIRST IMAGINATION ONLY).

THIS IS 4'33" (No.2) AND ALSO PT.3 OF A WORK OF WHICH ATLAS ECLIPTICALIS IS PT.1.

turn accepts whatever',[11] and looks toward a mode of attention, a 'performance' to be made by the listener, and one which could be realised quite independently of any concert-hall presentation such as Tudor's. Cage suggests:

> What really pleases me in that silent piece is that it can be played at any time, but it only comes alive when you play it. And each time you do, it is an experience of being very, very much alive.[12]

In his revision of *4'33"*, *0'00"(4'33" No. 2)* (1962), 'a solo to be performed in any way by anyone', Cage sought to clarify the implications of this invitation. Read as a description of an active looking and against the terms of *4'33"*, the frame Cage describes here is not dependent upon a given duration but a 'disciplined action' taken up by the viewer, in which a heightened attention ('maximum amplification') is exercised and 'all interruptions' accepted. Whereas *4'33"* is 'musical', *0'00"* accepts no such limitation, and while *4'33"* can be associated with a particular formal circumstance, here Cage bars any such simple definition. In this way, Cage defines a work which comes into being through the spectator's actions alone, which literally consists of and is defined by a committed self-reflexive attention.

Plainly, Cage's understanding of the terms by which such a 'work of art' is defined opposes any notion of the work's separation of itself from its context and the differentiation of one 'art-gender' from another. Where the identity of the 'work' is dependent upon only a mode of attention, then not only can the work of art have no independent existence but, by implication, the formal characteristics of the visual and performing arts converge, finding their common ground in the occasion of theatre, the event of their definition by the viewer. In this context, too, it becomes clear that for Cage the notion of the 'object' in which meaning inheres is a construction of the conventional and exclusive hierarchies that define the inherited languages of art. In playing upon the viewer's desire to perceive the elements of a work in a given, stable and so safe relationship, Cage argues, these hierarchies effect a distortion of an otherwise perfectly tangible reality:

> You say: the real, the world as it. But it is not, it becomes! It doesn't wait for us to change ... It is more mobile than you can imagine. You are getting closer to reality when you say that it 'presents itself'; that means it is not there, existing as an object. The world, the real, is not an object. It is a process.[13]

In this sense, conventional musical compositions deny their audience access to the actual nature of the sounds of which they are made up, rehearsing, instead, an understanding of the work and so the world as 'object'. Cage notes:

> When you listen to sounds that share a periodic rhythm, what you hear is necessarily something other than the sounds themselves. You don't hear the sounds – you hear the fact they're organized.[14]

It follows that for Cage, where 'art should introduce us to life'[15] as a process, a resistance to the presence of the object in art is fundamental to the value of the work. Such a resistance does not simply mean the pursuit of an ephemerality or the privileging of one kind of predetermination over another. Instead, it involves an undermining or disruption of the 'perceived' object and so an uncovering of the work's inherent instability; its dependency upon the attitude and intention of the viewer, the fact that 'through the way I place my intention, I create the experience that I have'.[16] Through his use of chance method in the process of composition and development of indeterminacy in performance itself, Cage sought to cast off conventional values and hierarchies and with them the ways of looking these conventions invite and imply. Thus, he tells us, through his early use of chance procedures drawn from the *I Ching*, he wished to come to 'a musical composition the continuity of which is free of individual taste and memory (psychology) and also of the literature and tradition of art'.[17]

Between chance and the personal image

The relationship between Cage's work and the various departures of the Judson Dance Theater is a complex one. In the first place, in utilising chance method for the selection as well as organisation of movement, the Judson dancers replay Cage's overturning of hierarchies. Most immediately, then, the distinctions upon which the conventional vocabularies of dance are based, classical or modern, are thrown into confusion. More particularly, where chance is used to determine the nature and selection of elements, the choreographer moves to collapse the conventional distinctions between that which is and is not 'proper' to the 'art dance'. Such consequences are apparent within *A Concert of Dance*. As a result of the chance procedures used in the composition of *Timepiece*, which was unaccompanied, Emerson recalls that 'to my utter horror ... I had to get over the fact that I could start the piece with forty seconds of stillness. One of the reasons that I liked the piece was that I learned I could do that.'[18] Where Elaine Summers introduced chance procedure into performance through the game structure of *Instant Chance*, similar 'natural rhythms' entered into the work. Thus, Banes observes, rather than seek to sustain a sense of 'performance', of presentation, the performers of *Instant Chance* were forced to concentrate 'on doing the task at hand – over and over', continually abandoning 'one movement for no obvious reason to throw their "dice" for the next instruction'.[19] Just as these transitions arise from the focus of the performers upon the playing of a game rather than the presentation of specific movement qualities, so the rules of the game themselves provide for a disruption of the 'performed' tasks. Again, Banes recounts:

> Though each performer is highly self-absorbed, there is some interaction. The instructions for this performance ... often had one dancer lifting his colleagues one at a time, or interrupting, or in other ways intervening in their movements ... The effect was that of a bratty child bothering his playmates.[20]

Instant Chance offers itself up as a game through which unpredictable actions and movements are found. In this way Summers pursues not only an indeterminacy with regard to the organisation of movement choices but, in certain respects, a giving up of her own control in order that apparently 'untransformed' elements may be offered to the viewer. Similarly, for Steve Paxton, such strategies complimented and extended his giving up of his own authority as choreographer. In *Proxy*, while his use of the photo-score served to disrupt the usual relationship between choreography and performance, his choice of movement also introduced an indeterminacy into the process of composition by calling on the idiosyncratic movements of his participants. Banes notes that the dance involved not only 'standing in a basin full of ball-bearings; getting into poses taken from photographs; drinking a glass of water; and eating a pear' but also 'a great deal of walking'.[21] Here the very ordinariness of movement such as eating or walking allows a giving up of specific controls. Paxton suggests:

> Walking is something you can't tamper with. If you say 'ordinary walking,' you get a wide range of materials. And the more you tamper with it, the less it has the quality of being just the thing. It starts to look like somebody with a problem on their mind or somebody with

an infirmity instead of just someone walking. I tried not to tamper with it too much, so that it wasn't too special and it just occurred.[22]

The association of chance method with such a breakdown of distinctions is evident in the earliest of the Judson explorations. In the first of Dunn's series of classes with just five participants, Paulus Berenson, Marni Mahaffay, Simone Forti, Steve Paxton and Yvonne Rainer,[23] a use of chance method served to confuse the notion of what was admissible and inadmissible as part of a dance presentation. For Mahaffay, Banes suggests, the classes offered an understanding of Cage's notion of silence, and, by implication, the idea that 'any movement is valid as a part of dance – "whether it's a cough, a sniffle, or natural movement"'.[24] Similarly, Paxton presented work consisting simply of removing furniture from an office at speed or 'sitting on a bench, eating a sandwich'.[25] Simone Forti's *See-Saw* and *Rollers*, which were performed as part of a programme of 'new happenings' at the Reuben Gallery in December 1960 in collaboration with Robert Morris and other artists, drew on children's activities and games to an analogous end. Seeing her own choices as a matter of placing 'an effective act within the interplay of many forces',[26] Forti used a see-saw and roller carts to place her performers in precarious relationships which threatened a loss of control, so focusing the participants' improvisations and introducing unpredictable qualities which would 'automatically become an element in their performance'.[27] In such work as this, Morris observes, the very complexity and difficulty of rules and relationships 'effectively blocked the dancer's performing "set" and reduced him to frantically attempting to respond to events – reduced him from performance to action'.[28]

In this work, then, where 'any movement is valid as a part of dance', the notion that the identity and meaning of a work is a matter of the formal properties it possesses, that there must be something 'within' a dance that separates it out from its mundane context, falls away. Rather than pursue a self-critical honing of dance toward the essence of the medium, a casting away of the 'unessential', these presentations throw out the attempt to differentiate between that which is and is not proper and necessary to dance. Such consequences are evident not only through the presentation of 'found' movement and everyday tasks, as well as the free combination of a wide range of departures and styles which characterised the Judson concerts, but also in direct challenges to the conventional distinctions between artistic media. So Trisha Brown, among others, was concerned to address 'dance' problems through a self-conscious exchange with other disciplines. In responding to Dunn's assignment to make a three-minute dance, she recalls:

> Dick Levine taught himself to cry and did so for the full period while I held a stopwatch instructed by him to shout just before the time elapsed, 'Stop it! Stop it! Cut it out!' both of us ending at exactly three minutes. That dance is a good example of the practice of substituting one medium, in this case acting/crying, to solve a dance problem.[29]

Here too, though, it is also important to set the role of chance method into context. Despite the importance of a use of chance to an overthrowing of prevailing assumptions and practice, aleatory processes clearly do not, in themselves, underpin and shape these various strategies. It is at this point, then, that significant differences between the Judson presentations and Cage's own work become evident.

As is clear from his silent pieces, where in Cage's work art seeks to 'introduce us to life', it does so by offering a discipline through which composer, performer and viewer may resist, in certain respects, their own imposition upon the materials they meet. For Cage, these notions are informed by an involvement with Zen Bhuddism. As a consequence of his studies with the Zen teacher D. T. Suzuki between 1946 and 1950, Cage came to shape his work through disciplines appropriate to the Zen pursuit of 'no-mind'. Distinguishing between *M*ind, or that which is beyond the intentions and will of the individual, and *m*ind, or the ego, Cage remarks:

> If one is involved just with Mind, and not with the arts, one sits cross-legged in order to come to no-mind. But if you're already, as I was, involved with music, then you have to control your likes and dislikes with something as strict as sitting cross-legged. So I used chance operations.[30]

While Cage's uses of aleatory processes are shaped by the nature and purposes of this discipline, for most of the choreographers associated with the Judson Dance Theater, as for many other artists drawing on Cage's work, chance method evidently effects a release from conventional hierarchies and introduces new concerns without establishing itself as a single means or set of parameters. The significance of this becomes quite apparent in that work which follows *A Concert of Dance*. While a second concert was constituted largely of work from the first presentation at the Judson Church, concerts three and four of January

1963 consisted of performances developed by the group following the end of Dunn's classes in the previous autumn. Stressing the pluralism of the group's work, the concerts introduced presentations which, in general, moved away from chance method and yet continued to be concerned in part with elements and patterns chance processes had offered an address to. These performances called on the work of untrained performers and everyday movements such as running and walking, as well as such compositional means as juxtaposition, repetition and structured improvisation, while incorporating monologues, tasks, the use of objects and even romantic music.[31]

In this way, even these early concerts marked not only a departure from the direct influence of Cage's methods but also from Dunn, whose approaches and aims coincided closely with Cage's. In a lecture written as early as 1961 or 1962, Yvonne Rainer gave voice to this difference, describing various meetings in her work between the chance operation and the 'image', the 'personal vision, fantasy, or dream and attendant atmosphere'. In doing so, she proposed a meeting between chance method and precisely the play of personal taste and intention Cage's disciplines were dedicated to overcoming. Rainer suggests:

There is no innate contradiction between the chance operation and the image.

Aside from the image possibilities in the use of chance – and by this I mean the assimilation of the results of a chance operation into one's own personal language and imagery – all this aside – it is possible for the chance result and the image to co-exist.

It is possible for the image to influence one's interpretation of the chance operation.

It is also possible for the image to be so strong and insistent that it makes other kinds of investigation unnecessary.

It is also possible – and very gratifying when it happens to me – for the chance operation to control certain aspects of a larger image. But here again is a situation where the image – also the experience and life of the artist – has been affected by the use of chance.[32]

Rainer's lecture clearly draws upon a sensibility that can be related to Cage's work, reflecting not only a concern to open the work to elements and influences beyond the author's control but also for the significance of chance to wider choices and experiences. At the same time, though, Rainer sees no conflict between the exercise of personal taste and the use of aleatory processes and is concerned for the variety of relationships that may exist between the two. Evidently, too, this openness was not simply a matter of Rainer's particular approach, but was an important aspect of the concerts themselves. In her review of concerts three and four, Jill Johnston concluded:

> The possibilities of form and movement have become unlimited. There is no way to make a dance; there is no kind of movement that can't be included in these dances; there is no kind of sound that is not proper for accompaniment.[33]

This very openness begs the question of precisely what notion of dance the Judson work marks out. Here, clearly, while aleatory processes have been instrumental in effecting a collapse of the oppositions upon which the notion of the self-contained and autonomous work depends, chance operations have not in themselves taken the place of this hierarchy as the means by which the work is defined. Indeed, it would seem that this work does not project itself toward the inherent and unique significance of dance-movement or attempt, after Cage, to produce its antithesis, a 'work' which, free of 'intention' and 'purpose', reaches toward another 'truth', to something quite beyond the claim to hierarchy or meaning.

Being seen: minimalism and process

Yvonne Rainer describes her *Trio A* of 1966 in terms analogous to those of minimal art. In her essay 'A Quasi Survey of Some "Minimalist" Tendencies in the Quantitatively Minimal Dance Activity Midst the Plethora, or an Analysis of *Trio A*' of the same year, Rainer emphasised her rejection of both formal and thematic development:

> Variation was not a method of development. No one of the individual movements in the series was made by varying a quality in any other...In the strict sense neither is there any repetition.[34]

In this context, and rather than emerge out of a focus upon the generation of movement-elements through tasks, actions in relation to objects, or rulegames, Rainer suggests, *Trio A*, which is comprised of many simple task-like actions performed in the mid-range of bodily extension, is constituted first of all through an attention to the 'look' of the performance as it unfolds before an audience. While the piece is constructed without variation of any of its elements, in its performance, Rainer notes, she allows no pauses between phrases, ensuring that 'each phrase merges immediately into the next with no observable accent'.[35] While a great variety of shapes occur, in their continuity, she suggests, 'no one part of the series is made any more important than any other'[36] as each is given an equal weight and so an equal emphasis. Here, and while Rainer averts her gaze from the audience in order that the sequence may seem 'worklike rather than exhibitionlike', the phrasing of both movement-elements and transitions serve to ensure:

> What is seen is a control that seems geared to the *actual* time it takes the *actual* weight of the body to go through the prescribed motions, rather than an adherence to an imposed ordering of time. In other words, the demands made on the body's (actual) energy resources appear to be commensurate with the task – be it getting up from the floor, raising an arm, tilting the pelvis, etc. – much as one would get up out of a chair, reach for a high shelf, or walk downstairs when one is not in a hurry.[37]

After Cage, such a presentation can be read as a deliberate frustration of the viewer's attempt to understand one element in terms of another. In her analysis of the piece, Rainer remarks that 'my *Trio A* dealt with the "seeing" difficulty by dint of its continual and unremitting revelation of gestural detail that did *not* repeat itself, thereby focusing on the fact that the material could not easily be encompassed'.[38] By its very complexity, *Trio A* resists the attempt to 'contain' it; to read it, predict it, to set its boundaries. It follows that the very 'difficulty' of reading the dance looks toward a disruption or a staving off of the 'object', the construction of a developing 'whole'.

While doing this, and in opposition to Cage's work, however, *Trio A* explicitly incorporates both classical and modern figures. Susan Foster notes that *Trio A* makes specific reference to 'the conventional lines of design-oriented dance' and offers 'fleeting glimpses of classical placement',[39] while Rainer's 'sustained, smooth transfer of weight' is, she suggests, 'reminiscent of the organic successivity of expressionist movement'.[40] Here, then, *Trio A* subjects quotations of familiar line and figure to this 'minimalism', treating conventional phrases as 'tasks' whose actual effort is to be exposed. In doing so, Sally Banes suggests, *Trio A* comes to operate 'dialectically', bringing 'classical lines and gesture into conflict with their own subversions'.[41] Rainer herself points to the 'reversal of a kind of illusionism'[42] out of which *Trio A* is constituted and acknowledges that her incorporation of conventional elements involves an inversion of the styles of performance they recall. In achieving the 'look' of *Trio A*, Rainer notes:

> one must bring to bear many different degrees of effort just in getting from one thing to another ... The irony here is ... [that] I have exposed a type of effort where it has been traditionally concealed and have concealed phrasing where it has been traditionally displayed.[43]

Such means qualify and extend Rainer's negotiation with the viewer. In exposing the actual effort of conventional phrases while placing them amongst simple task-like activities, Rainer specifically attacks the conventional distinctions between the 'natural rhythms' of functional movement and the 'transformed' or 'heightened' nature of 'dance-movement'. Yet such a treatment of quotation clearly goes further than an attack upon hierarchical vocabularies. In explicitly denying conventional phrases the disguise and elaboration upon which their usual significances depend, *Trio A* throws its own task-based mode of execution into relief. Through its play with expectation, its *denial* of conventional weight and significance to that which it appropriates, *Trio A* at once presents a critique of the nature and effect of conventional stylisation while exposing its own particular construction of movement-elements, its own 'minimalist style'. It follows that, here, the critique of style, of the 'giving' of meaning to movement-elements, extends to *Trio A*'s own means, as the series of denials it constitutes itself through are revealed as yet another manipulation and play with movement. In this way *Trio A* engages overtly with possible readings of movement, catching its elements between those 'styles' and so significances they recall and their construction as 'tasks' through a self-consciously minimalist mode of execution. Such a play with the 'reading' of movement is far from a revelation of that which is inherently 'significant' or legitimate within dance, but is an exposure of the dependency of movement for its character upon a negotiation between dancer and observer, upon an address to the nature and fact of its being read.

In contrast to Rainer's complex montages, Steve Paxton's concern with walking, which was established as early as 1962 in such pieces as *Proxy* and *Transit*, pursue a different kind of 'minimalism', not only through a giving up of the choreographer's authority but through a simplification of both the work and its elements. In *State* (1968), 42 performers presented themselves to an audience in 'a random, scattered group' and simply stood for two three-minute intervals, while in *Smiling* (1969) two performers smiled for five minutes.[44] For Banes, though, it is in *Satisfyin Lover* (1967) that Paxton presents the apotheosis of walking. Here, between 30 and 84 performers, divided into six groups, walk across an imaginary track ten feet wide, stretching from entrance to exit in a space, which, in its first performance, was 200 feet long. Three chairs, set in the centre of this area and slightly forward of the track, provide for an interruption of the walking as performers sit, stand and then return to their crossing of the space. While Paxton's score offers simply cues for activities, number of steps and the timing of pauses, his notes to performers emphasise the informal and individual nature of their actions:

> The pace is an easy walk, but not slow. Performance manner is serene and collected.
> The dance is about walking, standing, and sitting. Try to keep these elements clear and pure.
> The gaze is to be directed forward relative to the body, but should not be especially fixed. The mind should be at rest.[45]

Rather than transform individual movement-elements or establish qualities and patterns that might suggest a self-contained and articulate 'dance', Paxton facilitates an exhibition of walking, sitting and standing in the simplest possible way. Paxton's choices would seem to have been made precisely in order that the elements of *Satisfyin Lover* should remain not only unpredictable but, in their unself-conscious variety, acquire no significance, value or quality which could immediately distinguish them from the viewer's own act of walking or even presence in the space. It follows that the identity of such an activity as 'dance' becomes openly dependent upon the occasion of theatre. Reviewing a later presentation of *Satisfyin Lover*, the critic Jill Johnston focuses precisely upon this fact, attending to the very ordinary and apparently untransformed nature of movement-activity and its blurring of the distinction between 'movement' and 'dance-movement'. She draws attention to:

> the incredible assortment of bodies ... walking one after the other across the gymnasium in their any old clothes. The fat, the skinny, the

medium, the slouched and slumped, the straight and tall, the bow-legged and knock-kneed, the awkward, the elegant, the coarse, the delicate, the pregnant, the virginal, the you name it, by implication every postural possibility in the postural spectrum, that's you and me in all our ordinary everyday who cares postural splendour.[46]

Through its very simplicity, *Satisfyin Lover* makes visible the contingent nature of its identity as 'dance'. Rather than look inward, towards a legitimating core or interior quality, *Satisfyin Lover* looks outward, towards the viewer and her 'framing' of these activities as a dance.

On the basis of *Trio A* and *Satisfyin Lover*, one might readily read the 'pared-down' or 'minimal' dance of the Judson concerts as a resistance to those inherited languages which would stabilise the work, which would 'give' it meaning, in favour of a play of instability and contingency that might provoke an awareness of a dance's definition through the way in which it is seen. Indeed, what becomes evident through such a reading is the variety of means dedicated to such a self-reflexive negotiation with the observer.

Although usually associated with the 'cool' or 'analytical' aspects of the Judson performances, the work of Lucinda Childs, like that of Rainer herself, is characterised by a wide variety of means and a development through apparently radical change. In her own consideration of her work, though, Childs has emphasised a continuity which she describes first of all in terms of an attention to the viewer. Originally inspired by Cunningham and influenced by Cage and the choreographies of Robert Morris, Steve Paxton and Yvonne Rainer, Childs's early approaches were rooted in combining dance phrases with movement-activity in relation to objects and, later, in the juxtaposition of movement and language. In this context, and like Rainer, Childs sought to escape 'traditional dance vocabulary' through task-activity 'governed by the materials and subject to the limitations of their physical qualities'.[47] At the same time, though, Childs's monologues serve to set movement which might escape any conventional notion of choreographic pattern against a clear and obviously imposed structure. Childs notes:

The dialogues did not in and of themselves dictate action, but accompanied action as the activity in the dance drifted in and out of a context that was relevant to the content of the dialogue. And I determined the extent to which relevance between action and dialogue was sustained intermittently throughout the individual dances.[48]

In a piece such as *Street Dance* of July 1964 the disjunctive relationship between movement-activity and imposed structure is extended to the point where the audience's ability to 'see' the performance at all becomes dependent upon the monologue that frames it. Here, while the audience watches from a loft across the street, two performers engage in a six-minute sequence of activities entirely based on their 'found surroundings' and which are 'blended in with the other activity ... going on in the street'.[49] As Childs's taped voice describes the street in detail, the dancers engage in activities largely indistinguishable from the general activity around them, and punctuate their actions regularly, though momentarily, by pointing out that to which Childs's monologue refers. In this way, because at such a distance the viewer is unable to see the detail of that which the dancers point towards, Childs notes:

> the spectator was called upon to envision, in an imagined sort of way, information that in fact existed beyond the range of actual perception, so that a kind of cross-reference of perception tended to take place in which one mode of perceiving had to reconcile itself with the other to rule out the built-in discrepancy that the situation created.[50]

Street Dance plays on the discrepancy between that which the observer's attention is drawn towards and that which she can readily perceive, so provoking an awareness of looking. In doing so, though, *Street Dance* puts its own terms and parameters into question. Faced with a performance that is repeatedly lost to the unself-conscious activities of non-performers, and which is dependent for its distinction from the 'everyday' on a monologue which describes a place rather than an activity, these strategies would seem to put the very possibility of the definition of a 'work' into question. The purpose of the taped monologue is not so much to 'reveal' a dance as to put the observer into the position of defining the 'work', of negotiating between elements and means that have an ambivalent relationship to one another in a piece whose identity as a 'dance', let alone its particular parameters, are uncertain. Here, then, and in other such pieces where apparently 'everyday' or 'ordinary' movement-activities are set against a self-conscious frame, the observer is drawn toward an awareness of her own pivotal position in the definition of the piece.

Such a drawing of the viewer into a self-conscious process of definition underpins a range of strategies shaping Childs's work and is apparent from its inception. In *Geranium* of February 1965, a dance of four sections, Childs used the third section to announce the fact that there was no third section and offered instead 'theoretical reasons for dealing with the gap'.[51] In *Model* of August 1964, Childs's movement was accompanied by her description of a 'typical modern dance position':

It is uncomfortable to be in as well as difficult to get out of and ugly.
    The right foot is bent diagonally back toward the right and the left leg is bent diagonally back toward the left.
    It is an expressive position.
    Expressive for someone who has nothing to do.[52]

These commentaries play with the possible significance of structure, movement and dialogue, yet remain disarmingly self-reflexive. Here, while the significance of the lack of a third section becomes the substance of the third section, the 'typical modern dance position' is drained of its would-be 'expressivity' by Childs's description of the relationship between mechanics and purpose as well as the fact of the narrative itself. Such devices echo the quotations of *Trio A*, where the familiar phrase or line is denied its usual place and import, and is incorporated or appropriated in order that it may be subverted, put into question.

Formally, though, it is Childs's later work which converges with Rainer's. Beginning with *Untitled Trio* of 1968, Childs became concerned to apply a set of elements to a dance as variables, allowing identical phrase sequences to be repeated while being subject to 'reversals, subdivisions, inversions, reordering in space, and displacement from one dancer to another'.[53] In this way, and with seating on all sides in order to establish as many points of view as possible, Childs sought to create a situation in which 'the same thing is seen again and again but never in exactly the same way'.[54] In her solo *Particular Reel* (1973), Childs traversed 21 parallel lines, performing a three-minute phrase that covered one-third of the space, repeating it in reverse for the second third, and again in the original manner for the final third. Despite the apparent simplicity of the system the relationship between movement-activity and its organisation was such that the viewer was faced with a continually changing sequence. In *Particular Reel*, while a series of reversals allowed ends to link with ends and beginnings with beginnings, in the manner of 1234567654321234567, Childs's choice of movements for her original phrase served to introduce a complexity into this apparently simple structure, as the elements of the phrase mirrored and reversed one another. Childs notes:

While the dancer is fully cognizant of the particular adjustment she is abiding by, the spectator is not. He is introduced to the phenomena gradually during the passage of time, and the structure becomes apparent to him as configurations perceived outside the moment are matched up with those seen in the moment. While any configuration tends to dissolve in the memory as others replace it, the deliberate simplicity of the action tends to counteract that process. The perceptual bind that the viewer is drawn into, nevertheless, is reminiscent of the same kind of double focus provoked by the earlier pieces. Either he perceives that the same thing is different when it is not, or he perceives the same thing as the same through an awareness of the manner in which it has been removed from its original mode of presentation. In drifting between prediction and speculation, he is dislodged from any single point of view.[55]

Working its way through Childs's various kinds of presentations is a pursuit of a self-reflexive address to the process of looking. It is through such a focus that Childs's and Rainer's work may be seen as closely related despite their formal differences. *Particular Reel* operates by way of variation and elaboration, and so by those 'developments' *Trio A* rejects. Nevertheless, in so far as Childs's variations continually draw the spectator into readings from which she is dislodged, forcing a self-consciousness on behalf of the viewer as she views, these patterns serve an analogous function to Rainer's subversions of style.

In this context, aspects of Trisha Brown's later work can be read as exemplifying both the 'reductive' performance associated with the Judson presentations and a self-reflexive attention to the process of being seen. Rooted in her work with Ann Halprin on task-based choreography and, shortly afterwards, in her experimentation with chance and other methods in Dunn's classes, Brown's work has taken many departures and yet has tended to centre around the notion of 'improvisation within set boundaries'.[56] As her work has developed it has been upon the importance of these boundaries rather than particular movement choices, that her concerns have focused. In her 'Equipment Dances' of the late 1960s and early 1970s, such as *Man Walking Down the Side of a Building* (1969), Brown sought situations where the 'boundaries' of the piece, including its very difficulty, precluded movement choice. Here, where a dancer is equipped to walk down a seven-storey building:

Aside from the equipment and danger the piece was very direct. I knew when to start – it starts at the top. I knew where the dancer went – he went straight down. ... The movement that he did between top and the bottom was walking. There were so few choices; the structure, the set-up, made the choices. Now *that* comes out of my view on making and choreographing movement ... there are a thousand choices – I mean why is this better than that?[57]

Rather than concern herself with defining a dance through the presentation of particular movement qualities, Brown attends to the relationship between activity and frame and, through this, to the viewer's act of looking. In her review 'Walking on the Wall', Deborah Jowitt recorded her self-conscious vacillation between the 'uncanny' illusion of an everyday activity and the display of skill and equipment the frame itself necessitated:

> For dizzying moments at a time, you seem to be in a tower looking down on the foreshortened bodies of people promenading endlessly on two intersecting white streets. Sometimes you come down from the tower to watch the technique of it all – how they get into and out of the slings, how they pass, how they unstick a recalcitrant pulley, how they zoom around a corner.[58]

In this presentation no particular choice of movement-element is 'better' than any other in the sense that the definition of the piece is not, first of all, dependent upon any such choice. Indeed, in catching the viewer's attention between an acceptance of illusion and an attention to the frame, the Equipment Pieces would force a recognition of the dependence of these elements for what they 'are' on the manner of the viewer's own attention to them.

Consistently with this, and in her own discussion of her 'Accumulation Pieces', dances which in their performance continually evidence an accumulation of actions, Brown has clarified this point. Here, she suggests, while the choreographer is free to be 'seduced' by movement choices, 'the more important issue is how any movement is organized into a dance'.[59] In *Primary Accumulation* of 1972, Brown's dancers engaged in an 18-minute procedure whereby a sequence of 30 actions were accumulated one by one through the continual repetition of an extending string of movements, in the manner of 1; 1,2; 1,2,3; 1,2,3,4. Including movements 'based on formal arrangements of the body parts', 'gestures of universal meanings', 'eccentric actions' and actions with sexual overtones,[60] the procedure sought not only to demonstrate its own framing and reframing of material, but at moments deliberately called this process into question. Actions 3, 4 and 30, Brown notes, are familiar gestures performed in order to raise the question 'is she dancing or has she stopped?'[61] Just as it draws the viewer into a continual re-reading of movement-elements, at several moments *Performance Accumulation* presents activities which put into question whether or not a dance is continuing, yet which, in their repetition, are 'transformed' into dance-movement. In this way *Performance Accumulation* evidences its making as a 'dance', exposing a 'transformation' of 'functional', 'non-dance' activity into 'dance-movement' through a negotiation over framing and so over reading.

Like the Equipment Dances, the Accumulation Pieces suggest that a dance is defined through the way in which it is seen. Again, Brown's comments have reflected this position. In an interview of 1973, and in response to the suggestion that in her accumulation pieces she entered into a process of 'stripping movement to its core', Brown responded by putting the very possibility of such a 'reduction' into question, concluding that 'Most choreographers find a structure and anytime they make a new piece they make a new movement. Whereas I'm using the same movement and making new structures each time. The movement is immaterial.'[62]

If a dance's identity is a matter of circumstances, of 'framing', and so of the way it is seen, then the notion of 'stripping movement to its core' cannot make sense. In this context, neither movement nor dance can be said to have a 'core', for neither is in 'possession' of an identity that can be separated out from the particular meaning or meanings it acquires for those who meet it at the point at which it is met. Indeed, what flows from this position is that, because of the very contingent nature of its meaning and so identity, any element may become a dance or part of a dance by being brought into a negotiation with, or becoming subject to, that 'look', that 'reading', which holds the key to its possible definition.

Being read: Process to narrative

It is in terms of the definition of the dance and its elements through a self-reflexive attention to the process of being seen, that ostensibly 'minimal' performance finds itself on common ground with presentations which overtly incorporate familiar figures and conventions. On this basis, one can trace a consistent development rather than a transformation of means in the work of Yvonne Rainer and, later, Steve Paxton and Trisha Brown, as their work moves away from the overtly 'minimal' and towards an address to conventional dramatic continuities and theatrical forms and devices.

After the final version of *The Mind is a Muscle* in 1968, which had originally incorporated *Trio A* as its first part, Yvonne Rainer's work shifted direction. Following performances in 1968 and 1969 in which she sought to bring aspects of the rehearsal process into the performance itself, Rainer's *Continuous Project – Altered Daily* of 1969 initiated two years of improvisational work with the Grand Union, a collaborative group founded by the performers of the *Project* and which included Steve Paxton and Trisha Brown.

Rainer's dance piece was constructed after Robert Morris's 'process piece' *Continuous Project Altered Daily* of the same year. However, while for Morris the *Project* marked a direct extension of the concerns that had brought him to a 'minimalist' vocabulary, for Rainer the piece led to a departure from the formal conventions and critical vocabulary of minimalism.

In his essay, 'Some Notes on the Phenomenology of Making', Morris emphasised his concern for the process of 'art making', describing an art in which 'process becomes a part of the work instead of prior to it' and where 'forming is moved further into the presentation'.[63] For Morris such concerns stemmed from doubts surrounding the efficacy of the geometrical forms predominant within minimalist work and a desire to develop the logic of the minimalist object even further. Morris's introduction of non-rigid materials into his presentations from 1967 responded directly to the privileging of the cubic and the rectangular in the minimalist practice which he, among others, had defined. In his 'felt pieces', dating from 1967 and 1968, and consisting of sheets, strips or bundles of felt, Morris offered examples of work subject to an open-ended process of change. Shaped and reshaped by the accidents of transportation and exhibition, these objects promise a changing morphology limited only by the particular physical properties of the material itself.

Despite Morris's emphasis upon process, however, and while such 'sculpture' will be changed by the process of being shown, the felt pieces are inevitably presented as product, a particular result of a process now arrested. It is this tension between process and object that Morris's *Continuous Project Altered Daily* dramatises. In the form in which it was presented at the Castelli warehouse in January 1969,[64] the *Project* can be read as being caught between its material elements and the process of change to which they are subject. Installed in a single large room and ostensibly consisting of earth, water, grease, plastic, threads and felt distributed randomly across low wooden tables and the floor of the space, Morris's presentation consisted of the 'alteration' of these materials, first by adding elements and then by removing them.

For the viewer, admitted not to the actual removal of materials but to eight 'stages' of the work, stages documented by an accumulating series of photographs pinned to the wall, the piece sites itself between a process of making or altering and the promise of a resulting object. This 'work' is never 'realised' in the conventional sense, for the 'object' remains unfinished, in an intermediate stage, while its 'completion', the ending of the process of forming, is marked by the disappearance of the materials out of which it would seem to be comprised. The result of the process is then a series of pictures, a documentation explicitly at one remove from both the materials which were present and the hidden process of forming which led to their removal.

Developed over a period of a year from a 30-minute performance in March 1969 to a full two-hour presentation in March 1970, Rainer's *Continuous Project – Altered Daily* incorporated various kinds of material which by their nature transformed through the process of performance. Constructed of 'interchangeable units'[65] ranging from activities requiring the whole group of six performers to solos, duets and trios, which in their generation had been overseen by Rainer, the piece was an intensely collaborative presentation whose developing shape was determined in each individual performance by the performers themselves. Along with Rainer the group consisted primarily of Becky Arnold, Douglas Dunn, David Gordon, Barbara Lloyd and Steve Paxton, all of whom had been associated with the Judson experiments.

After Morris, Rainer not only relinquished control of her 'materials', the units of performance, but sought to put into question the notion of that which was finished or fully formed. In her detailed programme notes to the final presentation of the *Project* at the Whitney Museum, New York, in April 1970, Rainer set out the contrasting nature of the elements available to the dancers. These are characterised, first, by three 'levels of performance reality':

A. Primary: Performing original material in a personal style.

B. Secondary: Performing someone else's material in a style approximating the original, or working in a known style or 'genre'.

C. Tertiary: Performing someone else's material in a style completely different from, and/or inappropriate to, the original.[66]

In turn, elements available to the piece, and which would be realised in one of these modes, included rehearsal (including discussion and argument), run-through (a polished performance), working out (the creation of new material), surprises (elements introduced without the knowledge of all performers), marking (the performance of material in the absence of conditions necessary to a full presentation), teaching (of one performer by another) and 'behaviour'. Behaviour could emerge in four specific forms: actual (activities spontaneously occurring in predetermined situations); choreographed (observed and reproduced or stylised behaviour), professional ('the range of gesture and deportment visible in experienced performers'); and amateur ('the range of gesture and deportment visible in inexperienced performers'). For the individual performer, these elements may then again be qualified by their adoption of any of nearly 100 of what Rainer defines as 'roles and metamuscular conditions' which may or may not be visible in 'the execution of physical feats', including:

adolescent
angel
athlete
autistic child
angry child
Annette Michelson
bird
Barbra Streisand
Buster Keaton
brother
Betty Blythe
black militant
confidante
competitor[67]

Rainer's *Project* is evidently analogous to Morris's in important ways. Like Morris, Rainer seeks to withdraw aspects of her own control over the shape or final form of the material with which she works. The material, the elements of Rainer's work, not only finds form through the decisions of the dancers but is subject to shifting and transforming relationships brought about through the process of performing. In this way the act of performance itself provides for the development of 'behaviour' to 'performance', 'surprise' to 'working out', 'rehearsal' to 'run-through' or, potentially, any other development or interpenetration as the act of performance generates behaviours that may be formalised. In fostering such a process of making and transformation, too, the piece looks towards a tension between process and object, as the movement towards an 'object', towards a final form, is staved off and interrupted by the intrusion of new behaviours and incompletions which become subject to transforming levels of performance.

Through these very means, however, Rainer's *Project* also marks itself out as different in character from Morris's. As Morris makes clear, in allowing material to find its own form he looks towards a 'presence' that resists or is beyond a reading of internal relationships between parts. Ironically, though, for Rainer, a retreat as choreographer from the performer's self-determined interactions and development of material is a withdrawal from precisely the kind of controls and disciplines which might stave off a move towards the 'object' in this sense. Free of disciplines or controls, performers tend to interact on levels other than the formal, where a development and interweaving of performance elements, developing tasks, behaviours and references may imply or invite a reading of subject-matters, narratives, even relationships and 'character'. Indeed, Rainer herself clearly provides for this in a vocabulary which offers performers the opportunity to develop interactions through the quotation of style and genre, rehearsal behaviour, including spontaneous and formalised personal interaction, and the possibility of reference to role, character and states of being. Plainly, too, the documentation of the Grand Union's improvisations demonstrates that just such interactions became fundamental to the development of performances, as well as the audience's commitment to them.

In this way Rainer's *Project* looks towards a very different articulation of a tension between process and object than does Morris's work. Rather than resist the reading of internal relationships between figures or parts, Rainer releases the elements of the piece from a rigorous staving off of coherence and developing relationship. In doing so, the piece is allowed to create a space for a reading of continuities and development and yet at the same time acts to disrupt particular readings by the constant shifting and re-formation of that which is being read. Here, the possibility of the 'object', even of an object to be read through developing relationships and events, continually recurs, yet the very freedoms that give rise to the possibility of the object serve also to postpone its actual formation and so its final closure.

Through the *Project* Rainer sets in motion a mechanism for producing change, for promising and pursuing development and variation and at the same time deferring and displacing possible conclusions. Just as the *Project* fosters an active and divergent exchange between its elements, so it looks towards the displacement of one reading by another, a challenging, overlaying and juxtaposition of points of view. In this way, and like that performance which is ostensibly 'minimalist', the *Project* puts into question the possibility of separating the 'work' from its immediate circumstances, and so of identifying those properties which it is in possession of and by which it is defined. The *Project*'s very trans-formation of itself through performance is a reaching toward the contin-gencies and instabilities of the 'event', an attempt to allow itself to be seen to be penetrated by unstable and unpredictable exchanges and pro-cesses. In this way *Continuous Project – Altered Daily* emphasises and makes visible its own contingent nature as *performance*, offering not a 'thing', an 'object', but a series of developing and transforming frag-ments, displacements and exchanges.

Post-modern dance and the postmodern event

Underlying these various presentations is the notion of a performance which exhibits a dependence upon the occasion of theatre over and above any properties its particular movement-elements, structures or forms might definitively make claim to. In this context, 'dance', like any performance, might be best thought of as a sequence of strategies or bids set in a negotiation over frame, form and content. In these respects, and where it looks towards its own condition, dance comes to an asser-tion of dependence not independence, of fragmentation and contingency rather than unity and self-sufficiency. Where such work comes to be shadowed and even disrupted by the event of its being read, then it reveals a latent instability, a penetration by its immediate circumstances, and in doing so renders itself uncertain, liable to change. In these instances, post-modern dance can be read as looking toward a postmod-ern event; an event which shadows and challenges the move toward conclusion, which forces an instability, a vacillation between definition and displacement, and which reveals events, contingencies and negotia-tions. It is in the context of this notion of a 'postmodern event', too, and of the variety of strategies that may provoke it, that one might most use-fully return to that work which can be set directly against a 'postmodern style'.

Chapter 6

Telling Stories: Narrative Against Itself

> The response we make when we 'believe' a work of the imagination is that of saying: 'This is the way things are. I have always known it without being fully aware that I knew it. Now in the presence of this play or novel or poem (or picture or piece of music) I know that I know it.'[1]

In its presentation at the Performing Garage in New York, the Wooster Group's *Route 1 & 9 (The Last Act)* begins with 'THE LESSON (Upstairs): In Which a Man Delivers a Lecture on the Structure and Meaning of *Our Town*', the screening of a reconstruction of an *Encyclopaedia Britannica* 'teaching film' in which Clifton Fadiman introduces Thornton Wilder's play *Our Town* (1938). After Fadiman, Ron Vawter of the Wooster Group sets out 'Mr Wilder's art', demonstrating what he sees as the experience *Our Town* instils in its audience. Through an explication of Wilder's 'use of music, theme and variation, and of the condensed line or word',[2] Vawter traces the play's gentle reminder, through its portrait of the community of Grover's Corner, of the deeper 'truths' that underlie everyday experience.

In the Wooster Group's reconstruction, however, and while Vawter faithfully re-presents Fadiman's demonstration of the means by which Wilder's play 'helps us to understand and accept our existence upon the earth',[3] the language and construction of the 'teaching film' have been displaced. As the critic attempts to draw the viewer toward his own self-assured point of view, the tape sets out a subtle exaggeration of the means by which he gathers authority to himself and is framed by the film. The camera, David Savran notes, 'holds long static shots of the lecturer and pans portentously as he moves back and forth'.[4] As the lecture continues it 'zooms in for important "truths" and underscores them by spelling out catch phrases across the bottom of the television screen'.[5]

Here, and despite the fact that Vawter carefully gives voice to Fadiman's argument, the meaning and efficacy of the teaching film are put into question, as the Wooster Group shadow Fadiman's explication of *Our Town* with their own explication of his lecture. The result is doubly ironic. In analysing and revealing the purposes and effects of Fadiman's film, the Wooster Group show it to be a project with its own character and purpose, so setting it at a distance from its object. Paradoxically, though, in doing this they implicitly put the veracity of their own reproduction of Fadiman's film into question. Like Fadiman's lecture, the Wooster Group's tape speaks for its object by reconstructing it. In pointing toward Fadiman's displacement of that which he would speak for, then, his presentation of a 'simulation' which reveals what *Our Town* 'really means', so the Wooster Group draw attention to their own displacement of Fadiman's argument, their own participation in precisely such a project. In such a way, the Wooster Group's exercise not only mounts a critique of Fadiman's film but implicitly turns back against itself.

Through such means, the Wooster Group move in the opposite direction from the consensus the lecturer would seek to engender. Far from simply contradicting or opposing Fadiman's argument, which would only look towards another form of consensus, their re-presentation exposes and disrupts the means by which such agreements would be fostered, either by Fadiman or themselves. The result is a strategy that looks towards the uncertainties and instabilities suppressed by the lecturer's attempt to draw the audience towards that which 'we all know'. It is a strategy that fosters contention, that places itself into question just as it questions its object, that gives rise to conflicts and contradictions it does not offer to resolve.

Ambivalence and transgression: the Wooster Group and Karen Finley

In the controversy over *Route 1 & 9*, one of the things that was said was, 'There's no distance on it.' In other words, it was racist, because there wasn't a character or voice of authority saying, 'Look, this is a horrible thing. This is racist.' I suspect that if Spalding had been off to the side saying, in one way or another, 'I deplore this,' it would have been alright. Everyone would have said, 'Oh, this guy is dealing with his racism on the stage,' instead of the audience really having to deal with the racism unmediated.[6]

The Wooster Group's treatment of Fadiman's film exemplifies the equivocal attitude inscribed within their treatment of the various elements their work brings into collision. In *Route 1 & 9* these elements included the 'teaching film', extracts from *Our Town*, blackface routines once performed by the black comedian Pigmeat Markham, comedy-horror sequences as well as a pornographic tape. According to LeCompte, her interest in the Encyclopedia Britannica film, as with *Our Town* itself, was rooted in the ambivalent nature of her response to it. In conversation with David Savran, she recalled that:

> I liked the Clifton Fadiman film, but was bothered about liking it. It touched nostalgic chords of comfort for me that made me angry. It pressed two buttons simultaneously. And I found myself unable to accept either in comfort. I couldn't destroy it and I couldn't go with it and be satisfied. I wanted to dig more deeply into it.[7]

Ostensibly concerned with the community of Grover's Corner, a small town in turn-of-the-century New Hampshire, *Our Town* focuses upon two families, the Webbs and the Gibbs, whose children, Emily and George, promise themselves to each other in childhood, marry, and are parted by Emily's death in childbirth. Act one, 'Daily Life', contemplates the character of Grover's Corner and its community. Act two, 'Love and Marriage', brings the community together for the day of Emily and George's wedding. Act three, set on the day of Emily's funeral, places Emily amongst the dead, allowing her to reflect upon her life as she waits 'for the eternal part ... to come out clear'.[8]

Mediating between these fragments, and between the audience and the play, a Stage-Manager acts as narrator, manipulating the few items of scenery the play demands while setting its events in a broadening context. Speaking in past, present and future tenses concurrently, he traces events, experiences and desires which seem to find themselves repeated through and despite change; experiences which, by dint of their very ordinariness and familiarity, might transcend history and culture. Finally, in act three, the Stage-Manager draws the audience toward the realisation that:

we all know that *something* is eternal. And it ain't houses and it ain't
names, and it ain't earth, and it ain't even the stars ... everybody
knows in their bones that something is eternal, and that something has
to do with human beings ... there's something way down deep that's
eternal about every human being.[9]

Emphasising, after Gertrude Stein, the 'perpetual present' of action in
the theatre, Wilder sought a 'new drama' that would escape from what
he saw as naturalism's 'devitalizing' emphasis upon 'place', upon
'specification and localization'.[10] Yet in breaching fourth-wall illusionism, Wilder pursued not the overtly fragmented vision of much modern
art and literature but a form of work that could give direct voice to a
deeper unity underlying all experience. To this end, Wilder sought to
liberate theatre from what he saw as a concern for simple happenstance
in order that it might realise its capacity to carry 'the art of narration to a
higher power than the novel or epic poem'.[11] *Our Town* exemplifies the
combination of these elements, its strength lying, in Wilder's terms, not
in the veracity of particular incidents but 'in the succession of events ...
in the unfolding of an idea'.[12] Indeed, the importance of the particular
incidents within *Our Town* lies not so much in their individual weight as
in the fact that they are commonplace, a fact which, seen through the
metaphysical framework the Stage-Manager weaves, ties them to underlying and universal patterns and experiences.

In act three, then, it is through Emily's reflection upon what has
passed that the value of even the most ordinary moments of life is most
clearly articulated. For Emily, death does not mean the simple fulfilment
of that which underlay and was promised by life but, as her passions
drain from her, an understanding of the blindness of the living to the
value and vibrancy of every moment of life. Revisiting the living, this
realisation only brings her pain and she is forced to retreat from the
ignorance of those she has left behind. Returning to the grave, Emily
laments, 'Oh earth, you're too wonderful for anyone to realize you',
asking, finally, 'Do any human beings ever realize life while they live it?
– every, every minute?'[13]

With the end of 'THE LESSON (Upstairs)', the audience moves below
into the performance space itself. Here, the first live sequence begins,
and Part One of *Route 1 and 9* continues with 'THE LESSON
(Downstairs): In Which the Stage Hands Arrange the Stage for the Last
Act of *Our Town*'. Now, two white performers present the first of a
number of blackface sequences. In heavy makeup and blinded by their
overtly blacked-out sunglasses they take on the mantle of Wilder's

Stage-Manager, attempting to construct a forced-perspective, skeletal house which will act as the set for the last act of *Our Town* and which forms part three of *Route 1 & 9*. Moving clumsily around the space and near the audience they develop a slapstick double-act, while instructions for building the house and a routine between two (apparently black-faced) actors plays over loudspeakers.

With the construction of the house underway a few feet before the audience, a brief blackout signals the beginning of Part Two, 'THE PARTY: In Which the Stage Hands Call it a Day and a Telegram is Sent'. While the four televisions suspended above the performance area offer a panoramic view of the Manhattan skyline, the men continue to build. Two white women in blackface enter and, as 'Annie' and 'Willie', make a series of live telephone calls to order food for Annie's birthday party. Following a final call to 'Kenny' and 'Pigmeat', the two male performers transform into guests at the party and the performance itself shifts gear:

> Now transformed, the men pick up the liquor and join the women for the birthday party. 'ALL RIGHT LET'S GO,' Willie yells as the song *Hole in the Wall* explodes over the speakers. There follows the re-enactment of the Pigmeat Markham routine ... a wildly theatrical revel, a vaudeville of comedy and dance.[14]

As the party continues two more performers enter and, as Kenny and Pigmeat, perform a reconstruction of a Markham comedy routine from the 1960s. Armed with outsized bottles of rye and (mistakenly) castor oil, they joke, shout and pour drink on the floor, toasting each other over the music and dancing. As the music continues, Savran recounts, the performers stop one by one, 'because each has to go "send a telegram"', the meaning of which becomes clear 'when Pig defecates in his pants', providing the sequence with its punchline:

> PIG: Oh, me.
> WILLIE: Pigmeat.
> PIG: Oh, ho, ho, oh ho.
> . . . .
> WILLIE: Whatsa matter Pigmeat?
> PIG: Whadya mean?
> WILLIE: Don't tell me you gotta send a telegram too?
> PIG: No, no, I done sent mine.[15]

As this sequence ends the performers quieten and the focus of the piece shifts to the four video monitors raised 14 feet above the stage-floor. Once lowered to their foreground position, seven feet above the ground, extracts from the last act of *Our Town* begin to play simultaneously across all four monitors. With this, Part Three, 'THE LAST ACT (The Cemetery Scene): In Which Four Chairs are Placed on the Stage Facing the Audience to Represent Graves', begins. As fragments from *Our Town* draw the audience's attention, the blackface performers move quietly around the darkened stage engaging in a variety of tasks and interactions while trying not to distract the audience. As the action develops the blackface performers come to mimic not simply the calming tones of *Our Town* but Emily's reliving of her twelfth birthday. While Emily recounts the details of her party, the performers quietly play through Annie's birthday in the skeletal house. When Emily receives her birthday gift, Annie 'shows up wearing an extravagant blue-silk creation'.[16] At some point the men cross-dress, pulling dresses over their suits. As the fragments of *Our Town* come to an end, the party asserts itself once again. With Emily's closing lines another blackface routine forcefully disrupts the calm with a 'Ghoul Dance', a grotesque parody of Wilder's vision of the after-life:

Suddenly 'Jump the Line' sounds and the four, in what remains of their blackface, begin to dance furiously, shaking their skirts wildly, a horrible grimace on their faces. They approach the audience, blood streaming down their faces, their mouths gaping open to reveal vampire fangs.[17]

Finally, with the abrupt end of the routine, the performers sit passively, avoiding eye contact with the audience, and the beginning of Part Four, 'ROUTE 1 & 9', is signalled as three video tapes are shown simultaneously. On the upper monitors, now raised again high above the floor, are two tapes of the same sequence, 'In Which a Van Picks Up Two Hitchhikers and Heads South'. Here LeCompte drives a van out of the city, her male passenger smoking and drinking coffee. At some point in the journey the van stops and picks up a hitchhiking couple. Meanwhile at stage level, in the skeletal house, an old black-and-white television shows a third tape in which

the performers who played the hitchhikers are going through a series of sexual turns ... The sex sequences are graphic, the couple trying various positions. They are less concerned with performing for the camera than with allowing it to oversee them, much like a voyeur.[18]

As the videos end so *Route 1 & 9* comes to a close.

Self-evidently, read against *Our Town*, the collisions of texts and images which make up *Route 1 & 9* serve to violate the parameters and qualities of Wilder's vision. By taking Wilder's maxim to realise the value of each present moment literally and uncritically, *Route 1 and 9* would seem to reveal and parody the narrow parameters of *Our Town's* image of the 'universal'. Through the blackface the Wooster Group present much of what the inhabitants of Grover's Corner define themselves against, and which is represented in this denigrating image of the 'other'; a violent expression of physical vitality and energy, a celebration of sexuality and danger, a revelling in the body rather than the spirit. The pornographic tape similarly and graphically points toward the repressions upon which the 'innocence' of the community may rest, and which is given voice momentarily in Emily's apprehension at her marriage. Formally, too, *Route 1 & 9* explodes the hierarchies upon which Wilder's vision depends. In the Group's work, LeCompte suggests, 'the core is always dispersed',[19] while a combination and juxtaposition of radically different elements serves to undermine any single reading that might be made of the piece. It might follow that in opposition to *Our Town*, and rather than assert the 'right' perspective, *Route 1 & 9* emphasises conflict and difference, creating contentious and ambiguous relationships between values and perspectives that are resistant to any easy reading and resolution. By implication, the single most unequivocal critique of *Our Town*, as with Fadiman's lecture, then, may be its assumption of the right to such a 'totalising' view within which everything must find its place or be excluded.

Clearly, though, this conflict between perspectives and texts resists not only the assumptions inscribed within *Our Town* but also a reading based on such a simple opposition. Vawter's lecture, for example, not only questions the ground of Fadiman's authority but its own, while Fadiman's argument is rehearsed and offered all the same. Similarly, while the blackface may be read as an attack on the narrow confines of Wilder's vision of a small-town, white America, it does so while being held within denigrating representations of black people. At once, then, the blackface challenges *Our Town's* hegemony while condemning the white performers to re-enact its exclusivity before the Group's predominantly white, middle-class audience. Touching on the ironies of this position, LeCompte has acknowledged the double-edged nature of the image, arguing that for a white audience it 'is both ... a painful representation of blacks and also wild, joyous, and nihilistic and, therefore, freeing'.[20] Similarly, the pornographic tape hardly offers itself as an unequivocal release from the repressions it points toward. While, as Ron Vawter suggests, the presence of the tape may serve to set 'a little procreative act'[21] against Wilder's graveyard, it also remains an overtly and deliberately pornographic presentation[22] open to charges of abuse and obscenity.

Such ironies intrude upon each of the elements out of which *Route 1 & 9* is made up, as found material is wrong-footed or undercut through its reproduction. According to LeCompte, one key to the process by which the performance is compiled is a self-conscious reframing of found elements. She notes:

> When they act I use acting. When they perform, I use that. I frame other people's style in my frame so that it says something I want it to. I use their work in terms of the frame/context of the piece, which I set.[23]

In this way not only is a vocabulary of sharply contrasting styles and modes of work fostered within a single performance, but individual elements are placed on an ambivalent footing. In so far as a 'found' element or sequence is reproduced, the performance remains complicit with that which it reproduces. Yet the very fact of the material's reproduction puts it into question, as does its simultaneous and concurrent juxtaposition with like and unlike elements.

Specific strategies which LeCompte and the performers variously adopt extend this process, evidencing the displacement of material from the ground on which some aspect of its transparency, authority and so meaning depended. The first blackface routines, the comic building sequences, are placed on uncertain ground by the very fact of the performers' blindness. While clearly a source of much of the comedy, their handicap also slows the performance down, creating a tension between the routine and its painful pace and repetition, forcing a shifting and difficult relationship between the audience and the comedy. Similar tensions are also present in the readings of *Our Town*. LeCompte notes that as the group began to work with Wilder's text:

> I realised that when you took the Stage-Manager out of *Our Town*, it became a soap opera. So I took the last act and worked with Willem on separating it into scenes, close-up scenes with a soap opera feel.

We did improvs around a soap opera style, using TVs ... And from that we got a kind of rhythm. The actor's pacing is soap opera but the visual image is more 'portraiture', the actors speaking directly to the camera which serves as point of view.[24]

In this version of the cemetery scene, Wilder's representations are broken free of the Stage-Manager's narrative, while the actors' style of performance and the 'scenes' chosen offer a deliberately reductive view of the play. The visual image of 'portraiture' clarifies the tensions this treatment gives rise to. These close-ups seem to go too far, forcing the actor into an introverted, conversational mode, while creating a sense of entrapment or intrusion into the personal, the private. Reframed in this way, Wilder's representations of everyday life take on soap opera's overbearing concern for the ordinary and the trivial, seeming to give everyday events an attention and so significance they cannot bear. Ironically, in the absence of the Stage-Manager's explanations, Emily's reflections on her life seem confined to an intense and single-minded concern with precisely the idiosyncratic events Wilder set out to see beyond.

Such ironies are exacerbated by the juxtaposition of elements treated in this way. Constructed largely through a collage of found texts, actions and images, the Wooster Group would seem to put the formal and thematic boundaries of their performances into question. In a collage where 'Everything is equally weighted',[25] the resolution of a conflict between quotations, re-presentations and adaptations is staved off by their resistance to being read through each other. The very fact that such material is recognisably 'found' material, that it makes reference to 'other' histories and identities, aspects that the performance has not or cannot fully assimilate, leaves it in a sense unsorted, open to question in its relevance and consequence. The result is an open intertextuality, where the internal, self-supporting integrity of the 'work' is given over to a presentation which repeatedly sites itself in relation to pre-existing texts from whose vantage points elements of the collage may be variously read.

The significance of this becomes clearer in the effect of the blackface. In the context of *Route 1 & 9* this equivocal figure, which, historically, has been employed both to reinforce and subvert racial stereotype,[26] becomes subject to competing points of view. The reversals brought about through the blackface house-building, party and ghoul dance may be read as representing the blackface as that which *Our Town* excludes. In their re-enactment by white performers, however, the blackface routines might be taken as an *act* of exclusion, the presentation of images not sufficiently distanced from the denigration they recall and continue to rehearse. After the New York State Council on the Arts (NYSCA) and other critics of the piece, one might cite the live telephone calls as a wilful confusion of crude caricature and the quotation and contextualisation of a theatrical image. Indeed, this very reading of the piece reputedly cost the Wooster Group some 40 per cent of their grant funding from the NYSCA.[27]

While the stubborn independence of the individual elements and texts foster such conflicting readings, the Wooster Group themselves frame their performances in such a way as to call into question their independence from one another. *Route 1 & 9*, the Group make clear, is Part One of a trilogy, *The Road to Immortality*, of which *L.S.D. (... Just the High Points ...)* (1984) forms Part Two, while *Frank Dell's The Temptation of Saint Anthony* (1987) comprises Part Three. This trilogy follows the pattern established by their first sequence of pieces, *Three Places in Rhode Island*, which consisted of *Sakonnet Point* (1975), *Rumstick Road* (1977), *Nyatt School* (1978) and *Point Judith (An Epilogue)* (1979). Only the short dance pieces *Hula* (1981) and *For the Good Times* (1983) along with the play *North Atlantic* (1984) have fallen outside this pattern. For LeCompte, it seems, such sequences reflect and grow out of the fact that the perspective from which choices are made shifts and may be turned back on itself. In self-consciously seeking to create a body of work, LeCompte would appear not to elaborate a particular position or developing argument so much as deliberately attack or remake her own vocabulary. She notes that 'I'm always remaking the vocabulary, constantly rewriting it. Things are reversed and totally destroyed, and we go back on what we did in previous pieces.'[28]

Consistently with this the blackface recurs in Part Two of *L.S.D.* in which, initially, the Group performed an hysterical 30-minute rendering of *The Crucible*, later replaced by Michael Kirby's play *The Hearing* following the intervention of Arthur Miller.[29] Here, the Group implicitly set their own 'transgression' in *Route 1 & 9* against Miller's treatment of Tituba, the black servant. Through their presentation of a black role conventionally played by a black actress by a white performer in blackface, the Wooster Group mount a critique of both Miller's unselfconscious reference to stereotype and an unthinking acceptance of this treatment and its implications. In turn, as the white performer goes on to play 'white' roles while still wearing the remnants of her blackface makeup, the conventional meanings and references of the blackface are challenged through an overt disjunction between its history and the roles the blackfaced performer takes up.

Here, then, the reworking of material serves to heighten the uncertainties the process of reframing and the conflict between texts fosters. As readings multiply and turn back on each other, this 'body of work' enters into conflict with itself. According to Ron Vawter, one key to the performances lies in precisely the way in which elements are combined to create a space open to meanings of various kinds:

> An event which can be interpreted only one way inhibits and limits the possibility. It's not that we're deliberately trying to make pieces which are mute. Just the opposite. I often see a piece as an opportunity for meaning, rather than an expression of a single meaning.[30]

Such strategies not only put into question that material which is incorporated or reproduced but, through the construction and displacement of perspectives, provoke conflicts and contradictions which unsettle or interrupt moves toward a single reading or point of view. At the same time, though, and despite the overtly social and political reference much of this material makes, this resistance to unity and synthesis also effects a resistance to the giving of social and political *meaning*. In this respect, *Route 1 & 9* may be identified with formal strategies through which the process of negotiation, the move towards meaning, is exposed, and where the meaning of particular images is disrupted, postponed, staved off. In doing so, however, it seems that *Route 1 & 9* risks pursuing a confusion of the politically radical and the reactionary or, at least, a deliberate provocation of a conflict between these two possibilities. Such a presentation inevitably becomes uncomfortable, by its nature open to charges of an unthinking complicity with the material it incorporates.

Perhaps even more so than the Wooster Group, Karen Finley's appropriations of languages of abuse, denigration and pornography have provoked a sharply divided critical and popular response. Since *The Constant State of Desire* (1986), in particular, Finley's work has been read both as a capitulation to male violence and objectification, and a powerful transgression and challenge to the construction of sexual difference.[31] More controversially, the piece has been condemned, despite acknowledgements of Finley's 'feminist intentions', first as an exploitation of the popular taste for obscenity and secondly for relying on arcane references to feminist theory incapable of 'full comprehension' by the 'average' spectator.[32]

The Constant State of Desire is typical of the fractured nature of Finley's performances, consisting of a series of monologues punctuated by improvised exchanges with the audience. Her published text[33] breaks the piece down into five sections: *Strangling Baby Birds, Enter Entrepreneur, Two Stories, Common Sense* and *The Father in All of Us*. As in much of Finley's other work, these stories intertwine painful descriptions of sexual abuse with, by turns, an angry and despairing mourning for the dying implicitly bound up with the consequences of AIDS. In the course of this, Finley's concerns spill over towards racism and the abuse of minorities, to the abandonment of the homeless, of addicts, and to the marginalised. In her later monologue, *We Keep Our Victims Ready* (1990), these broader political concerns become explicit as accounts of sexual abuse, the persecution of AIDS victims and of artists themselves are set against images of the Nazi death camps.

Rather than offer a coherent critique of a process of marginalisation, or of sexual objectification, subordination and abuse, however, Finley's performances operate first and foremost on a direct and powerful emotional level, though by no means one which is straightforwardly cathartic. In particular, Finley's appropriations of pornographic imagery and language serve to call into question not only the distance and perspective an audience might wish to establish in an address to such material, but her own implication in the processes of objectification and abuse she ostensibly attacks.

The Constant State of Desire begins with the recollection of a woman's dreams; she imagines killing baby birds, an image which slips quickly into that of the woman herself caged and watched over by her family. The dream is then a dream of falling and of crying without being able to give voice, and one, like others of being beaten and tortured, that is given importance and picked over by doctors: 'the same doctors who anaesthetized her during the birth of her children .... who called her an animal as she nursed ... who gave her episiotomies. No more sexual feelings for her during and after childbirth.'[34]

The monologue rapidly turns toward self-blame, however, and, now in the first person, present tense, to a mourning of the death of television stars, the suicide of her father, the report of an abortion and an incestuous rape. The father committed suicide, Finley reports, 'because he no longer found me attractive'. She concludes, 'you can tell that I prefer talking about the fear of living, as opposed to the fear of dying'.[35]

With this the tack of Finley's text shifts again. In performance, Finley takes off her clothes, smashes eggs in a clear plastic bag and then uses a child's soft toy as an applicator to smear the yellow liquid over herself. Finally she sprinkles glitter and confetti over her body and wraps herself in paper boas.[36] This completed, the second monologue, *Enter*

Entrepreneur, signals a vitriolic attack on the art-consuming yuppie, mapping out his consumption of abuse as art and culminating in a vivid description of the castration of Wall Street traders who 'don't miss their balls 'cause they're too busy fucking me with everything else they got'.[37] Finley completes her 'sweet revenge' by boiling their testicles, rolling them in dung and selling them as 'Easter eggs to gourmet chocolate shops'.[38]

Two Stories shifts the ground again, recounting the abuse of a woman by her husband and setting this against a sexual assault by burglars 'at gunpoint in front of her own children and pets'.[39] This in turn slips into an account, in the first person, present tense, of a son's resentment of his father's rejection of him as he leaves for Vietnam. *Common Sense* then initiates an attack on Freud, which moves toward a more overtly political account of women's exclusion, marginalisation and a self-destructive internalisation of these processes. Finally, Freud is inverted as Finley traces the archetypal father's jealousy 'when he discovered woman's ability to have multiple orgasms'.[40] Finley teases the men in her audience: 'Okay, I know that some of you guys like to let us know that you can fuck more than once. But I need no time to refuel. *So maybe it's womb envy instead of penis envy.*'[41]

In her final monologue, *The Father in All of Us*, which is divided into several parts, Finley readdresses the concerns running through the piece but in a more graphic and difficult way. 'My First Sexual Experience' sets out a violent parody of the privileging of Oedipal drives and desires and the definition of woman in terms of lack. The piece begins with Finley's description of birth itself as a sexual experience, after which she takes on the mantle of a male 'motherfucker' who uses a baby as a substitute penis to abuse his indifferent mother. This is followed by 'Refrigerator', which returns to a description of sexual abuse, setting out a distressing account of a father's assault on his daughter. Sitting her in the refrigerator:

> he leans down to the vegetable bin, opens it and takes out the carrots, the celery, the zucchini, the cucumbers. Then he starts working on my little hole, my little, little, hole. My little girl hole. Showing me 'what it's like to be mamma' ... Next thing I know I'm in bed crying, bleeding. I got all my dollies and animals around me. I've got Band-Aids between their legs. If they can't protect me, I'll protect them.[42]

'The Father in All of Us' then turns explicitly to AIDS as Finley again gives voice to the son whose sexuality and death is rejected by his father. Images of violent sexual abuse are then set against accounts of addicts and the homeless abandoned on the street. Finally, in a gentler tone but no less bitter a parody, Finley speaks as a yuppy in search of a 'religious experience', but who finds only dying friends and a 'White Man's Guilt', a self-indulgent discomfort borne of exploitation and privilege.

Like *Route 1 & 9*, *The Constant State of Desire* is constructed through shifting perspectives, while Finley's relationship to the material she engages with remains an ambivalent one. Through her rehearsal of violent and even pornographic imagery and language, Finley couches her performance and her presentation of herself in the terms of a violent sexual objectification and abuse. Paradoxically, and despite her verbal assaults on the abusers, Finley's performances have been read as capitulating through the very terms by which she tells her stories with that which she bitterly attacks. Indeed, one may even argue that any such engagement can only be politically self-destructive as, by its nature, an appropriation of male languages of objectification and abuse speaks to a male audience first and is bound in its reception by the assumptions that generate and sustain its terms. For a critic such as Jill Dolan, powerful as Finley's performance evidently are, they remain limited, even self-defeating:

> There is not much potential for radical change in Finley's work because ... she is still caught within the representational system to which she refers. Although male spectators are challenged and confronted in Finley's work, her aims are achieved by abusing herself under representational terms that remain operative from the male point of view. Finley perverts the strippers position, but remains defined by its traditional history.[43]

Yet the very extreme and surprising nature of Finley's appropriations, as well as the shifting and fragmented nature of her monologues, can be read as resisting such an accommodation. Far from offering herself as a passive object, Finley takes on and incorporates these languages into her performance in such a way that she becomes active through them. Here, one can argue, by re-enacting the violence of the male subject she subverts the terms of his objectification, appropriating the language that would define her as a passive victim and throwing it back at her audience. Importantly, too, as she engages in this process Finley effects a continual change of ground and identity, taking on and disposing, variously and unpredictably, of male and female voices, and the personas of abused, abuser, victim and protagonist. In doing so, she overtly resists the spectator's reading of 'character' as a unifying force, and particularly a reading of herself as an empathetic figure or victim in relation to which the various experiences she recounts might be placed.

In performance, the tensions between these poles become even more apparent, as Finley's shifts of narrative voice and the clash between texts are themselves framed within improvised and revealing exchanges with the audience.[44] This rapport looks toward a dual effect, at once standing in tension with the aggressive and sometimes abusive nature of her monologues while evidencing the process of her performance, the construction of the 'act' itself. At the time of her performance of *The Constant State of Desire* Finley articulated this tension, making a distinction in her work between 'experimental theatre', material which had become fixed and was repeatable, and a 'performance procedure' which can be prepared for but is not rehearsed.[45]

Caught between these two poles, Finley's performances of her monologues set themselves against conventional theatrical and dramatic criteria. Indeed, in important respects it is more appropriate to read Finley's performance against Body Art's exposure of the physical and psychological vulnerability of the artist or a concern with a process of making than the actor's realisation of a text. Charged with presenting a 'bad' performance, Finley has responded by arguing that in such circumstances the exposure of her own struggle to perform becomes part of her subject-matter:

> for that reason I thought it was the best night: people could see me as I am. I showed that a performance is really hard to do. I think it's my duty as a performer to be completely honest, to show them what I'm going through.[46]

Such a reading of Finley's performance begins to turn away from an attention simply to the material she appropriates and towards a framing and treatment of this material through formal strategies. From this point of view, and while the influences acting on the Wooster Group and Karen Finley are diverse, their work can be usefully set against treatments of narrative defined through self-conscious appropriations of conventional theatre forms and figures. Here, narrative is treated as a figure with certain formal consequences, and one whose effect is to be questioned through its displacement in an address to its place and effect in an active negotiation over identity and meaning.

Resisting narrative

Yvonne Rainer's final theatre-piece was a two-hour multi-media perform-ance, *This is the story of a woman who...*, first presented in March 1973. Like *Grand Union Dreams* and her film *Lives of Performers* of 1972, which marked the culmination of her work with the Grand Union, this presentation pursued the increasingly open address to dramatic con-vention that characterised the development of her work through perform-ance and toward an exclusive concern with film. Yet despite open references to narrative, 'persona', and an interaction between 'characters', in this work Rainer's use of conventional form and figure is always qualified by a displacement or subversion of the continuities such ele-ments would seem to look towards.

Set in a simply defined rectangular space, *This is the story of a woman who ...* incorporates film and slide projections, before which the three performers, originally Rainer herself, Shirley Soffer and John Erdman, variously interact with each other and tell their stories to the audience. While Rainer and Erdman alternate between sitting on a pair of chairs at the rear, interacting with each other around the space and on a mattress placed downstage right, Soffer sits before a microphone near the audience, ostensibly taking on the role of narrator.

Soffer's entry signals the beginning of the piece. As she takes her seat behind the microphone thunder is heard, then the sound of rain. As the rain sounds, one of three projections that may be made in sequence or simultaneously across the back wall shows Soffer in what seems to be various family photographs. The photographs are replaced by a title, 'Inner Appearances', which cues Erdman's entry. At first singing to him-self, Erdman vacuums the space and a sequence of 15 texts are projected in a broken rhythm. Sporadically, Erdman interrupts his task to stand still or sit on a chair or the mattress. The sense of time, Rainer suggests, 'is protracted and melancholy'.[47] The texts offer what seem to be self-conscious and discontinuous accounts of Erdman's thoughts, but ones that are in the third person and that weave in and out of an implied fic-tional context. They reflect on 'the character's mask', his 'growing irri-tation', the fact that 'before the performance he ran into someone he hadn't seen for a year'.[48] In turn, this meeting is absorbed into a narrat-ive in which Erdman has been left by his wife or lover. The text recounts an incident in which 'the character' hides in a doorway to avoid the new couple. Finally, Erdman sits on a chair at the rear and the text concludes by putting itself into question: 'Cliché is, in a sense, the purest art of intelligibility; it tempts us with the possibility of enclosing life within beautifully unalterable formulas, of obscuring the arbitrary nature of imagination with an appearance of necessity.'[49]

As the piece continues to unfold, various narrative voices intrude unpredictably upon one another. While Soffer, sitting before the microphone, remains silent, a tape of Erdman's voice plays, offering an account of a woman's loss, possibly her feelings at being left by her partner. Soffer takes over the narrative, describing a scene from a relationship, an exchange rooted in suspicion. Meanwhile, Rainer and Erdman develop a sequence of 'stop-motion poses in relation to each other and the objects'.[50] The lights fade and the text returns, describing both a breaking up and a reconciliation. Soffer reads the first four of nine 'paragraphs' which she announces as such and numbers them. She recounts a woman's visit to the Pantheon, a cathedral, against projected illustrations of cities, gardens and anonymous places. Fragments of incidents or experiences unfold variously. The slide projections offer dialogue as a film of an ocean and beach is superimposed over the left-hand slide image; Soffer delivers a monologue in the first person, present tense of being lost in a city, the victim of unwanted attentions. As Rainer and Erdman enact a slow-motion fight scene, the distinctions between narrative lines and identities threaten to be further confused as Soffer steps into the performance space proper:

> Shirley stands downstage centre with microphone and says 'That's her fantasy. If it were mine I'd do it differently.' She has a screaming fit, then says, 'I just can't do it tonight.' John starts to rearrange the chairs. Shirley goes to him and says 'Her unrelenting inten ...' Yvonne looks up from where she has been shuffling papers, stands up, coughs, watches Shirley lie down on the mattress.[51]

In this way, the elements constituting the performance continually invite a reading of narrative continuity and yet resist the actual construction of a single or even predominant narrative. Ironically, this disruption of the reading of narrative is achieved first of all through the clear and specific claim of each narrative voice. In this piece, individual voices and texts re-narrativise each other, either directly or through the redrawing of analogous events, experiences and themes. As if to compound this, the particular identity of these voices proves to be elusive. Repeatedly, what is narrated are the experiences, feelings and points of view of the 'other', which may or may not be Rainer, Erdman or Soffer's 'characters'. Thematically, this may be read as an evasion of responsibility, a measuring of one's own actions in terms of another's. Formally, however, it means that the narrative voice fails to identify its own position, but concerns itself with redrawing the position of others. Paradoxically, only Soffer, as the external voice of the 'narrator', speaks of herself directly, intruding, at this point, into that which she would ostensibly draw a frame around and lead the audience through.

The equivocal nature of this invitation to read the 'story' of a woman or her experiences is echoed, too, in the relationship between narrative and the performers' actions and interactions. In the first scene, incorporating Erdman's 'dance' *Inner Appearances*, Rainer suggests, 'The dance consisted of cleaning, vacuuming the performance space. Drama and psychological meaning were conveyed by slides of typescript dealing with the state of mind of a character ... The dancer becomes a persona related by spatial proximity to the projected texts.'[52]

Erdman presents his dance while his proximity to the projected texts invites a reading of the dancer as 'persona'. The nature of the text, which announces its own construction of a fiction and use of cliché, at once extends an invitation to read his presence through its terms and yet maintains a self-conscious distance from Erdman's activities. Typically, this scene does not offer unequivocal representations of character or dramatic incident but actions, texts, images and commentaries which stand in self-conscious, uncertain and shifting relationships to one another.

As the piece continues, and once Soffer has joined Rainer and Erdman, the conflict between the status and nature of the narrative voices intensifies. As Soffer engages directly with the two 'characters', a tape of Rainer's voice seems to take on what was Soffer's role. In turn, a film of Soffer in bed further draws her into the relationship that seemed to be Rainer and Erdman's. Finally, the text 'She showed him her dance', signals the incorporation of a series of overt quotations into the piece. Rainer performs an earlier dance-piece, *Three Satie Spoons*; 40 stills of the shower scene from Hitchcock's *Psycho* are set against 'paragraph seven', in which Soffer tells the story of a woman leaving, nauseated, from a film-theatre. Rainer and Erdman make a series of approaches to each other against a text which concludes by falling overtly into cliché: 'His performance was magnificent. Afterwards she wept. Then she slept. As a pool of warm water spreading in the sunlight.'[53]

The intrusion of such quotations and references extend and intensify the series of displacements the narrative voices effect. The 'cliché' Rainer's texts incorporate may advance the 'story' and its meanings, yet, as they do so, they declare themselves to be second hand, formulaic. Rainer's overt appropriations offer similar positions from which

readings may be at once made and questioned. The sequence from
Psycho may parallel or parody the 'woman's' experiences, inviting a re-
reading of a relationship or her partner's actions, or even be taken as a
fantasy or dream. Prefaced and shadowed by the text, 'She shows him
her dance', Rainer's performance of *Three Satie Spoons* gains a new
ambiguity, perhaps offering itself as a metaphor for some kind of
exchange between them. Whatever readings these elements invite or
accommodate, however, they pointedly resist incorporation into a
formal or thematic whole both by their obvious *difference*, their formal
and stylistic independence from the elements in relation to which they
are placed, and by the histories and references they bring with them.

In this piece, then, Rainer's elements repeatedly invite the reading of
a narrative. At the same time, though, the sequence of claim and
counter-claim, of parallel and reversal, within which these narrative
appropriations and conventions are bound, continually undercut and displace the ground on which such a narrative might be followed through.
Here, ironically, it is the very narrative voices that invite a reading of the
piece in terms of an unfolding whole that resist integration into such a
whole, that speak for others and will not be spoken for.

In fact, for Rainer, it seems that the more such figures come into play,
the more sharply their unifying effect should be resisted. Rainer has
argued that 'the more meanings get spelled out for an audience in terms
of specific narrative information, the stronger the need for 'opening up'
things at another level with ambiguous or even ambivalent clues and
signs'.[54] As narrative strategies emerge and develop in Rainer's work, so
the particular narrative comes to be shadowed by that which it cannot
encompass. Competing narrative voices displace one another, to be
exposed as figures which would establish a continuity through which the
'other' would be silenced or spoken for. Narrative patterns are revealed
by events which escape their logic, undermining the transparency of
cause-and-effect. Overt quotations intrude formally and thematically,
setting the narratives against which they are placed in relation to others
beyond the piece itself.

Rainer's late performances offer examples of a range of work that in
incorporating narrative comes to interrogate the nature and consequence
of the act of narration. Here, the reading of representation and continuity
is at once invited and disrupted, as the act of narration is revealed to be
the act of reading one element through another, of having one voice
speak for another.

For Joan Jonas, whose early performances had been linked to the
aftermath of the Judson experiments, video, television and a developing

use of mask, role and narrative provided a very specific route away from the influence of minimal art.[55] Her first explicit appropriations of narrative emerged in *The Juniper Tree* (1976), and were developed through *Upside Down and Backwards* (1979), *Double Lunar Dogs* (1980), which drew on science-fiction, and *Volcano Saga* (1989), which incorporated Icelandic myth. An engagement with theatre convention and dramatic narrative is also evident in her work as a performer with the Wooster Group, first in *Nyatt School* (1978) and more recently in *Brace Up!* (1990).

Upside Down and Backwards begins with a recording of Jonas's own version of two Grimm Brothers' fairy tales, *The Frog Prince* and *The Boy Who Went Out to Learn Fear*. Yet the telling of the stories is disrupted, as *The Frog Prince* is presented in reverse order and the two stories are collaged together paragraph by paragraph:

> My stomach is full and I am tired, so carry me to your satin bed and we will lie together. The girl was afraid of the cold green frog but her father gave her angry looks, so, picking the frog up and holding him at arm's length, she went to her room and put him in a corner, but as she lay down he crawled over and threatened to tell her father if she did not take him to bed.
>
> In the dry and empty land there was a boy who had never known fear. Not the darkest night, the desert snakes, or the twisting winds. They wanted him to earn a living but he said that first he would like to learn fear. They didn't understand. One night they tried to frighten him in the old adobe bell tower, but he just got angry, so his father kicked him out of the house. 'No son of mine ...'[56]

Despite Jonas's intervention into the continuity of each story, the tone of her text is immediately recognisable. Although the collage confuses the content of the individual fables, the juxtaposition serves to heighten a sense of their common symmetry, rhythm and pattern. Ironically, though, while Jonas's reading of the stories reveals something of their formal nature, so it also serves to deny each narrative the possibility of establishing a single, unified and developing order.

Following the first two paragraphs Jonas enters the performance area. At the end of the sequence, she 'sits and plays a tune backwards on a music box, in which the paper roll has been reversed'.[57] The second part of the performance then begins, in which Jonas engages in a series of activities presented before three large paintings which dominate the stage. As she moves gradually from left to right, and so from one

painting to another, leaving a trail of objects behind her, a soundtrack
sets fragments of 1950s rock-and-roll against contemporary music, film
soundtrack and television. The soundtrack plays moments of *Let Me In*
by the Sensations; a fragment of a Cocteau film with the sound of frogs
croaking as a woman repeats '*Je t'aime*'; a tune from a music box, then
the same tune in reverse; the song *Yesyesyes* by the rock group The Res-
idents. Meanwhile Jonas translates her formal strategy of 'doubling'
into recurrent images of a double or doubles which shadow elements
drawn from the two fables. Manipulating her props, Jonas sets herself
against her double, a woman's head on a pole; she plays with a skeleton,
undressing it and dancing with it; she superimposes the image of a boy
painted on to glass over the skull. In the course of these activities
another double narrative is presented. Here, as Jonas papers the floor
with photocopies of landscape photographs, two soundtracks play
simultaneously in which she describes, in the first person, present tense,
activities, sights and impressions of two places. As she distributes the
photocopies, so she repeats the fragments of the tapes. The places echo
those from the fables, a woodland and a dry, arid place. The impression
they give, Jonas notes, is 'ominous' suggesting 'a loss of innocence'.[58]

Finally, moving backwards from left to right, Jonas reads from the
two intercut fairy-tales again, but this time they have been collaged
sentence by sentence:

> I am tired, so carry me to your bed and we will lie together. He was
> not afraid of the darkest nights, the desert snakes or the twisting
> winds, but she was, and so, picking him up, she threw him against the
> wall, and, as he fell, he turned into a man.[59]

Clearly, these fables are juxtaposed and their imagery reproduced and
echoed in such a way as to disrupt either narratives' ability to stabilise
the relationship between images and so circumscribe their meaning. Yet,
prefaced as they are by their sources within narrative, Jonas's images
refer back to narrative at the very moment at which they escape its
strictures.

This unravelling, in which the unifying function of narrative is disrupted through the presentation of explicitly narrative elements, has paradoxical consequences. While these images are clearly drawn from and
offered in relation to the fables, they are freed of the structures upon
which the stability of their meanings seemed to depend. The result is
neither a free flow of images nor a narrative continuity, but elements
torn between the two: between the narrative structures they recall and

the wide range of associations and references their freedom from narrative order makes apparent. Jonas extends this play on narrative by her extensive incorporation of quotations and appropriations. For the spectator, offered a ground and order that is put into question, the readings of these elements becomes difficult, continually under threat of displacement. Here, the centred perspective the narrative would promise is displaced, undermined by a free play of reference and allusion taken from the narrative and yet set against its closure.

In both *This is the story of a woman who ...* and *Upside Down and Backwards* narratives and narrative conventions are presented in such a way that their claim to authority is challenged. Yet this challenge to narrative is not simply a matter of competing or conflicting narratives, or even the successive displacement of one narrative by another. Here narratives are resisted or disrupted in such a way that the nature of their move toward unity and containment is made visible. Ironically, this work reveals the formal function and effect of the narrative voice by setting narrative elements against the move towards narrative closure, by deploying narrative voices against each other in such a way that the *event* of narration, the move toward containment, is frustrated and so made apparent.

A postmodern politics?

Read through such terms, the conflicts which *Route 1 & 9* and *The Constant State of Desire* so evidently foster can be seen as acutely and explicitly political extensions of this disruption of the move towards narrative closure. Like other Wooster Group performances, *Route 1 & 9* persistently disrupts not only the meaning of the stories it appropriates, such as Fadiman's lecture, *Our Town*, the Markham routines and, elsewhere, *The Crucible* or *Three Sisters*, but the stories it tells of these appropriations. Just as the authority of Fadiman's lecture is undermined, as is Wilder's claim to universality in *Our Town*, so the Wooster Group's own narrative claims come into question. Repeatedly, the Wooster Group implicate their own presentations in the processes they expose and critique. Indeed, such implication is inescapable where this critique is mounted against the claim to narrative voice and authority.

Like Rainer's late work, too, and consistently with this exposure of a struggle between narrative voices, these strategies bring the conflict between narrative possibilities on to a formal level. *Route 1 & 9* refuses to privilege the position of the viewer, resisting, through its self-conscious ironies and shifts of ground, any unself-conscious reading which would construct itself beyond the struggle between texts and perspectives. Indeed, this piece evidently effects a dangerous instability with regard to meaning in order that the viewer might contend with this struggle. The treatment of the blackface exemplifies this process. Subject to competing narratives, the blackface comes to occupy a space torn between meanings, a space which conflicting possibilities threaten to occupy in an impossible way. In reading the blackface, the viewer must enter into the struggle between voices and meanings, as a determination of what it *means* involves the giving of ascendency to one narrative over another. It may, then, be here that the most acutely uncomfortable aspects of *Route 1 & 9* lie as, if the re-enactment of the blackface is taken to be an act of degradation, the very collision between narratives begs the question of where the responsibility for that degradation actually lies.

Such a struggle between narrative claims is not a matter of articulating political meanings, but of making visible a politics of who speaks and who is spoken for. In this way, and far from reading the collision between texts as an attempt to shrug off responsibility for meaning, the paradoxical positions this work repeatedly strikes may be read as precipitating an 'event' with regard to meaning; the contesting of meaning, the struggle between narrative possibilities. By implicating themselves in this process of claim and counter-claim, the Wooster Group's strategies turn away from the question of *the meaning* and toward the *act* of making meaning.

In *The Constant State of Desire*, Finley, too, provokes such a struggle. Like the Wooster Group, her continual shifts of voice and narrative mode operate not simply on a thematic but a formal level, undercutting the position of the spectator and drawing her into a conflict between narratives and representations. So Finley's various narrative voices put each other into question, while her attack upon the 'sexuality of violence'[60] is made through an appropriation of languages whose rehearsal threatens to invite a reading through the very terms she would condemn.

In contrast to the Wooster Group, though, the space these conflicting narratives threaten to occupy is that marked out by Finley herself. At stake in *The Constant State of Desire* is a reading or construction of Finley as an active subject or her objectification and abuse through the terms she replays. In this context Finley's mode of performance gains a special significance. Rather than present a simple sequence of monologues, Finley shadows their presentation by her own steps in and out of a performance, her vacillations between formal and informal relationships with the audience. Here, Finley's concern to show that 'performance is hard to do', to trace out the *act* of performance, puts into question the claim of her various narratives to the ground she herself occupies. *The Constant State of Desire* not only offers differing voices and perspectives, threatening to block together conflicting narrative possibilities, but shadows this with the *event* of her telling, an event which is beyond the terms of any narrative. Through these means Finley moves to stave off a narrative closure, to place herself beyond the reach and so terms of the languages she uses and, in using, parodies.

Such a preoccupation with a performance's coming into being, with a shadowing of the performance by the act of performance, is evident too in the Wooster Group's work. Commenting on the incorporation of dances combining ballet exercises and flamenco at the end of *L.S.D.*, as four of the Wooster Group performers stand in for 'Donna Sierra and the Del Fuegos', a dance group who, it appears, have failed to turn up, LeCompte draws attention to just such a moment:

> To watch the dancer drop out to prepare for the next Raga was the most exciting thing for me – to watch that transformation. This dance was a kind of play on that. Kate Valk picks up these idiot ragas – there's nothing to them – but the whole thing is about the change of persona. From the preparation to the execution of the dance with such incredible aplomb. That's what dancing is about! It doesn't matter what you do, it's how you do it.[61]

Through specific devices, such as Willem Dafoe's dripping of glycerine into his eyes before the audience in order that he might 'cry' in *L.S.D.* or the handicapping of the blackface performers, as well as through the clash of performance styles itself, the Wooster Group's performances threaten to shadow and disrupt that which is being performed with the act of performance. Such strategies are concerned with those events which cannot be encompassed *within* narrative, that cannot be represented, and which shadow and qualify representation, that mark out or make visible the fact and limitation of representation. Indeed, in these respects, these performances attempt to qualify their engagement in their various discourses through a concern for 'figure', a concern for the event of the telling, of that aspect of narrative which discourse can neither encompass nor escape but would suppress.

Clearly, the Wooster Group and Karen Finley's performances are constructed towards a dangerous instability with regard to their meanings. Yet these presentations engage in a decidedly political resistance to narrative closure and, with this, a making visible of the nature and consequences of the narrative act. The effect of such a resistance is not to be found in a particular import or articulation of a point of view, but occurs as a destabilising of that which is 'assumed', of that which would appear to the audience as something which is already 'known'. Operating in this way, as a series of intrusions and disruptions, this performance also resists the attempt to divorce its 'meanings' or political value from its immediate contexts. LeCompte's own notion of the political effect of the Wooster Group's work seems to echo this idea. Commenting on her interest in *The Crucible*, which was incorporated into early versions of *L.S.D.*, she observes that:

> I felt we could do this play better than anyone in creation because of our particular distance. It's a distanced political play that takes its power from the situation in which it was written, not from the internal relationships. That is so often the way in which our work is conceived.[62]

Such a description of the political value of certain kinds of formal strategies clearly has a wider resonance. After Lyotard, and simply in order to be consistent, one cannot confine such a notion of the 'political' to that work which incorporates overtly social and political narratives and images. In so far as the Wooster Group's and Karen Finley's performances effect a disruption of the 'meaningful', upsetting the hierarchies and assumption that would define and stabilise the formal and thematic parameters of their work, their strategies echo Kaprow's, Brecht's and the Judson dancers' attacks on the stability of the 'object'. Although formally quite distinct from a quotation and subversion of 'texts', these earlier presentations nevertheless intervened into reading, playing on and problematising the viewer's desire for 'completion' and closure. Although eschewing narrative, they similarly called into question the authority of the 'work', just as they rendered uncertain the status and meaning of that which the viewer encountered 'through' it. Such presentations may readily be set against Lyotard's understanding of the significance of aesthetic transgression, and the playing out of the resistance to the 'illusion' of totalisation for which he calls. 'The price to pay for such an illusion', Lyotard argues 'is terror', and he concludes that:

> the nineteenth and twentieth centuries have given us as much terror as we can take. We have paid a high enough price for the nostalgia of the whole and the one ... Let us wage a war on totality.[63]

In conclusion, then, and in something of the spirit of a resistance to closure, these ideas serve to turn attention back towards that work which has already been considered in this book, and which, although removed to one degree or another from a social and political 'content', nevertheless intrudes upon and disrupts the unself-conscious move toward closure.

Conclusion

Postmodernism and Performance

As it is taken here, the postmodern is not the property of a particular form or vocabulary. In so far as the postmodern in art may be identified with an unstable 'event' provoked by a questioning that casts doubt sharply upon even itself, then one characteristic of the postmodern would be its resistance to any simple circumscription of its means and forms. As a disruption of 'foundation' or a striving toward foundation, this postmodernism is best thought of as an *effect* of particular strategies played out in response to certain expectations. Indeed, the limitation of 'postmodern' means or the abstraction of predominant or defining 'post-modern' forms can only move against those instabilities which one might wish to identify as postmodern, so drawing the postmodern implicitly back towards foundation and the modern. It follows, then, that a description of 'postmodernism' must be given over to an account of postmodernism*s*, and so to an acknowledgement of the multiple means by which particular kinds of contingencies are revealed.

This view of diverse and multiple postmodernisms is one that lends itself to an address to those kinds of presentations and activities in the arts which corrupt conventional divisions and categories, or that are resistant to the very modes of looking and reading which they invite. For these reasons, the postmodernism debate can readily be used to provide a framework of ideas through which to explore and test that reaching towards theatre which springs from interdisciplinary practices and sensibilities. Importantly, too, this idea of the 'postmodern event' allows an exploration of connections between very obviously divergent kinds of work which meet in a making visible of the unsteady agree-ments and circumstances upon which the work of art and its meanings depend.

In looking towards these points of contact between differing forms, practices and ideas, however, this study does not attempt to observe connections between 'postmodernism' and 'performance' in any impar-tial way. In this book, the postmodern is overtly defined and 'limited' in order to allow a particular address to take place. It follows that, to be consistent, a project which looks towards the production of such 'post-modern' instabilities must also invite a questioning of its own terms and limits. One might challenge, then, the ways in which the exclusions this book makes serve to construct a predominant view, moving implicitly towards a circumscription of ideas, means and forms. In looking towards performance which is touched on but not considered in detail here, one might both use and challenge the move towards categories this study effects. Thus Laurie Anderson's performance, *United States*, of 1983, might be read as resisting a consideration either through a dis-ruption of narrative, after the Wooster Group, or as an attack on the effi-cacy of the sign, after Richard Foreman. Yet Anderson's appropriations and displacements of popular imagery and her telling of paradoxical stories around these images might be considered by setting these two readings against each other, using and challenging the distinctions between them.

Indeed, the resistance to category that underlies this notion of the post-modern might be set against the implicit privileging, here, of perform-ance as a 'primary postmodern mode'. If the postmodern occurs as a disruption of discourse and representation, then it cannot be associated in any exclusive way with a particular form or mode. If the 'postmodern event' occurs as a breaking away, a disruption of what is 'given', then 'its' forms cannot usefully be pinned down in any final or categorical way. In this case, where the postmodern is represented in one way, where 'its' means are defined, then the 'postmodern event' will come into play at the very moment this limitation, and so the move toward closure, is disrupted. Such definitions cannot arrive at the postmodern, but can only set out a ground which might be challenged.

To 'use' the postmodern, though, and so to deliberately 'limit' it, might not be, quite, to define it. Limiting the postmodern might be more like a local activity, one that tacitly acknowledges its own parameters as much as it strives to confine the postmodernism debate. Rather than seek to *totalise* and so *possess* the term, to hold it within a particular cat-egorical and formal definition, such a limitation might look towards an interrogation of its own terms and assumptions. This invitation is more consistent with the 'postmodern' as it is taken here than could be any particular definition of postmodern forms or features, as it is an invitation that calls for a resistance to a drawing of the postmodern back towards the foundation it would disrupt.

Notes

Notes to the Introduction

1. G. Vattimo, *The End of Modernity* (Oxford, 1988) p. 2.
2. See, for example, J. B. Alter, 'A Critical Analysis of Suzanne K. Langer's Dance Theory', *Dance Research Annual*, vol. XVI (1987) pp. 110–19; and M. Sheets-Johnstone, 'On the Nature of Theories of Dance', *CORD Dance Research Annual*, vol. X (1979) pp. 3–29.

Notes to Chapter 1

1. Although the development of 'postmodern' design can be traced back, at least, to the work of Robert Venturi in the early 1960s (see R. Venturi, *Complexity and Contradiction in Architecture* (New York, 1966), Portoghesi argues that modern design had become untenable by 1968. In *What is Post-modernism?*, 2nd edn (London, 1987) Charles Jencks, tongue-in-cheek, dates the 'Death of Modernism/Rise of Post-modernism' from the dynamiting of the Pruitt-Igoe housing complex in St Louis in 1972.
2. P. Portoghesi, *Postmodern: The Architecture of Postindustrial Society* (New York, 1982) p. 11.
3. Ibid., p. 12.
4. Ibid., p. 7.
5. Ibid.
6. U. Conrads, *Programmes and Manifestos on Twentieth Century Architecture* (London, 1970) p. 74.
7. C. Jencks, *Post-modernism: The New Classicism in Art and Architecture* (London, 1987) p. 330.
8. H. Klotz, *The History of Postmodern Architecture* (London, 1988) p. 421.

9. See, particularly, C. Jencks, *What is Post-modernism?*, 2nd edn (London, 1987) and *Post-modernism: The New Classicism in Art and Architecture* (London, 1987).
10. Jencks, *Post-modernism*, p. 268.
11. Ibid., p. 271.
12. Ibid., p. 272.
13. Ibid.
14. Ibid.
15. Ibid., p. 338.
16. Ibid., p. 345.
17. Ibid., p. 340.
18. Ibid., p. 345.
19. Conrads, *Programmes and Manifestos*, p. 95.
20. See Klotz, *History of Postmodern Architecture*, p. 20.
21. Conrads, *Programmes and Manifestos*, p. 25.
22. Le Corbusier, *Towards a New Architecture* (London, 1927) p. 20.
23. L. Hutcheon, *A Poetics of Postmodernism* (London, 1988) p. 3.
24. Ibid., p. 92.
25. Ibid., p. 108.
26. Ibid., p. 107.
27. J. Kalb, 'Ping Chong: From *Lazarus* to *Anna into Nightlight*', *Theater*, vol. XIV, no. 2 (1983) pp. 68–75, esp. p. 68.
28. N. Carrol, 'A Select View of Earthlings: Ping Chong', *Drama Review*, vol. XXVII, no. 1 (1983) pp. 72–81.
29. See, for example, H. Papaport, ' "Can You Say Hello?": Laurie Anderson's *United States*', *Theatre Journal*, vol. XXXVIII, no. 3 (1986) pp. 339–54.
30. See, for example, W. W. Demastes, 'Spalding Gray's *Swimming to Cambodia* and the Evolution of an Ironic Presence', *Theatre Journal*, vol. XXXXI, no. 1 (1989) pp. 75–94.
31. See N. Kaye, 'Richard Schechner: Theory and Practice of the Indeterminate Theatre', *New Theatre Quarterly*, vol. V, no. 20 (1989) pp. 348–60.
32. Hutcheon, *Poetics of Postmodernism*, p. 11.
33. J. Derrida, *Of Grammatology* (London, 1976) p. 7.
34. For Derrida's discussion of Saussure and structural linguistics see, particularly, *Of Grammatology*, pp. 27–73.
35. See, for example, H. Foster, 'Wild Signs: the Breakup of the Sign in '70s Art', in J. Tagg (ed.), *The Cultural Politics of Postmodernism* (New York, 1989).
36. J. Baudrillard, *The Ecstasy of Communication* (New York, 1987) p. 11.

37. J. F. Lyotard, *The Postmodern Condition: A Report on Knowledge* (Manchester, 1984) p. xxvii.

38. Ibid., p. xxiv.

39. B. Readings, *Introducing Lyotard: Art and Politics* (London, 1991) p. 69.

40. Ibid., p. 79.

41. See O. Paz, *Children of the Mire* (Harvard, Mass., 1974), Ch. 1: 'A Tradition Against Itself'.

42. Lyotard, *Postmodern Condition*, p. 79.

43. Readings, *Introducing Lyotard*, p. 74.

44. Baudrillard, *Ecstasy of Communication*, p. 11.

45. See T. Docherty, *After Theory: Post-modernism/Post-Marxism* (London, 1990). Docherty uses the term 'backward glance' to indicate the construction of a legitimating historical perspective.

46. U. Eco, *Reflections on 'The Name of the Rose'* (London, 1985) p. 67.

47. S. Lash, *Sociology of Postmodernism* (London, 1990) p. 157.

48. Ibid., p. 173.

49. See, particularly, M. Fried, 'Art and Objecthood', in G. Battcock (ed.), *Minimal Art: A Critical Anthology* (New York, 1968).

Notes to Chapter 2

1. See, for example, S. Banes, *Democracy's Body: Judson Dance Theater, 1962–1964* (Ann Arbor, Mich., 1983); and R. Goldberg, *Performance Art* (London, 1988) pp. 141–3.

2. C. Greenberg, ' "American-type" Painting', in C. Greenberg, *Art and Culture: Critical Essays* (Boston, Mass., 1965) p. 210.

3. C. Greenberg, 'After Abstract Expressionism', *Art International*, vol. VI, no. 8 (1962) pp. 26–30, esp. p. 30.

4. Greenberg, ' "American-type" Painting', p. 209.

5. Ibid., p. 210.

6. C. Greenberg, 'After Abstract Expressionism', *Art International*, vol. VI, no. 8 (1962) pp. 26–30, esp. p. 30.

7. C. Greenberg, 'Modernist Painting', *Art and Literature*, vol. 4 (1965) pp. 193–201, esp. p. 194.

8. Ibid., p. 193.

9. Ibid., p. 195.

10. C. Greenberg, 'Avant-garde and Kitsch', in Greenberg, *Art and Culture*, pp. 5–6.

11. Greenberg, 'Modernist Painting', p. 200.

12. V. Acconci, *Recorded documentation by Vito Acconci of the exhibition and commission for San Diego State University*, April–May 1982 (audio cassette) (San Diego, Cal., 1982).

13. M. Fried, 'Art and Objecthood', in G. Battcock (ed.), *Minimal Art: A Critical Anthology* (New York, 1968) p. 125.

14. Ibid., p. 145.

15. Ibid., p. 135.

16. Ibid., p. 141.

17. Ibid., p. 142.

18. L. Alloway, 'Rauschenberg's Development', in Smithsonian Institute, *Robert Rauschenberg* (Washington, D.C., 1976) p. 3.

19. Ibid., p. 5.

20. Greenberg, 'After Abstract Expressionism', p. 26.

21. M. Crichton, *Jasper Johns* (London, 1977) p. 40.

22. A. Kaprow, *Assemblages, Environments and Happenings* (New York, 1966) p. 159.

23. Ibid., p. 165.

24. Ibid., p. 169.

25. First emerging in New York in 1961 under the organisation of gallery owner George Maciunas, 'Fluxus' became a name under which a continually growing and changing number of American and European artists presented concerts and published books and proposals. Characterised above all by an eclecticism and informality, Fluxus might be best described as a manner of work or a certain kind of sensibility. In describing Fluxus 'art-amusement' as 'the fusion of Spike Jones, Vaudeville, gag, children's games and Duchamp', Maciunas went some way toward identifying the spirit of their activities.

26. The Reuben Gallery, *George Brecht: toward Events*, announcement of exhibition (New York, 1959).

27. C. Oldenburg, *Store Days* (New York, 1967) p. 200.

28. A script and documentation of *18 Happenings in 6 Parts*, among a range of other early presentations, is published in M. Kirby, *Happenings* (New York, 1965).

29. See, for example, J. Cage, 'An Interview', *Tulane Drama Review*, vol. x, no. 2 (1965) pp. 50–72.

30. See Fried, 'Art and Objecthood', p. 124. Fried notes his disagreement here with his earlier view of modernism set out in his article 'Three American Painters'.

31. Fried, 'Art and Objecthood', pp. 123–4.

32. See, particularly, D. M. Levin, 'Postmodernism in Dance: Dance, Discourse, Democracy', in H. J. Silverman (ed.), *Postmodernism – Philosophy and the Arts* (London, 1990). Levin draws on Greenberg and Fried to argue that the modernist work is one which reveals, reflects upon and displaces those conditions which have served to define the work of art under a particular set of (contingent) historical conditions. Levin goes on to argue that, in its deconstruction of the modern, the modernist work comprises a first phase of postmodernism, and one that gives way to the specifically postmodernist. Levin defines postmodernism in art in terms of an historical break from the modern and a subsequent and general chronological development.

33. Fried, 'Art and Objecthood', p. 123.

34. A. Kaprow, 'Self-Service: a Happening', *Drama Review*, vol. XII, no. 3 (1968) pp. 160–4, esp. pp. 161–4.

35. R. Kostalanetz, *The Theatre of Mixed Means* (New York, 1968) p. 112.

36. Kaprow, *Assemblages, Environments and Happenings*, p. 193.

37. A. Kaprow, 'Education of the Un-artist, Part Two', *Art News*, vol. LXXI, no. 3 (1972) pp. 34–9, 62, esp. p. 35.

38. A. Kaprow and R. Schechner, 'Extensions in Time and Space', *Drama Review*, vol. XII, no. 2 (1968) pp. 153–9, esp. p. 154.

39. Ibid., p. 153.

40. Kaprow, 'Self-Service: a Happening', pp. 160–4.

41. Ibid., p. 161.

42. Kaprow and Schechner, 'Extensions in Time and Space', p. 154.

43. Ibid.

44. A. Kaprow, 'The Happenings are Dead: Long Live the Happenings', *Artforum*, vol. IV, no. 7 (1966) pp. 36–9, esp. p. 39.

45. Ibid.

46. *Three Aqueous Events* was originally published in George Brecht's *Water Yam* (Fluxus: New York, 1962). According to Brecht, a first edition of approximately 60 cards was expanded to an edition of 105 or 110 in 1964 or 1965. Other sources for Brecht 'event-scores' include H. Ruhe (ed.), *Fluxus: the most radical and experimental art movement of the sixties* (Amsterdam, 1979); and *Film Culture*, vol. 43 (1966).

47. H. Martin, 'An Interview with George Brecht by Henry Martin', in H. Martin, *An Introduction to George Brecht's Book of the Tumbler on Fire* (Milan, 1978) p. 84.

48. See, for example, I. Lebeer, 'An Interview with George Brecht by

Irmilene Lebeer', in Martin, *An Introduction to George Brecht's Book*, p. 87.

49. From my own correspondence with the artist, December 1983.
50. Martin, *An Introduction to George Brecht's Book*, pp. 27–8.
51. G. Brecht and A. Kaprow, 'Excerpts from a discussion between George Brecht and Allan Kaprow entitled: "Happening and Events"', in H. Sohm (ed.), *Happenings and Fluxus* (Cologne, 1971) pages unnumbered.
52. Martin, *An Introduction to George Brecht's Book*, p. 10.
53. See M. Kirby, *Happenings* (New York, 1965) p. 21.
54. Lebeer, 'Interview with George Brecht'.
55. A. Kaprow, 'Non-theatrical Performance', *Artforum*, vol. XIV, no. 9 (1976) pp. 45–51, esp. pp. 49–50.
56. Martin, *An Introduction to George Brecht's Book*, pp. 10–11.
57. J. Van der Marck, 'George Brecht: an Art of Multiple Implications', *Art in America*, vol. LXII, no. 4 (1974) pp. 48–57, esp. p. 51.
58. Martin, 'An Interview with George Brecht by Henry Martin', pp. 77–8.
59. Ibid., p. 77.
60. M. Alocco and B. Vautier, 'A Conversation About Something Else: an Interview with George Brecht by Marcel Alocco and Ben Vautier', in Martin, *An Introduction to George Brecht's Book*, pp. 69–70.
61. M. Nyman, 'An Interview with George Brecht by Michael Nyman', in Martin, *An Introduction to George Brecht's Book*, p. 120.

Notes to Chapter 3

1. See, particularly, T. Shank, *American Alternative Theatre* (London, 1982). Shank groups Wilson and Kirby together on the grounds that 'form or structure' are 'the predominant content of their work' (p. 123). See also R. Schechner, 'The Decline and Fall of the (American) Avant-garde', in R. Schechner, *The End of Humanism* (New York, 1982). Schechner argues that work by Foreman, Wilson and others in the 1970s heralded a 'formalist deep freeze ... great work was done, but it was cut off; it did not manifest significant content' (p. 18).
2. N. Kaye and M. Kirby, unpublished interview, New York, April 1990.
3. M. Feingold, 'An Interview with Richard Foreman', *Theatre*, vol. VII, no. 1 (1975) pp. 5–29, esp. p. 25.

4. Ibid., p. 10.
5. N. Kaye, 'Bouncing Back the Impulse: an Interview with Richard Foreman', *Performance*, vol. 61 (1990) pp. 31–42, esp. p. 32.
6. S. Brecht, *The Theatre of Visions* (Frankfurt am Main, 1978) pp. 21–2.
7. Ibid., p. 26.
8. Ibid., p. 28.
9. Ibid., p. 45.
10. R. Foreman, 'How to Write a Play', in R. Foreman, *Reverberation Machines: The Later Plays and Essays* (New York, 1985) p. 222.
11. M. Kirby, 'Structural Analysis/Structural Theory', *Drama Review*, vol. XX, no. 4 (1976) pp. 51–68, esp. p. 53.
12. R. Foreman, *Ontological-Hysteric Manifesto I*, in K. Davy (ed.), *Richard Foreman: Plays and Manifestos* (New York, 1976) p. 69.
13. R. Foreman, *Pandering to the Masses: A Misrepresentation*, in B. Marranca (ed.), *The Theatre of Images* (New York, 1977) pp. 15–36.
14. Ibid., p. 26.
15. Ibid., p. 16.
16. Ibid.
17. Ibid.
18. See K. Davy, 'Review: Foreman's Pandering', *Drama Review*, vol. XIX, no. 1 (1975) pp. 116–17, esp. p. 117.
19. Marranca (ed.), *The Theatre of Images*, p. 12.
20. R. Foreman, 'How Truth . . . Leaps (Stumbles) Across Stage', in Foreman, *Reverberation Machines*, p. 198.
21. R. Foreman, 'How I Write My (Self:Plays)', *Drama Review*, vol. XXI, no. 4 (1977) pp. 5–24, esp. p. 21.
22. Foreman, *Ontological-Hysteric Manifesto I*, p. 76.
23. Foreman, 'How I Write My (Self:Plays)', p. 13.
24. Foreman, 'How Truth . . . Leaps (Stumbles) Across Stage', p. 198.
25. R. Foreman, *Ontological-Hysteric: Manifesto II*, in Davy (ed.), *Richard Foreman: Plays and Manifestos*, p. 137.
26. Ibid., p. 145.
27. Foreman, 'How to Write a Play', p. 224.
28. As well as being instrumental to innovations in dance (see Chapter 5), chance method was of particular importance to Fluxus work and many early Happenings. Several of George Brecht's 'event-scores' explicitly draw on Cage's methods.
29. Foreman, *Ontological-Hysteric Manifesto I*, p. 68.
30. R. Foreman, '14 Things I Tell Myself', in Foreman, *Reverberation Machines*, p. 215.

31. Foreman, 'How Truth ... Leaps (Stumbles) Across Stage', p. 199.
32. K. Davy, 'Foreman's *Vertical Mobility* and *PAIN(T)*', *Drama Review*, vol. XVIII, no. 2 (1974) pp. 26–37, esp. p. 34.
33. Ibid., p. 35.
34. Kaye, 'Bouncing Back the Impulse', p. 34.
35. Foreman, *Ontological-Hysteric Manifesto I*, p. 68.
36. K. Davy, 'Kate Manheim on Foreman's Rhoda', *Drama Review*, vol. XX, no. 3 (1976) pp. 37–50, esp. p. 43.
37. Ibid.
38. Ibid.
39. Foreman, *Ontological-Hysteric Manifesto I*, p. 70.
40. Foreman, *Ontological-Hysteric: Manifesto II*, p. 143.
41. Kaye, 'Bouncing Back the Impulse', p. 39.
42. Foreman, 'How to Write a Play', p. 229.
43. Kaye and Kirby, unpublished interview.
44. Ibid.
45. M. Kirby, *First Signs of Decadence* (Schulenburg, 1986) p. xiii.
46. Ibid., p. vi.
47. Ibid., p. xiii.
48. Kaye and Kirby, unpublished interview.
49. Kirby, *First Signs of Decadence*, p. x.
50. Ibid, p. viii.
51. Kaye and Kirby, unpublished interview.
52. Kirby, *First Signs of Decadence*, p. 19.
53. Ibid., p. 24.
54. Ibid., p. 15.
55. Ibid., p. 30.
56. Ibid., p. xi.
57. Kaye and Kirby, unpublished interview.
58. Kirby, *First Signs of Decadence*, p. 13.
59. Ibid., p. 19.
60. Ibid., p. 34.
61. Ibid., p. 23.
62. Brecht, *Theatre of Visions*, pp. 54–5.
63. Ibid., p. 55.
64. L. Shyer, *Robert Wilson and his Collaborators* (New York, 1989) p. 6.
65. Brecht, *Theatre of Visions*, p. 115.
66. O. Trilling, 'Robert Wilson's *Ka Mountain*', *Drama Review*, vol. XVII, no. 2 (1973) pp. 33–47, esp. p. 44.
67. Shyer, *Robert Wilson*, p. 7.
68. Brecht, *Theatre of Visions*, p. 55.

69. Trilling, 'Robert Wilson's *Ka Mountain*', p. 44.
70. Shyer, *Robert Wilson*, pp. 6–7.
71. Brecht, *Theatre of Visions*, p. 55.
72. Ibid.
73. Ibid., pp. 56–7.
74. Ibid., p. 58.
75. Ibid., p. 210.
76. Ibid., p. 390.
77. Ibid., p. 172.
78. Wilson's early work was performed by a changing company of largely untrained performers. Wilson used the idiosyncratic qualities of his performers in the manner of 'found' elements in the construction of his collages. See, in particular, Shyer, *Robert Wilson*; and B. Simmer, 'Sue Sheehy', *Drama Review*, vol. XX, no. 1 (1976) pp. 67–74.
79. Brecht, *Theatre of Visions*, p. 420.
80. Ibid., p. 419.
81. J. Donker, *President of Paradise: A traveller's account of Robert Wilson's 'the CIVIL warS'* (Amsterdam, 1985) pp. 23–4.
82. In particular, the King of Spain in *The King of Spain* (1969), Sigmund Freud in *The Life and Times of Sigmund Freud* (1970), Joseph Stalin in *The Life and Times of Joseph Stalin* (1973), Queen Victoria in *A Letter for Queen Victoria* (1974), Einstein in *Einstein on the Beach* (1976), Thomas Edison in *Edison* (1979), Rudolph Hess in *Death, Destruction and Detroit* (1979) and Abraham Lincoln in *the CIVIL warS* (1984).
83. For example, *A Letter for Queen Victoria* (1974) and *The Golden Windows* (1982).
84. Shyer, *Robert Wilson*, p. 80.
85. Brecht, *Theatre of Visions*, p. 274.
86. Ibid., p. 277.
87. Shyer, *Robert Wilson*, p. 216.
88. Donker, *President of Paradise*, p. 117.
89. Brecht, *Theatre of Visions*, p. 420.
90. Ibid., p. 425.
91. Foreman, '14 Things I Tell Myself', p. 213.

Notes to Chapter 4

1. L. Horst and C. Russell, *Modern Dance Forms* (San Francisco, 1961) p. 16.

2. See, for example, M. B. Siegel, 'Modern Dance at Bennington: Sorting It All Out', *Dance Research Journal*, vol. XIX, no. 1 (1987) pp. 3–9.

3. Ibid.

4 J. H. Mazo, *Prime Movers* (London, 1977) p. 121.

5. Ibid., p. 123.

6. Ibid., p. 184.

7. S. L. Foster, *Reading Dancing: Bodies and Subjects in Contemporary American Dance* (Berkeley, Cal., 1986) p. 150.

8. Horst and Russell, *Modern Dance Forms*, p. 23.

9. Ibid., p. 24.

10. Ibid.

11. See S. Banes, *Democracy's Body: Judson Dance Theater, 1962–1964* (Ann Arbor, Mich., 1983) p. 3.

12. Ibid., p. 3.

13. Ibid., p. xviii.

14. Ibid.

15. S. Banes, *Terpsichore in Sneakers: Post-modern Dance*, 2nd edn (Middletown, Conn., 1987) p. xiv.

16. See J. Hendricks (ed.), *Fluxus Etc.: The Gilbert and Lila Silverman Collection* (Bloomfield Hills, Mich., 1981) Part 3, a chronology of Fluxus performance.

17. See Banes, *Democracy's Body*, pp. 131–2.

18. M. Fried, 'Art and Objecthood', in G. Battcock (ed.), *Minimal Art: A Critical Anthology* (New York, 1968) p. 140.

19. Ibid.

20. Foster, *Reading Dancing*, p. xiv.

21. Ibid., p. xvi.

22. C. Sachs, *World History of the Dance* (New York, 1937) p. 447.

23. J. Martin, *Introduction to the Dance* (New York, 1939) p. 224.

24. Ibid., p. 32.

25. Horst and Russell, *Modern Dance Forms*, pp. 13–14.

26. Ibid., p. 13.

27. Foster, *Reading Dancing*, p. xvi.

28. S. K. Langer, *Feeling and Form: A Theory of Art* (London, 1953) p. 23.

29. Ibid., p. 39.

30. Ibid.

31. Ibid., p. 31.

32. Ibid., p. 67.

33. Ibid., p. 45.

34. Ibid., p. 46.
35. Ibid., p. 45.
36. Ibid., p. 84.
37. Ibid., p. 71.
38. Ibid., pp. 71–2.
39. Ibid., p. 72.
40. Ibid.
41. Ibid., p. 73.
42. Ibid., p. 178.
43. Ibid., p. 175.
44. Ibid., p. 205.
45. Ibid., p. 184.
46. Ibid., p. 59.
47. J. Martin, *The Modern Dance* (New York, 1933) p. 84.
48. Ibid., p. 4.
49. Ibid., p. 6.
50. Ibid.
51. Ibid., pp. 7–8.
52. Ibid., p. 15.
53. Ibid., p. 31.
54. Ibid.
55. Ibid., p. 33.
56. Ibid., p. 35.
57. Ibid., p. 91.
58. Ibid., p. 90.
59. Ibid., p. 85.
60. Ibid., p. 86.
61. Ibid., p. 47.
62. Langer, *Feeling and Form*, p. 175.
63. Horst and Russell, *Modern Dance Forms*, p. 117.
64. Ibid., pp. 117–18.

Notes to Chapter 5

1. S. Banes, *Democracy's Body: Judson Dance Theater, 1962–1964* (Ann Arbor, Mich., 1983) p. 1.
2. Ibid., p. 2.
3. Ibid., p. 7.
4. Ibid., p. 39.
5. Ibid., p. 11.

6. Ibid., p. 44.
7. Ibid., p. 65.
8. Ibid., p. 58.
9. N. Kaye, unpublished interview with John Cage, London, May 1985.
10. J. Cage, 'Experimental Music', in J. Cage, *Silence: Lectures and Writings* (London, 1968) p. 8.
11. J. Cage, 'Lecture on Nothing', in Cage, *Silence*, p. 111.
12. J. Cage and D. Charles, *For the Birds* (London, 1981) p. 153.
13. Ibid., p. 180.
14. Ibid., p. 201.
15. Ibid., p. 52.
16. Kaye, unpublished interview.
17. J. Cage, 'To Describe the Process of Composition Used in *Music of Changes* and *Imaginary Landscape No. 4*', in Cage, *Silence*, p. 58.
18. Banes, *Democracy's Body*, p. 43.
19. Ibid., p. 47.
20. Ibid.
21. Ibid., pp. 59–60.
22. Ibid., p. 60.
23. Ibid., p. 7.
24. Ibid., p. 8.
25. Ibid., pp. 8–9.
26. S. Forti, *Handbook in Motion* (New York, 1974) p. 36.
27. Ibid., p. 44.
28. R. Morris, 'Notes on Dance', *Tulane Drama Review*, vol. x, no. 2 (1965) pp. 179–86, esp. p. 179.
29. A. Livet (ed.), *Contemporary Dance* (New York, 1978) p. 45.
30. Kaye, unpublished interview.
31. Banes, *Democracy's Body*, pp. 87, 90–1.
32. Ibid., p. 78.
33. Ibid., p. 86.
34. Y. Rainer, *Work, 1961–73* (Nova Scotia and New York, 1974) pp. 67–8.
35. Ibid., p. 66.
36. Ibid., p. 67.
37. Ibid.
38. Ibid., p. 68.
39. Foster, *Reading Dancing*, p. 175.
40. Ibid., p. 176.
41. Banes, *Terpsichore in Sneakers*, p. 44.

42. Rainer, *Work, 1961–73*, p. 67.
43. Ibid.
44. Banes, *Terpsichore in Sneakers*, p. 61.
45. S. Paxton, score and notes for *Satisfyin Lover*, in Banes, *Terpsichore in Sneakers*, p. 71.
46. Banes, *Democracy's Body*, p. 60.
47. L. Childs, 'Lucinda Childs: a Portfolio', *Artforum*, vol. 11 (1973) pp. 50–7, esp. p. 50.
48. Ibid.
49. L. Childs, 'Notes: '64–'74', *Drama Review*, vol. XIX, no. 1 (1975) pp. 33–6, esp. p. 33.
50. Ibid.
51. Childs, 'Lucinda Childs', p. 56.
52. Ibid., p. 55.
53. Childs, 'Notes: '64–'74', p. 34.
54. Ibid.
55. Ibid., pp. 34–5.
56. Livet, *Contemporary Dance*, p. 44.
57. E. Stefano, 'Moving Structures', *Art and Artists*, vol. VII, no. 10 (1974) pp. 16–25, esp. p. 17.
58. D. Jowitt, *Dance Beat: Selected Views and Reviews* (New York, 1977) p. 117.
59. T. Brown, 'Three Pieces', *Drama Review*, vol. XIX, no. 1 (1975) pp. 26–32, esp. p. 29.
60. Ibid.
61. Ibid.
62. Stefano, 'Moving Structures', p. 2 0.
63. R. Morris, 'Some Notes on the Phenomenology of Making', *Artforum*, vol. VIII, no. 6 (1970) pp. 62–4, esp. p. 63.
64. See, for example, M. Compton and D. Sylvester, *Robert Morris* (London, 1977) pp. 114–17.
65. Rainer, *Work, 1961–73*, p. 125.
66. Ibid., p. 130.
67. Ibid., p. 131.

Notes to Chapter 6

1. T. Wilder, *Our Town, The Skin of Our Teeth, The Matchmaker* (London, 1987) p. 7.

2. W. Coco, 'Review: *Route 1 & 9*', *Theatre Journal*, vol. XXXIV, no. 2 (1982) pp. 249–52, esp. p. 250.

3. D. Savran, *Breaking the Rules: The Wooster Group* (New York, 1988) p. 15.

4. Ibid., p. 21.

5. Ibid., p. 22.

6. Ibid., p. 30.

7. Ibid., p. 14.

8. Wilder, *Our Town*, p. 76.

9. Ibid.

10. Ibid., p. 11.

11. R. J. Burbank, *Thornton Wilder*, 2nd edn (New York, 1978) p. 72.

12. Ibid.

13. Wilder, *Our Town*, p. 89.

14. Savran, *Breaking the Rules*, p. 25.

15. Ibid., p. 27.

16. Coco, 'Review: *Route 1 & 9*', p. 251.

17. Savran, *Breaking the Rules*, p. 36.

18. Ibid., p. 43.

19. Ibid., p. 53.

20. Ibid., p. 31.

21. Ibid., p. 44.

22. According to Elizabeth LeCompte and Ron Vawter, the tape was developed before *Route 1 & 9* and derived from an interest in the nature of performance in pornographic film and the desire to make something 'private and possibly obscene'. See Savran, *Breaking the Rules*, pp. 41–5.

23. L. Champagne, 'Always Starting Anew: Elizabeth LeCompte', *Drama Review*, vol. XXV, no. 3 (1981) pp. 19–28, p. 25.

24. Savran, *Breaking the Rules*, p. 34.

25. Champagne, 'Always Starting Anew', p. 25.

26. See Savran, *Breaking the Rules*, pp. 26–33. The history and use of the blackface is widely charted. See, in particular, B. Ostendorf, *Black Literature in White America* (Totowa, N.J., 1982) ch. 3.

27. See Savran, *Breaking the Rules*, p. 10. Savran reports that an NYSCA memo concluded that '*Route 1 & 9* constituted in its blackface sequences harsh and caricatured portrayals of a racial minority'.

28. Champagne, 'Always Starting Anew', p. 36.

29. See, for example, D. Savran, 'The Wooster Group, Arthur Miller and *The Crucible*', *Drama Review*, vol. XXIX, no. 2 (1985) pp. 99–109.

30. Savran, *Breaking the Rules*, pp. 53–4.
31. See, for example, E. Fuchs, 'Staging the Obscene Body', *Drama Review*, vol. XXXIII, no. 1 (1989) pp. 33–58.
32. See, particularly, C. Schuler, 'Spectator Response and Comprehension: the Problem of Karen Finley's *The Constant State of Desire*', *Drama Review*, vol. XXXIV, no. 1 (1990) pp. 152–8.
33. Karen Finley's *The Constant State of Desire* has been published in three forms, reflecting the changing nature of the piece in performance. This discussion draws principally on the later publication in Finley's *Shock Treatment* (San Francisco, 1990), with some reference to her earlier publication of 'The Constant State of Desire' in *Drama Review*, vol. XXXII, no. 1 (1988) pp. 139–51. The earlier text includes stage-directions. Another version of the text is published in L. Champagne, *Out from Under: Texts by Women Performance Artists* (New York, 1990).
34. Finley, *Shock Treatment*, p. 3.
35. Ibid., p. 5.
36. Finley, 'The Constant State of Desire', p. 140.
37. Finley, *Shock Treatment*, p. 9.
38. Finley, 'The Constant State of Desire', p. 142.
39. Finley, *Shock Treatment*, pp. 9–10.
40. Ibid., p. 15.
41. Ibid.
42. Ibid., pp. 20–1.
43. J. Dolan, *The Feminist Spectator as Critic* (Ann Arbor, Mich., 1988) p. 67.
44. See, for example, M. Robinson, 'Performance Strategies: Interviews with Ishmael Houston-Jones, John Kelly, Karen Finley, Richard Elovich', *Performing Arts Journal*, vol. X, no. 3 (1987) pp. 31–56.
45. R. Schechner, 'Karen Finley: a Constant State of Becoming', *Drama Review*, vol. XXXII, no. 1 (1988) pp. 152–8, esp. p. 155.
46. Robinson, 'Performance Strategies', p. 44.
47. Y. Rainer, *Work, 1961–73* (Nova Scotia and New York, 1974) p. 251.
48. Ibid.
49. Ibid., p. 253.
50. Ibid., p. 257.
51. Ibid., p. 263.
52. P. Hulton, 'Fiction, Character and Narration: Yvonne Rainer', *Dartington Theatre Papers*, 2nd series, no. 7 (Dartington Hall, Devon, 1978), pp. 5–6.

53. Rainer, *Work, 1961–73*, p. 271.
54. Hulton, 'Fiction, Character and Narration', p. 12.
55. See N. Kaye, 'Mask, Role and Narrative: an Interview with Joan Jonas', *Performance*, vols 65–6 (1992) pp. 49–60.
56. J. Jonas, *Scripts and Descriptions* (Berkeley, Cal., 1983) p. 99.
57. Ibid.
58. Ibid., p. 103.
59. Ibid., p. 107.
60. Schechner, 'Karen Finley', p. 153.
61. A. Aronson, 'The Wooster Group's *L.S.D. (... Just the High Points ...)*', *Drama Review*, vol. XXIX, no. 2 (1985) pp. 65–77, esp. p. 73.
62. Ibid., p. 71.
63. J. F. Lyotard, *The Postmodern Condition: A Report on Knowledge* (Manchester, 1984) pp. 51–2.

Select Bibliography

From postmodern style to performance

Apignanesi, L., (ed.), *Postmodernism* (London, 1989).
Baudrillard, J., *Simulations* (New York, 1983).
——, *The Ecstasy of Communication* (New York, 1987).
——, *Cool Memories* (Paris, 1987).
——, *America* (London, 1989)
Benjamin, A., (ed.), *The Problems of Modernity: Adorno and Benjamin* (London, 1989).
Benjamin, W., *Illuminations* (London, 1968).
Birringer, J., *Theatre, Theory, Postmodernism* (Bloomington and Indianapolis, 1991).
Blau, H., *Blooded Thought* (New York, 1982).
——, *The Eye of Prey: Subversions of the Postmodern* (Bloomington and Indianapolis, 1987).
——, *The Audience* (Baltimore, Md, 1990).
Bradbury, M., and McFarlane, J. (eds), *Modernism: 1890–1930* (London, 1976).
Burgin, V., *The End of Art Theory: Criticism and Postmodernity* (London, 1986).
Butler, C., *After the Wake: An Essay on the Contemporary Avant-garde* (Oxford, 1980).
Calinescu, M., *Five Faces of Modernity: Modernism, Avant-garde, Decadence Kitsch, Postmodernism* (London, 1987).
Calinescu, M., and Fokkema, D. (eds), *Exploring Postmodernism* (Amsterdam and Philadelphia, 1990).
Carroll, D., *Paraesthetics: Foucault, Lyotard, Derrida* (London, 1987)
Carrol, N., 'A Select View of Earthlings: Ping Chong', *Drama Review*, vol. XXVII, no. 1 (1983) pp. 72–81.
Cheetham, M. A., with Hutcheon, L., *Remembering Postmodernism: Recent Trends in Canadian Art* (Oxford, 1991).
Connor, S., *Postmodernist Culture: An Introduction to Theories of the Contemporary* (Oxford, 1989).
Conrads, U., *Programmes and Manifestos on 20th Century Architecture* (London, 1970).

Demastes, W.W., 'Spalding Gray's *Swimming to Cambodia* and the Evolution of an Ironic Presence', *Theatre Journal*, vol. XXXXI, no. 1 (1989) pp. 75–94.

Derrida, J., *Of Grammatology* (London, 1974).

——, *Writing and Difference* (London, 1978).

Docherty, T., *After Theory: Post-modernism/Post-Marxism* (London, 1990).

Eco, U., *Reflections on 'The Name of the Rose'* (London, 1985).

——, *Travels in Hyperreality* (London, 1986).

——, *The Open Work*, 2nd edn (London, 1989).

Featherstone, M. (ed.), *Postmodernism* (London, 1988).

Ferguson, R., Olander, W., Ticker, M., and Fiss, K., *Discourses: Conversations in Postmodern Art and Culture* (New York, 1990).

Fokkema, D. W., and Bertens, J. W. (eds), *Approaching Postmodernism* (Amsterdam and Philadelphia, 1986).

Foster, H. (ed.), *Postmodern Culture* (London, 1983).

Gaggi, S., *Modern–Postmodern: A Study in Twentieth Century Arts and Ideas* (Philadelphia, Penn., 1989).

Goldberg, R., *Performance Art* (London, 1988).

Harvey, D., *The Condition of Postmodernity* (London, 1989).

Hassan, I., *The Dismemberment of Orpheus: Toward a Postmodern Literature* (Madison, Wisc., 1982).

——, *The Postmodern Turn: Essays in Postmodern Theory and Culture* (Columbus, Ohio, 1987).

Hutcheon, L., *A Poetics of Postmodernism: History, Theory, Fiction* (London, 1988).

——, *The Politics of Postmodernism* (London, 1989).

Huyssen, A., *After the Great Divide: Modernism, Mass Culture, Postmodernism* (Indianapolis, 1986).

Jameson, F., *Postmodernism, or, The Cultural Logic of Late Capitalism* (Durham, 1991).

Jencks, C., *What is Post-modernism?*, 2nd edn (London, 1987).

——, *Post-modernism: The New Classicism in Art and Architecture* (London, 1988).

——, *The Language of Postmodern Architecture* (London, 1977).

Kalb, J., 'Ping Chong: From *Lazarus* to *Anna into Nightlight*', *Theater*, vol. XIV, no. 2 (1983) pp. 68–75.

Kaplan, E. A., *Rocking Around the Clock: Music Television, Postmodernism and Consumer Culture* (London and New York, 1987).

—— (ed.), *Postmodernism and Its Discontents: Theories, Practices* (London, 1988).

Kaye, N., 'Richard Schechner: Theory and Practice of the Indeterminate Theatre', *New Theatre Quarterly*, vol. V, no. 20 (1989) pp. 348–60.

Klinkowitz, J., *Rosenberg, Barthes, Hassan: Postmodern Habit of Thought* (Athens, Ga, 1988).

Klotz, H., *The History of Postmodern Architecture* (London, 1988).

Krauss, R. E., *The Originality of the Avant-garde and Other Modernist Myths* (London, 1985).

Kroker, A., and Cook, D., *The Postmodern Scene: Excremental Culture and Hyper-aesthetics*, 2nd edn (London, 1988).

Lash, S., *Sociology of Postmodernism* (London, 1990).

Lawson, H., *Reflexivity: The Post-modern Predicament* (London, 1985).
Le Corbusier, *Towards a New Architecture* (London, 1927).
Lyotard, J.-F., *Discours, Figure* (Paris, 1971).
——, *The Differend: Phrases in Dispute* (Manchester, 1990).
——, *The Postmodern Condition: A Report on Knowledge* (Manchester, 1984).
——, and Thebaud, J.-L., *Just Gaming* (Manchester, 1985).
Madan, S., *An Introductory Guide to Post-structuralism and Post-modernism* (Athens, Ga, 1988).
Milner, A., Thompson, P., and Worth, C., *Postmodern Conditions* (Oxford, 1990).
Newman, C., *The Post-modern Aura* (Evanston, Ill., 1985).
Nicholson, L. J., *Feminism/Postmodernism* (London, 1990).
Norris, C., *What's Wrong with Postmodernism?: Critical Theory and the Ends of Philosophy* (London, 1990).
Papaport, H., ' "Can You Say Hello?": Laurie Anderson's *United States*', *Theatre Journal*, vol. XXXVIII, no. 3 (1986) pp. 339–54.
Paz, O., *Children of the Mire: Modern Poetry from Romanticism to the Avant-garde* (Cambridge, Mass., 1974).
Perloff, M. (ed.), *Postmodern Genres* (Norman, Okla, 1988).
Portoghesi, P., *Postmodern: The Architecture of Postindustrial Society* (New York, 1982).
Readings, B., *Introducing Lyotard: Art and Politics* (London, 1991).
Sayre, H., *The Object of Performance* (Chicago, 1989).
Schechner, R., *The End of Humanism* (New York, 1982).
Schleifer, R., *Rhetoric and Death: The Language of Modernism and Postmodern Discourse Theory* (Chicago, 1990)
Shapiro, G., *After the Future: Postmodern Times and Places* (New York, 1990).
Silverman, H. J. (ed.), *Postmodernism – Philosophy and the Arts* (London, 1990).
Tagg, J. (ed.), *The Cultural Politics of Postmodernism* (New York, 1989).
Trachtenberg, S. (ed.), *The Postmodern Moment: A Handbook of Contemporary Innovation in the Arts* (Westport, Conn., 1985).
Turner, B. S. (ed.), *Theories of Modernity and Postmodernity* (London, 1990).
Ulmer, G. L., *Applied Grammatology: Post(e)-Pedagogy from Jacques Derrida to Joseph Beuys* (Baltimore, md, 1981).
Vattimo, G., *The End of Modernity* (London, 1988).
Venturi, R., *Complexity and Contradiction in Architecture* (New York, 1966).
——, and Scott-Brown, D., *Learning from Las Vegas*, rev. edn (London, 1971).
Wakefield, N., *Postmodernism: The Twilight of the Real* (London, 1990).
Wright, E., *Postmodern Brecht: A Re-presentation* (London, 1988).

Theatricality and the modernist work

Battcock, G., *Minimal Art* (New York, 1968).
——, with Berger, R., and Glusberg, J., *The Art of Performance* (New York, 1979).
——, and Nickas, R. (eds), *The Art of Performance: A Critical Anthology* (New York, 1984).

Brecht, G., *Chance Imagery: A Great Bear Pamphlet* (New York, 1966).
——, and Fillou, R., *Games at the Cedilla, or The Cedilla Takes Off* (New York, 1967).
Bronson, A. A., and Gale, P., *Performance by Artists* (Toronto, 1979).
Buettner, S., *American Art Theory, 1945–1970* (Ann Arbor, Mich., 1981).
Cage, J., *Silence: Lectures and Writings* (Middletown, Conn., 1961).
Calder, J. (ed.), *New Writers Four* (London, 1967).
Crichton, M., *Jasper Johns* (London, 1977).
Fluxus, *1962 Wiesbaden Fluxus 1982* (Berlin, 1982).
Goldberg, R., *Performance Art* (London, 1979).
Greenberg, C., *Art and Culture* (Boston, Mass., 1965).
——, 'After Abstract Expressionism', *Art International*, vol. VI, no. 8 (1962) pp. 26–30.
——, 'Modernist Painting', *Art and Literature*, vol. 4 (1965) pp. 193–201.
Hansen, A., *A Primer of Happenings and Time/Space Art* (New York, 1965).
Hendricks, J. (ed.), *Fluxus Etc., The Gilbert and Lila Silverman Collection* (Bloomfield Hills, Mich., 1983).
Henri, A., *Environments and Happenings* (London, 1974).
Inga-Pin, L., *Performance, Happenings, Actions, Events, Activities, Installations* (Padua, 1978).
Johnson, E. H., *American Artists on Art* (New York, 1982).
Kaprow, A., *Assemblages, Environments and Happenings* (New York, 1966).
——, *Some Recent Happenings: A Great Bear Pamphlet* (New York, 1966).
——, 'The Happenings Are Dead: Long Live the Happenings', *Artforum*, vol. IV, no. 7 (1966) pp. 36–9.
——, *Untitled Essays and Other Works: A Great Bear Pamphlet* (New York, 1967).
——, 'Self-Service: a Happening', *Drama Review*, vol. XII, no. 3 (1968) pp. 160–4.
——, 'Education of the Un-artist, Part One', *Art News*, vol. LXIX, no. 10 (1971) pp. 28–31.
——, 'Education of the Un-artist, Part Two', *Art News*, vol. LXXI, no. 3 (1972) pp. 34–9, 62.
——, 'Education of the Un-artist, Part Three', *Art in America*, vol. LXII, no. 1 (1974) pp. 85–91.
——, 'Non-theatrical Performance', *Artforum*, vol. XIV, no. 9 (1976) pp. 45–51.
——, and R. Schechner, 'Extensions in Time and Space', *Drama Review*, vol. XII, no. 2 (1968) pp. 153–9.
Kostalanetz, R., *The Theatre of Mixed Means* (New York, 1968).
Loeffler, C. E., and Tung, D. (eds), *Performance Anthology: Source Book for a Decade of Californian Performance Art* (San Francisco, 1980).
Martin, H., *An Introduction to George Brecht's Book of the Tumbler on Fire* (Milan, 1978).
——, and Brecht, G., *A Conversation with George Brecht by Henry Martin* (Bologne, 1979).
Oldenburg, C., *Injun and Other Histories: A Great Bear Pamphlet* (New York, 1966).
——, *Store Days* (New York, 1967).
——, *Raw Notes* (Halifax, Nova Scotia, 1973).

Ruhe, H. (ed.), *Fluxus: the most radical and experimental art movement of the sixties* (Amsterdam, 1979).
Sohm, H. (ed.), *Happenings and Fluxus* (Cologne, 1970).

Kirby, Foreman, Wilson

Alenikoff, F., 'Scenario: a Talk with Robert Wilson', *Dance Scope*, vol. X, no. 1 (1975–61) pp. 11–21.
Andriessen, L., and Wilson, R., *Die Materie: Libretto* (Amsterdam, 1989).
Aronson, A., 'Wilson's *Dollar Value of Man*', *Drama Review*, vol. XIX, no. 3 (1975) pp. 106–10.
Baracks, B., 'Einstein on the Beach', *Artforum*, vol. XV, no. 7 (1977) pp. 30–6.
Bigsby, C. W. E., *A Critical Introduction to Twentieth Century American Drama*, vol. 3, *Beyond Broadway* (Cambridge, 1985).
Brecht, S., *The Theatre of Visions: Robert Wilson* (Frankfurt am Main, 1978).
Cage, J., Foreman, R., and Kostalanetz, R., 'Art in the Culture', *Performing Arts Journal*, vol. IV, nos 1 & 2 (1979) pp. 70–84.
Carroll, N., 'The Mystery Plays of Michael Kirby', *Drama Review*, vol. XXIII, no. 3 (1979) pp. 103–12.
Davy, K., 'Foreman's *Vertical Mobility* and *PAIN(T)*', *Drama Review*, vol. XVIII, no. 2 (1974) pp. 26–37.
——, 'Review: Foreman's *Pandering*', *Drama Review*, vol. XIX, no. 1 (1975) pp. 116–17.
——, 'Kate Manheim as Foreman's Rhoda', *Drama Review*, vol. XX, no. 3 (1976) pp. 37–50.
——, *Richard Foreman and the Ontological-Hysteric Theatre* (Ann Arbor, Mich., 1981).
—— (ed.), *Richard Foreman: Plays and Manifestos* (New York, 1976).
Deak, F., 'Robert Wilson', *Drama Review*, vol. XVIII, no. 2 (1974) pp. 67–80.
Donker, J., *The President of Paradise: A Traveller's Account of Robert Wilson's 'the CIVIL warS'* (Amsterdam, 1985).
Feingold, M., 'An Interview with Richard Foreman', *Theater*, vol. VII, no. 1 (1975) pp. 5–29.
Flakes, S., 'Robert Wilson's *Einstein on the Beach*', *Drama Review*, vol. XX, no. 4 (1976) pp. 69–82.
Foreman, R., '*Vertical Mobility*', *Drama Review*, vol. XVIII, no. 2 (1974) pp. 38–47.
——, 'How I Write My (Self: Plays)', *Drama Review*, vol. XXI, no. 4 (1977) pp. 5–24.
——, 'Hotel for Criminals', *Theater*, vol. VII, no. 1 (1975) pp. 30–55.
——, 'The American Imagination', *Performing Arts Journal*, vol. IV, nos 1 & 2 (1979) pp. 177–99.
——, *Reverberation Machines: The Later Plays and Essays* (New York, 1985).
——, 'Film is Ego: Radio is God', *Drama Review*, vol. XXXI, no. 4 (1987) pp. 149–76.
Glass, P., 'Notes: *Einstein on the Beach*', *Performing Arts Journal*, vol. II, no. 3 (1978) pp. 63–70.

Kaye, N., 'Bouncing Back the Impulse: an Interview with Richard Foreman', *Performance*, vol. 61 (1990) pp. 31–42.

Kirby, M., 'On Acting and Not Acting', *Drama Review*, vol. XVI, no. 1 (1972) pp. 3–15.

——,'Richard Foreman's Ontological-Hysteric Theatre', *Drama Review*, vol. XVII, no. 2 (1973) pp. 5–32.

——, 'Manifesto of Structuralism', *Drama Review*, vol. XIX, no. 4 (1975) pp. 82–3.

——, 'Structural Analysis/Structural Theory', *Drama Review*, vol. XX, no. 4 (1976) pp. 51–68.

——, *Photoanalysis: A Structuralist Play* (Seoul, 1978).

——, *First Signs of Decadence* (Schulenburg. 1986).

——, *A Formalist Theatre* (Philadelphia, 1987).

Langton, B., 'Journey to Ka Mountain', *Drama Review*, vol. XVII, no. 2 (1973) pp. 48–57.

Marranca, B., *Theatrewritings* (New York, 1984).

—— (ed.), *The Theatre of Images* (New York, 1977).

Nodal, A., and De Bretteville, S. L. (eds), *Robert Wilson's 'CIVIL warS': Drawings, Models and Documentation* (Los Angeles, 1984).

Monk, E., '*Film is Ego: Radio is God*, Richard Foreman and the Arts of Control', *Drama Review*, vol. XXXI, no. 4 (1987) pp. 143–8.

Nahston, E., 'With Foreman on Broadway', *Drama Review*, vol. XX, no. 3 (1976) pp. 83–100.

Quadri, F., 'Robert Wilson: It's About Time', *Artforum*, vol. XXIII, no. 2 (1984) pp. 76–82.

Rouse, J., 'Robert Wilson, Texts and History: *CIVIL warS*, German Part', *Theater*, vol. XVI, no. 1 (1984) pp. 68–74.

Savran, D., *In Their Own Words: Contemporary American Playwrights* (New York, 1988)

Scarpetta, G., 'Richard Foreman's Scenography: Examples of his Work in France', *Drama Review*, vol. XXVIII, no. 2 (1984) pp. 23–31.

Schechner, R., 'Richard Foreman on Richard Foreman', *Drama Review*, vol. XXXI, no. 4 (1987) pp. 125–35.

Shank, T., *American Alternative Theatre* (London, 1982).

Shyer, L., *Robert Wilson and His Collaborators* (New York, 1989).

Simmer, B., 'Robert Wilson and Therapy', *Drama Review*, vol. XX, no. 1 (1976) pp. 99–110.

——, 'Sue Sheehy', *Drama Review*, vol. XX, no. 3 (1976) pp. 67–74.

Trilling, O., 'Robert Wilson's *Ka Mountain*', *Drama Review*, vol. XVII, no. 2 (1973) pp. 33–47.

Wilson, R., 'I Thought I Was Hallucinating ...', *Drama Review*, vol. XXI, no. 4 (1977) pp. 75–8.

——, '*I Was Sitting on my Patio This Guy Appeared I Thought I Was Hallucinating*', *Performing Arts Journal*, vol. IV, nos 1 & 2 (1979) pp. 200–18.

——, *Robert Wilson: From a Theatre of Images* (Cincinatti, Ohio, 1980).

——, *The Golden Windows: A Play in Three Parts* (Munich, 1982).

——, and Knowles, C., 'The Dollar Value of Man', *Theater*, vol. IX, no. 2 (1978) pp. 91–109.

Dance

Alter, J. B., 'A Critical Analysis of Susanne K. Langer's Dance Theory', *Dance Research Annual*, vol. XVI (1987) pp. 110–19.

Banes, S., *Democracy's Body: Judson Dance Theater, 1962–1964* (Ann Arbor, Mich., 1983).

——, *Terpsichore in Sneakers: Post-modern Dance*, 2nd edn (Middletown, Conn., 1987).

——, 'Vital Signs: Steve Paxton's *Flat* in Perspective', *Dance Research Annual*, vol. XVI (1987) pp. 120–34.

Beardsley, M. C., 'What is Going on in Dance?', *Dance Research Journal*, vol. XV, no. 1 (1982) pp. 31–6.

Brown, T., 'Three Pieces', *Drama Review*, vol. XIX, no. 1 (1975) pp. 26–33.

——, 'All of the Person's Person Arriving', *Drama Review*, vol. XXX, no. 1 (1986) pp. 149–70.

Brown, T., Brunel, L., Mangolte, B., and Delahaye, G., *l'atelier des chorégraphes Trisha Brown* (Paris, 1987).

Carrol, N., and Banes, S., 'Working and Dancing: a Response to Monroe C. Beardley's *What is Going on in Dance?*', *Dance Research Journal*, vol. XV, no. 1 (1982) pp. 37–41.

Childs, L., 'Notes' 64–'74', *Drama Review*, vol. XIX, no. 1 (1975) pp. 33–6.

——, 'Lucinda Childs: a Portfolio', *Artforum*, vol. 11 (1973) pp. 50–7.

Chin, D., 'Talking with Lucinda Childs', *Dance Scope*, vol. XIII, nos 2 & 3 (1979) pp. 70–81.

Croce, A., *Afterimages* (New York, 1977).

Cunningham, M., *Changes: Notes on Choreography* (New York, 1968).

——, *The Dancer and the Dance* (London, 1985).

Fancher G., and Myers, G., *Philosophical Essays on Dance* (New York, 1981).

Forti, S., *Handbook in Motion* (Nova Scotia and New York, 1974).

Foster, S., 'The Signifying Body: Reaction and Resistance in Postmodern Dance', *Theatre Journal*, vol. XXXVII, no. 1 (1985) pp. 44–64.

——, *Reading Dancing: Bodies and Subjects in Contemporary American Dance* (Berkeley, Cal., 1986).

Goldberg, R., 'Space as Praxis', *Studio International*, vol. 977 (1975) pp. 130–5.

——, 'Performance: the Art of Notation', *Studio International*, vol. 982 (1976) pp. 54–8.

Gordon, D., 'It's About Time', *Drama Review*, vol. XIX, no. 1 (1975) pp. 43–52.

Goldwater, L., *Primitivism in Modern Art* (London, 1986).

Graham, M., *The Notebooks of Martha Graham* (New York, 1973).

Grand Union, 'The Grand Union', *Dance Scope*, vol. VII, no. 2 (1973) pp. 28–32.

Hay, D., 'Dance Talks', *Dance Scope*, vol. XII, no. 1 (1977–8) pp. 18–22.

Hecht, R., 'Reflections on the Career of Yvonne Rainer and the Value of Minimal Dance', *Dance Scope*, vol. VIII, no. 1 (1973–4) pp. 12–25.

Horst, L., *Pre-classic Dance Forms* (New York, 1968).

——, and Russell, C., *Modern Dance Forms* (San Francisco, 1961).

Humphrey, D., *The Art of Making Dance* (New York and Toronto, 1959).

Johnston, J., *Marmalade Me* (New York, 1971).

Sheets-Johnstone, M., 'On the Nature of Theories of Dance', *CORD Dance Research Annuʌ l*, vol. X (1979) pp. 3–29.

Kaprilian, M. H., 'What Makes Art Art?', *Dance Research Journal*, vol. XIX, no. 1 (1974–5) pp. 10–12.

Kirby, M., *The Art of Time* (New York, 1969).

——, 'The New Dance: an Introduction', *Drama Review*, vol. XVI, no. 3 (1972) pp. 115–16.

Langer, S. K., *Feeling and Form: A Theory of Art* (London, 1953).

Livet, A., *Contemporary Dance* (New York, 1978).

Lorber, R., 'The Problem with the Grand Union', *Dance Scope*, vol. VIII, no. 2 (1973) pp. 33–4.

Manning, S., 'Modernist Dogma and "Post-modern" Rhetoric: a Response to Sally Banes' *Terpsichore in Sneakers*', *Drama Review*, vol. XXXIV, no. 4 (1988) pp. 32–9.

Martin, J., *The Modern Dance* (New York, 1933).

——, *Introduction to the Dance* (New York, 1939).

Mazo, J. H., *Prime Movers* (London, 1977).

McDonagh, D., *The Rise and Fall and Rise of Modern Dance* (New York, 1970).

Michelson, A., 'Yvonne Rainer, Part 1: The Dancer and the Dance', *Artforum*, vol. XII, no. 5 (1974) pp. 57–63.

Morris, R., 'Notes on Dance', *Tulane Drama Review*, vol. X, no. 2 (1965) pp. 179–86.

Nadel, M. H. and Miller, C. N., *The Dance Experience: Readings in Dance Appreciation* (New York, 1978).

Paxton, S., 'The Grand Union', *Drama Review*, vol. XVI, no. 3 (1972) pp. 128–34.

Percival, L., *Experimental Dance* (London, 1971).

Rainer, Y., 'Yvonne Rainer Interviews Anne Halprin', *Drama Review*, vol. X, no. 2 (1965) pp. 142–67.

——, *Work, 1961–73* (Nova Scotia and New York, 1974).

——, with Hulton, P., and Fulkerson, M., *Dartington Theatre Papers*, series 2, Number 7: *Yvonne Rainer* (Dartington Hall, Devon, 1978).

Sachs, C., *World History of the Dance* (New York, 1937).

Segal, M., 'Yvonne Rainer: Holding a Mirror to Experience', *Studio International*, vol. 982 (1976) pp. 41–3.

Schmit, S., 'Off Off Broadway: Three Chances at Judson', *Village Voice*, 8 March 1962.

Siegel, M. B., 'Modern Dance Before Bennington: Sorting It All Out', *Dance Research Journal*, vol. XIX, no. 1 (1987) pp. 3–9.

Smith, K., 'David Gordon's *The Matter*', *Drama Review*, vol. XIX, no. 1 (1972) pp. 117–27.

Sommer, S. R., 'Equipment Dances: Trisha Brown', *Drama Review*, vol. XIX, no. 1 (1972) pp. 135–41.

——, 'Trisha Brown: Making Dances', *Dance Scope*, vol. XI, no. 2 (1977) pp. 7–18.

Stefano, E., 'Moving Structures', *Art and Artists*, vol. VIII, no. 10 (1974) pp. 16–25.

Steinman, L., *The Knowing Body: Elements of Contemporary Performance* (Boston, Mass., 1986).

Sulzman, M., 'Choice/Form in Trisha Brown's *Locus*: a View from Inside the Cube', *Dance Chronicle*, vol. II, no. 2 (1978) pp. 117–30.

Telling stories

Aronson, A., '*Sakonnet Point*', *Drama Review*, vol. XIX, no. 4 (1975) pp. 27–35.

——, 'The Wooster Group's *L. S. D. (... Just the High Points ...)*, *Drama Review*, vol. XXIX, no. 2 (1985) pp. 65–77.

Auslander, P., 'Toward a Concept of the Political in Postmodern Theatre', *Theatre Journal*, vol. XXXIX, no. 1 (1987) pp. 20–34.

——, 'Task and Vision: Willem Dafoe in *L. S. D.*', *Drama Review*, vol. XXIX, no. 2 (1985) pp. 94–8.

Bierman, J., '*Three Places in Rhode Island*', *Drama Review*, vol. XXXIII, no. 1 (1989) pp. 13–30.

Borden, L., 'Trisha Brown and Yvonne Rainer', *Artforum*, vol. XI, no. 10 (1973) pp. 79–82.

Bos, S., 'Interview with Joan Jonas', *De Appel Bulletin*, vol. 1 (1985).

Burbank, R. J., *Thornton Wilder*, 2nd edn (New York, 1978).

Carr, C., 'Karen Finley', *Artforum*, vol. XXVII, no. 3 (1988) p. 148.

Champagne, L., 'Always Starting Anew: Elizabeth LeCompte', *Drama Review*, vol. XXV, no. 3 (1981) pp. 19–28.

——, *Out From Under: Texts by Women Performance Artists* (New York, 1990)

Christie, I., '*Lives of Performers*', *Monthly Film Bulletin*, vol. XXXX, no. 520 (1977) p. 101.

Coco, W., 'Review: *Route 1 & 9*', *Theatre Journal*, vol. XXXIV, no. 2 (1982) pp. 249–52.

——, and Gunawarda, A. J., 'Responses to India: an Interview with Yvonne Rainer', *Drama Review*, vol. XV, no. 3 (1971) pp. 139–42.

Coe, R., 'Four Performance Artists', *Theater*, vol. XII, no. 2 (1982) pp. 76–85.

Dimmick, K., 'Who's Afraid of LSD?', *Theater*, vol. XVI, no. 2 (1985) pp. 92–6.

Dolan J., *The Feminist Spectator as Critic* (Ann Arbor, Mich., 1988).

Erickson, J., 'Appropriation and Transgression in Contemporary American Performance: the Wooster Group, Holly Hughes and Karen Finley', *Theatre Journal*, vol. XLII, no. 2 (1990) pp. 225–36.

Finley, K., *Shock Treatment* (San Francisco, 1990).

——, 'The Constant State of Desire', *Drama Review*, vol. XXXII, no. 1 (1988) pp. 139–51.

Forte, J., 'Women's Performance Art: Feminism and Postmodernism', *Theatre Journal*, vol. XXXX, no. 2 (1988) pp. 217–36.

Fuchs, E., 'Performance Notes: *North Atlantic* and *L. S. D.*', *Performing Arts Journal*, vol. VIII, no. 2 (1984) pp. 51–5

——, 'Staging the Obscene Body', *Drama Review*, vol. XXXIII, no. 1 (1989) pp. 33–58.

Gray, S., 'About *Three Places in Rhode Island*', *Drama Review*, vol. XXXIII, no. 1 (1989) pp. 31–42.

——, and LeCompte, E., 'The Making of a Trilogy', *Performing Arts Journal*, vol. III, no. 2 (1978) pp. 81–91.

——, '*Rumstick Road*', *Performing Arts Journal*, vol. III, no. 2 (1978) pp. 92–115.

Hart, L., 'Motherhood According to Finley: *The Theory of Total Blame*', *Drama Review*, vol. XXXVI, no. 1 (1992) pp. 124–34.

Howell, J., 'The Constant Stage of Desire', *Artforum*, vol. XXV, no. 7 (1987) pp. 130–11.

Hulton, P., 'Fiction, Character and Narrative: Yvonne Rainer' (interview), *Dartington Theatre Papers*, 2nd series, no. 7 (Dartington Hall, Devon, 1978).

Jonas, J., 'Seven Years', *Drama Review*, vol. XIX, no. 1 (1975) pp. 13–17.

——, *Joan Jonas' Stage Sets* (Philadelphia, 1976).

——, *Scripts and Descriptions, 1968–1982* (Berekeley, Cal., 1983).

——, and White, R., 'Interview with Joan Jonas', *View*, vol. II, no. 1 (1979) whole issue.

Jong, C. de, 'Organic Honey's Visual Telepathy', *Drama Review*, vol. XVI, no. 2 (1972) pp. 63–5.

Kaye, N., 'Mask, Role and Narrative: an Interview with Joan Jonas', *Performance*, vols 65–6 (1992) pp. 49–60.

King, B., *Contemporary American Theatre* (London, 1991).

Koch, S., 'Performance: a Conversation', *Artforum*, vol. XI, no. 4 (1972) pp. 53–8.

LeCompte, E., 'The Wooster Group Dances', *Drama Review*, vol. XXXIX, no. 2 (1985) pp. 78–93.

Michelson, A., 'Yvonne Rainer, Part 2: Lives of Performers', *Artforum*, vol. XII, no. 6 (1974) pp. 30–5.

Nadotti, M., 'Karen Finley's Poison Meatloaf', *Artforum*, vol. XXXVII, no. 7 (1989) pp. 113–16.

Rainer, Y., *The Films of Yvonne Rainer* (Indianapolis, 1989).

——, *Work, 1961–73* (Nova Scotia, 1974).

Riering, J., 'Joan Jonas: Delay Delay', *Drama Review*, vol. XVI, no. 3 (1972) pp. 142–51.

Robinson, M., 'Performance Strategies: Interviews with Ishmael Huston-Joanes, John Kelly, Karen Finley, Richard Elovich', *Performing Arts Journal*, vol. X, no. 3 (1987) pp. 31–56.

Savran, D., 'The Wooster Group, Arthur Miller and *The Crucible*', *Drama Review*, vol. XXIX, no. 2 (1985) pp. 99–109.

——, *The Wooster Group, 1975–1985: Breaking the Rules* (New York, 1988).

Schechner, R., 'Karen Finley: a Constant State of Becoming', *Drama Review*, vol. XXXII, no. 1 (1988) pp. 152–8.

Schuler, C., 'Spectator Response and Comprehension: the Problem of Karen Finley's *Constant State of Desire*', *Drama Review*, vol. XXXIV, no. 1 (1990) pp. 131–45.

Stofflet, M., 'Joan Jonas and Cultural Biography', *Artweek*, 7 June 1980, p. 5

——, 'Jonas' Futurism', *Artweek*, 6 July 1980 p. 5.

Welling, J., 'Joan Jonas Performance', *Artweek*, 12 April 1975, p. 4.

Wohl, D., 'The Wooster Group's *North Atlantic*', *Theatre Journal*, vol. XXXVI, no. 3 (1984) pp. 413–15.

Index

Abstract Expressionism, 25
Acconci, Vito, 24, 27
Acker, Kathy
  Birth of the Poet, 13
  Lulu, 13
Actor, the, 57–8; *see also* Performer
Aestheticism, 59–60
AIDS, 129, 130–1
Aleatory process, *see* Chance method
Allen, Maud, 72
Alocco, Marcel, 44
Anderson, Laurie
  United States, 12, 145
Andrews, Raymond, 47, 62–6
Architecture, 4, 5–9, 71
Arnold, Becky, 114
Assemblage, 30, 31, 35
Audience,
  and the modernist work, 77
  see also Performer *and* Viewer
Avant-garde, 21, 26

Banes, Sally, 2, 74–7, 88, 90–1, 99,
    105–6
Baudrillard, Jean, 17, 21
Bauhaus, 8, 90
Berenson, Paul, 100
Blackface, 64–5, 120, 121–8, 140–1;
    see also Racism
Body Art, 24, 27, 132
Body, the
  and historical modern dance, 72–3,
    77–8, 85–6
  and Robert Wilson, 63
  and the Wooster Group, 124

Bofill, Ricardo, 5
Brecht, George, 33, 35, 76, 90, 142
  The Case, 31–2
  Three Aqueous Events, 40–5, 41 *ill.*
  Three Yellow Events, 41 *ill.*
  Two Signs, 41 *ill.*
  Water Yam, 40
  Word Event, 41 *ill.*
Brecht, Stefan, 62–3, 65, 67
Bricolage, 12
Brown, Trisha,
  'Accumulation Pieces', 111
  'Equipment Dances', 110, 112
  *Man Walking Down a
    Building*, 110–11
  Primary Accumulation, 111–12

Cage, John
  and dance, 74, 90–3, 98–103, 104,
    107
  and Happenings and Fluxus, 90
  and Michael Kirby, 46
  and musical vocabulary, 94–8
  and Richard Foreman, 53
  and Robert Wilson, 48
  and Zen Bhuddism, 101
  Black Mountain College event, 32–3
  4'33", 93, 94–5 *ill.*, 97, 101
  0'00" (4'33" No. 2), 96 *ill.*, 97–8,
    101
Chance method
  and dance, 74, 90–2, 98–103, 110
  and music, 93–8
  and personal taste, 101–3
  and theatre, 46–7, 53

see also Cage, John
Character
  fragmentation of, 50–2, 66
  reference to, 116, 134–5
  subversion of, 12, 55, 64, 132
Childs, Lucinda, 75, 107
  Geranium, 108
  Model, 109
  Particular Reel, 109–10
  Street Dance, 108
  Untitled trio, 109
Chong, Ping, 11, 13
Cliché, 133, 135
Closure, 16
  desire for, 142
  resistance to, 29, 40, 43, 45, 54,
      61–2, 116–17, 141–3, 145
Coetzee, J. M.
  Foe, 10
Combine, 29–30
Corner, Philip, 76
Criticism
  and its object, 20–1
  and modern dance, 77–9, 84–9
  and postmodern dance, 71, 74–7
  and the postmodern, 3–4, 22, 145–6
  in dance, 2
  modernist, 2, 78–9
Cunningham, Merce, 32, 74, 90, 107

Dafoe, Willem, 125, 141; *see also*
    Wooster Group, the
Dance, *see* Historical modern dance
    and Historical postmodern dance
Davis, William, 74, 91
Decadence, 59–60
de Kooning, Willem, 25
Denishawn Company, 72
Derrida, Jacques, 14–17
Dine, Jim, 30, 33
Docherty, Thomas, 22
Documentation, 113–14
Dolan, Jill, 131
Duchamp, Marcel, 19, 43
Duncan, Isadora, 72, 77–8
Dunn, Douglas, 114
Dunn, Judith, 74, 91
Dunn, Robert, 74–5, 90–2, 101–2,
    110

Eco, Umberto, 21
Emerson, Ruth, 74
  Narrative, 92
  Timepiece, 91, 98–9
Environment, 30–2, 35, 37, 93
Erdman, John, 133–5
Excess, *see* Postmodernism

Fable, 137–9
Feminism, 128
Finley, Karen, 141–2
  The Constant State of Desire, 12,
      128–32, 139, 140–1
  We Keep Our Victims Ready, 12,
      129
Fluxus (group of artists), 31–2, 40, 76,
    90
Foreman, Richard, 13–14, 24, 46, 48,
    69
  Angelface, 47
  *Pandering to the Masses: A
      Misrepresentation*, 49–56, 70
Formalism
  and modernist programme, 26, 53
  and realism, 47, 57–8, 61, 70
  and theatre, 46–7, 56, 58–62
  in painting, 25–6
Forti, Simone
  Rollers, 100
  See-Saw, 100
Found object, 29, 31
  material, 11, 12, 125–6
  movement, 99–100
  surroundings, 108
Fowles, John, 9
Freud, Sigmund, 130
Fried, Michael, 2–3, 24, 31, 71, 76–7,
    84, 88
  critique of minimal art, 26–8
  defence of the modernist work, 33–5
Fuller, Loie, 72

Game, 11, 31, 39–40, 99, 100, 104
Garcia, Marquez Gabriel, 9
  One Hundred Years of Solitude, 10
Gordon, David, 74–5, 114
  Helen's Dance, 91–2
Gorky, Ashille, 25
Graham, Martha, 71–4

Primitive Mysteries, 78
Grand Union, The, 113, 116, 133
Grass, Gunther, 9
  The Tim Drum, 10
Gray, Spalding, 13, 120
Greenberg, Clement, 2, 28–9, 33, 71,
  76–7, 83–4, 87–8
  definition of the modernist
    work, 25–6
Grooms, Red, 33
Gropius, Walter, 8

Halprin, Ann, 110
Hansen, A1, 33
Happenings, 30–3, 35–40, 46, 75–6,
  90, 100
Hay, Alex
  Rafladan, 91
Hay, Deborah
  Rafladan, 91
Herko, Fred, 75
  *Once or Twice a Week I Put on
    Sneakers to Go Uptown*, 91
Higgins, Dick, 33, 76
Historical modern dance, 2, 24, 109
  and authenticity, 73, 78
  and everyday activity, 87–8
  and expressionism, 72–4, 84, 86
  and modern art, 73–4, 78
  and postmodern dance, 71–4
  and rejection of classical dance, 64,
    71–2, 77–8
  and rejection of free dance, 72, 84
  and the modernist work, 77–86,
    87–9
Historical postmodern dance, 2–3, 9,
  12, 14, 53, 71
  and a rejection of modern dance
    styles, 89, 74–7
  and attention to being seen, 105,
    107–8, 110, 112, 116–17
  and stylisation, 104–5
  and the conventional vocabulary of
    dance, 98–101, 104–5, 107,
    109
  and the everyday, 87–9, 108, 111–12
  and the modernist work, 87–9, 100–1
History
  and Robert Wilson, 67–8

and the modernist work, 5, 20,
    25–6, 34–5
  and the postmodern, 8, 9–10, 13–14,
    20–2
Hollein, Hans, 5
Holm, Hanya, 71
Horst, Louis, 72–4, 78, 89
Humphrey, Doris, 71–5
  Shakers, 78
Hutcheon, Linda, 9–10, 19–20, 22–3

I Ching, 98
Indeterminacy
  in choreographic process, 92–3, 99
  in performance, 92, 98
Interdisciplinarity, 3, 24
  and dance, 75, 100–1
  and theatre, 28, 97, 144–5
  opposition to, 25–6, 28, 82–4, 86
Intertextuality, 10, 13, 126–7

Jencks, Charles, 6–9, 11, 19–21, 23,
  71
Johns, Jasper, 29
  Tango, 30
Johnston, Jill, 103, 106–7
Jonas, Joan, 13–14, 24, 136
  Double Lunar Dogs, 137
  The Juniper Tree, 137
  Upside Down and Backwards, 12,
    137–9
  Volcano Saga, 137
Jowitt, Deborah, 111
Judd, Donald, 27, 49
Judson Dance Theater, 71, 74–6, 90,
  102–3, 110, 114, 136, 142
  A Concert of Dance, 91–3, 98–101

Kaprow, Allan, 30–1, 43, 90, 142
  18 Happenings in 6 Parts, 32–3
  Self Service, 35–40
Kirby, Michael, 24, 42, 46, 48
  Eight People, 47
  First Signs of Decadence, 47, 56–62,
    70
  The Hearing, 127
Klotz, Heinrich, 6–7, 9
Knowles, Christopher, 47–8, 67
Kostalanetz, Richard, 36

Langer, Suzanne K., 2, 78
  and the modernist work, 83–4, 87–9
  nature of dance, 82–3
  theory of art, 77, 79–84, 88–9
Language
  and significance in art, 79–80
  game, 18–19
  quotation of, 140
  subversion of, 67–8
  see also Structural linguistics
Lash, Scott, 21
LeCompte, Elizabeth, 11, 120, 123–5,
    127, 141; *see also* Wooster
    Group, the
le Corbusier, 8–9
Levine, Dick, 101
Lloyd, Barbara, 114
Louis, Morris, 25
Lyotard, Jean-François, 17–20, 22,
    142–3

Mabou Mines
  Red Horse Animation, 12
Mahafay, Marni, 100
Manheim, Kate, 55
Martin, Henry, 40–3
Martin, John, 2, 77–9, 84–8
McDowell, John Herbert
  Overture, 91
Meaning
  and the postmodern dispute with
      foundation, 14–17
  and the art-object, 32, 97–8
  contingency of, 61, 107, 112, 142
  disruption of, 70, 128, 138, 140,
      142
  multiplicity of, 17, 63–4, 66, 69,
      128
  presence of, 14–17
  production of, 15, 56, 69–70, 128,
      132, 140
  undecidability of, 16–17, 58–62, 140
Mekas, Jonas, 47
Metakinesis, 85–6
Metanarrative, *see* Modern, the *and*
    Postmodernism
Mies van der Rohe, Ludwig, 6
Miller, Arthur
  The Crucible, 127, 139, 142

Minimal art, 14
  and dance, 76, 103–7, 112
  and process art, 113–4
  and theatre, 46–9, 69–70
  and theatricality, 26–8
  and the event of the work, 33–5
  and the modernist work, 24
Modern, the
  and the Enlightenment, 25–6
  and the recourse to
      metanarrative, 18, 34–5
  disruption of, 6, 17
  in art, 2, 121
  in dance, *see* Historical modern
      dance
Modernist
  architecture, 5–9
  discourses, 3
  painting, 2, 21, 25–6, 34, 76
  performance, 87–9
  programme, 3, 26, 53
  projection towards foundation, 1–4,
      13–14, 17, 21, 33, 76, 144
  sculpture, 2
  stylisation, 7, 8–9
  work of art, 2, 17, 24–8, 33–5; *see*
      also Historical modern dance
      and Historical postmodern
      dance
Modernity, 1–2
Monk, Meredith, 11
  Education of a Girl Child, 13
  Vessel, 13
Moore, Charles, 5
Morris, Robert, 24, 27, 75–6, 100–7
  felt pieces, 113
  *Continuous Project Altered
      Daily*, 113–16
Multi-media performance, 11, 12, 14,
    75, 133–6; *see also* Wooster
    Group, the
Music
  and attack on autonomy of art, 93–8
  and symbolic nature of art, 80
  see also Cage, John

Narrative
  and historical postmodern
      dance, 76, 116–17

and history, 20
and literature, 9–10
and narrativity, 18, 139, 49, 52
and the postmodern condition, 18–19
claim to authority, 139–41
disruption of, 12–13, 121, 132, 133–9
fragmentation of, 138–40, 49, 50
of modernity, 6
of the modernist work, 4, 34–5
voice, 132, 134–6, 139, 140–1
Newman, Barnett, 25
New School of Contemporary Art, 90
New York State Council on the Arts, 127
Noland, Kenneth, 25
Non-objective art, 25–6, 77

Object, the
and chance method, 93–8
and dance, 87–9, 104
and modernist performance, 88–9
and objecthood, 27–8, 30, 81, 84
and perception, 44, 53, 97–8
and place, 32
and process, 97–8, 113–14, 116
and theatre, 23, 142
and theatricality, 35
and the event of being read, 44, 56
disruption of, 28–33, 53–4, 93, 97–8, 104, 142
in art, 23, 97
in music, 98
see also Found object
Objet trouvé, *see* Found object
Oldenburg, Claes, 30, 33
The Store, 32
Olitski, Jules, 25
Olsen, Charles, 32
Ontological–Hysteric Theatre, *see* Foreman, Richard

Painting, 29–30, 33–4l; *see also* Modernist *and* Postmodern
Parody, 13, 124, 131, 141
as perfect postmodern form, 22–3
Paxton, Steve, 74–5, 91, 112–14
Proxy, 92–3, 99–100, 105

Satisfyin' Lover, 106–7
Smiling, 106
State, 106
Transit, 92, 105
Perception, *see* Object, the *and* Structure
Performance
and the everyday, 37–40, 87–8, 99–100, 102, 106–8, 111–12
and the postmodern, 3, 22–3, 71, 145
as unravelling of discrete work, 32–3, 35–45, 88–9
style, 50–2, 55, 57–8, 62–4, 65, 86, 104–6, 110, 114–15, 125–6
the act of, 115, 132, 140–1
Performance art, 12, 14, 24
Performer
presence of, 55, 76
relationship with audience, 50–2, 55, 116, 120, 125, 128–9, 132, 140–1
Performing Garage, 118; *see also* Wooster Group, the
Pollock, Jackson, 25
Pop Art, 32
Pornography, 12, 59, 120, 123–5, 128–9, 131
Portoghesi, Paolo, 5–6, 9
Postmodern
architecture, 4, 5–9, 71
art, 1, 3–4, 13
dance, *see* Historical postmodern dance
drama, 3
event, 19–20, 22–3, 70, 117, 140, 144–6
film, 9
genre, 14
limitation of the, 4, 145–6
literature, 9–10
music, 9
painting, 3, 9
politics, 128, 131–2, 139–43
sculpture, 3, 9
style, 5–14, 23, 117
television, 9
theatre, 1, 3–4
video, 9

Postmodernism
  and authenticity, 4
  and excess, 20, 23
  and legitimacy, 1–2
  and meaning, 14–20
  as anti-foundational disruption, 3–4,
      17, 21–3, 144
  as conflation of signifier and
      referent, 17
  as confusion of category, 19, 22
  as disruption of unitary sign, 17
  as incredulity toward
      metanarrative, 18–19
  as play with fiction, 6
  as subversion of terms in play, 17,
      19–20
  emergent rules of, 6, 8
  implication in the modern, 2 19
  see also Criticism *and* History *and*
      Transgression
Postmodernity, 1
Primitivism, 78
Process, 56
  and dance, 92, 113–17
  and the object, 97–8
  art, 113–14, 116
  of performance, 132

Quotation
  of dance, 92, 104–5, 109, 135–6
  of film, 135–6
  of language, 140
  of narrative, 136, 139
  of performance, 121–2, 124–5
  of popular images, 12
  of style, 6–8, 116, 125–6
  of text, 11–12, 118–24, 142, 13
  of theatre convention, 132–3, 136
  postmode. n, 13
  see also Blackface

Racism, 119–20, 126–9
Rainer, Yvonne, 13–14, 24, 75, 100,
    102, 107, 112, 139
  *Continuous Project – Altered
      Daily*, 113–17
  *Dance for 3 People and 6
      Arms*, 92
  Divertissement, 91–2

Grand Union Dreams, 133
Lives of Performers, 133
Ordinary Dance, 92
Rose Fractions, 12
The Mind is a Muscle, 113
*This is the Story of a Woman
    who ...* , 12, 133–6
Three Satie Spoons, 135–6
Trio A, 103–5, 109–10, 113
Rauschenberg, Robert, 28, 30, 32, 76
  White Paintings, 29
Readings, Bill, 19
Realism, 53
  and chance method, 47
  see also Formalism
Representation, 29, 124, 131
  act of, 126–7
  disruption of, 52–3, 57, 136, 140–1,
      145
  in dance, 85–6
  modernist rejection of, 26
Richards, Mary Caroline, 32
Rossi, Aldo, 5
Rothko, Mark, 25
Rothlein, Aileen, 75
Rulegame, *see* Game
Rushdie, Salman, 9
  Shame, 10

Sachs, Curt, 2, 77–9
St Denis, Ruth, 72
Saussure, Ferdinand de, 14–16
Savran, David, 119–20, 122 ,
Scenography
  and Richard Foreman, 51–2, 55
  and Robert Wilson, 66
Schechner, Richard, 38
  Don Juan, 13
Schneemann, Carolee
  *Environment for Sound and
      Motions*, 76
Scothorn, Carol, 92
Sculpture, 2–3, 9
Serial sculpture, *see* Minimal art
Sexual
  abuse, 129–32, 141
  objectification, 128–9, 131, 141
Significant form, 79–81
  in dance, 82–9

in the work of art, 80–1
Sign, the, 70, 145
 and modernism, 17
 functioning of, 14–17
 and the work of art, 16–17
Simulacrum, 17
Smith, Jack, 47
Soffer, Shirley, 133–5
Stein, Gertrude, 121
Stella, Frank, 27, 49
Stern, Robert, 5
Still, Clyfford, 25
Stirling, James
 Neue Staatsgalerie, 7–8
 Strada Novissima, 5–6
Structure
 and choreography, 73–4, 107–12
 and meaning, 54, 61–2, 68–9
 and perception, 46, 48, 57–8, 108–12
Structuralist Theatre, *see* Kirby,
  Michael
Structuralist Workshop, *see* Kirby,
  Michael
Structural linguistics, 14–15
 and transcendental signified, 16–17
Stylisation, 2, 7–9
Summers, Elaine, 75
 Instant Chance, 92, 99
 Overture, 91
 The Daily Wake, 92
Sutton, Sheryl, 62–4
Suzuki, D. T., 101

Task
 in dance, 88, 99, 102–5, 107, 110
TAU Group, 3
Theatre, 3
 and resistance to modernist
  work, 71, 77, 87–9
 representational, 46, 52, 57
Theatre of Images, *see* Foreman,
  Richard *and* Wilson, Robert
Theatricality
 and dance, 106–7
 and literalist sensibility, 27–8
 and minimalism, 24, 27–8, 33
 and the object, 35
 and the postmodern, 3, 23, 117
 and Wilson, Robert, 65

Totalisation, 18–19, 124, 142, 145
Transgression, 119–20, 22, 127, 128,
  142
Tudor, David, 93–7

Vattimo, Gianni, 1–2
Vautier, Ben, 44
Vawter, Ron, 118–19, 124–5, 128; *see
  also* Wooster Group, the
Venturi, Robert, Rauch, John and
  Brown, Scott Denise
  (partnership), 5
Video, 136–7
Viewer, the, 114, 119
 and the act of reading, 46, 48–9, 52–6,
  105, 116–17, 128, 131–2
 and the definition of the
  work, 39–45, 106–12
 and self-reflexive attention, 56,
  61–2, 93, 97–8, 108
 as performer, 36–40
 assumptions of, 142
 negotiation with, 105
 position of, 139–40
 presence of, 29–32
 see also Performer

Watts, Robert, 76
Whitman, Robert, 30, 33
Wiedman, Charles, 71–2
Wilder, Thornton
 Our Town, 11, 118–26, 139
Williams, Nigel, 9
Wilson, Robert, 13–14, 24, 46, 70
 A Letter for Queen Victoria, 48, 65,
  67
 Deafman Glance, 47, 62–9, 70
 Einstein on the Beach, 48, 68
 *KA MOUNTAIN AND GUARDenia
  TERRACE*, 63, 65
 the CIVIL warS, 66, 68
 The $ Value of Man, 48
 The Golden Windows, 67
 The King of Spain, 47–8, 67
 *The Life and Times of Joseph
  Stalin*, 48
 *The Life and Times of Sigmund
  Freud*, 47, 65–7
Wooster Group, the

Brace Up!, 11, 137
For the Good Times, 127
*Frank Dell's Temptation of St
    Anthony*, 11, 127
Hula, 127
*L.S.D. (...Just the High
    Points...)*, 11, 127–8, 141–2
North Atlantic, 127
Nyatt School, 11, 127, 137
Point Judith, 11, 127
Route 1 & 9 (The Last Act), 11,
    118–28, 131, 139–40
Sakonnet Point, 127
The Road to Immortality
    (trilogy), 127

Three Places in Rhode Island
    (trilogy), 11, 127
Work of art
    and the sign, 16–17
    contingency of the, 23, 27, 31–5,
        44–5, 70, 89, 97–8, 103, 145
    the auratic, 3
    the authority of, 142
    the autonomous, 2, 3, 14, 24, 34,
        79–84, 88–9, 93
Wright, Frank Lloyd, 8

YAM Festival, 76

HYMNODY
PAST AND PRESENT

By the same Author :

The Church in France, 1789–1848.   8s. 6d.

The Church in France, 1848–1907.   12s. 6d.

The New Commandment.   An enquiry into the social precept and practice of the Ancient Church.   6s.

London : S.P.C.K.

HYMNODY
PAST AND PRESENT

BY

C. S. PHILLIPS

M.A., D.D.

CHAPLAIN OF THE COLLEGE OF ST. NICOLAS,
CHISLEHURST

FORMERLY FELLOW AND LECTURER OF SELWYN
COLLEGE, CAMBRIDGE

LONDON
SOCIETY FOR PROMOTING
CHRISTIAN KNOWLEDGE

NEW YORK: THE MACMILLAN COMPANY

First published, 1937

MADE IN GREAT BRITAIN

PREFACE

THE subject of Christian hymnody is so vast that any attempt to deal with it (as here) in a popular, practical and succinct way must necessarily approach it from a particular angle. It should therefore be made clear that the present book treats of it with special reference to the hymns of all ages and countries that are in use among English (and, more particularly, Anglican) Christians to-day.

Within these limits the book aims at setting before the general reader the main results of scholarly research on the subject with which it deals. Its author can make no claim to be a researcher at first hand himself. But he has for many years taken a warm interest in the history and the use of hymns : and he has done his best to equip himself for his task by a diligent study of the best and latest authorities on its subject-matter, both English and foreign. The notes containing his references to these have been relegated to the end of the volume, so that the ordinary reader need not be distracted by them ; while at the same time those who would go deeper into the subject are given assistance towards doing so. The works to which he is chiefly indebted are set forth at the head of the notes in question : and to their writers, living and dead, the author here makes the grateful acknowledgments that are fitting.

So far as individual hymns are concerned, the book takes as its basis the three hymn-books which at the present time are in most general use in the Church of England, viz. *Hymns Ancient and Modern*, the *English Hymnal*

PREFACE

and *Songs of Praise,* together with the recently published *Plainsong Hymn Book.* These are on occasion referred to for brevity's sake as *A.M., E.H., S.P.* and *P.H.B.* respectively. In the case of hymn-numbers * denotes *Hymns Ancient and Modern,* ** the *Plainsong Hymn Book,* † the *English Hymnal* and ‡ *Songs of Praise.* It may be added that up to the end of chapter iv references to *Songs of Praise* have not been inserted, for the reason that such of the famous hymns of earlier ages as appear in that book have in certain cases been so altered that the versions can hardly be said to represent the originals.

COLLEGE OF ST. NICOLAS,
        CHISLEHURST,
                Eastertide, 1937.

CONTENTS

			PAGE
Preface	. . . . . .	.	vii
Introduction.	Concerning Hymns in general	.	1

Part I. HISTORICAL

Chap.	I.	The Early Church . .	.	11
,,	II.	Hymns of the Eastern Church	.	27
,,	III.	Latin Hymnody . . .	.	47
,,	IV.	Latin Hymnody (continued) .	.	68
,,	V.	German Hymnody . .	.	99
,,	VI.	The Metrical Psalters . .	.	123
,,	VII.	English Hymnody up to the time of Watts	.	148
,,	VIII.	The Methodist and Evangelical Movements	.	171
,,	IX.	The Oxford Movement and After	.	198
,,	X.	New Ideas in the Twentieth Century		229

Part II. PRACTICAL

,,	XI.	Towards a Policy . . .	.	249
,,	XII.	Some Practical Counsels .	.	260
Notes	. . . .	.	271

CONTENTS

PART III. APPENDICES

PAGE

Appendix A. A brief note on Hymn-metres . 279

„ B. A Table to illustrate the Development of the Hymnal Scheme of the English Mediaeval Breviaries . 281

„ C. Office Hymns from "Neo-Gallican" Breviaries 286

„ D. English Hymns in common use based on the Psalms . . . 289

Index of Subjects 291

Index of Hymn-titles (English) 297

INTRODUCTION

Concerning Hymns in general

" There is a style and manner suited to the composition of hymns which may be more successfully or at least more easily attained by a versifier than by a poet. They should be Hymns, not Odes, if designed for public worship and for the use of plain people. Perspicacity, simplicity and ease should be chiefly attended to : and the image and colouring of poetry, if admitted at all, should be indulged sparingly and with great judgment. The late Dr. Watts, many of whose hymns are admirable patterns in this species of writing, might, as a poet, have a right to say that it cost him labour to restrain his fire and to accommodate himself to the capacity of common readers."

So wrote Cowper's friend, the Reverend John Newton, in his preface to the *Olney Hymns*, dated Feb. 15, 1779. His explanations were, by his own admission, largely made in self-defence — to meet the possible charge that, unlike Dr. Watts, he was *not* a poet. But it is interesting to note that, over a century later, his view was echoed — from the opposite side, so to speak — by one whose poetic qualification even his most carping critic will not seriously deny. Not long before his death, Tennyson, in a conversation with Dr. Warren, President of Magdalen, remarked : "A good hymn is the most difficult thing in the world to write. In a good hymn you have to be commonplace and poetical. The moment you cease to be commonplace and put in any expression at all out of the common, it ceases to be a hymn."[1]

The two judgments recorded above will help to make clear the scope of the present book. It is a book on hymns, not on religious poetry. Many of the greatest examples of the poetic faculty at work on the loftiest subject of all will find no place in its pages — for the simple reason that, though poetry, they are not hymns. On the other hand, the great bulk of the compositions that *do* concern us are hardly more than verse, and sometimes not even very good verse. They may have the appeal that comes from the sincere expression of deeply felt emotion : but the high imaginative flight that makes great poetry is not theirs — and indeed they would be less suited for their purpose if it were. No hymn that has attained to world-wide fame and popularity bears the name of any poet of the first rank. The hymns that are classics in their own line are the work of men who have been notable for their piety rather than for their literary accomplishment. It may occasionally happen that a hymn-writer includes in his make-up a spark of the genuine poetic fire. This is specially true of one whom some would place at the head of all English hymn-writers — Charles Wesley. But even in his case the poetic inspiration was very uncertain and spasmodic : and if his countless hymns sometimes contain real poetry it is more by accident than by design, for his aim was not literature but edification. When he showed himself a poet, it was simply because he could not help it.

What then *is* a hymn — in the sense, that is, in which we are mainly concerned with such things in the pages that follow ?

Two elements in the required definition are too obvious to need much comment. First, a hymn is concerned with the expression of religious feeling of some kind. St. Augustine's definition — *hymnus cantus est cum laude Dei*, "a hymn is a song with praise of GOD" [2] — is clearly too much restricted, at least for modern usage : for hymns express many other moods of the soul besides praise. But whatever it be, the feeling expressed must be of a religious character : and (seeing that our subject is Christian hymns) it must also be consonant with the kind of religious outlook associated with the Christian faith and practice.

Secondly, a hymn should be cast in a metrical or at least a rhythmic form. Prose passages may sometimes be described as "hymns", as e.g. when St. Paul's great outpouring in 1 Cor. xiii. is called "a hymn in praise of love": but with such we cannot concern ourselves here. The rhythmic structure of a hymn need not be cast in the strict mould of formal prosody, though in modern hymns it practically always is. But some rhythmic basis there must be, in a hymn as in a poem.

To this extent, then, a hymn is the same as a religious poem. But we have already seen that for our present purpose the two need to be differentiated. This differentiation may be made (as Newton suggested) along two lines.

1. First, a hymn is a religious poem that is "designed for public worship". This naturally includes the idea of its being sung to a musical setting. As St. Augustine says, a hymn is a "song" — we may add, a communal song. Even those who do not actually join in singing it are regarded as associating themselves in mind and heart with what the singers sing for them. So, too, even those religious bodies which have been most hostile to the use of music in worship have made an exception in the case of hymns, or at least of metrical versions of the Biblical psalms. Thus the present book, while mainly concerned with the words of hymns, will hardly be able to avoid some consideration of the tunes to which they are set. It must be remarked, however, that when we speak of a hymn as "designed for public worship", we mean "designed" only in the sense of "adapted" — not necessarily that it was written, at least primarily, for such a purpose. The Jewish Psalter, in the form in which we have it, is a collection of sacred lyrics for liturgical use — "the hymn-book of the Second Temple", it has been called. But this does not mean that all the psalms that compose it, or indeed more than a minority, were written with a view to such use. Many of the most beautiful and poignant of them are obviously the expres-

sion of some intensely personal and individual emotion, written in an innermost chamber for no human eye save the writer's. "In the Psalms", says Dean Church, "we see the soul in the secret of its workings — loving, hoping, fearing, despairing, exulting, repenting, aspiring".[3]

But such emotions are, in a greater or less degree, the common property of mankind; though only a few can give them adequate verbal expression. Thus it was only natural that these classic voicings of a universal experience should be laid hold of eagerly by those who could feel, but could not utter their feeling: and, inasmuch as the emotions in question are the stuff and staple of man's religious life, that these psalms, originally written by one man for himself, should become part of the public worship of the Jewish and afterwards of the Christian Church. In the same way many of the most famous hymns were written to express the writer's religious mood of the moment: and indeed to not a few of them are attached stories, true or legendary, concerning the circumstances that inspired them. It would be too much to say that there was never an idea in the writer's mind of their being sung in public: for the individualistic type of religion fostered e.g. by the Methodist and Evangelical Revivals favoured this personal type of hymn. But before such lyrics can come properly within the category of "hymns", they must have proved in practice their suitability for communal use.

The case is otherwise, of course, with hymns specifically written for use in public worship: but, rather oddly, the most popular hymns are not usually of this type, nor are they very easy in any case to find in large numbers. It is a valid criticism of most hymn-books that "I" hymns are far too numerous. But the fault is less that of the compilers than of those who write and (still more) of those who sing hymns.

2. Secondly, a hymn (at least if it is to be of practical value) must be "designed for the use of plain people".

INTRODUCTION

It would be too much to say that this description is applicable without exception to all the hymns of which we are to speak. The later Greek hymns were highly elaborate compositions designed for the edification of a religious *élite* rather than of the multitude. Again, in the West, as the languages of modern Europe developed and Latin ceased to be in common use, the Office Hymns and Sequences can have conveyed little to the ordinary worshipper, who even in the Middle Ages successfully vindicated his right (though within strict limits) to express his devotion in vernacular canticles that he could understand. But so far as our own current use of hymns is concerned, the need of simplicity and general intelligibility cannot be ignored. The Christian Church is a democratic body in which the "foolish" are of not less account than the "wise". The former, too, are by far the more numerous. As Dr. Neale says, "Church hymns must be the life-expression of all hearts."[4] The desire of our reformers to raise the level of the hymns we sing is a very laudable one: and it is obvious that we must be exceedingly chary about introducing into our hymn-books material that we know to be of slight literary or musical value simply because it is popular. It may also be conceded that as education advances even an average congregation may come to enjoy singing hymns of a poetic quality that is at present "above their heads". But a hymn-book that is nothing more than an anthology of religious poetry wedded to tunes in an elaborate and unfamiliar idiom defeats its own ends. The ideal hymn is harmonious and dignified in its language and moves gracefully in its prosody: but it is at the same time simple and free from all elaboration both of thought and expression — such a hymn as 'O GOD, our help in ages past.' Here we have no word or image that even the simplest can fail to understand. Yet the total effect is of a sober magnificence that makes the hymn worthy of the greatest and most moving occasions.

5

It is important, too, that not only the language and imagery of a hymn but also its sentiment should be suited to the ordinary worshipper. Nothing is more pernicious than to put on the lips of people phrases that they do not and cannot mean. It is a real objection to many Victorian hymns — and even more to many of the hymns of the Methodist Revival — that they express sentiments which, however sincere in those who wrote them, are not sincere when voiced secondhand by the ordinary Churchgoer. But the same objection applies to many religious poems which some would substitute for the "old favourites". Emily Bronte's superb 'No coward soul is mine' is just as inappropriate to the average "man in the pew" as 'O Paradise, O Paradise' : and the argument against its use as a hymn cannot be evaded by pleading its literary excellence. It is possible to make out a case for a sparing use of such things on the ground that they provide people with an ideal to aim at — or at least to admire. But we must always be on our guard against the insincerity which is the greatest enemy of real religion.

At the same time it should not be forgotten that even "ordinary" people vary widely in their temperament and circumstances, and also that every individual may at times have to pass through experiences that set him apart from the mass of his fellows. For example, hymns in preparation for death may be very unreal on the lips of the young and healthy. Yet there are circumstances in which such hymns may be most appropriate, both for communal and even more for private use. To old people who have been confined to the house for years their hymn-book may mean a great deal ; for it is usually the only book of sacred verse which they possess. Again, it is not unusual to hear a hymn like Bonar's 'Thy way, not mine, O Lord' condemned as "defeatist". Yet, after all, it reflects the earthly lot of a large number of our fellow human-beings, and when sung by a gathering of tired and worn working-class mothers may have an intense pathos. If, however, hymns with a particular appeal of this kind are included in a hymnal, the preface should make it clear that its contents are not all suitable for use at the ordinary Sunday services.

A word may be added here concerning the scope and purpose of the present book. Its treatment of its subjects is primarily historical, seeking to give an account of the development of Christian hymnody throughout the ages — not, of course, a complete account, but one that keeps specially in view those writers and those hymns of all periods which figure in the hymnals in use among English Churchpeople (and, indeed, in those of English Christians generally) to-day. Even so, the field is so enormous that we shall often be compelled to confine ourselves to the best-known names in the various departments of our study and to their most conspicuous productions. But it is hoped that the reader will at least obtain a general conspectus of a large subject which will help him to a more intelligent and interested participation in the hymns that he sings.

This, however, is not all. Our aim is in part practical — not only to inform but also to guide. Of all the parts of Christian worship the hymns make the widest popular appeal. But for that very reason it is important that we should give careful attention to the question of the hymns that we are to use. We shall deal with this question further at the end of the book. For the present it is sufficient to point out that it can only be dealt with properly against a background of knowledge — knowledge, first, of the history and range of Christian hymnody and, secondly, of the criteria that should be applied in judging individual hymns. It is the author's modest hope that he may do a little to help his readers to better their equipment in both directions.

PART I

HISTORICAL

CHAPTER I

THE EARLY CHURCH

IN every race and age religious emotion has found utterance in music and song. This was even more than usually to be expected in the case of a religion so enthusiastic, and often even ecstatic, as we know the Christianity of the first age to have been. As Dr. Frere has said, "The Christian Church started on its way singing."[5] But when we go on to ask what actually were the songs it sang, we confront a question to which it is not easy to give a satisfactory answer.

I

On one point at least we may speak with assurance. St. Paul in a well-known passage bids the Ephesians "speak to one another in psalms and hymns and spiritual songs" (Eph. v. 19; cf. Col. iii. 16). It is natural to assume that on the lips of a Jew the word "psalms" bears its customary meaning; though it would hardly be safe to treat this as certain. But at least there can be no doubt as to the prominent and indeed primary place which the Jewish psalter held in the song of the youthful Church, as in that of all Christian ages since. That Church had its roots deep in the Jewish past from which it arose: and along with the other Scriptures of the Old Covenant it took over its sacred song as well. To the first disciples, as to their Master, the Psalms were a treasure of inestimable worth that was known by heart. No doubt He and they would often repeat them together: and the "hymn" which they sang before leaving the Upper Chamber for Gethsemane (St. Mark xiv. 26) was almost certainly the *Hallel*, consisting of

Pss. cxii.–cxviii. The Psalms, too, formed an integral part of
the worship of those synagogues of the Diaspora through
which the Gospel was first spread outside Palestine. Thus
through the Christians of Jewish race they would become
known (in the Greek translations) to their fellows who
were drawn from among the Gentiles : and when, in consequence of the split between the Church and the Synagogue, the former began to organize a worship entirely its
own, it was in the Psalms that the faith and devotion of its
members continued to find expression. So, too, at a later
date, the due recitation of the Psalter was one of the two
main objects with which the "Divine Office" came into
existence, the other being the regular reading of Holy
Scripture. [6]

It would appear, further, that along with the words of
the Psalms the Christian Church took over from the
Jewish the manner of their musical performance. The
origin of the ancient music of the Church called "plainsong" is a question of extreme obscurity : and our present
state of knowledge does not allow us to say with certainty
whether or not it is ultimately derived from the "cantilla-
tion" practised in the Temple and synagogues. But however it may be with the music itself, there is no doubt
that both the earlier and the later *methods* of chanting the
psalms practised in the Christian Church had Jewish antecedents. [7] The former method is called "responsorial" and
consists of a solo recitation by the precentor interspersed
with occasional responses by the choir or congregation.
The latter, the "antiphonal" method (traditionally said to
have been originated by St. Ignatius at Antioch, but more
probably introduced there in the fourth century and
thence rapidly extended over both East and West), consists in the chanting of the verses by two choirs alternately.
Both these types of psalmody were practised by the Jews —
indeed, the structure of some of the psalms clearly pre-
supposes the one or the other.

The Jewish antecedents of Christianity are nowhere more in evidence than in the earliest of its sacred lyrics — those to be found in the opening chapters of St. Luke's Gospel. These ("the Messianic Psalms of the New Testament," as they have been called) — viz. the *Magnificat*, *Benedictus* and *Nunc dimittis* — partake of the strongly Hebraic character of the whole Gospel of the Infancy in which they are embedded. The *Magnificat* bears a close resemblance to the Song of Hannah in 1 Sam. i. : and they may all have been originally composed in Aramaic. But they stand by themselves; and, in literary form at least, represent rather the close of an old era than the beginning of a new. It is possible that the Jewish-Christian communities of Palestine had their religious lyrics similarly framed on the model of the Jewish Psalms. But as the main current of the Christian propaganda advanced into the world of the Mediterranean, it moved further away from its Hebrew origins and became more and more impregnated with Hellenic elements. Thus it would be only natural that the sacred song of the Gentile churches should reflect this development. Yet even so the Biblical influence was unescapable : and, here most of all, the Oriental element would seem to have always dominated the Greek. It is true that the old Hellenic religion had its "hymns" no less than the religion of Israel. The so-called "Hymns of Homer" were already old in the time of Thucydides : and later centuries witnessed the production of the Hymns of Callimachus (IIIrd century B.C.), the famous *Hymn to Zeus* of the Stoic Cleanthes (quoted by St. Paul on Mars' Hill) as well as the hymns associated with the Orphic mysteries. But we have no reason to suppose that these products of Paganism had any influence on the hymnody of the Christian Church. It is possible, again, that the Graeco-Asiatic mystery-religions that were so widespread and so influential in the Roman Empire during the first centuries of Christianity may have affected its sacred song, as well as other departments of its life. But we have no material evidence of this : and in any case the character of these religions was rather Oriental than Greek. As Lord Selborne said, "For the origin and idea of Christian hymnody we must look, not to Gentile, but to Hebrew sources." [8] Yet a religion possessed by so furious a vitality as was primitive Christianity was bound to find fresh modes of expression for its love and worship, and, whatever its debt to the old, to blossom forth also into the new.

II

Of what nature then were the "hymns and spiritual songs" of which St. Paul speaks — the songs which the Church used in addition to the psalms bequeathed to it by Israel and which expressed its new environment and outlook ? Here we are largely in the region of surmise. The Church quickly began to create for itself a new authoritative literature of its own, by the side of what it had inherited from Judaism. But in this literature as we possess it poetry is not included, except in an indirect and incidental way. However, it seems not impossible to extract a certain amount of material on which conjecture may be based.

It may be well at the outset to warn the reader who is unfamiliar with the subject that, neither now nor for a long time to come, must he expect to find much resemblance between a "hymn" and the kind of composition that he is wont to associate with the name. For us a hymn is a poem written in clearly marked "verses" of definite metrical structure and adorned to a greater or less extent by regularly recurring rhymes. But it was several centuries before hymns came to assume this shape anywhere ; and in a large part of the Christian Church they never assumed it at all. The early Christian hymns are rather of the nature of rhythmic and poetical prose : and even when, in

Greek-speaking countries at a considerably later date, a quasi-metrical scheme was evolved for such things, it bore no resemblance to what the modern Englishman would call "poetry".

With this *caveat*, we may begin by noting the fairly general agreement among scholars that in certain rhythmically phrased passages of St. Paul's Epistles we have what are probably quotations from early Christian hymns. The clearest instance is found in Eph. v. 14: "Awake, thou that sleepest, and arise from the dead and Christ shall give thee light." Others are 1 Tim. iii. 16, 1 Tim. vi. 15–16 and the other "faithful sayings" in the Pastoral Epistles (1 Tim. i. 15, 2 Tim. ii. 11–13). Again, in the description of the heavenly worship in the Apocalypse we find more than one lyrical outpouring of praise and adoration set upon the lips of the angels and the redeemed. Such are the "Holy, holy, holy" and "Worthy art Thou" in Rev. iv. 8, 11, and the "Worthy is the Lamb" in Rev. v. 9, with the "Blessing and glory and honour and power" that follows. It is not unreasonable to suppose that in these "hymns" we have a reflection of the liturgical language familiar to the ears of worshippers on earth : a language which, if this be the case, was full of echoes of the Old Testament. Conversely, these songs, consecrated by their setting and by the universal reverence accorded to the book in which they appear, must have had a potent influence on the course of liturgical development in the future. They are, as Dr. Burn has said, "the types of future hymnody". 9

In trying to visualize the worship in which such "hymns and spiritual songs" played a part, we must beware of postulating any such rigidly fixed liturgical formulae as came to be the rule at a later date. We know that in the earliest days the custom of "tongue-speaking" introduced an anarchic element into the Church's worship that caused it to be frowned upon by St. Paul and finally to fall into

15

desuetude. And, even when this had taken place, the high honour paid to the "prophet" gave wide scope for the personal inspiration of the individual. Such is the situation portrayed in the *Didache*, in which we seem to have a picture of a Church-life that by the time the book was written had become mostly a thing of the past, but still survived in the more remote parts of the Church.[10] The striking formulae for the thanksgivings over the bread and wine (§ 9) and the thanksgiving after communion (§ 10) may be taken as specimens of the way in which the prophets were in the habit of fulfilling their task in celebrating the Eucharist. In all these the rhythmical and imaginative quality associated with poetry is clearly marked: and the last is couched in the form of three definite strophes, each ending with the same conclusion. It may be roughly translated as follows:

We give thanks to Thee, Holy Father,
>for Thy holy name which Thou hast made to tabernacle
>>in our hearts
>and for the knowledge and faith and immortality
>which Thou hast made known unto us through Jesus
>>Thy Son;
>>To Thee be glory for ever and ever.

Thou, LORD Almighty, hast created all things for Thy Name's
>>sake
>and hast given food and drink to men for their enjoyment,
>that they might give thanks unto Thee;
>but on us Thou hast bestowed spiritual food and drink
>>and eternal life through Thy Son:
>Above all we give thanks to Thee because Thou art
>>mighty;
>>To Thee be glory for ever and ever.

Remember, O LORD, Thy Church
>to deliver it from all evil and to perfect it in Thy love.
>Sanctify it and gather it together from the four winds into
>>Thy kingdom
>which Thou hast prepared for it.
>>For thine is the power and the glory for ever and ever.

Let grace come and let this world pass away.
    Hosanna to the GOD of David.
If any be holy, let him come : if any be not, let him repent.
    Maran-atha.
        Amen.

"Here," says Dom Leclercq, "we have the rudiments of rhythmical prayer in the first century : and if these prayers are not hymns in the sense that the word has assumed in liturgical language, they are, we may say, the sources and models of Christian hymnography." [11]

Nor did this rhythmical style of prayer cease when the "charismatic" ministry gave way to a localized and official one. It is certain that down to the third century a wide liberty of improvization was left to the celebrant. In Justin Martyr's account of the Liturgy in his time (c. 150) we are expressly told that the President offered prayer "to the best of his power".[12] But such improvizations tended to assume a distinctive "liturgical" style that marked them off from other and less sacred utterances. In the days of transition "the bishops" (to quote Dom Leclercq again) "must have regarded it as a point of honour not to improvize with less abundance and facility than the prophets who were hierarchically inferior to them".[13] Thus the tendency to a rhythmic and poetic phraseology (an easy matter on Greek lips) was maintained. It is generally agreed that in the long and beautiful intercession in chaps. 59–61 of Clement of Rome's Epistle to the Corinthians (c. 96) we have an example of such "Eucharistic prayer".[14] The same rhythmical effect is to be seen in certain grandly phrased passages in the glorious Epistle to Diognetus (§§ 7, 9, 11, 12), of which a brief citation may serve as a specimen :

He (i.e. the Word of GOD) is the Eternal, Who to-day is
        reckoned a Son,
    Through Whom the Church is made rich

17

And grace is unfolded and multiplied in the saints,
    giving understanding,
    revealing mysteries,
    proclaiming times,
    rejoicing in the faithful,
    bestowing gifts on them that seek,
to whom the pledges of faith are not broken
nor the decrees of the fathers transgressed.

In the offering of such prayer the congregation was not content simply to "stand and wait", but would associate itself with the action of the celebrant by various forms of response. It is quite possible that the prayer of St. Clement just mentioned was not a simple monologue, but was rather of the nature of a *litany* — a form which we know to have been already employed in pagan worship and which has an obvious psychological value in producing a cumulative emotional effect.[15] Each clause of the long intercession would be said first by the celebrant and then repeated by the congregation after him. Or the faithful might intervene by means of the method of "acclamation" (i.e. the repetition of brief liturgical formulae again and again), of which we catch echoes in the Apocalypse and which still survives in the Eastern Church.[16] "The early Christians," as Dom Cabrol has pointed out, "loved these formulae and used them as an expression of greeting, a token of union, a sign of recognition, almost as a password".[17] Such cries as 'Amen', 'Maranatha', 'Hosanna', 'Alleluia' and 'Kyrie eleison' would punctuate the course of the rite: or the congregation would make its contribution in the shape of a brief familiar refrain. In the *staccato* clauses of the final lines of the *Didache* thanksgiving quoted above we seem to hear these acclamations piling up in a swelling *crescendo* of fervour.

This use of the "refrain" was already familiar in some of the psalms of the Old Testament: and we have alluded to the further development of it in the earliest type of psalmody practised in the Christian Church, viz. the so-called *cantus responsorius*, in which during the reading of a psalm the congregation would intervene from time to time with an identical response called the *hypopsalma* — "the simplest form of Christian prose hymnography in the Greek language".[18] It is further illustrated by one of the earliest Christian hymns to have come down to us *in extenso* — the poem that closes the *Banquet of the Ten Virgins* by Methodius (see below, p. 26), in which each stanza is followed by a short refrain called ὑπακοή. It is likely that some of these "refrains" have survived in the shorter of the early Christian hymns mentioned in the last section of this chapter.

In addition to these "acclamations" we have abundant grounds for believing that the congregation would sometimes contribute more extended "hymns" on their own account. In early Christianity the truth that "the Spirit is given to *every* man to profit withal" was strongly emphasized : and thus those who had the poetic gift would find a warm welcome awaiting the products of their inspiration, which would be gladly taken over and used by their fellow-worshippers. St. Paul, speaking to the Corinthians concerning individual contributions to their common worship, says : "When ye come together, each one hath a *psalm*, hath a teaching, hath a revelation, hath a tongue, hath an interpretation" (1 Cor. xiv. 26). It is from "hymns" of this sort which had attained to a specially wide currency that the quotations in the Apostle's letters mentioned above are presumably taken. It may even be that the very abundance in which such hymns were produced, and the consequent rapidity with which the earlier ones tended to be supplanted by others, explain (together with their inconspicuous origin) their general failure to survive. We have clear evidence that in the second and third centuries these *psalmi idiotici* or private psalms existed in large numbers.[19] Describing the Christian *Agape* (or "Love-feast") Tertullian (*c.* 200) says : "Each man is stirred to sing songs publicly to GOD either from the Holy Scriptures or of his own invention according to his ability." [20] An interesting passage in the Church historian Eusebius gives a quotation from an anonymous controversial work written against the second-century heretic Artemon, in which the author speaks of "psalms and odes such as from the beginning were written by believers, hymns to the Christ, the Word of GOD, calling Him GOD".[21] Another passage in Eusebius tells of Nepos, an Egyptian bishop (apparently of the third century), as the author of an "abundant psalmody" that won wide acceptance.[22] The epithet *idiotici* would seem to imply that such "psalms" or hymns were originally produced for purposes of private devotion. It was of such use that St. Paul was apparently thinking when he gave his admonition to the Ephesians — even as he and Silas in prison at Philippi are described as "praying and singing hymns unto GOD" (Acts xvi. 25). But there would be nothing surprising in their forcing their way into public worship, at least locally — especially in an age when the forms of worship were still fluid. We can readily believe that there was objection to their finding a home within the sacred enclosure of the Eucharist : and, indeed, Justin Martyr in his description makes no mention of either psalms or hymns as a part of that service. But there would be other occasions for their use : and it was in this fashion, we may presume, that, by the operation of the principle of "the survival of fittest", a few of them finally won their way to universal use and became a permanent part of Christian worship.

In this connection we may note the much-debated passage in Pliny's Letter to Trajan (*c.* 105), in which, describing the habits of the Christians in his province of Bithynia, he speaks of them as "assembling together early in the morning and singing by turns (*invicem*) a song to Christ as a god".[23] In this "song" some have seen a Messianic psalm : others (including the great French scholar Duchesne) have preferred a primitive form of the Morning Hymn that was to develop later into the *Gloria in excelsis*.[24] Others, again, would hold that the word used for "song" (*carmen*) is employed in its technical sense of "incantation" and refers to the priest's consecration of the Eucharist, to which the people made response. But all this must remain a matter of speculation in view of the vagueness both of the terms used and of Pliny's knowledge of the subject.

Besides their obvious value in voicing and stimulating devotion, a second motive for the use of hymns, which was to have immense importance again and again in later ages, would seem to have become operative to some extent at a very early date. The heretical sects quickly discovered the value of poetry as a means of disseminating their doctrine among the masses : for poetry is at once attractive in itself and easy to remember, especially when it is set to tunes of a popular kind. We know from Tertullian that the Gnostics Marcion and Valentinus resorted to this device in the middle of the second century : [25] and a generation later the Syrian Gnostics also adopted it with great success, as we shall see. Nor did the Church disdain to meet the challenge in a similar way. Irenaeus (*c.* 180) tells us how "a presbyter" whom he had known in his youthful days at Ephesus had taught him a short poem directed against the Gnostic Markos.[26] Probably, too, many of the *psalmi idiotici* were written with a similar purpose. Human nature being what it is, it was only to be expected that the heretics should object to their own weapon being thus turned against themselves. Thus Paul of Samosata, the heretical Bishop of Antioch (260–70), suppressed "the psalms which were sung there in honour of our Lord Jesus Christ" on the ground that "they were new and the work of new men" [27] — a proof, incidentally, that by this time in the great city of Antioch at any rate the use of non-scriptural hymns was an established custom. For this suppression (among other offences) the bishops of his province condemned and deposed him (269) ; thus giving an implicit sanction to the practice that he had withstood. In the next century, as we shall see, the Arian controversy was to give it wide extension on both sides of the fray.

III

The account here given of the hymnody of the pre-Constantinian Church is an attempt to weave into a coherent whole the scattered and often obscure references to the subject found in the literature of the period. It is necessarily therefore incomplete and contains a considerable element of speculation and surmise. From these quicksands the reader may turn with relief to a brief consideration of those hymns that have actually come down to us to which an early if not primitive date may be safely assigned. Yet even here he will not immediately find the ground firm under his feet. It has been claimed that in the recently discovered *Odes of Solomon*, written in Syriac, we have the earliest specimens of Christian hymnody that are in existence. Dr. Rendel Harris, their discoverer, maintains that here is nothing less than a lost hymn-book of the Apostolic, or at least the sub-Apostolic, Church. According to him they were written in Greek by a Jewish Christian towards the end of the first century and are the private poems of a non-sacramental mystic.[28] On the other hand, Archbishop Bernard, who edited them in *Texts and Studies*, considers that the Syriac is probably the original form, that they were written not long before A.D. 200, and that they are "baptismal hymns for use in public worship, either for catechumens or for those who have recently been baptized".[29] These two estimates are sufficiently opposed in themselves : but the question is further complicated by the fact that Harnack considered the *Odes* to be a Christian recension of Jewish originals, while others detect in them signs of Gnostic inspiration.[30] Their great beauty and interest cannot be denied : and if (as seems now to be the prevailing opinion) they really are of Christian origin, we may regard them as furnishing excellent examples of the *psalmi idiotici* spoken of above. But having regard to the obscurity that surrounds them and to the fact that, even if their provenance be Christian, they have left no trace behind in Christian worship, we may be excused if we give them no more than passing mention.

The case is otherwise with what had usually been regarded hitherto as the earliest Christian hymn that has come down to us, at least as a complete whole — the beautiful *Φῶς ἱλαρόν* ('Joyful Light'). Here we have something which is not only of great antiquity and indubitably Christian origin, but has occupied an honoured place in the worship of the Eastern Church since a very early period. It has been attributed to the martyr Athenagoras (*c.* 180) : but this seems to rest on a mistake. There can be no doubt, however, that it is very old : for St. Basil, writing *c.* 370, speaks of it thus : "We cannot say who is the father of these expressions at the Thanksgiving at the Lighting of the Lamps : but it is an *ancient* formula which the people repeat : and no one has ever yet been accused of impiety for saying, 'We hymn the Father and the Son and the Holy Spirit of GOD.' " [31] Whether originally written for public worship or for private use, it had already by St. Basil's time become part of the Vesper Office held "at the lighting of the lamps" and therefore called in Greek *ἐπιλύχνιον* and in Latin *Lucernarium*. It still forms part of the Evening Office of the Eastern Church. It has been translated by many hands ; the best-known renderings being the unmetrical rhymed version by John Keble, 'Hail, gladdening Light,' *18, and Robert Bridges's translation, 'O gladsome Light,' †269, written to fit the exquisite tune by Bourgeois for the metrical version of *Nunc dimittis* in the Genevan Psalter.

Another early hymn is that found in the *Apostolical*

Constitutions (IVth century) — again as part of the Vesper
Office. Dom Leclercq considers it to be of the third
century at the latest.[32] It may be translated thus:

We praise Thee, we hymn Thee, we bless Thee for Thy
great glory, Lord King, Father of Christ the Immaculate
Lamb that taketh away the sins of the world. Thou art worthy
to be praised, Thou art worthy to be hymned, Thou art
worthy to be glorified, Who art God and Father through the
Son in the Holy Spirit for ever and ever. Amen.

The reader will at once notice the resemblance to the
Gloria in excelsis. This, too, is a non-Scriptural hymn of
early date; its opening words being suggested by the
Angelic Song heard by the shepherds on the night of
Christ's nativity. The *Apostolic Constitutions* (where it
appears in a longer form than in the Roman Liturgy)
reveal it as being in use in the East at the Morning Office
in the fourth century, and in an earlier form it may be
much older. Concerning its structure Dom Cabrol says:
"The rhythm is free: but the harmonious arrangement of
the phrases and their subsidiary clauses, especially striking
in the Greek, seems based on a studied succession of
syllables and accents and even rhyme, the use of which
gives greater symmetry to the cadence."[33] It has never
been used at Mass in the East: but it appears in the Roman
Mass from the beginning of the sixth century — at first,
however, only on Sundays and festivals and for use by the
Bishop alone.[34] The Triumphal Hymn or *Sanctus*, on the
other hand, forms part of the Mass in both East and
West: but it is virtually a Scriptural composition.

Another very ancient hymn is the so-called *Trisagion*,
which may be translated thus:

Holy God, Holy and Mighty, Holy and Immortal, have
mercy upon us.

Its earliest attestation is by the Council of Chalcedon
(451): but it is undoubtedly of much earlier date.[35] Even

more interesting is an ancient Easter song which survives in the Greek service-book called the *Pentecostarion*, and which Cardinal Pitra tells us was still sung in the original Greek at the Easter solemnities in Rome in the ninth century. It may be taken as an example of the "acclamations" spoken of above. Its effect is incommunicable in an English translation ; so it may be given in Pitra's Latin version :

> *Pascha* (i.e. Passover)
> *Sacrum nobis hodie apparuit !*
> *Pascha novum, sanctum !*
> *Pascha mysticum !*
> *Pascha augustissimum !*
> *Pascha, Christus Redemptor !*
> *Pascha immaculatum !*
> *Pascha magnum !*
> *Pascha fidelium !*
> *Pascha quo portae nobis*
> *Paradisi aperta sunt !*
> *Pascha*
> *Omnes sanctificans fideles !*
> *Romae Papam tu, Christe, conserva.*[36]

All these ancient hymns have survived in the public worship of East or West. It remains to mention three others of the same period which have come down to us, though neither now nor (so far as we know) at any time have they been used for liturgical purposes.

The first is a Hymn to Christ attached to the *Paedagogus* of Clement of Alexandria (170–220), beginning Στομίον πώλων ἀδαῶν, 'Bridle of colts untamed.' [37] It is thus the earliest Christian hymn that can be definitely dated. Unlike the "rhythmical" hymns mentioned above it is written in a classical metre (Anapaestic dimeter), and in this way (as we shall see) lies off the main track on which Eastern hymnody was to proceed. The second is the "Amherst papyrus", so-called because it was discovered in the library of Lord Amherst in Norfolk.[38] This may be dated about the end of the third century and is written in anapaests. (For an explanation of this and other metrical terms used in this book the reader is referred to Appendix A.) "It has been described", says Baumstark, "as a versified ethical catechism of early Christendom, although it might quite as fitly be regarded as a hymn forming part of the liturgy of initiation addressed to the newly baptized." Its great interest in the history of hymnody lies in two directions. First, its anapaests are regulated as much by accent as by quantity. Thus it marks an early stage in the process, common to the hymnody of both East and West, by which accent came to be the regulating principle of prosody in place of the vowel-quantity of the old classical metres. Secondly, we have here the earliest extant example of the alphabetic acrostic which, already employed frequently in the Hebrew psalms, was to be so marked a feature of Eastern hymnody. In the initial letters of the lines the letters of the Greek alphabet in their order appear three times over.

The last of these three hymns has been already referred to — the hymn beginning Ἄνωθεν παρθένοι, 'Up, maidens !', that closes the *Banquet of the Ten Virgins* ascribed to Methodius (d. 311).[39] In this curious work ten virgins are represented as engaging in a kind of competition in declaring the glory of their state. Finally Thekla, the victor, chants a psalm to which the others respond by a brief refrain :

I keep myself chaste for Thee, and wielding light-bearing torches, O Bridegroom, I will go to meet Thee.

Here we have the use of the refrain for the first time in any extant hymn. In addition, the iambics of the verses are not less accentual in character than the anapaests of the "Amherst papyrus" ; while the acrostic also reappears, each of the 24 stanzas beginning with the successive letters of the alphabet. Thus three of the most characteristic features of late Greek hymnody — accentual versification, acrostic and refrain — are already anticipated.

CHAPTER II

HYMNS OF THE EASTERN CHURCH

THE earliest products of Greek hymnody have been dealt with in the preceding chapter. It must be remembered that the fact that they are in Greek does not necessarily imply that their use was confined to the Eastern portions of the Roman Empire. In the first Christian centuries Greek, not Latin, was the usual language of worship not only in the East but also in a large part of the Christianized West. The earliest surviving literature emanating from the Church of Rome was written in Greek: and it is certain that Greek continued to be its liturgical language until the middle of the third century. It was in this way, possibly, that hymns written in Greek like the *Gloria in excelsis* [40] and the *Te decet laus* (*see* p. 24) became part of the worship of the Western Church; to retain their position in a translated form when the change from Greek to Latin took place. Still more interesting is the case of the *Trisagion*, which survives in the Roman rite (in the Good Friday Reproaches) in its Greek as well as its Latin form: '*Agios o Theos, Agios ischyros, Agios athanatos, eleison imas.*' A similar Greek survival is the *Kyrie eleison;* and we have seen how until the ninth century the *Pascha* acclamations continued to be sung at Rome in Greek.

From the middle of the fourth century onwards the hymnodies of East and West part company and proceed on widely different lines. Yet in both cases there is a great extension in the use of hymns, which soon become for the first time a definitely recognized part of the Church's

27

worship. This extension, too, is in each case largely prompted by the same cause — the fight against heresy. We have already spoken of the use of hymns by the early heretics as a means of winning a popular currency for their doctrines. Of those who exploited this method none was so thorough or so successful as the Syrian Gnostic, Bardesanes, at the end of the second century. He and his son Harmonius produced a "Gnostic psalter" of 150 hymns. It was to meet this challenge that, more than a century later, the celebrated Ephraem Syrus (?307–373) composed his Syriac hymns.[41] Ephraem lived at Edessa and ranks as the most famous of the theologians who wrote in Syriac. In one of his writings he thus complains :

> In the resorts of Bardesanes
> There are songs and melodies ;
> For seeing that young people
> Loved sweet music,
> By the harmony of his songs
> He corrupted their morals.

To counteract the "poisoned sweetness" of these songs Ephraem, we are told, "gathered the daughters of the Convent", and for them, as they met daily in the churches of Edessa, "he, like a spiritual harpist, arranged different kinds of songs and taught them the variation of chants until the whole city was gathered to him and the party of the adversary was put to shame". These hymns of Ephraem — with their strophes, refrains and "rhythmical" structure based not on quantity but on accent and on the presence of an equal number of syllables in corresponding lines — would appear to have had considerable influence in determining the form not only of Syriac hymnody, but of Greek hymnody too.[42] Besides hymns in the more ordinary sense Ephraem also cultivated a literary *genre* of his own called "metrical homilies", in which he attacked not the Bardesanites only but other forms of heresy as well. A number of his hymns have been translated into

English, though none has come into common use with the exception of Dr. Burkitt's 'Receive, O Lord, in heaven above' †194. As a writer of Syriac hymns he had many successors, but none of equal fame.

At the period when Ephraem in further Syria was coping with the relics of Gnosticism, the main body of the Empire was in the throes of a conflict between orthodoxy and the new heresy called Arianism. Its founder, Arius, used from the outset songs set to popular tunes to propagate his ideas. "The workers of the port," says Duchesne, "the sailors, the idlers and the common people knew these songs and deafened the faithful of Alexandria with them." [43] The earliest and greatest of the opponents of Arius, the austere St. Athanasius, was apparently content, so far as we know, to denounce the frivolity and unseemliness of this practice and did not attempt to organize a counter-crusade of song. But during the fourth century it would seem that the custom of singing hymns in the churches was widely spread in the East : for we know, on the authority of St. Augustine, that at Milan in 386 the same custom was introduced in the West "after the use of the Eastern provinces".[44] On the other hand, the 59th canon of the Council of Laodicea [45] (held between 343 and 381) allowed the liturgical use of nothing save Holy Scripture and forbade the singing of *psalmi idiotici* — presumably to avoid the risk of contaminating the orthodoxy of the faithful by means of heretical hymns. "This prohibition, however," says Dom Leclercq, "would not appear to have been very widely observed." [46] In any case it is certain that at the end of the same century the alternative method of "not allowing the devil to have all the good tunes" was again boldly resorted to at Constantinople. When St. Chrysostom became Bishop there in 398, the Arians were not allowed to worship within the city walls. They made up for this, however, by coming into the city on the evenings of Saturdays, Sundays and the greater festivals and assembling in the public porticoes and other places of common resort. Here they passed the night in singing hymns (with *acroteleuteia* or refrains) in which they set forth the Arian doctrines and hurled taunts at the orthodox. These performances attracted large crowds : and by way of counteracting their influence Chrysostom, with the support and at the expense of the Empress Eudoxia, initiated solemn nocturnal processions for the chanting of hymns with such ceremonial adjuncts as silver crosses and lighted candles. These competitive demonstrations not unnaturally led to riot and bloodshed, with the result that the Arian hymn-singings were forbidden by law. Their orthodox rivals, on the other hand, became a permanent institution.[47]

One of Chrysostom's immediate predecessors in the see of Constantinople, Gregory of Nazianzus (d. *c.* 390), the life-long friend of St. Basil, had already voiced the orthodoxy of the Councils of Nicaea and Constantinople in a number of poems written in the closing years of his chequered life. Like our own Bishop Ken, he had been compelled by the political vicissitudes of the time to resign his see (381) and to go into retirement (in a cell in his native city Nazianzus) : and, like him, too, he solaced his enforced leisure with the writing of sacred poetry. His poems, written almost entirely in the classical metres, reach a high level of excellence : and a number of them have been translated into English by the Rev. A. W. Chatfield in his *Songs and Hymns of the Greek Christian Poets* (1876).[48]

Another Christian poet of slightly later date was Synesius (*c.* 365–414). A genial country gentleman of philosophic tastes living in Cyrene in North Africa, he went in 397 to Constantinople, where he vainly tried to induce the Emperor Arcadius to take steps to meet the growing barbarian menace. After his return he was gradually converted to Christianity ; and in 410, much against his will, he allowed himself to be made Bishop of Ptolemais. Here (to quote Gibbon's characteristic comment) "the philosophic bishop supported with dignity the character which he had assumed with reluctance".[49] Even as a Christian he remained a good deal of a Neoplatonist : and his orthodoxy has been called in question. But his ten *Odes*, written in various classical metres, are of great interest and beauty in their presentation of Christian doctrine as seen through the eyes of a Platonist philosopher. Mrs. Browning even went so far as to call Synesius "the chief, for all true and natural gifts, of all our Greek Christian poets" ; and adds, "These Odes have, in fact, a wonderful rapture and ecstasy".[50] She herself translated two of them : and all ten were translated by Mr. Chatfield. One of his versions (of the 10th Ode), 'Lord Jesus, think on me' *185 †77, finds a place in most modern hymnals : but the translator himself has told us that it is more a paraphrase than an exact translation. More characteristic of Synesius's thought is another version from the same hand which appears in *A.M.* 'Lift up thyself, my soul' *661. This is a really fine hymn, not only noble both in thought and language but of a characteristically Hellenic type hardly represented otherwise at all in our hymn-books. It helps, too, to fill the serious gap arising from the deficiency of hymns addressed to the Father as compared with those addressed to the Incarnate Son.

Neither the hymns of Gregory nor those of Synesius succeeded in finding a place in the public services of the Eastern Church. They were hardly adapted for the purpose in any case : and their employment of the classical metres of Greece set them outside of the lines on which Greek hymnody was destined to develop. With a single exception (the three Iambic Canons of St. John Damascene) the service-books of the Eastern Church include no hymns written in those metres. The character of the vast body of hymns that they contain is rather Oriental than

31

Hellenic, alike in matter and literary form : their filiation proceeds from other sources than Greek poetry. At the period when these hymns were produced classical Greek was dying out : moreover, as Neale says, "in the decline of the language accent was trampling down quantity". The line was no longer based on the arrangement of long- and short-vowelled syllables into various types of metrical "feet", but on the alternation of accented and unaccented syllables, of *arsis* and *thesis* ; the classical distinction between long and short vowels tending more and more to disappear.[51] The change (as we shall see) was common to both Greek and Latin hymnody : but in the case of the former it was no doubt encouraged by the influence of Syriac hymnody, which was accentual in prosody from the beginning.[52] Another influence operating in the same direction was that of the elaborate prose of the later Greek rhetoricians. There is good reason to believe that some of the earlier Greek "rhythmical" hymns were nothing else than combinations of extracts from the homilies of the Greek Fathers. In an instruction by St. Dorotheus (IVth century) to his monks in Palestine we find a commentary on the successive lines of a hymn on the Resurrection which turns out on examination to be simply a cento of passages from an Easter homily of St. Gregory of Nazianzus (382). "The rhythmic movement of the phrases," says M. Petrides, "was accentuated in such a way that one had only to join to them an appropriate melody to obtain a hymn worthy to figure in the Paschal office." [53] Another of St. Dorotheus's instructions comments on a hymn to Martyrs which has a similar origin.

It was under these influences that the *Troparia* were produced which from the fifth century onwards achieved an immense and increasing popularity in the worship of the Eastern Church. In their earliest form these *Troparia* would appear to have been short hymns consisting of a single stanza. To the old-fashioned and strict-minded they seemed a mere "luxury of devotion" to be frowned upon. Cardinal Pitra has collected three quaint stories to this effect,[54] in all of which monks who have become enamoured of the new form of singing are rebuked by a holy and austere abbot, who, while admitting that such things may be tolerable for the secular clergy and the laity, regards them as a violation of ancient tradition and unworthy of the ascetic life of a monk. At the same time the stories reveal that even in the monasteries this prejudice was more and more breaking down.

Of these early *Troparia* a large number survive: and many find a place in the Greek service books, though they are not always easy to identify. Two of them, presumably dating from the sixth century, have achieved immense fame and become enshrined within the Mass itself. The first is the *Cherubic Hymn* sung in the chief Eastern Liturgies before the "Great Entrance". This is generally ascribed to the time of the Emperor Justinian: it was inserted in the Liturgy in the reign of his successor Justin II (565–78).[55] It runs as follows:

Let us who mystically represent the Cherubim and sing the thrice-holy hymn to the quickening Trinity lay by at this time all worldly cares, that we may receive the King of glory, invisibly attended by the angelic orders. Alleluia, Alleluia, Alleluia.

In this connection we may notice that in the Liturgy of the Church of Jerusalem, commonly called the Liturgy of St. James, this Cherubic Hymn is accompanied by a prayer, to be said by the Priest, which, as freely translated by the Rev. G. Moultrie, has become well-known in the guise of the Eucharistic hymn, 'Let all mortal flesh keep silence' †318 (Dr. Mason's 'Not a thought of earthly things' *717 is an alternative version). Another prayer from the same Liturgy (to be said by the Deacon before the Priest goes to the sacristy after the service) has been similarly paraphrased in metrical form as the hymn 'From glory to glory advancing' †310. It must be repeated, however, that in their original form these hymns are not hymns at all but prayers.

Besides the Cherubic Hymn another hymn, presumably of the same period, is attributed to the pen of the Emperor Justinian himself, beginning with the words 'Ο μονογενὴς υἱός.[56] It may be translated thus:

Only-begotten Son and Word of GOD, Immortal, Who didst vouchsafe for our salvation to take flesh of the holy Mother of GOD and ever-Virgin Mary, and didst without mutation become Man and wast crucified, Christ our GOD, and by death didst overcome death, being one of the Holy Trinity and glorified together with the Father and the Holy Spirit; Save us.

This has become familiar to many English congregations in Dr. T. A. Lacey's metrical translation, †325.

Such simple single-stanza *Troparia*, varying widely both in the number and in the length of their lines, continue to figure largely in the Greek service-books, especially after the first group of psalms in the Night-Office, and are called by various names according to their character and use. But as time went on the stanzas were multiplied, thus forming hymns of considerable length. Sometimes a number of *Idiomela* or single-stanza *Troparia* were strung loosely together into a long hymn called a *Stichera*. But more usually the constituent *troparia* were welded into an artistic whole with a definitely articulated structure in the form called a *Contakion* — after the rolls (*contakia*) from which they were sung by the precentor. It is this poetic form which is associated with the "Middle Period" of Greek hymnody that brought to birth its most beautiful and distinguished products — the "golden age of Byzantine hymnody", as it has been called.[57] Unfortunately the service-books (called *Tropologia*) in which these hymns were collected were destroyed wholesale by the Iconoclast reformers of the eighth and ninth centuries. Thus the hymns in question entirely disappeared except for certain fragments that were rescued from oblivion and incorporated into the later service-books. The so-called "contakia" in these presumably represent the mutilated remains of the old *Contakia*.[58]

Fortunately, however, a considerable number of the latter have chanced to be preserved in three MSS. Tropologia at Moscow, Rome and Turin, where they remained unknown for centuries until they were discovered by Cardinal Pitra, who published a collection of them in 1876.[59] The most distinguished of the writers of this school is the deacon Romanus, called the Melodist. Unfortunately there is wide discrepancy of opinion as to his date. He is said to have come to Constantinople "in the reign of Anastasius". But there were two emperors of that name : Anastasius I (491–518) and Anastasius II (713–9) — a difference of two centuries. Pitra declared for the former. But the German scholar Crist argued [60] (very reasonably, as it seems) that this would set Romanus back in the first, formative period of Greek hymnody when (so far as we know) nothing but *Troparia* and *Idiomela* existed ; though as against this it might be urged that in Methodius's *Hymn of the Virgins* we have a very early composition which is not only as elaborate as Romanus's *Contakia* but is actually constructed on similar lines. The prevailing opinion is to follow Crist's choice of the later date.[61] If this be correct, Romanus flourished just before the first outbreak of the Iconoclastic controversy.

In addition to his discovery of these hymns Pitra has also the credit of having found the long lost key to their prosodic structure and that of the later Greek hymns generally. Before his time it was generally believed that the hymns of the Greek service-books were not really poetry at all, but "measured prose". Neale definitely expressed this view in the preface to his *Hymns of the Eastern Church* published in 1862.[62] But even before Neale wrote Pitra had stumbled on the secret. He himself has told the story in his *Hymnologie de l'Eglise grecque* (1867).[63] In 1859 the future Cardinal, then a Benedictine of Solesmes, visited St. Petersburg (now Leningrad). Here he came across an old MS. containing at the end a "Canon of eight Odes" (a term explained below, p. 39), the text of which was divided up throughout at frequent intervals by red dots. Taking each Ode separately and comparing its strophes with one another, he found that in every strophe the *number of syllables* in each corresponding division thus marked off was the same, though these numbers differed widely from one another, some of the divisions or "lines" being much longer than others. An examination of other MSS. revealed the presence of similar divisions marked on precisely the same plan. Thus, says Pitra, "the pilgrim was in possession of the syllabic system of the hymnographers".

This system worked as follows. At the beginning of every Ode was a strophe called *heirmos*, usually a strophe taken from an earlier hymn (in which case only the first line was indicated). This served as the pattern-strophe for the whole Ode, regulating at once (1) the melody to which the Ode was sung, (2) the number of syllables in each clause or 'line', (3) the beat of the accentuation, this last ignoring the distinction between long and short vowels observed in the classical metres. The 'lines' may vary from 3 to 13 syllables, and the strophes from 3 to 33 "lines" in each. The strophes following the *heirmos* are called *troparia* : and the whole Canon is knit together by an acrostic supplying the initial letters of the successive strophes. This acrostic is sometimes alphabetic and sometimes indicates either the name of the author or the theme of his poem. Another feature is the *ephymnion* or refrain closing each *troparion*.

The Canons and Odes thus analysed by Pitra belong to a later period of Greek hymnody than the *Contakia* of Romanus and his school : but the principles of construction are much the same in the latter as in the former. In the *Contakia*, however, the *heirmos* is preceded by a brief strophe called the πρόασμα.[64] In Pitra's opinion these earlier hymns are superior to the later Odes and Canons in freshness and animation. In particular they have a markedly dramatic character which is completely absent from their successors. He suggests that (like some of the earlier Sequences in the West) they were actually sung with dramatic accompaniments as a substitute for the theatrical performances of pagan times.[65] He gives a description of the most celebrated of Romanus's *Contakia*. It is a Christmas hymn and consists of 24 long strophes. The first is the "proem" and differs in structure from the rest, though it concludes with the refrain that is to end all the other strophes : 'New-born Child, Who wast GOD from before all ages.' The second is the *heirmos*, which provides the mould for all the other strophes and also starts the acrostic. The latter consists of the words, τοῦ ταπεινοῦ ʽΡωμανοῦ ὕμνος, "The hymn of humble Romanus." The first strophe gives a description of the scene and characters of the Nativity. Later, the Virgin addresses the Divine Infant, after which the Magi appear and a dialogue ensues between the Virgin, Joseph and them. Then the Magi present their gifts ; and the hymn concludes with an intercession by the Virgin.

Next in importance to Romanus as a representative of this 'Middle Period' of Greek hymnody may be reckoned the Patriarch Sergius of Constantinople (610–41), author of the famous hymn called the *Akathistos*. It was originally written as a thanksgiving to the Blessed Virgin for the defence of Constantinople against the Persians ; and was so called because it was always sung standing. It is not unlike the hymns of Romanus in some respects : but its form is rather different. It has been translated by Dr. G. R. Woodward, but its subject-matter makes it unsuitable for Anglican worship.

However great the merits of Romanus and his school, it

is unnecessary to do more than pay a passing tribute to their historical interest : for, with a single exception (a Christmas *Contakion*, 'Bethlehem hath opened Eden'[66]), none of their hymns has been translated into English and the one exception has never come into use. The same treatment may be accorded to Sophronius, Patriarch of Jerusalem (629). His Anacreontic hymns, written in Iambic dimeter, never made their way into the service-books : but a few of the others, written in the accustomed "rhythmical" style, have found a place there. None of these, however, has been translated.

The case is otherwise with the later school of hymnody which came into existence on the ruins of its predecessor and, in the teeth of triumphant Iconoclasm, sought to do all over again its work of using sacred song to bear witness to and safeguard the orthodox faith. This is the hymnody that supplies the originals of those translations of Neale's from the Greek [67] which have become so popular in our English hymnals. It is the hymnody which has displayed its voluminous richness for nearly a thousand years in the Greek service-books that form what may be called the "Eastern Breviary". Neale calculates that "on a moderate computation" these Offices "comprise five thousand closely printed quarto pages in double columns of which at least four thousand are poetry".[68] They are arranged in 18 volumes : (1) 12 volumes of *Menaea*, one for each month (Gk. μήν), corresponding to the Proper of Saints in the Western Breviary ; (2) the *Parakletike*, containing the ferial Offices arranged according to a recurring system of eight weeks ; (3) the *Octoechus*, containing the Offices for Saturday evening and Sunday from the preceding (the term '*Octoechus*' is derived from the Eight "Modes" (ἦχοι) in which the music of the ferial Offices of each of the eight weeks in turn is written) ; (4) the *Triodion*, containing the services for Lent and the three Sundays preceding it — so named because the Odes in it are usually arranged in groups of three ; (5) the *Pentecostarion*, containing the services for the seasons of Easter and Pentecost ; (6) the *Euchologion*, containing the Occasional Offices ; (7) the *Horologion*, containing the Hours of Prayer.

The general principles on which this vast body of hymns is constructed have been already described in our account of Pitra's discovery. The most characteristic feature of the system is the *Ode*. An *Ode* (like Romanus's *Contakion*) consists of a *heirmos* followed by a varying number of *troparia*, of which the *heirmos* (usually a strophe of older date) supplies the model. The concluding strophe of an Ode usually celebrates the Blessed Virgin and is therefore called the *Theotokion*, Theotokos meaning "Mother of GOD." The Odes in their turn are arranged in groups, occasionally of two or four but usually of three or (in the case of the great Festival Canons) of eight. The eight Odes forming a Canon are threaded on an acrostic, usually in verse. These Canons are sung at Lauds. Their constituent Odes were written to accompany the Scriptural Canticles that originally formed part of that service. These Canticles were at first nine in number : but the second (the Song of Moses in Deut. xxxii) was omitted because its minatory character made it unsuitable for festivals, and the corresponding Ode vanished too. Hence the number eight. In course of time the other Canticles also practically disappeared, while the Odes remained.[69]

It may conduce to greater clearness if we append a literal translation of an Ode. It is the first of the eight Odes comprising the most celebrated of all the Festival Canons — St. John Damascene's great Easter Canon, of which more will be said shortly. The reader will be already well-acquainted with it in Neale's metrical version. The present rendering is necessarily very clumsy : and it is of course impossible to reproduce the "syllabic" arrangement. It must suffice to repeat that in the original Greek the number of syllables in the first line of every

stanza is the same, and so on through succeeding lines.
(The number of these syllables is indicated in brackets.)

Heirmos

The Day of Resurrection ! (8)
Rejoice we, all peoples ! (5)
The Passover of the Lord, the Passover ! (7)
For from death unto life (8)
And from earth unto heaven (6)
Christ our GOD (5)
Hath brought us over (7)
Singing a triumph-song (7)

Troparia

Let us purify our hearts (8)
And we shall behold, (5)
In the light unapproachable (7)
Of the Resurrection, Christ (8)
Sending forth His rays, and (6)
His greeting ' All hail ' (5)
We shall hear clearly, (7)
Singing a triumph-song (7)

Let the heavens in fitting fashion (8)
Make rejoicing (5)
And let the earth be glad. (7)
Let the world exult, (8)
Both all that is visible (6)
And invisible ; (5)
For Christ is risen, (7)
Our joy everlasting (7)

A word must now be said concerning the circumstances
which gave rise to the movement resulting in the efflorescence of this amazing outburst of sacred song. In the
third decade of the eighth century the Emperor Leo the
Isaurian set himself to put down what seemed to him the
excessive and idolatrous veneration paid to images in the
Eastern Church. The faith and arms of Islam were spreading with terrifying rapidity : and his motive was largely to
wipe out a reproach that seemed to make Christianity
easily vulnerable by its stern monotheism. In the long

drawn-out struggle that followed under Leo and his successors the Church for the most part vehemently opposed
the imperial policy : and the contest more and more
assumed the character of a defence of her independence
against the encroachments of the civil power. The heart
and soul of the anti-Iconoclast party was the monks : and
their resistance found its most formidable strongholds in
two monasteries — first, the Laura of Saint Sabas near
Jerusalem, set "like an eagle's nest" on a crag overlooking
the wild valley of the Kedron, and secondly (at a rather
later date) the famous monastery of St. John the Baptist
in Constantinople, commonly called the Studion (or
Studium) after the name of its founder, Studios. The leading figures in both these centres of opposition were not
only theologians but poets as well : and in their hands
hymnody was once again made to serve the interests of
orthodoxy against the wiles of "heresy".

Even before the Iconoclastic controversy began Jerusalem had produced a hymn-writer of note in St. Andrew
of Crete (660–732), who before becoming Archbishop of
that island had been a monk in the Holy City, though not
at St. Sabas. Whether or not he was the inventor of the
Canon, his are the earliest Canons that survive : and a
number of them are still found in the Greek service-books.
The most celebrated is the so-called "Great Canon",
which runs to no less than 250 strophes and is still sung in
Lent — mercifully for the singers, only once in its entirety.
Part of it was translated by Neale ('Whence shall my tears
begin?'). He wrote *Triodia* and *Idiomela* as well : and Neale's
translations include two sets of *Stichera* — for Palm Sunday
and Maundy Thursday. In publishing his well-known
Lenten hymn 'Christian, dost thou see them ? ', Neale
described it as translated "from a Stichera of St. Andrew
of Crete" : but no Greek original has been found.

At St. Sabas the two greatest names — the greatest in
later Greek hymnody — are those of St. Cosmas (d. *c.* 760)

and St. John of Damascus (d. before 754).[70] To both (along with others) is given the title of "the Melodist" — a term which appears to include the musician's art as well as the poet's. To John is attributed the arrangement of the Octoechus according to the Eight Modes. The two saints were connected by close personal ties. Cosmas was the adopted son of John's father: and the two lads were educated together under the care of another Cosmas, who was a hymn-writer too and in company with whom they later joined the Laura of St. Sabas together. Cosmas became Bishop of Maïuma in 743: but John had his head-quarters at Jerusalem till the end of his life. Neale describes him as "the last but one of the Fathers of the Greek Church and the greatest of her poets". The latter honour would in fact seem rather to belong to Romanus: but when Neale wrote he was undiscovered. John was the author of an elaborate theological treatise called *The Fountain of Knowledge*, and also wrote three celebrated *Orations* defending the cause of the icons against their opponents. It is, however, in virtue of his gift of wedding clear-cut dogma to the poetic art that he has exercised his greatest influence on posterity. In this he was the superior of Cosmas, in whom the theologian for the most part dominated the poet. Cosmas's chief work was a number of Canons for the Festivals: but these pale before the grand series of similar compositions that came from John's pen and represent the high-water-mark of his achievement. They are six in number and celebrate the festivals of Christmas, the Theophany, Pentecost, Easter, St. Thomas's (i.e. Low) Sunday and the Ascension. The first of these are in Iambic metre: the others are in the usual "rhythmical" form. In not a few of the Festival Canons "the Odes of the several Canons by St. Cosmas and St. John of Damascus are interwoven, brotherlike, ·with one another". Besides his Odes and Canons John wrote numerous *Idiomela* as well.

In his translations from the Greek hymns Neale properly gave special attention to the works of John and Cosmas. The former's masterpiece — the so-called "Golden Canon" or "King of Canons" for Easter — he has rendered *in extenso*. The first of its eight Odes provides one of the most joyous and popular of our Easter hymns : '['Tis] the Day of Resurrection' *132 †137. The last Ode of the same Canon appears in E.H. : 'Thou hallowed chosen morn of praise' †138. The four Odes translated from the Canon for St. Thomas's Sunday include another famous Easter hymn (Ode 1) : 'Come, ye faithful, raise the strain' *133 †131. The *Idiomela* for All Saints, 'Those eternal bowers', appeared in the 1904 edition of Hymns A. and M. (622). A *Stichera* beginning 'Take thy last kiss' is an exquisite threnody on the departed soul (taken from the Burial Office in the *Euchologion*), but is rather a sacred lyric than a hymn in our sense of the word. The *Euchologion* also provides the original of Mr. Athelstan Riley's 'What sweet of life endureth' †360 — from the Burial Office for Priests. Neale further translated the eight Odes of the Canon for Christmas Day by St. Cosmas : but these have not come into use as hymns. A cento, however, from the same writer's Canon for the Transfiguration provides the hymn 'In days of old on Sinai' *460.

At Constantinople an elder contemporary of Cosmas and John — like them at once poet and defender of the icons — was Germanus (634–734), Patriarch of Constantinople and author of (among other things) the original of the now familiar Christmas carol, 'A great and mighty wonder' †19. But the fame of the imperial city as a home of hymn-writers is centred in the great monastery of the Studium and belongs to a later stage in the Iconoclastic controversy. Its sternly ascetic Abbot, St. Theodore (*c.* 759–826), was a foremost champion of the icons, in defence of which he found a more than dubious ally in the cruel and unscrupulous Empress Irene. He wrote an exultant Canon sung on "Orthodoxy Sunday" (the 1st Sunday in Lent) celebrating the victory of their cause. This has been translated by Neale ('A song, a song of gladness'), as also another Canon (for Sexagesima) on the Last Judgment — described by him as "the finest Judgment Hymn of the Church till the *Dies Irae*". More famous still was St. Theophanes (*c*. 800–850), who is considered by Neale to "hold the third place among Greek hymn-writers". Neale translated a *Stichera* and *Idiomela* of his : but neither is suitable for use as an English hymn. Two other hymn-writers, one certainly, the other probably, to be connected with the Studium, remain to be mentioned. The first is St. Theoctistus (*c*. 890), author of the "Suppliant Canon", of which a portion has been translated by Neale as the beautiful hymn 'Jesu ! Name all names above' *775 †418, and also of the original of the Lent hymn, 'Sweet Saviour, in Thy pitying grace' *490. The second is St. Anatolius, who wrote 'Fierce was the wild billow' †388, and the *Stichera* for St. Stephen's Day, 'The Lord and King of all things' †32. The Greek original from which Neale made 'The day is past and over' *21 †276 is ascribed by him to St. Anatolius (whom incidentally he confused with a saint of the same name who lived some centuries earlier) : but it is actually a metrical portion of the Late Evening Service of the Orthodox Church.[71]

To the "Sabaites" and "Studites" may be added a third group of monastic hymn-writers of the same school of hymnody. These lived in the South of Italy and Sicily, where many opponents of Iconoclasm had taken refuge from persecution. To this group belongs Joseph the Hymnographer (*c*. 810–883), though he left his native Sicily as a young man and passed his life in Constantinople and elsewhere. He is wrongly called "Joseph of the Studium" by Neale, who confused him with another Joseph (of Thessalonica), who lived at the Studium and also wrote hymns.[72] He is the most prolific of the Greek hymnographers : Pitra says that he wrote more than a thousand. Neale had a poor opinion of his powers, accusing him of tawdiness and verbiage ; though he contrived to base on centos from Joseph's Canons two of the best of his own hymns : 'Stars of the morning' *423 †245 and 'Let our choirs new anthems raise' *441 †187. On the other hand, Joseph's 'alphabetic' Canon on the Ascension has been ranked as "probably the finest hymn extant" on that theme.[73]. It was translated by Neale, who reproduced the alphabetic acrostic. Two other of Neale's hymns, 'O happy band of pilgrims' and 'Safe home, safe home in port,' were described by him in the first edition of his *Hymns of the Eastern Church* as "after Joseph of the Studium" : but in the second edition he admitted that "they contain so little from the Greek that they ought not to have been included" as translations. The same admission is made in regard to 'Art thou weary ? '.[74]

Another well-known hymn-writer of this school was St. Methodius (d. 836) — not to be confused with his much earlier namesake, the author of the *Banquet of the Virgins*. The art of writing Greek hymns persisted in Italy long after it had almost died out elsewhere. A colony of Greek monks at Grottaferrata, near Tusculum, carried it on into the twelfth century.[75] A further hymn-writer, who belonged to none of the groups mentioned above, is Metrophanes, Bishop of Smyrna (d. *c*. 910), author of eight Canons to the Holy Trinity. From one of these Neale extracted the cento 'O Unity of threefold Light' †163.

Mention should be made in conclusion of a number of hymns in *E.H.* taken from the Greek service-books, of which it is impossible to assign the author or even with any certainty the date. They are as follows : 'Behold, the Bridegroom cometh' (†3=*641), from the Ferial Midnight Office at the beginning of the *Horologion* ; 'O King, enthroned on high' †454, from the *Pentecostarion* ; 'Thou, Lord, hast power to heal' †349, from the Office of

Anointing; and two Litanies — the Litany of the Deacon, 'GOD of all grace' †652 and the "Great Collect", 'LORD, to our humble prayers attend' †650.

The main defect of Greek hymnody is a "defect of its quality". The weakness of most modern hymns is a tendency to be unduly subjective, to concentrate on the moods and needs of the human ego rather than on the splendour and beauty of GOD and His revelation in Christ. This weakness the Greek hymns entirely avoid.

The most remarkable characteristic of Greek hymnody (it has been said [76]) is its objectiveness, with which is connected its faculty of sustained praise . . . This habit of thought has, however, its disadvantages. By its discouragement of the development of human emotion, aspiration and benefit the range of subjects and reflection is narrowed : and in the later poets the repetition of the same types, epithets and metaphors issues in sameness, conventional diction and fossil thought. It is impossible to avoid the conviction that the great bulk of Greek hymns would have had a richer value if it had sought for inspiration in the deep spiritual analysis of St. Paul, or the interpretation of the changing moods of the soul which are of such preciousness in the Psalms.

None the less the fundamental "quality" remains : and these dogmatic, essentially liturgical and profoundly "Catholic" hymns nobly help in filling a void that is only too conspicuous in most of our hymn-books.

CHAPTER III

LATIN HYMNODY

THE beginnings of Latin hymnody are considerably later than those of Greek. During the first two and a half Christian centuries Greek, not Latin, was the liturgical language in Rome and Italy; while in Gaul and Africa there is no trace of hymnody before Constantine I. It was not until the fourth century was well on its way that it began to develop, and then apparently as a deliberate borrowing of Eastern usage. The earliest experiments in Latin hymn-writing are associated with the name of St. Hilary (d. 368), of whom the Spanish liturgist, St. Isidore of Seville, tells us (*c.* 633) that he was "the first who flourished in composing hymns in verse".[77] An unflinching opponent of Arianism (he earned the title of *Malleus Arianorum*), he was exiled to Phrygia by the Emperor Constantius in 356. For six years he remained in a region where hymns were in common use : and it was presumably in imitation of what he found there that he wrote the earliest Latin hymns of which there is record. In a letter attributed to him [78] (which, however, is now generally regarded as spurious) he informs his daughter, Abra, that he is sending her two hymns of his own composition, for morning and evening. St. Jerome, too, tells of a *liber hymnorum* composed by Hilary.[79] Some twenty years later (as we have already mentioned in passing) the custom of singing hymns in the churches was definitely initiated in the West (386). St. Augustine tells the story, in connection with his own delight in these hymns :

What tears did I shed over the hymns and canticles when the sweet sound of the music of Thy Church thrilled the soul ! . . .

47

The Church of Milan had but recently begun to practise this kind of consolation and exhortation, to the great delight of the brethren, who sang together with heart and voice. It was about a year from the time when Justina, mother of the boy Emperor Valentinian, entered upon her persecution of Thy holy man Ambrose, because he resisted the heresy into which she had been seduced by the Arians. The people of GOD were keeping ward in the church, ready to die with their bishop. Then it was that the custom arose of singing hymns and psalms, after the usage of the Eastern provinces, to save the people from being utterly worn by their long and sorrowful vigils. From that day to this it has been retained : and many, I might say all, Thy flocks throughout the rest of the world now follow our example.[80]

In certain quarters, however, a prejudice against hymns in worship seems to have lingered — a prejudice which we may connect with the growing authority of the Bible as against the Tradition that preceded it. St. Hilary found that in his time the Gauls disliked hymns.[81] In Spain as late as 561 the Council of Braga decreed that "outside of the psalms . . . of the Old and New Testament no poetical composition shall be sung in church" (canon 12). On the other hand, the Council of Agde (in Gaul) ordered in 506 the daily singing of hymns both morning and evening (c. 30) : while in 567 the Council of Tours permitted the use not only of "Ambrosian hymns" but of others as well, "on condition that the names of the authors are inscribed at the top" (c. 23). Even in Spain the prejudice against hymns finally died out : for in 633 the 6th Council of Toledo decreed : "Let none of you henceforth object to hymns composed in praise of GOD : but let Gaul and Spain celebrate them alike. They are to be excommunicated who dare to reject hymns" (c. 13).[82]

The Latin hymnody of the West was to assume a very definite form of its own. But this form was not discovered quite immediately. To the earliest period, the period of experiment, belongs the greatest of all Latin non-Scriptural hymns, the *Te Deum laudamus*. The date and author-

ship of this were long in dispute : for the story which tells
that it was improvized by St. Ambrose and St. Augustine
when the former baptized the latter is, of course, a mere
legend. But it is now generally held to have been written
by Niceta, missionary Bishop of Remesiana, in Dacia, at
the end of the fourth century; though some recent
scholars allege reasons for believing that the first part of it
is of considerably earlier date.[83] The earliest testimony to
its liturgical use is in the Rule of St. Benedict in the first
half of the sixth century.

'The hymn in its original form concludes with the words
"in glory everlasting"; the subsequent verses being suf-
frages in the form of versicle and response that came to be
appended to it. It is written in prose: but its three
"strophes" are clearly marked and have a very definite
structure, as will be seen from the following setting-out of
it in the original Latin, based on Dr. Burn :

Te Deum laudamus, te Dominum confitemur,
Te aeternum Patrem omnis terra veneratur.
Tibi omnes angeli, tibi coeli et universae potestates,
Tibi Cherubin et Seraphin incessabili voce proclamant :
    Sanctus, Sanctus, Sanctus Dominus Deus Sabaoth,
    Pleni sunt coeli et terra majestatis gloriae tuae.

Te gloriosus apostolorum chorus,
Te prophetarum laudabilis numerus,
Te martyrum candidatus laudat exercitus.
Te per orbem terrarum sancta confitetur ecclesia :
    Patrem immensae majestatis,
    Venerandum tuum verum et unigenitum Filium,
    Sanctum quoque Paraclitum Spiritum.

Tu rex gloriae, Christe, tu Patris sempiternus es Filius,
Tu ad liberandum suscepturus hominem non horruisti Virginis uterum,
Tu, devicto mortis aculeo, aperuisti credentibus regna coelorum,
Tu, ad dexteram Dei sedens in gloria Patris, judex crederis esse
    venturus.
    Te ergo quaesumus tuis famulis subveni,
    Quos pretioso sanguine redemisti ;
    Aeterna fac cum sanctis tuis gloria munerari.

The *Te Deum* is a masterpiece that had no successor. In the hymns of St. Hilary we have a different sort of experiment, not masterly at all but equally unprolific. It was formerly the custom to attribute to Hilary some seven or eight hymns that have survived, including the Lenten Office Hymn *Jesu, quadragenariae* : but it is now agreed that none of these can be reckoned as his. In 1884, however, a MS. was discovered at Arezzo, containing Hilary's treatise *De mysteriis* followed by three hymns with the heading *Incipiunt hymni ejusdem* — "here begin hymns by the same author". All three are more or less incomplete : but it is now commonly agreed that all are genuinely from Hilary's hand.[84] The first two are constructed on an alphabetic acrostic — one among other signs of Eastern influence. The third is in the metre known as Trochaic tetrameter — the rhythm to which the marching-songs of the Roman legionaries were set ; and both in form and thought bears a curious resemblance to the great *Pange lingua* in that metre by Venantius Fortunatus, who was Hilary's successor some 200 years later as Bishop of Poitiers and wrote his biography. The same metre — but in stanzas of two lines instead of three — is also employed in a very ancient hymn, *Hymnum dicat turba fratrum*, which is described as Hilary's in the seventh-century Irish MS. called the *Antiphonary of Bangor*. Here there is more dispute as to Hilary's authorship than in the case of the Arezzo hymns : but a strong body of opinion pronounces in its favour.[85] None of these hymns, however, was destined to pass into general use in the West. They were not really of the stuff of which popular songs are composed ; but were rather (as Dr. Frere says) "the work of a pioneer who has not found the way along which progress is ultimately to be made".[86]

Very different is the case of St. Ambrose (340–397), who has been described as "the main founder of the original, simple, dignified, objective school of popular Latin hymnody which for so many ages prevailed over the Roman Empire and is still in use in the Divine Offices all over Europe".[87] It was to Ambrose, along with the great monastic leaders (Benedict, Caesarius) of a rather later period, that the vanquishing of the Western prejudice against hymns as non-Scriptural was due. His personal prestige was enormous. He was a man of vast energy and dauntless courage — it will be remembered how he refused communion to the great Emperor Theodosius until he had done penance for the massacre of thousands of innocent persons at Thessalonica. Of noble birth and eminent at once as leader of men, as administrator and as theologian (he ranks as one of the four "Western Fathers"), Ambrose raised his see to a position of such authority that it has been said by Duchesne that in his time and that of his immediate successors "the Western episcopate acknowledged a double hegemony : that of the Pope and that of the Bishop of Milan".[88] It is thus not surprising that his hymns at once achieved so great a vogue that the Arians accused him of having "bewitched the people".[89] Their form was austerely simple and was couched in the metre called Iambic dimeter — whence later hymns framed in similar fashion came to be called "Ambrosian".[90] The matter, too, corresponds to the form. As Archbishop Trench has said :

The passion is there, but it is latent and represt. . . . [There is] no softness, perhaps little tenderness ; but . . . a rock-like firmness, the old Roman Stoicism transmuted into that nobler Christian courage which encountered and at length overcame the world.[91]

Of the numerous hymns formerly attributed to St. Ambrose [92] the authenticity of three is beyond possibility of cavil : for they are quoted textually by his contemporary and friend, St. Augustine. These are : a morning hymn, *Aeterne rerum conditor*; [93] an evening hymn, *Deus creator omnium*,[94] 'Creator of the earth and sky' †49 ; and a hymn

for the third hour, *Jam surgit hora tertia*.⁹⁵ In regard to a
fourth Augustine's attestation is doubtful : but we have
early and wide evidence from other sources. This is
Intende qui regis Israel,⁹⁶ which, with v. i omitted, figures
as the great Christmas hymn, *Veni redemptor gentium*, 'Come,
Thou Redeemer of the earth' †14=**19=*55. To these
four may be added two others which also have very early
attestation, viz. another morning hymn, *Splendor paternae
gloriae*,⁹⁷ 'O splendour of GOD's glory bright' †52=*2
**2, and a hymn for Epiphany, *Inluminans altissimus*.⁹⁸

A second group of eight hymns may also be assigned
with some confidence to St. Ambrose, despite the lack of
such early attestation as is forthcoming in the case of the
first group. Both groups equally form part of the traditional collection of hymns in use at Milan ; the hymns of
the second group, like those of the first, are written in
Iambic dimeter and consist of eight verses of four lines
each ; while they exhibit many resemblances in thought
and expression to St. Ambrose's prose writings. Of these
eight hymns one is for Easter, six are for saints' days, while
the eighth, *Aeterna Christi munera*,⁹⁹ 'The eternal gifts of
Christ the King', supplies the two hymns bearing that
title found in most Western Breviaries (though, rather
strangely, not in that of Sarum) ; one selection of lines
providing the hymn for Apostles, **81, *430, †175, and
another that for Martyrs, **87=*444.

Concerning a third group of hymns — four in number
— popularly attributed to St. Ambrose there is more
doubt. All are in current use both in the Breviary and in
our English hymn-books. They are : (1), (2), (3) the well-
known hymns for Terce, Sext and None, *9–11 **4–6,
†255, 261–2, and (4) the hymn for Virgins, *Jesu corona
Virginum*, 'Jesu, the Virgins' crown' *455, †192, **95.¹⁰⁰
They form part of the Milanese tradition and resemble
the authentic hymns of Ambrose in metre and style ; but
besides the difference in the number of verses (three or

four instead of eight) there are external reasons that militate against our regarding them as his.

Such questions in any case are of secondary importance. The essential facts stand firm, that not only do we owe to St. Ambrose the recognition of hymns as an integral part of the public worship of the Western Church, but also that it was he who laid down the lines on which Latin hymnody was mainly to develop in the centuries succeeding.

Composed (says the accomplished historian of Christian Latin poetry, Mr. F. J. E. Raby) with the practical aim of expounding the doctrines of the Catholic faith in a manner sufficiently simple to capture the imagination of the unlearned, the hymns of Ambrose possess at the same time the admirable qualities of dignity, directness and evangelical fervour. . . . [They] reflect the mind of the great teacher of the Latin Church.[101]

Some 100 hymns survive of the so-called "Ambrosian" kind — the work of Ambrose himself and of his imitators during the next 200 years. These hymns represent the staple type of the Latin Office Hymns; and were to be distributed broad and wide among the Breviaries of every part of Western Christendom. "St. Ambrose," says M. Gastoué, "fixes henceforth a literary and musical form of which the rhythm and the melodies are easily remembered : the Ambrosian hymn is musically a true type of the *chanson populaire*." [102] However little like it they may seem to our modern ears, these early hymns were in fact genuine folk-songs, and continued to be so as long as Latin remained a living language. It was only later that they became perforce a "poetry of the church and cloister" : [103] and even then their metrical and verse structure was to perpetuate itself in the vernacular hymnody of many lands. What else is the "Long Measure" in which so many of our hymns are written than the "Ambrosian hymn" in an English guise ?

The typical form of these hymns, then, is a series of verses of four lines each, written in Iambic dimeter. The metres of classical prosody were now for the most part abandoned. To some extent, as Archbishop Trench suggests, this may have been because of their association with Paganism and its preoccupation with the merely finite and temporal.[104] But the principal reason, no doubt, lay in the general breakdown, in the decay of the old classical culture, of the distinctions in the quantity of vowels and of the metrical structures based upon them. These structures were even more precarious in Latin than in Greek. The classical metres were not indigenous in Italy, but had been introduced as a copying of Greek models. Their scansion always involved an element of elaboration and artificiality : and, as the domination of the classical tradition loosened amid the decay of the old Roman polity, a simpler and more natural type of prosody (which no doubt had existed all along in the songs of the people) began to assert itself — a prosody based not on quantity but on accent.[105] In this connection it must be remembered that the hymns of the Church were not written for the literary delectation of the cultured few, but to meet the devotional needs of the people. Thus it was natural that these hymns should conform more and more to the new type of accentual versification : and the triumph of this was assisted by the ease with which its simple and obvious metrical structures could be made to serve the purposes of congregational singing. Along with this substitution of accent for quantity went another change — the introduction of rhyme. This is not yet present in the authentic hymns of Ambrose : but it is found in hymns of a slightly later date. "It was," says Archbishop Trench, "the well-nigh instinctive result of the craving after periodic recurrence, proportion, limitation, the desire to mark and make distinctly noticeable to the ear those limits and restraints which the verse, for its own ultimate good, imposes upon itself."[106]

In a classical metre like the hexameter this object had been secured by the fixed dactyl and spondee at the end of a line : in the accentuated verse the same purpose of marking the close was achieved by the use of rhyme. "Indeed," as Dr. Guest pointed out long ago, "no people have ever adopted an accentual rhythm without also adopting rhyme." [107] A further recommendation of rhyme, especially in a day when books were scarce and costly, was the assistance that it lent to memory.

The example of Ambrose determined not only the form of Latin liturgical hymnody but its spirit as well. It is a spirit grave, severe, and giving little scope for the poetic imagination to soar. Alike to the student of pure letters and to the connoisseur in religious emotions, these ancient hymns of the Church will appear as somewhat of a valley of dry bones. Their rugged and often pedestrian diction is wedded to an uncompromising practical morality and to an austerely objective concentration on the dogmas and mysteries of the Faith. "These solemn old hymns," says Dr. Bigg, "are strong because they are not the outpouring of individual emotion but an attempt to realize the majesty of GOD." [108] They represent the reaction of ascetic Christianity from the license and frivolity of Paganism, the "purging out of the old leaven" that had to precede the return of a now sanctified gaiety to the world in the joyous carollings of the Franciscan revival.[109] Their analogues in the world of art are the stern and massive outlines of Romanesque architecture and the stiff, grim, almost intimidating mosaics that stare at the beholder from the apses and friezes of the churches of Ravenna. In poetry and art alike we are conscious of a failure of the old technique : but this is not the whole secret of the change — there is an element of deliberate choice as well. The essential quality of both is *hieratic* : they breathe the spirit of the great and austere pontiffs and abbots who were rebuilding the old *imperium* of Rome into a new shape and so laying the foundations of the mediaeval Church.

This does not mean that the Christian poetry of the age between Ambrose and Gregory the Great was incapable of clothing itself in a more genial and imaginative guise. Indeed the most famous writers of hymns in order of time after Ambrose was a poet of very different calibre. But Prudentius was hardly in intention a hymn-writer at all. His poems were to contribute considerably to the hymnaries of the Western Church, but only after undergoing a process of selection and abbreviation. Rather, he was a Christian lyrist of the same kind as George Herbert and John Keble. His purpose is not to provide a vehicle of liturgical devotion, but to voice the sentiments evoked in a pious and meditative soul by a contemplation of the mysteries and practices of the Faith and the achievements of its heroes. In their original form his poems are too long to be suitable for use as hymns. They are also framed too closely on the model of the classical tradition, the metres of which they employ in considerable variety; though even here we see the vanquishing of quantity by accent in frequent violations of correct usage such as e.g. *delībutus* and *margāritum*. Within his own rather restricted limits, Prudentius is a genuine poet, with real qualities of grace and tenderness mingled with a kind of "fairy-tale" romanticism. Dr. T. R. Glover even goes further and describes him as "the first really great Christian poet"; and adds: "The more one studies his contemporaries, the more one admires him. Spiritually and intellectually he far outstrips the heathen poets, and in poetic insight, grace and mastery of his materials he is far above the Christians." [110] But for this very reason he lies outside the main current of early Western hymnody.

What little information we have concerning Prudentius is derived from his own writings. Born *c.* 348, he was a native of northern Spain, and after practising at the Bar entered the civil service, in which he rose to a position of some importance. In his 57th year he retired and devoted himself henceforth to using in the service of Christ the poetic faculty with which he was endowed. He himself did not overrate this. In the preface to the *Peristephanon* he writes as follows (I use Dr. Glover's beautiful translation with his permission) :

> Yet has Christ a need of me,
> Though but a moment's space I have my station ;
> Earthen vessel though I be
> I pass into the Palace of Salvation.
>
> Be the service ne'er so slight,
> GOD owns it. Then, whatever Time is bringing,
> This shall still be my delight
> That Christ has had the tribute of my singing.[111]

Not long after his retirement he went to Rome to present some petition to the Emperor Honorius. The journey he turned into a pilgrimage, visiting every famous shrine on the way and in Rome itself. The fruit of his experiences was the collection of 14 poems called *Peristephanon* or 'Martyr-Garlands'. These display a true Spaniard's love of the saints and of the gory details of their martyrdoms, besides throwing much light on the devotional practices of the age. Another collection of 12 poems is called *Cathemerinon*, 'The Christian's Day,' and deals with the duties and observances of the devout life. It is from these books that the hymns of Prudentius are derived which have passed into liturgical use. His other poems are didactic theological treatises, written in passable hexameters, and need not concern us here.

In the curtailed form in which they appear in the Latin Breviaries a number of Prudentius's poems have been translated into English and are widely used. The finest of all, perhaps, is the grand, rolling Christmas hymn in Hilary's Trochaic tetrameter, *Corde natus*,[112] 'Of the Father's love begotten' *56 **146=†613. The refrain

Saeculorum saeculis, 'Evermore and evermore,' is not part of the original, but was added when it was adapted for liturgical use. Other familiar hymns of his are *O sola magna urbium*, 'Earth hath many a noble city' *76=†40, and the hymn for Holy Innocents, *Salvete flores martyrum*,[113] 'Sweet flow'rets of the martyr band' *68=†34. The Latin versions of these are both centos from no. 12 in the *Cathemerinon*, beginning *Quicunque Christum quaeritis*. Another well-known hymn from Prudentius is the Sarum Compline hymn for Passiontide, *Cultor Dei memento*,[114] 'Servant of GOD, remember' †104 **45. This is part of no. 6 of the *Cathemerinon*, of which another cento, *Ades Pater supreme*, is the original of 'Father, most high, be with us' *493 (with its lovely tune from the German collection of 1533 called *Melodiae Prudentianae*). In addition, *E.H.* provides translations of the three Breviary Office hymns for use at Lauds, *Ales diei nuntius*,[115] 'The winged herald of the day' †53; *Nox et tenebrae et nubila*,[116] 'Ye clouds and darkness, hosts of night' †54; *Lux ecce surgit aurea*,[117] 'Lo! golden light rekindles day' †55; together with a hymn for Martyrs, *Beate Martyr, prospera*, 'Blest Martyr, let thy triumph-day' †185, and the more elaborate and philosophical hymn for the departed, *Deus ignee fons animarum*,[118] 'Father of spirits, Whose Divine control' †352. This last was described by Archbishop Trench as "the grandest of them all".

Two contemporaries of Prudentius have contributed to our hymn-books. One is St. Paulinus of Nola (353–431), the gentle and humble patrician of Gaul who, to the distress of his old teacher Ausonius, forsook the world and retired to Spain, thence to remove later to Nola in Campania, where he ended his days as parish priest of the shrine of Nola's saintly bishop Felix. Paulinus was devoted to Felix's memory and wrote every year a poem to help pilgrims to honour it. An excerpt from one of these poems beginning *Ecce dies nobis* is the original of 'Another year completed' †195. The other poet is [Caelius] Sedulius, who wrote about the middle of the fifth century. We know little about him : but it would appear that he remained a pagan until his later years and was subsequently ordained priest. Among other poems he wrote a long one in Iambic dimeter on the life of Christ called *Paean alphabeticum de Christo* and beginning *A solis ortus cardine*.[119] This is written in the form of an alphabetic acrostic : e.g. the 2nd verse begins *Beata auctor saeculi*, the third *Clausae puellae viscera*, and so on. A cento of this is the original of the Christmas Office hymn, 'From east to west, from shore to shore' *483 †18 **20 : but the translation does not pre-serve the alphabetic scheme. Another cento from the same poem (beginning with v. 8) is the Epiphany Office Hymn, *Hostis Herodis impie*, 'How vain the cruel Herod's fear' *75 **29=†38. Both of these were in general use in the Western Breviaries.

Passing from the fifth to the beginning of the sixth century we may notice in passing Ennodius, Bishop of Pavia (473–521). A number of what Mr. Walpole calls his "laboured and unpoetical" hymns [120] have survived : but none is the original of any English hymn. Of more interest is his contemporary Elpis, said to have been the wife of the famous philosopher Boethius.[121] She is re-putedly the author of the Office Hymn for St. Peter and St. Paul, *Aurea luce et decore roseo*, 'With golden splendour and with radiant hues of morn' †226, which, if this doubt-ful attribution be correct, has the distinction of being the only Office Hymn written by a woman. Both these names, however, pale into insignificance beside that of another hymn-writer of the second half of the same century, Venantius Fortunatus, author of several of the most famous among Latin hymns.

Fortunatus was born *c.* 530 at Treviso in northern Italy. While a student at Ravenna he was threatened with blindness : but his sight was restored (as he believed) through the application of oil taken from the lamp that burned before the altar of St. Martin of Tours in a Ravennese church. This led him to go on pilgrimage to the saint's shrine at Tours : and in Gaul he remained for the rest of his days — "a kind of halcyon on the dangerous Frankish seas", to borrow Miss Helen Waddell's charming description of him.[122] At first he journeyed here and there in leisurely fashion, visiting the houses of the great, whose hospitality he repaid by writing graceful trifles in verse, and following for a time the royal train of King Sigebert of Austrasia. But in 567 he met the fascinating ascetic, Rhadegunda, Clotaire of Neustria's "reluctant queen", who had retired to Poitiers and founded a monastery there. Captivated by her spiritual charm he settled down by her side and later became a priest. He was finally made Bishop of Poitiers, *c.* 598, and died a few years later.

The poetical work of Fortunatus varies widely both in quality and in range. Trench speaks of him as "one of the last who, amid the advancing tide of barbarism, retained anything of the old classical culture".[123] But his is a decadent classicism — it could hardly be otherwise : indeed Mr. Raby prefers to regard him "not as the last of the Roman but as the first of the mediaeval poets".[124] In his troubadour days, as we have said, he composed a good deal of light verse : but later he consecrated his muse to religious subjects, in treating which he rose, at his best, to heights of genuine inspiration, being sometimes rugged and grand, sometimes lilting and fanciful and gay. In the former manner his greatest achievement is the Passiontide Office Hymn at Vespers, *Vexilla Regis prodeunt*,[125] 'The Royal banners forward go' *96 †94 **44, written after the "Ambrosian" fashion in Iambic dimeter in verses of 4 lines. This famous hymn is said to have been composed on the occasion of the solemn reception of a relic of the True Cross which the Emperor Justin II had given to Rhadegunda for her convent of Sainte Croix at Poitiers

(Nov. 19, 569). Certainly its stately processional movement well befits such a solemnity; and explains too the
immense popularity which the hymn, wedded to its
superb plainsong melody, enjoyed at the time of the
Crusades. In Neale's translation (more or less altered) it
finds a place in most Church hymnals: but a far finer
version is that which appeared in Walter Blount's Roman
Catholic manual, *The [Compleat] Office of the Holy Week*
(1670 and 1687). A much altered form of this was
included in *The Office of the Blessed Virgin Mary* (1687),
from which it was adopted by *Church Hymns* (1903) and
the *Oxford Hymn Book*. But the original form is far superior
and, as it is very difficult of access, is here reprinted:

> Abroad the Regal Banners fly;
> Now shines the Crosses mystery:
> Upon it life did death endure,
> And yet by death did life procure.
> Who, wounded with a direful spear,
> Did, purposely to wash us clear
> From stain of sin, pour out a flood
> Of precious water, mixed blood.
> Fully accomplisht are the things,
> David, in faithful Meeter, sings:
> Where he to nations does attest,
> GOD on a tree his reign possest.
> O lovely and refulgent tree,
> Adorn'd with purpled majesty;
> Cull'd from a worthy stock, to bear
> Those limbs which sanctified were.
> Blest tree, whose happy branches bore
> The wealth, that did the World restore:
> The beam, that did that body weigh,
> Which rais'd up Hell's expected prey.
> Hail Cross, of hopes the most sublime,
> Now in this mourning Passion-time;
> Improve religious souls in grace;
> The sins of criminals efface.
> Blest Trinity, Salvation's spring;
> May every soul Thy praises sing:
> To those Thou grantest conquest by
> The holy Cross Rewards apply.   Amen.[126]

Another great hymn by Fortunatus, believed to have been written for the same occasion, is the Office Hymn at Mattins and Lauds in Passiontide, *Pange lingua gloriosi proelium certaminis*,[127] 'Sing, my tongue, the glorious battle.' This is written in Trochaic tetrameter, and must be distinguished from St. Thomas Aquinas's hymn with the same three opening words, which is clearly modelled on it. It was translated by Neale. His version, much altered, is used in *97 **43. (†95 is a mainly new translation, †96 Neale's original.) In using the hymn it is well to remember that v. 2 is based on a purely legendary story that the tree from which the Cross was made sprang from a seed of the Tree of Life in the Garden of Eden, and also that v. 3 in the words

> To the traitor's art opposing
> Art yet deeper than his own

suggests a mode of presenting the doctrine of the Atonement (sometimes irreverently nicknamed the "mousetrap" theory) which has been obsolete for centuries — a criticism that applies to v. 5 of *Vexilla Regis* as well. A third hymn by Fortunatus deals with the same subject of the Cross, *Crux benedicta nitet*.[128] It is " a beautiful weaving in of the image of the true Vine with the fact of the Crucifixion." Neale's version in a shortened and considerably rewritten form appears in **118, 'Lo! the blest Cross is displayed.'

In the last-named hymn, written in elegiacs (i.e. alternate hexameters and pentameters) and "full of that strange and novel beauty with which Christian mysticism was learning to adorn the measures borrowed from the ancient world", the other, more picturesque and luxuriant side of Fortunatus's talent is revealed, notably in the lines that have been thus translated :

Strong in thy fertile array, O Tree of sweetness and glory,
Bearing such new-found fruit 'mid the green leaves of thy boughs,

Stately thou rearest thy head by the streams of the clear-
  running waters,
Shedding from flower-deck'd boughs leaves for the healing
  of men.

But this side finds its fullest expression in the great Processional Proses, beginning *Salve festa dies*, which were
widely used in the Middle Ages all over Europe and in their
various English forms have won much popularity in the
last generation or so. They are taken from a long poem in
elegiacs on the Resurrection, beginning *Tempora florigero
rutilant distincta sereno.*[129] The complete poem paints a
glowing picture of the coming of spring, regarded as a
symbol of the New Life which came to the world with the
rising of Christ from the tomb and as the tribute of Nature
to her triumphant LORD. Though the subject of the poem
thus refers really to Easter, three separate centos are found
in the Sarum Processional — for Easter, Ascension and
Whitsunday respectively. The refrain of the first is by
Fortunatus himself, while those of the other two are
adapted to fit the festival they serve. The cento for Whitsunday (apart from the refrain) has no reference to the
coming of the Holy Spirit, though it presents a joyous
picture of the countryside in early summer. For this
reason, presumably, a very inferior substitute of much
later date was provided in the York Processional. *A.M.*
provides a translation of the three Sarum forms in clear-
cut heroic couplets by Dr. A. J. Mason, *650, 652, 653 ;
while *P.H.B.* supplies a version of the same three in the
elegiacs of the original by the present writer, **149, 151,
152. It may be noted that the plainsong melody proper to
all the *Salves* is one of exquisite and haunting beauty,
though some may find it a little deficient in the quality
of *joy*. *E.H.* gives the Sarum Proses for Easter and Ascension, †624, 628, the York one for Whitsuntide, †630.
These are written in the original metre by different translators, and are wedded to the well-known tune Dr.

Vaughan Williams composed for them. In addition to the three already mentioned the Sarum Processional provided *Salves* for Dedication, Corpus Christi, the Visitation, and the Name of Jesus : but these are of later date and very inferior, and have nothing to do with Fortunatus. *A.M.* and *E.H.* provide versions of that for Dedication, *747 †634, *P.H.B.* of those for Dedication and Corpus Christi, **155, 161 ; though the latter is rather a free treatment of selected parts of its very debased original than a translation in the strict sense.

Before leaving Fortunatus, we may add that there appears to be some reason for attributing to him the ancient hymn in honour of the Blessed Virgin, *Quem terra, pontus, aethera*,[130] 'The GOD Whom earth and sea and sky' *449 †214 **106.

One other name remains to be mentioned at this point — a name among the most illustrious in Christian history — that of Fortunatus' contemporary, Pope Gregory the Great (540–604). The services rendered by Gregory to the codification and reform of the Church's music are beyond dispute ; even if subsequent generations chose to regard him as wholly responsible for a work which in fact he only began and set upon the lines on which it was to run. It was only natural, therefore, that tradition should assign to this "most versatile of Popes" a place among the writers of those Office Hymns (both words and music) which in his time and after were rapidly winning an established place in Christian worship. His Benedictine editors credit him with eight hymns, including several which in their English guise are in common use to-day (viz. †50 ; the Sapphic †165=‡3 ; *87=†66 ; †68=*89 ; †51=**7=*38). But none of these attributions rests on any satisfactory evidence : though (as we shall see) it is by no means forbidden to believe that the great Pope included the writing of hymns among his other accomplishments (*see below*, p. 71).

Of the names that have been mentioned Prudentius is the only one that does not belong to Italy or Gaul — and he was a hymn-writer only, as it were, by accident. The prejudice against hymns, we have seen, lingered longer in Prudentius's native country of Spain than elsewhere. But, once having come into line, Spain seems to have elected to compensate for its late start by a special addiction to hymns and fertility in composing them. Its liturgy — called first 'Old Spanish', then 'Gothic', finally (after the Arab conquest) 'Mozarabic' — was specially rich in hymns : and the collection of these which it embodied bears a decided national character. The figure most prominently identified with this liturgy was St. Isidore of Seville, who "seems", says Dreves, "to have done for the Spanish liturgy what Gregory did for the Roman".[131] He was a younger contemporary of the famous Pope (d. 636) and was himself a writer of hymns. With the obsolescence of the Mozarabic Liturgy, however, the majority of its hymns were to pass out of use.

Less important in a general way than the Spanish, but to the English student of greater interest, is another distinctively national collection that came into existence about the same time near our own shores in the Celtic Church of Ireland. Though situated on the furthest outskirts of the Christendom of that time, the Church founded by Palladius and Patrick was to prove second to none in devotion and missionary ardour. From its earliest days it would appear to have been fertile in sacred song. The name of Patrick himself is associated with a celebrated song called *Lorica* or "Breastplate". It was not written in Latin but in Irish : but for convenience' sake something may be said about it here. Opinion is divided as to whether it is really his : but the majority of scholars see no reason why it should not be.[132] It is the best and probably the earliest of a number of similar "charm-hymns" which were a Christianized form of the old pagan runes intended

65

to ward off evil. An ancient Irish preface [133] to it describes its use :

It is a corslet of faith for the protection of body and soul. . . . Whosoever shall sing it every day with pious meditation on GOD, devils shall not stay before him . . . . It will be a safeguard against every poison and envy. It will be a defence to him against sudden death. It will be a corslet to his soul after dying.

The same preface thus describes the occasion of its composition :

Patrick chanted this when the ambushes were set against him by [King] Loegaire that he might not go to Tara to sow the faith, so that [he and his monks] seemed before the liers-in-wait to be wild deer.

It is becoming well-known in Mrs. Alexander's translation 'I bind unto myself to-day' *655 †212. (The opening words of the original really mean 'To-day I arise.') But a finer though less exact version, "preserving", says Dr. Todd, "the tone and spirit of the original", is that made by the Irish poet James Clarence Mangan, [134] the author of that terrible and unforgettable poem, *The Nameless One*. Its irregular metrical structure, however, makes it unsuitable for use as a hymn.

The earliest form of this *Lorica* is given in the eleventh-century MS. of the Irish *Liber Hymnorum* preserved at Trinity College, Dublin. But hymns are also to be found in a much older Irish MS. — the famous *Antiphonary of Bangor* [135] (not the Welsh Bangor, but the Irish Bennchar), which dates from the end of the seventh century and is the oldest hymnal MS. in existence. This includes 12 hymns, of which one is the hymn ascribed to St. Hilary, *Hymnum dicat turba fratrum*, already mentioned, and another, in praise of St. Patrick, is attributed to the saint's friend and fellow-worker, St. Sechnall. But by far the most interesting of all is the 8th hymn, *Sancti venite*, [136] which has become celebrated in Neale's translation, 'Draw nigh and take the

Body of the Lord' *313 †307. This is shown by its title to be an *Antiphona* or *Communio ad accedentes*, to be used "when the priests" (of whom there would be many in an Irish monastery) "make their communion". The legendary story of its origin is thus given in the thirteenth-century Irish MS. called the *Lebhar Breac*, which describes how Patrick and Sechnall had a quarrel that was ended by mutual explanations:

> So then they made peace: and while they were going round the cemetery they heard a choir of angels chanting at the offering in the church, and this is what they chanted, the hymn whose beginning is *Sancti venite, corpus Christi*, etc. Wherefore from that time forward this hymn is sung in Ireland when one goes to Christ's Body.[137]

In *S.P.* a mangled version of Neale's translation (‡268) is set to a singularly lovely old Irish melody appropriately christened 'St. Sechnall'.

Among the Irish saints the next most famous after Patrick, the great St. Columba, was also a sacred poet. His hymn, *Altus Prosator* (in reality rather a "cosmogonical and eschatological poem"), is an alphabetical composition of 24 stanzas and is to be found in the Irish *Liber Hymnorum*.[138] The significance of its ancient preface describing how it was written in return for a gift of "Hymns for the Week" sent by Gregory the Great will be considered in the next chapter. Had this gift anything to do with "the book of hymns for the week" written by the hand of Columba, concerning which his biographer, Adamnan, has a story to tell? Adamnan tells, too, how after the saint's death, "the mattins hymns being ended", his body was borne into the church.[139]

CHAPTER IV

LATIN HYMNODY (*continued*)

I

WE have examined the beginnings of Western hymnody and passed in review its leading exponents between the fourth and the seventh centuries. We have now to trace the process by which hymns were not only constituted an integral part of the Church's services but came to be arranged in an ordered sequence for use at different times and seasons. It should be understood that hymns for a long time had no place in the Eucharist. The sung portions of the Mass were confined to Scripture (mainly to the psalms) and to such quasi-Scriptural unmetrical texts as the *Sanctus* and (later) the *Gloria in excelsis*, with the Creed. It was in connection with the Hour-services, which by the end of the fourth century were well on the way to becoming a regular institution in the larger churches, that hymns established themselves as a normal element in Divine worship. The evolution of these services was greatly stimulated by the monastic movement that spread rapidly over Western Europe during the fifth century and found its patriarch and law-giver in St. Benedict in the sixth. It was then that the seven "Canonical Hours" assumed their permanent shape in the following sequence : (1) the night-service called *Nocturns* (later called *Mattins*), followed by *Lauds* at daybreak ; (2) *Prime* in the early morning ; (3), (4), (5) *Terce, Sext* and *None*, at 9, 12 and 3 respectively ; (6) the evening service called *Vespers* ; (7) *Compline*, before retiring to rest. Of all these services hymns formed a part : and the Rules of St.

Benedict (530) and of others gave explicit directions to this effect.

The tracing of the successive stages in the assignment of specific hymns among these various Offices is a complicated and technical question which it is impossible to deal with adequately within the limits of this book. Those who are interested in the subject are referred to Dr. Frere's lucid and detailed treatment of it in the Introduction to the *Historical Edition of Hymns A. and M.*[140] It must suffice to summarize briefly the conclusions there advanced.

The earliest cycle of hymns for the different Offices of the week was the creation of the monasteries and was well-known in the time of St. Benedict and of his fellow-legislators, St. Caesarius of Arles and St. Aurelian. Further, the learned German Jesuit, Father Blume,[141] has shown that this "primitive monastic" cycle is identical (so far as it goes) with that found in a group of five of the earliest existing hymnal MSS., written in the ninth century. In its earliest form it fell into two parts — one for Eastertide, the other for the rest of the year. We have here the beginning of that distinction between "Proper" and "Common" which was later to receive wide extension in regard to all parts of the services. The hymns of this cycle include all the five hymns appropriate to the scheme that appear in the two classes of the hymns of St. Ambrose which are indubitably his, viz. *Jam surgit, Hic est dies, Aeterne rerum, Splendor paternae, Deus Creator* (*see above*, p. 51). Here appears, too, the Compline hymn, *Christe qui lux es et dies*,[142] 'O Christ, Who art the Light and Day' *95 †81 **41, which thus belongs to the earliest stratum of Western hymnody. Apart from these the list includes no hymns that have become familiar in English guise. Later the cycle was extended to 36 hymns in all by the addition of a number of hymns for the seasons,[143] which include for Christmas St. Ambrose's *Intende qui regis Israel*=*Veni Redemptor gentium*; for Easter, *Ad cenam Agni providi*, 'The

Lamb's high banquet' *128 **54=†125, and *Aurora lucis rutilat*,[144] 'Light's glittering morn' *126 **53=†123; and (for the first time) a saint's day hymn, St. Ambrose's *Aeterna Christi munera* (for Martyrs).

This cycle, however, was comparatively short-lived. It was presumably brought to England by the Benedictine St. Augustine of Canterbury, and the three hymns that appear in the eighth century Canterbury Psalter in the British Museum — "the first English hymnal", as it has been called — are proved by internal evidence to belong to it. But by the ninth century a new cycle had come into existence, at first side by side with the old. For Blume goes on to show that besides the above-mentioned group of ninth-century MSS. containing the "primitive monastic cycle" there is a second, contemporary group, which provides a cycle that is entirely different. These MSS., unlike the others, are all of Irish or English origin — for which reason Dr. Frere christens the cycle contained in them the "Anglo-Irish cycle". Further, it is this new cycle which forms the nucleus and basis of the hymnal-scheme of all the subsequent Western Breviaries and of the Roman Breviary of the present day. It would appear, then, that by the end of the ninth century the "Anglo-Irish" cycle had won so complete a victory over its predecessor that the latter vanished entirely from the field.

The only features common to the two cycles are the undisputed hymns of St. Ambrose, the Compline *Christe qui lux es* and the two Easter hymns, *Ad cenam Agni* and *Aurora lucis*. In the new cycle there appear for the first time a second Compline hymn, *Te lucis ante terminum*,[145] 'Before the ending of the day' *15 †264 **9, and the current hymns for Terce, Sext and None,[146] *9–11 **4–6 †255, 261–2, with *Jam surgit* (Terce) from the earlier cycle as an "extra". There are also included the ferial hymns for the various days of the week at Vespers, Mattins and Lauds[147] (of which *E.H.* provides versions of the Vespers

70

and Lauds series, †49, 51, 58–62 ; 50 (M), 52–7), including
3 by Ambrose and 3 by Prudentius. In the section for
saints' days all the hymns included except one are found
in English versions in *E.H.*, viz. 180, 183, 175 (*430),
192 (*455), 182 (*756), 191.[148] The last two, written in
Asclepiads and Sapphics respectively, mark the first
appearance of hymns in the old classical metres instead of
the Ambrosian Iambic dimeter.

So far we seem to be on a fairly solid ground of facts.
But when we go on to seek the explanation of this sudden
and complete disappearance of a cycle consecrated by
some four centuries of use, we enter the region of speculation and surmise. The provenance of the MSS. in which
the new cycle is first found suggests that it had its origin
in the British Isles. Blume finds further support for this
theory in a statement made in an ancient Irish preface [149]
to St. Columba's hymn *Altus Prosator*, which represents
the hymn as written in return for a set of hymns "for every
night in the week" sent to the saint by Gregory the
Great. These hymns, it is suggested, are none other than
the hymns for Vespers that appear for the first time in the
"Anglo-Irish cycle" and may well have been, at least in
part, from the hand of Gregory himself. The suggestion is
ingenious and interesting ; though of course it falls very
far short of being proved. But we may admit that, if
Gregory really had a hand in the new cycle, this would be
an enormous recommendation of it and would greatly
help its victory over its predecessor — at first in our own
islands and then, when it was carried by Irish and English
missionaries to the Continent, all over the West and even
in Rome itself.

As a provision of "ferial" hymns for the week the new
cycle was practically complete from the beginning : and
here it received few additions. A Canterbury hymnal of
the later tenth century, which forms part of the so-called
"Bosworth Psalter" in the British Museum, adds four new

hymns — two as summer alternatives to the others at
Mattins and Lauds respectively, the Sapphic hymns,
Nocte surgentes and *Ecce jam noctis* ; [150] and two hymns for
Compline, *Jesu redemptor saeculi* and Prudentius's *Cultor
Dei* (*see above*, p. 58). To these the Sarum Use added two
further Compline hymns, *Jesu nostra redemptio* and *Salvator
mundi* : and the six were distributed among different
seasons. All six appear in *P.H.B.*, viz. 9 (ferial), 23 (Christmas), 41 (Lent), 45 (Passiontide), 58 (Easter), 62 (Ascension). The Mattins hymn appears, too, in *P.H.B.* as 'Let
hearts awaken' (3). *A.M.*, too, has all six Compline hymns,
but the Passiontide one follows the alternative cento of
Prudentius's original mentioned above (p. 58). *E.H.*
contains four of the six Compline hymns (264, 81, 104, 144)
and the Mattins *Nocte surgentes* (165).

It was to meet the requirements of the Church's year
that the original cycle was to undergo a wide and progressive expansion. Herein, in fact, lay the special *rationale*
of the liturgical hymn — "to define" (as Dom Cabrol
says) "the meaning of feasts or offices and in the concert
of Divine praise to strike the note of the liturgical muse"
— not (he adds) in any wise to serve as "a kind of Christian
Psalter", for "the Christian Psalter is the Psalter of
David".[151] The requirements in question were of two
kinds — those concerned with the ecclesiastical seasons
and those concerned with Saints' days. At first, with a few
exceptions, provision was made for *classes* of saints only.
Thus, apart from these exceptions, the earlier division was
into two sections — "Proper of Seasons" and "Common
of Saints", to use the later technical terms. In regard to
both of these the development was tolerably uniform all
over Western Europe. But later the small group of *individual* saints recognized at first swelled into a vast multitude, whose claim to separate recognition produced a third
division — "Proper of Saints." Here local considerations
largely held sway : and there is a wide range of variation.

It is obviously impossible to deal with all the hymns that appear under these various categories in the mediaeval hymnals of Europe. Our concern here is only with the English Uses ; and especially with those hymns that have won a vernacular currency in our modern English hymn-books. Even so we shall not inflict on the reader's patience what would be little more than a dry catalogue of hymns. Those who are sufficiently interested in the subject are referred to the lists in Appendix B at the end of the volume, where the development of the scheme of English Office Hymns is summarily set forth, so far as the "Common of Seasons", the "Proper of Seasons" and the "Common of Saints" are concerned, together with the provision made for the most important feasts of individual saints. The list is arranged in three parallel columns, containing (1) the hymns in the Anglo-Irish cycle, (2) the Office Hymns prescribed in the tenth-century "Canterbury Hymnal" mentioned above, (3) the Office Hymns in the Sarum Breviary. The few hymns found in the Primitive Monastic Cycle which survived into these later lists are indicated by the letters P.M.

An examination of these lists will show that most of the hymns in the Canterbury Hymnal were retained in the Sarum books, though a certain number dropped out : while, on the other hand, additions were made, most of them presumably hymns written since the earlier list was compiled. The most striking omission is the beautiful "farewell to Alleluia" — *Alleluia dulce carmen*, 'Alleluia, song of sweetness' *82 †63 **32 — which has won considerable favour with English congregations in Neale's version. The singing of this hymn formed part of a set of quaint and picturesque ceremonies. In the Church of Toul in north-east France the custom of "burying" Alleluia in a coffin with full funeral rites was observed as late as the fifteenth century. But in most places the ceremonies died out much earlier ; and the hymn disappeared with them.[152] In the Mozarabic rite a similar practice was connected with the singing of the hymn (also found in the English Anglo-Saxon hymnals) *Alleluia piis edite laudibus*,[153] 'Sing Alleluia forth in duteous praise' *296 — sung in this case not before Septuagesima but on the first Sunday in Lent. Here again the hymn died out with the ceremonies accompanying it.

A further development of the English Office Hymns was due to the emergence of new festivals in the Kalendar. Chief among these is Trinity Sunday, the observance of which began in England earlier than elsewhere (the Low Countries possibly excepted) — in the tenth or eleventh century. About the same time, too, it became customary to observe the festival of a church's Dedication. This gave room for the *Urbs beata Hierusalem*, 'Blessed city, heavenly Salem' *396 †169–70 **78 — that "rugged but fine old hymn", as Trench calls it, which is found in the oldest extant MSS. of the ninth century and is probably considerably older still.[154] In the thirteenth century began the observance of Corpus Christi (instituted by Pope Urban IV in 1264), which led to the inclusion of three hymns written by St. Thomas Aquinas, of which more will be said shortly. The Feast of the Transfiguration and that of the Most Sweet Name of Jesus were later still (XIVth or XVth century).

The same closing centuries of the Middle Ages also produced a vast crop of hymns in honour of individual saints. In England, it is true, the number of these was not large : but abroad (to quote Dr. Frere) "the long row of volumes of Dreves and Blume, *Analecta Hymnica Medii Aevi*, show what immense labour was spent on the Continent in providing second-rate festivals with third- or fourth-rate hymns".[155]

With such foreign developments we are not here concerned. But even confining ourselves, as we must, to the provision made in our own country to meet the more outstanding liturgical requirements, we are confronted with a fairly large corpus of hymns — one, too, that, as a result of the Catholic Revival, is copiously if not completely represented in our Church hymnals. The value of these ancient hymns in their English dress will be variously assessed, and largely according to the store that we set by the idea of historical continuity in the Church's life and worship. To many the majority of them will appear heavy and dry and remote from the needs of the modern world. To others their use, at least in moderation, will be valuable as a link with the *Ecclesia Anglicana* of an earlier day and also as supplying the objective and dogmatic element that most modern hymns lack. From the musical point of view, too, these hymns afford what many will regard as a welcome opportunity for introducing an element of plainsong into the services — and plainsong in its most attractive and easily digested form. Many of the plainsong hymn-tunes are of exquisite and haunting beauty : and to ears attuned to our latter-day musical idiom they may hope to make an appeal to which Victorian ears were mostly insensible. In this connection attention may be drawn to Mr. J. H. Arnold's admirable little treatise, *The Approach to Plainsong through the Office Hymn.*

In any case, in weighing the claims of these ancient hymns upon our attention and use, due regard must be paid to the fact that those familiar with them only through the medium of a translation can form but a very inadequate idea of their real quality. For the structure and genius of the Latin and English languages are entirely different. To begin with, Latin abounds in deep and broad vowel-sounds ; while in English (at least of the "cultivated" variety) the lighter, "thinner" vowels predominate. Again, Latin words are usually longer than their English equivalents, with the result that a translation lacks the rolling sonority of the original. It is this grand polysyllabic quality that makes Latin so incomparable as a liturgical language. No doubt our Book of Common Prayer has an immense literary beauty of its own : but the predominance of short words makes it a different sort of beauty from that of the Latin services. Compare the effect of the following clauses from the *Gloria in excelsis* in Latin and English respectively :

Laudamus te, benedicimus te, adoramus te, glorificamus te, gratias agimus tibi propter magnam gloriam tuam.

Here we have 15 words, of which only 4 are monosyllables.

We praise Thee, we bless Thee, we worship Thee, we glorify Thee, we give thanks to Thee for Thy great glory.

Here are 21 words, of which no less than 18 are monosyllables.

The same difficulty occurs in the case of hymns ; but with the additional disadvantage that, in order to reproduce the line- and verse-structure of the Latin, it is necessary to make up for the shortness of the English words by a continual "padding" of the sense. This is even allowing for the fact that in English the grammatical "persons" and "cases" are represented by pronouns and prepositions respectively and not by inflections — a characteristic which in itself increases the monosyllabic effect. Take e.g. verse 1 of one of the most famous Latin hymns, setting it side by side with the English translation :

Jesu dulcis memoria,	Jesu ! the very thought is sweet ;
Dans vera cordis gaudia :	In that dear name all heart-joys meet.
Sed super mel et omnia	But oh ! than honey sweeter far
Dulcis eius praesentia.	The glimpses of Thy presence are.

Here are 15 words in the Latin to 26 in the English, with 4 monosyllables in the former and 21 in the latter. Further, in line 1 'very' is a makeweight, in line 2 'in that dear Name' is a repetition, while in lines 3 and 4 'far' and 'the glimpses of' are additions which involve the total sacrifice of *et omnia*. Let it be added that all this is not intended to cast the slightest reflection on Neale's version. It merely serves to emphasize the obvious fact that the particular quality of the Latin original largely (however inevitably) evaporates in translation — and all the more when we add to the other handicaps the loss of the booming Latin vowels. *Experto crede !*

Nor is this all. If Latin is more imposing in effect, it is at the same time easier to manipulate. The order of words in an English sense is with rare exceptions the "natural" order of "subject, verb, object". But in Latin it may be largely varied at the will of the writer. It is this, incidentally, that helps to give Latin its epigrammatic, "lapidary" quality which is one among other reasons why such a composition as the *Lauda Sion* is virtually untranslatable. Again, in the case of the mediaeval Latin hymn-writers the sense of verbal "flow" is assisted by the less emphatic stress of the accentuation — a quality that has been inherited by the Romance languages derived from Latin. One of the greatest difficulties of the Englishman in learning to speak French well is to acquire the characteristic "evenness" of its accentuation. It has been reasonably argued that it was the desire to obviate still further a "jog-trot" effect that prompted the repeated assignment in plainsong of the "neums" or note-groups to the weak and not to the strong syllables. The result seems strange to our ears when these melodies are sung to those English translations which in this and other respects stretch them on a "Procrustean bed". A further consequence of this less marked accentuation is the license given to the mediaeval hymn-writer (and frequently used by him) to indulge in what modern prosody (like that of classical Latin) would describe as flagrant "false quantities". E.g. line 2 of the ancient Easter hymn, *Aurora lucis*, runs thus :

Coelum laudĭbus intonat.

which is as though an English poet were to scan 'radiance' as 'radīance'.

Such, then, are the largely insuperable difficulties in the way of him who would translate these old Latin hymns into tolerable English verse. They do not indeed make his task futile : for many hymns that have won great and well-deserved popularity are of this sort. But such hymns must be judged on their own literary merits, which are bound to be in great measure different from the merits of the originals. And if no decent version exist, it is better to forego the use of a hymn altogether, however ancient and venerable it may be in the language in which its author wrote it. Many of the translations in the mid-Victorian Anglo-Catholic hymnals do credit to the respect for antiquity of those who wrote and sang them. They say less for their literary taste.

II

Of the Office Hymns that we have been describing the vast majority are anonymous. Even the date of each is largely a matter of conjecture. It is obvious that any hymn must be at least as old as the date of the MS. in which it first makes its appearance. An early date seems to be indicated by the inclusion of a hymn in the traditional "Ambrosian" collection at Milan ; and also by the style of versification, if this is metrical rather than accentual. But further than this we cannot go. In regard to a small minority, however, it is possible to name the author. Of these authors some have been already spoken of — those who lived up to the end of the sixth century. We may now say something concerning those who lived subsequently to that date.

The earliest of these in order of time is an Englishman, the Venerable Bede (673–735). Besides the York Office hymn at Mattins for Ascension, *Hymnum canamus gloriae*, 'Sing we triumphant hymns of praise' † 146 **61, a number of other hymns by him survive, of which two are becoming familiar in English : the lilting hymn for Holy Innocents, *Hymnum canentes gloriae*, 'The hymn for conquering martyrs raise' †35, and a hymn written in honour of St. John the Baptist, *Praecursor altus luminis*, 'The great forerunner of the morn' *415=†225. Historian, biographer, exegetist, philosopher, mathematician, as well as sacred poet, Bede was the greatest scholar of his time in Europe — a living encyclopaedia of all the learning of his age. His whole life was passed in a monastery — first at Wearmouth and then at Jarrow. Yet he was in touch with all the events of his time ; and in this way was able to collect the materials of the work on which his fame chiefly rests — his great *Ecclesiastical History of the English Nation*. At the end of this he gives a list of his own works, which includes "A Book of Hymns in several sorts of metre or rhyme."

In the later part of the eighth century Western Europe passed from the darkness and brutality of the Merovingian period into the comparative sunlight of the so-called "Carolingian Renaissance", which found its centre in the court of the Emperor Karl the Great (or "Charlemagne") and its famous "palace school", with the great English scholar Alcuin at its head. Alcuin himself was a sacred poet : and the majority of his circle seem to have practised hymn-writing, though not apparently to any marked extent — perhaps (as Dreves suggests) owing to the fact that the Roman liturgy, which at this time was spreading rapidly throughout the West in place of the old local rites, had not yet admitted the use of hymns.[156] Even Charlemagne himself has been numbered among hymn-writers, by the attribution to him of *Veni Creator Spiritus* : but this is no longer taken seriously. Three poets, however, who at various times came within his orbit are worthy of mention.

The first is the Italian Paul the Deacon (?730–?799). He had been tutor to a Lombard princess, and after the fall of the Lombard monarchy in 774 entered the celebrated monastery of Monte Cassino. The total loss of his property led him to make appeal to Charlemagne, who as the price of granting his suit insisted on his bringing his poetic gifts to adorn his own court. Later he was allowed to return to Monte Cassino, and wrote his *History of the Lombards*. He is reputedly the author of the Sapphic hymn in honour of John the Baptist, *Ut queant laxis*, 'Let thine example, holy John, remind us' †223=**108, though his authorship has been questioned.[157] This hymn is of special interest to musicians because the tune associated with it provided the "sol-fa" nomenclature of the notes of the scale. The tenth century musical theorist, Guido of Arezzo, observed that the half verses of this melody began in turn with these notes in an ascending order, thus:

He therefore named these notes by the syllables on which they fall in the hymn, and (with the addition of *si*, and with *do* sometimes substituted for *ut*) they are in use to this day.

A younger contemporary of Paul was St. Theodulph of Orleans, author of the Palm Sunday hymn, 'All glory, laud, and honour', concerning which more is said below. But the best-known name in Carolingian hymnody is that of Hrabanus Maurus[158] (*c.* 776–856). Brought up at the great monastery of Fulda, he studied at Tours under Alcuin, returning later to Fulda to become head of the monastery school. He became Abbot in 822, then (847) Archbishop of Mainz. The two Office Hymns for Michaelmas, *Tibi, Christe, splendor Patris*, 'Thee, O Christ, the Father's splendour' †241=**119, and *Christe, sanctorum decus angelorum*, 'Christ, the fair glory of the holy angels' †242=**121, have been attributed to him, as well as that for the Purification, *Quod chorus vatum*, 'All prophets hail thee' †208= **101 : but there is considerable doubt in each case.[159] On the other hand, there are cogent grounds for solving definitely in his favour the vexed question of the authorship of one of the most famous of all hymns, *Veni Creator Spiritus*,[160] which has been ascribed to a number of writers, including not only Charlemagne but St. Ambrose and St. Gregory the Great.

Of the *Veni Creator* there are a number of translations into English. The best-known is the beautiful 'Come, Holy Ghost, our souls inspire' *157 †153 **65, by Bishop John Cosin (1564–1672). This appeared for the first time in his *Collection of Private Devotions in the Ancient Church* (1627), and was later accorded the honour of inclusion in the services for the Ordination of Priests and the Consecration of Bishops in the Prayer Book of 1661. It is, however, rather a "skilfully condensed paraphrase" than a translation in the strict sense. Another paraphrase, but far from condensed, is provided for alternative use in the same services, 'Come, Holy Ghost, Eternal GOD' *508. This, in dull Common Measure, is a very pedestrian affair and is considerably more than twice the length of the original. It appeared (in rather a different form from the present) in both the Ordinals of Edward VI. Closer translations than either of these are that by Robert Bridges, 'Come, O Creator Spirit, come' †154, and one based on Caswall, 'Come, Holy Ghost, Creator blest' *347 **66. Dryden's 'Creator Spirit, by Whose aid' †156, is another expanded paraphrase : but it is a good one of its kind, and its eighteenth-century style and its shape (6 lines instead of

4) make it an appropriate vehicle for Attwood's elegantly beautiful tune, written for Cosin's version for use at an Ordination in St. Paul's in 1831. The plainsong melody (probably the most familiar of all such melodies to English ears) has been associated with the hymn since the latter's first known appearance, but is itself older than the hymn and was previously used for an Easter hymn by St. Ambrose.[161]

In addition to his own reputation as a hymn-writer Hrabanus Maurus is further interesting as supplying the link between Charlemagne's "palace-school" and the famous poetical and musical "School of St. Gall", which will be mentioned in more than one connection in these pages.

By the eleventh century the cycle of Office Hymns was tolerably complete, so far as the provision made for the major requirements of the Church's year was concerned. We need only mention three more writers, all represented in our English hymnals. St. Fulbert of Chartres, author of the Easter hymn, *Chorus novae Hierusalem*, 'Ye choirs of new Jerusalem' †122=**52=*125, was a distinguished scholar and poet, who became Bishop of Chartres *c*. 1007 and died in 1028. Of him Mr. Raby has said that "he made the cathedral school [of Chartres] the intellectual glory of eleventh-century France. . . . He exercised a magical influence over his pupils. Alike as Master and as Bishop he was pre-eminent in his generation".[162] Philippe de Grevia (d. 1236), Chancellor of the church of Paris, wrote the long hymn *Collaudemus Magdalenae*, 'Sing we all the joys and sorrows' †230–1=‡111 (abbreviated), assigned by Sarum in three portions to St. Mary Magdalene's day. The last, the great St. Thomas Aquinas, will be dealt with in the next section when we come to speak of his Sequence for Corpus Christi, *Lauda Sion*. A word may be added concerning another famous hymn, *Jesu dulcis memoria*, 'Jesu, the very thought is sweet' *177 †238

**115. This was long attributed to St. Bernard of Clairvaux (1091–1153): but the ascription cannot be substantiated, and its real authorship remains an unsolved mystery.[163] In its liturgical form it is a cento taken from a long poem of over 50 stanzas. The lovely plainsong melody originally belonged to the Christmas hymn, *Christe Redemptor omniun*, †17 **21. In the period immediately preceding the Reformation another cento, beginning with the same first line, was adopted in England as a Sequence at Mass, and in the printed editions of the Sarum Gradual, issued in 1527, 1528 and 1532, is set to the beautiful melody known as the 'Rosy Sequence' †238.

Before concluding this section it is necessary to speak of a number of Latin hymns which do not come within the category of Office Hymns but have enjoyed wide use and fame and are familiar in English versions. We have already spoken of the Processional Proses of Fortunatus and his imitators, beginning *Salve festa dies*. Another great processional is that for Palm Sunday, *Gloria, laus et honor*. This is said to have been written by the distinguished poet and prelate St. Theodulph, Bishop of Orleans[164] (d. 821) in the prison at Angers in which he was confined by King Louis the Pious, and to have been sung by him through the window of his cell while the King was passing in the Palm Sunday procession, with the gratifying result that he was at once set at liberty. The story is apocryphal: but Theodulph's authorship of the hymn need not be questioned. The ceremonial attending the singing of it as part of the Palm Sunday solemnities was minutely laid down in the mediaeval rites. At Sarum the first four verses were to be sung by seven boys standing in 'a very elevated position on the south side of the church'.[165] Neale produced two translations of parts of the Latin original, which ran to 39 verses. One, 'Glory and honour and laud', is in the original elegiac metre and forms the basis of the version in **148 (†621 gives an abbreviated version).

The other, 'All glory, laud and honour' *98 †622 is in
7.6.7.6., and is that in general use. The familiar modern
tune to this had originally nothing to do with Palm
Sunday, but is that of the German chorale, *Valet ich will dir
geben* ('Farewell, I gladly bid thee,' *The Choral Book*,
137). This, a hymn for the dying, was written by Valerius
Herberger in 1613 during a pestilence that devastated the
town of Fraustadt where he lived, the melody being supplied by his precentor, Melchior Teschner. The original
associations of the tune are thus completely different from
those evoked by Neale's "cheerful and festive" hymn.
But hymn-tunes are plastic things : and much depends on
pace and manner of performance.

The joys of the heavenly Jerusalem were a favourite
theme with mediaeval hymn-writers. We have already
spoken of *Urbs beata*. Less well known but hardly less
ancient is *O beata Hierusalem*, 'O Jerusalem the blissful'
*602. This is of Mozarabic origin and may be traced back
at least to the ninth century. More generally popular than
either are two compositions that were both written in the
twelfth century. One of these, *O quanta qualia*, 'O what
their joy and their glory must be' *235 †465 **153, is the
work of St. Bernard's *bête noir*, the celebrated theologian
Pierre Abelard [166] (1079–1142), at one time the idol of
the schools of Paris. It formed part of a complete hymn-
book that he wrote for the Abbey of the Paraclete, of
which his wife, Heloïse, was abbess, and was designed for
use at Vespers on Saturday evening. The familiar majestic
tune sung to Neale's version has nothing to do with
Abelard's hymn, but is an adaptation, made to fit the
former in the *Hymnal Noted* of 1854, from a late plainsong
melody of the seventeenth or eighteenth century which
appears in Aynès's edition (1808) of La Feillée's *Méthode
de Plain Chant* as a setting of a hymn in a different metre
(Alcaics), *Regnator orbis*.[167] Besides Neale's version there
is a beautiful rendering of Abelard's original in Miss

Waddell's *Mediaeval Latin Lyrics*, beginning 'How mighty are the Sabbaths', which has already been taken over for use as a hymn by the *Clarendon Hymnal*.

Of slightly later date than Abelard's poem is the composition represented by a well-known quartet of English hymns : 'Brief life is here our portion,' 'The world is very evil,' 'For thee, O dear, dear country' and 'Jerusalem the golden' *225–8 †371, 495, 392, 412. These are taken from a partial translation by Neale of an immensely long poem written *c.* 1145 by a monk of Cluny called Bernard of Morval or Morlaas (Bernard of *Morlaix* is certainly wrong). The original poem was not a hymn at all. It was entitled *De contemptu mundi*,[168] and was "a bitter satire on the fearful corruptions of the age", to which its glowing pictures of the glories of heaven served as a contrast. It was written in a lilting metre called the dactylic hexameter, complicated by a rhyming system that made it so difficult to manage that the author says that only by a special inspiration could he have maintained it through so long a poem. The opening line of the whole is scanned thus :

Hóra novíssima ‖ témpora péssima ‖ súnt : vigilémus,

or in a not very successful mid-Victorian translation :

Thése are the látter times, ‖ thése are not bétter times ; ‖ lét us stand wáiting.

We have already referred to the new note that came into Christian song through the influence of St. Francis. Bishop Creighton has said that "Francis was a poet whose life was his poem". In his early years he had been a gay young troubadour : and the troubadour spirit never left him, though after his conversion it was transfigured and lifted to a higher plane. Walter Pater and Emile Gebhart have written of the anticipation of the Renaissance proper which occurred at the end of the twelfth and beginning of the thirteenth centuries, "a Renaissance within the middle age itself''. Of this earlier Renaissance St. Francis was a genuine product, though very much after his own fashion. In him and his first followers the note of *joy* returned to Christianity — joy in Nature, joy in the simple yet august sanctities of human life and destiny, joy in the all-embracing Love of GOD of which all these are a reflection. It is the spirit to which Francis himself gave utterance in his *Canticle of the Sun* (written in Tuscan), and which in his followers gave birth to the copious and lovely carol-literature of the later Middle Ages. The latter is represented in collections of carols rather than in our hymn-books : but St. Francis's canticle is becoming known in Mr. Draper's metrical translation, 'All creatures of our GOD and King' ‡439. At the same time in Francis, unlike other representatives of the Renaissance earlier and later, the joy is achieved not by ignoring the harsher side of man's life but by accepting and transcending it. The troubadour is also the saint of the Stigmata. The power of Francis to help his suffering fellow-mortals lay precisely in his perception of the *value* of suffering, as shown in the sufferings of Christ and his own joyful self-identification with them. Thus we are prepared for a second note in Franciscan hymnody — its concentration on the Passion of the Redeemer and its tragic accompaniments. It is fitting that the *Stabat mater*, 'At the Cross her station keeping' *117 **47=†115, should have come (in all probability) from the pen of a Franciscan lay brother Jacopone da Todi [169] (d. 1306). It is no less characteristic that the writer of this poignant portrayal of anguish, human and Divine, should have been a sort of Brother Juniper — a holy buffoon, "a fool for Christ's sake". A second familiar hymn on the Passion, *In passione Domini*, 'In the LORD's atoning grief' *105, was written by another Franciscan, the *Doctor Seraphicus* St. Bonaventura (1221–74), who wrote it for an Office of the Holy Cross, it is said, at the suggestion of King Louis IX of France. Finally, it was a

French Franciscan friar, Jean Tisserand (d. 1494), who wrote the Easter hymn *O filii et filiae*, 'O sons and daughters, let us sing' *130=†626. This joyous composition, "modelled" as it is "on the Provençal *cantinella*",[170] may be regarded as a kind of last flaming up of the troubadour spirit in Church hymnody before the Middle Ages expired.

The close of the mediaeval period hardly presents an impressive spectacle so far as "official" Christianity is concerned. More and more such vital personal religion as it can show tends to take refuge in those groups of humble, pious souls who were the real precursors of the coming Reformation. Among these the "Brethren of the Common Life" in the Low Countries stand out conspicuous. It was in this *milieu* that the author of the *Imitatio Christi*, Thomas à Kempis (1380–1471), lived and died. To him there seem to be good grounds for ascribing the originals of several hymns in our English books. Of these the best-known is *O amor quam ecstaticus*, 'O love, how deep, how broad, how high '*173 †459 **72. Others are *En dies est dominica*, ' Again the LORD's own day is here' *35; *Quisquis valet numerare*, 'If there be that skills to reckon' †250 **122= *619; *Hierusalem luminosa*, 'Light's abode' *232 †431 **154; and *In domo Patris*, 'Our Father's home eternal' †252.[171]

III

It has been remarked earlier in this chapter that for a long time the introduction of hymns into the public worship of the West was confined to the Breviary Offices, and that their use was rigidly excluded from the Mass. When, here too, after the lapse of centuries, they made their appearance, it was by a side door (so to speak) and in a specialized shape. During the eighth and ninth centuries a practice [172] arose of supplementing the austerely simple "Gregorian" chant with phrases and melodies of a much more ornate character, perhaps derived from Byzantine sources. These were interpolated into the existing chants and at first simply involved the attachment of long florid "melismatic" passages to single syllables of the verbal text. These interpolations were called *Tropes*. As, however, such passages were hard to memorize, a further custom developed of fitting words to them : so that now we have interpolations not only in the music but in the text itself. The words thus added were normally in Latin ; though in France at a later date they were sometimes written in the vernacular. The earliest specimens of French popular religious songs were produced in this way. The melody of the hymn *O filii et filiae* mentioned above was in its origin that of a Trope sung in Provençal and inserted in the Epistle for Easter Day, *Ab Madalene un matin*, to which the Latin words by Tisserand were fitted some two centuries later.[173]

Such Tropes were largely to die out in time. But in one position in the Mass they held their ground. Of the new melodies a special elaboration characterized those attached to the *Alleluia* following the Gradual sung between the Epistle and the Gospel. The final syllable -a, already protracted in an ornate vocal flourish or *jubilus*, was now further extended by a much longer melody called *Sequela*. It was these *Sequelae* (originally wordless) which when provided with a verbal text produced the type of hymn known as a *Sequence*.

The fitting of words to Tropes appears to have originated in the ninth century in northern France. But when — through the flight from the Northmen (it is said) of a monk of Jumièges, who carried his choir books with him — it reached the great abbey of St. Gall in Switzerland, the local chroniclers, who were masters of self-advertisement, claimed it as their own. It is a monk of St. Gall, Notker surnamed *Balbulus* (or 'Stammerer'), whose name is specially connected with the earlier type of

Sequences, so-called because, whereas other Tropes were interpolations, this kind *followed* the Alleluia. Such compositions were at first non-metrical in character, having to follow the free rhythm of the music to which they were fitted. But as each phrase of this was wont to be repeated twice and the practice was "a syllable to a note", the result was "rhythmical prose in binary form".[174] For this reason in France Tropes (including the Sequences) were usually known as "Proses", though in fact they were much less prosaic than the products of Germany, St. Gall, etc.

These compositions became extremely popular, and their number rapidly increased in both France and Germany. In course of time, in addition to new words to old music, new music came to be composed as well. It is unfortunately impossible to say which of the St. Gall Sequences that have survived are to be attributed to Notker himself.[175] The so-called "Alleluiatic Sequence", *Cantemus cuncti melodum*, 'The strain upraise' *295 †494, is usually regarded as his : but this is uncertain. Other examples of the earlier non-metrical type of Sequence called after him "Notkerian" are to be seen in English guise in our hymnals. The most famous is the Easter Sequence, *Victimae Paschali*, 'Christians, to the Paschal Victim' **56=†130. This is, incidentally, of great importance in the history of the drama. Its form and character lent themselves easily to dramatic representation : and its use in this way helped to originate the later "Mystery-plays" of the Middle Ages.[176] The authorship is ascribed to Wipo (d. 1050), a native of Burgundy (or perhaps Swabia) and chaplain to the Emperors Conrad II and Henry III. Another early specimen is the Sarum Sequence for the first Sunday in Advent, *Salus aeterna*, 'Saviour eternal' †10 **18. This is already found in a Bodleian MS. of *c.* 1000. We may mention, too, the Prose for the Holy Innocents, *Sedentem in supernum*, 'To GOD enthroned in heaven' **128 ; the beautiful Christmas Prose, *Laeta-*

bundus, 'Come rejoicing' †22=**24 ; the Prose for Whit-suntide, *Laudes Deo devotas*, 'Sing to GOD your praises' **68 ; and that for Martyrs, *Mirabilis Deus*, 'How wondrous is GOD' **90. These show graceful *French* musician-ship.

As time went on, the practice of fitting words to existing music gave place to the alternative method of writing the words first and setting them to music afterwards. It was only natural that the words should assume a metrical rhymed structure analogous to that of the Office hymns. The "binary" form, however, persisted. The character-istic shape of the later type of Sequence is a stanza of 6 lines falling into two groups of 3. The first 2 lines of each group rhyme with one another ; while the final lines (the 3rd and 6th of the stanza) rhyme also. To compositions of this type the word "Prose" was no longer applicable : and the alternative name "Sequence" became general.

It is this metrical formula that is associated specially with the name of Adam of St. Victor,[177] the most famous of the later Sequence-writers. Trench goes further and calls him "the greatest of the sacred Latin poets of the Middle Ages". He was certainly among the most prolific, though it is not easy to decide which of the Sequences ascribed to him are actually his. Gautier's edition of 1853 credited him with 106 : but in the latest edition by Misset and Aubry (1900) [178] this number shrinks to 45. Not much is known about his life. He is described as *Brito*, which may mean either a Breton or an Englishman. About 1130 he entered the great abbey of St. Victor on the outskirts of Paris, where he was a contemporary of the two great "Victorine" theologians, Hugh and Robert. His death is variously dated 1172 and 1192. His work is distinguished by stateliness of versification, skilful rhyming and a re-markable knowledge of Scripture and its "typological" application. Several of Gautier's 106 Sequences appear in *A.M.* and *E.H.*, of which only those here preceded

by an asterisk are accepted as Adam's by Misset and
Aubry. Those in *A.M.* are : for St. Stephen's Day, *Heri
mundus exultavit*, 'Yesterday with exultation' *64; for
Evangelists, *Jucundare, plebs fidelis*, 'Come, pure hearts, in
sweetest measure' *434, and *Plausu chorus laetabundo*,
'Come sing, ye choirs exultant' *621 ; for Apostles, *Stola
regia laureatus*, 'In royal robes of splendour' *620. The two
last are not in the metre of the original, which is that
described above. *E.H.* has three : 'Come sing, ye choirs'
†179, and two others : *Supernae matris gaudia*, 'Joy and
triumph everlasting' †200 — written by Robert Bridges
to fit the Genevan Psalm tune 42 — and *Hierusalem et Sion
filiae*, 'Sion's daughters, sons of Jerusalem' †172.

None of Adam's Sequences, however, can compare in
popularity with the Sequence for Whitsunday, *Veni,
sancte Spiritus*, 'Come, Thou Holy Spirit, come' *156
**67=†155. This has been variously attributed, but is
most probably the work of Cardinal Stephen Langton,
Archbishop of Canterbury (d. 1228).[179] Another celebrated Sequence is that in the Mass of the Dead, *Dies irae,
dies illa*, 'Day of wrath, O day of mourning' *398 **143=
†351; though it was not written for this position and was a
long time winning it in general use. It is generally
ascribed to Thomas of Celano, a disciple and friend of
St. Francis, one of the early *Lives* of whom he wrote.[180]
The original version ended with the line '*gere curam mei
finis*', the 7th from the end : the remainder being made up
later of verses from the Response *Libera me*. The current
translation of it is by the Rev. W. J. Irons, who made it
after hearing the *Dies irae* sung at the Requiem in Notre
Dame for Archbishop Affre of Paris, who was shot on the
barricades during the Revolution of 1848.[181]

The same thirteenth century also produced the majestic
and highly dogmatic Sequence for Corpus Christi, *Lauda
Sion Salvatorem*, 'Praise, O Sion, praise thy Master' **134=
†317. This is the work of the greatest theologian of the

Middle Ages, St. Thomas Aquinas (?1227–1274).[182] At the request of Pope Urban IV he wrote in 1263 a series of hymns for the proposed Mass and Office of Corpus Christi. For the former he wrote the Sequence in question, for the latter the three Office hymns, *Pange lingua gloriosi Corporis mysterium*, 'Now, my tongue, the mystery telling' *309 **125=†326, *Sacris sollenniis*, and *Verbum supernum prodiens*, 'The Word of GOD proceeding forth' *311 †330 **126. A fifth hymn, *Adoro te devote*, 'Thee we adore, O hidden Saviour' *312 †331 **133, is usually ascribed to Aquinas, but his authorship is not certain. It was not written for liturgical use, but became widely popular and is not less so in England in Bishop Woodford's translation.

One more Sequence may be mentioned, *O beata beatorum*, 'Blessed feasts of blessed Martyrs' *440 †184, which belongs to the fourteenth century and is of German origin. Neither this nor the *Dies irae* is in the normal later Sequence form.

The number of Sequences in use at the close of the Middle Ages was enormous, as may be seen by a glance at the (by no means complete) list given in Julian's *Dictionary of Hymnology*, which fills ten large pages of very small type.[183] With the increase in number went a grave deterioration in quality — a deterioration that marked the music as well. "There was," says Dr. Frere, "a magnificence about the earlier rhythmical melodies which was entirely lacking in the prim and conventional formulas which made up most of the later Sequence melodies."[184] These considerations helped to sharpen the disfavour with which Rome had at all times regarded them. The liturgical reformers of the Council of Trent decided therefore to make practically a clean sweep of them. In the Roman Missal of 1570 only four were allowed to remain, viz.: *Victimae Paschali* (Easter), *Veni sancte Spiritus* (Pentecost), *Lauda Sion* (Corpus Christi), and *Dies irae* (Requiem). To these was added in 1727 a fifth, *Stabat mater*, which was

turned into a Sequence for the Friday after Passion
Sunday.

IV

We have spoken at considerable length of the heritage
bequeathed to us by the Latin hymn-writers of the Middle
Ages. Our indebtedness to Latin hymnody, however, is
by no means confined to this. Many familiar hymns
"translated from the Latin" represent originals that were
never sung in England at all, but were written on the
Continent by poets of the Roman obedience subsequently
to the Reformation. For in the sphere of hymnody, as in
that of private devotion, the divisions of Christendom are
of small account.

The instinct of the Counter-Reformation, like that of
the Reformation in England, was towards liturgical unity.
The Roman Breviary issued by the Council of Trent in
1568 put an end to the infinite and confusing variety of
the local diocesan Uses. But a century later, and notably
in France, the tendency towards variation once more
asserted itself. The Gallican Church of the reign of Louis
XIV was intensely conscious of its "national" character;
and, while of course remaining in communion with the
Holy See, was by no means unready to show its independence of it, especially in view of the protracted quarrel
between Rome and the Monarchy that raged at the time.
Further, its leaders were largely men of refined and
scholarly tastes, whose contact with the Court and the
cultivated world made them well aware of the spirit and
the needs of the brilliant age they lived in. To such men
the existing Breviary Offices appeared open to criticism
both in matter and in manner. In particular, the lessons
contained many legends that revolted the rising sense of
historical criticism; while the ancient hymns seemed
barbarous in language and versification. It was these combined motives that led to the appearance at the end of the

seventeenth and the beginning of the eighteenth centuries of what are called the "Neo-Gallican Breviaries".[185] The earliest of these was issued by Archbishop Harlay of Paris in 1680. Two others may be specially mentioned : the Cluniac Breviary (for the use of the great abbey of Cluny in Burgundy), issued in 1686, and a revised edition of the Paris Breviary issued by Archbishop Vintimille in 1736.

With these Breviaries we are concerned only in their hymnological aspect. Even the compilers of the Breviary of the Council of Trent had felt their sense of elegant Latinity, formed by the Renaissance, shocked and affronted by the "barbarism" of the ancient Office Hymns, and had handled them roughly by way of "improving" them. In the neo-Gallican Breviaries the more drastic step was taken of largely abolishing them altogether and providing new ones. Fortunately a number of accomplished scholars and versifiers were available to undertake the task. On the score of craftsmanship the hymns they produced were much superior, generally speaking, to the old. At the same time their range of subject was wider, their mood more subjective, emotional and suited to the age for which they were written. Thus "they are to be classed with modern hymns rather than with old hymns, in spite of their language".[186] The Breviaries containing them remained in use until far into the nineteenth century : and it was with them that the earlier English translators (who were also, generally speaking, the more accomplished) were specially familiar, particularly after Newman published his *Hymns from the Paris Breviary* in 1838. For this reason, combined with their more modern outlook, they figure largely in the English collections. A complete list of the versions of these hymns in *A.M.*, *E.H.* and *P.H.B.* is given in Appendix C at the end of this volume.

It remains to say something here concerning the leading figures in this school of hymn-writers and the best-known among the hymns we owe to them. Prominent among the contributors to the Paris Breviary of 1680 and the Cluniac of 1686 were the two brothers de Santeuil. One, Claude (1628–84), was attached to the seminary of St. Magloire, the other, Jean Baptiste (1630–97), was a Canon of St. Victor (both in Paris) ; for which reason their names were Latinized into "Santolius Maglorianus" and "Santolius Victorinus" respectively. Of Claude's only one hymn is represented in our collections : *Prome vocem, mens, canoram*, 'Now, my soul, thy voice upraising' *103 †623. His brother has no less than 10 in *A.M.*, and has particularly helped to swell the repertory of hymns for Saints' days. Of his hymns three are particularly popular in English versions : *Divine crescebas puer*, 'The heavenly Child in stature grows' *78=†46 : and the two for Apostles, *Supreme quales arbiter*, the original of Isaac Williams' splendid 'Disposer supreme' *431 †178, and *Coelestis aulae principes*, 'Captains of the saintly band' *432 †177.

Other contributors to the 1680 and 1686 Breviaries were Nicolas le Tourneaux (1640–86), author of the Epiphany hymn, *Emergit undis*, 'The Son of Man from Jordan rose' *487 ; and Guillaume de la Brunetière (?–1702), who wrote a finely dramatic hymn on the Conversion of St. Paul, *Quae gloriosum*, 'What cause compelling' **99= *405. To the Paris Breviary of 1680 Charles Guiet (1601–64) contributed *Patris aeterni suboles coaeva*, original of 'O Word of GOD above' *395 †171.

Most of the above hymns found a place in the revised Paris Breviary of 1736. Chief among the new contributors to this was Charles Coffin (1676–1749), Principal of the College Dormans-Beauvais in the University of Paris, of which latter he became Rector in 1718. To him we owe no less than 19 hymns in *A.M.*, not a few of which have won wide popularity. We may mention here the two Advent hymns, *Instantis adventum Dei*, 'The Advent of our King' *48 †11, and *Jordanis oras praevia*,' On Jordan's banks' *50 †9; *Jam desinant suspiria*, 'GOD from on high hath heard' *58=†27, and *Quae stella sole pulchrior*, 'What star is this?' *77 †44, for Christmas and Epiphany respectively; two hymns for Septuagesima, *Te laeta mundi Conditor*, 'Creator of the world' *83=†64, and *Rebus creatis nil egens*, 'O GOD, the joy' *489; the hymn on St. John Baptist, *Nunc suis tandem*, 'Lo! from the desert homes' *414; the evening hymn, *Labente jam solis rota*, 'As now the sun's declining rays' *13 †265; together with *O fons amoris Spiritus*, 'O Holy Spirit, Lord of grace' *208 †453, and *O quam juvat fratres*, 'O LORD, how joyful 'tis to see' *273=†398. These, surely, form a decidedly impressive list. The hymns on the six week-days of creation in *A.M.* (39–44) are also by Coffin.

To the same Breviary Sebastien Besnault contributed two hymns for the Circumcision, which was not provided for in the mediaeval series (*70, *71 †36). An anonymous contribution is the original of the familiar 'Conquering kings their titles take', *Victis sibi cognomina*, *175 †37.

Besides these major Breviaries the French diocesan Breviaries of the eighteenth century have given a number of hymns to our collections. Two of these may be mentioned. From the Meaux Breviary (1713) comes the Sapphic hymn, *Lapsus est annus*, not very worthily represented by the dull jog-trot of 'The year has gone beyond recall' *72; from the Breviary of Bourges (1734), *Pugnate, Christi milites*, original of the popular 'Soldiers, who are Christ's below' *447 †480. The latter has become wedded in its English form to a French melody of far earlier date. This first appears in an Office for the Circumcision written by Pierre de Corbeil, Archbishop of Sens (d. 1222), as the music of a hymn celebrating the ass that carried the Blessed Virgin into Bethlehem.[187]

The liturgical revival of the seventeenth century in France even produced new Sequences as well as new Office Hymns. An example of these is *Sponsa Christi*, 'Bride

of Christ' *618=†253. It was written by Jean Baptiste des
Contes (1601–79), Dean of Paris, and first appeared in the
Paris Missal of 1665.

There remain to be mentioned the best-known of a
number of hymns of continental Roman Catholic origin
derived from various sources. *O Deus, ego amo te*, 'My GOD,
I love Thee' *106 †80, is usually attributed to the great
Jesuit missionary, St. Francis Xavier (1506–52); but it
seems to be really a Latin translation of a Spanish sonnet
of unknown origin.[188] Of German collections the *Maintzisch Gesangbuch* (1661) has *O esca viatorum*, 'O food of men
wayfaring' †321=*314; and *Simphonia Sirenum* (1695)
provides *Dignare me, O Jesu*, 'Jesu, grant me this, I pray'
*182 †413, and *Finita jam sunt proelia*, 'The strife is o'er'
*135 †625. *Quicunque certum quaeritis*, 'All ye who seek for
sure relief' *112=†71, is from an eighteenth-century
Office of the Sacred Heart; while the beautiful *Sol
praeceps rapitur*, 'The sun is sinking fast' *17 (**8 is a
translation in the original metre), is apparently a product
of the early nineteenth century.

Finally, something must be said concerning two hymns
of which, on account of their wide use and popularity, we
should much like to know the history; but that history
still remains very obscure, as regards both words and
music. The first is *Veni, veni, Emmanuel*, 'O come, O come,
Emmanuel' *49=†8. This is obviously a versification of
five of the "Great O's", the Antiphons sung from very
early times before the Magnificat at Vespers on the days
preceding Christmas Eve. But the date of this versification
is uncertain. Neale, who translated it, ascribed it to the
twelfth century: but there seems to be no proof whatever
of this. It has been traced back as far as a collection of
1710 called *Psalteriolum Cantionum Catholicarum*. The origin
of the tune is no less mysterious. On its first appearance in
the *Hymnal Noted* (1854) it was described as "from a
French Missal in the National Library at Lisbon": but

no trace of this has been found. It appears to be an adaptation of a plainsong *Kyrie*.[189]

The other is the splendid Christmas hymn, *Adeste fideles*, 'O come, all ye faithful' *59 †28.[190] This would seem to be a French product of the late seventeenth or early eighteenth century : but, rather oddly, the English sources in which it first appears are earlier than the French. It is given (with its tune), under the heading 'Another Prose on the Nativity of our LORD', in a book published in London in 1782 called *An Essay on the Church Plain Chant*, containing a collection of music sung in Roman Catholic chapels in England. (We may note in passing that in the same book appear for the first time four tunes that have become exceedingly familiar — 'Veni Sancte Spiritus,' 'Melcombe' (originally a setting of *O salutaris*), 'Alleluia dulce carmen' and 'St. Thomas' (both set to *Tantum ergo*) — of which the first two are certainly and the third possibly by Samuel Webbe (1740–1816), organist of the Sardinian Chapel, who probably edited the book.) *Adeste fideles* has also been found in a collection of MS. music at Stonyhurst, dated 1751. In the French version it is longer than in the English : and the extra verses in *E.H.* 614 are from this source. The current translation is based on one made by the Rev. F. Oakeley in 1841 for Margaret Chapel, now All Saints, Margaret Street. The tune has been ascribed to John Reading, Organist of Winchester College, 1680 ; but without the slightest evidence. Whatever its ultimate origin, the hymn as we have it is one of the most priceless legacies of the early Anglo-Catholic Revival to posterity.

CHAPTER V

GERMAN HYMNODY

WITH the coming of the Reformation an entirely new chapter in the history of hymnody begins. To the leaders of the movement in all countries no principle was more fundamental than that which required that public worship should be in the vernacular, "to the end that the congregation may be thereby edified", as Cranmer's preface to the 1549 Prayer Book puts it. And not only must Divine service be intelligible to the people, but they must be encouraged to participate actively in it themselves in "psalms and hymns and spiritual songs" in their own tongue. In this department, indeed, even the mediaeval Church had been compelled to tolerate exceptions to its use of Latin as the sole liturgical language. In the "tropes" and *cantiques* of France, in the *Leisen* of Germany, in the *Laudi Spirituali* of the Franciscan revival in Italy (of which *Discendi amor santo*, 'Come down, O Love divine' *670 †152 ‡177, by Bianco da Siena, d. 1434, is an example), and, above all, in the "carols" of all countries, the common people had been allowed to lift up their voices in the language that they knew. But the use of such things was kept within close limits, and was confined for the most part to "extra-liturgical" occasions: to pilgrimages, to mission preachings and to the popular services and ceremonies connected with the great feasts of the Church. So far as the Mass and the Divine Office were concerned, the hymnal element was normally confined to the Latin Sequences and Office Hymns, in which the people could hardly be expected to take a part.

99

Now, however, in those countries where the Reformation triumphed, all was to be changed. It is true that the latitude permitted as regards the *kind* of hymns used varied considerably according to the particular form that the Reformation assumed. In the Calvinist churches of France, Switzerland, Scotland and of certain parts of Germany the use of hymns was for a long time confined to metrical translations of the Psalms and other passages of Scripture : and the same was largely true of our own Church. In Lutheran Germany, on the other hand, encouragement was given from the outset to the production of entirely new and original poetical compositions for use in public worship. Luther himself was foremost in setting the example. A great lover of music and steeped in the folk-song and traditional vernacular hymnody of his race, he saw clearly how much could be done to rouse enthusiasm and to assist the dissemination of his views by means of simple popular hymns set to well-known tunes, whether of religious or secular origin. Here, then, once again, as in the days of Arianism and Iconoclasm, the singing of hymns was to be made a vehicle for spreading and per-petuating a particular kind of theological teaching ; and with such success that a contemporary Romanist com-plained that "the whole country is singing itself into this Lutheran doctrine". It must be remembered, too, that in thus furbishing anew an ancient weapon of propaganda the Reformers had at their disposal a mighty resource unknown to their predecessors. The invention of printing had made possible the cheap and indefinite multiplication of hymn-books : and, in consequence, we see a continuous stream of these pouring from the presses in all the countries of the Reform.

I

From a purely musical point of view it would be hard to deny to the hymns of Lutheran Germany pride of place over all others. The words of these hymns, however, are normally on a much lower level than the music. The best of them, indeed, are models of what hymns should be — whether as represented by the simple, forthright sturdiness of Luther and his associates in the "heroic" phase of the German Reformation or by the mingled fervour and tenderness of Paul Gerhardt. But these are the exception and not the rule even in the case of the hymns of the sixteenth and seventeenth centuries; while those of the eighteenth century in their weak sentimentality are often models, rather, of what hymns should *not* be.

In any case the limits imposed by the scheme of the present book preclude any very extended treatment of these hymns. For, as Robert Bridges has said, " attempts to introduce the German chorales into England have never, so far as I know, been successful", "owing, I suppose", he adds, "to a difference in the melodic sense of the two nations".[191] And as without their tunes the words are for the most part devoid of any great claim to attention, especially through the distorting medium of a translation, this has meant that the Lutheran influences which, owing to the circumstances of the time in which it was compiled, have left a definite mark on the Prayer Book are but slightly represented in our hymnals. To the musical public, of course, a large number of the German "chorales" are becoming increasingly familiar in the magnificently elaborated form in which Bach worked them up in his two *Passions* and innumerable Church-cantatas. But that public is limited : and so far as the services of the Church are concerned Bridges's statement seems likely to remain true — no doubt for the reason that he suggests. On the other hand, so notable a mass of hymnody cannot be passed over without some attempt to give at least a brief general view of it, not only for historical reasons, but also because it has given us a certain number of hymns which are hardly less popular in England than they are in Germany.[192]

The first beginnings of Church music in Germany are associated with the name of the Emperor Charlemagne (768–814). He was an enthusiastic admirer of the Roman chant and founded schools for teaching it at Aachen, Fulda and elsewhere in the German portion of his dominions. If the testimony of John the Deacon, the ninth-century biographer of Gregory the Great, is to be trusted, the Roman cantors sent to instruct them found their pupils decidedly raw material :

> These mountainous bodies (he says) whose voices roar like thunder, cannot imitate our sweet tones : for their barbarous and ever-thirsty throats can only produce sounds like those of a loaded waggon passing over a rough road.[193]

Here possibly, however, speaks the voice of racial prejudice : the Italians have always been severe critics of German vocal methods ! In any case, in the course of the next hundred years the Swiss monastery of St. Gall, along with a group of neighbouring houses, managed to accumulate wide fame as a musical centre. We have already seen the part played by it in the development of the Latin Sequences. Linked also with the same great monastery is the name of the author of one of the two earliest specimens of sacred poetry in the German language. Both of these are Lives of Christ — the one, called the *Heliand*, the work of a Saxon priest (*c.* 830), the other written about forty years later by Otfrid of Weissenburg, who had been a monk both at Fulda and St. Gall. It is interesting to note that Otfrid was largely responsible for the introduction into German poetry of the rhymed stanza (imitated from the Latin Office Hymns) in place of the earlier German alliterative metre in which the *Heliand* was composed.[194]

Such large-scale efforts of German sacred poetry were

for a long time without successors. During the next two centuries the literature of Germany was almost exclusively in Latin. On the other hand, it was at this period that the first small beginnings of vernacular hymnody appeared. In the worship of the Church the contribution of the people was confined to the saying of *Kyrie eleison*, *Christe eleison*, at intervals during the Latin service, sometimes as many as two or three hundred times. Not long after the development of the "Notkerian" Sequences, the clergy had the idea of providing a kind of imitation of them in the German language, so as to give the congregation something less monotonous to sing. In these compositions, written in irregular verse, each stanza ended with *Kyrie eleison*, for which reason they came to be known as *Leisen*. They were not sung, however, during the Mass, but only at pilgrimages and on similar occasions. The first verse of the earliest of them, written early in the tenth century in honour of St. Peter, has been translated by Miss Winkworth thus:

> Our dear LORD of grace hath given
> To St. Peter power in heaven,
> That he may uphold alway
> All who hope in him and say
> > *Kyrie eleison.*
> > *Christe eleison.*[195]

As time went on the number of these *Leisen* (or *Leiche* as they were also called) increased largely. At the great festivals they were even sung during the Mass itself. One of the most celebrated is that for Easter, *Christ ist erstanden*, of which Luther said that "after a time one tires of singing all other hymns, but the *Christ ist erstanden* one can always sing again". A number of different versions of it exist, of which the earliest belong to the twelfth century. It may be interesting to give here the first verse of a translation by the English Reformer Bishop

Coverdale in his *Goostly Psalms and Spiritualle Songs* (*see* p. 151):

> Christ is now risen agayne
> From his death and all his payne;
> Therefore will we mery be
> And rejoyse with hym gladlie.
>   Kirieleison.

It was on this hymn that Luther based his own Easter hymn, *Christ lag in Todesbanden*, described in the book in which it first appeared as "The hymn *Christ ist erstanden* improved". Luther's version of words and melody was used by Bach in one of the most resplendent of his Church Cantatas, 'Christ lay in death's dark prison'. An adapted arrangement of the earlier form of the tune is appropriately set to 'Jesus lives!' in †134 ‡155.

Concurrently with the production of original hymns of this kind a number of the more famous Latin hymns and Sequences were translated into the vernacular — a practice that appears to have been more or less confined to the German-speaking lands. These, too, were sung in church, though it would seem that generally speaking their use was discouraged except on extra-liturgical occasions.

In the closing centuries of the Middle Ages the German Sequences sung at Easter and Whitsuntide were expanded into longer hymns. The same centuries also produced a great output of carols for various occasions, in Germany as in other countries. These lie outside the scope of this book: but two may be mentioned in passing, both on account of their intrinsic beauty and because they have become familiar in England in Dr. G. R. Woodward's beautiful arrangements, viz. *Es kommt ein Schiff geladen*, 'There comes a galley laden,' by the famous fourteenth-century preacher and mystic, Johann Tauler; and the lovely *Es ist ein Ros entsprungen*, 'The noble stem of Jesse' (Cowley Carol Book, series i, 31, 19). Many of these carols exhibit a quaint mixture of Latin and German lines, as in the well-known *In dulci jubilo* (*ibid.* 12). In our hymnals the popular tune 'Quem pastores laudavere' *622 †543 ‡540, is such a carol-melody, and another, 'Ave Virgo virginum' *679 †131 ‡144, is a late mediaeval German tune of similar origin. A third, 'Ave Hierarchia', was shortened and adapted by W. H. Monk into the familiar tune to 'LORD, Thy word abideth'.

Now, too, arose a custom later followed by Luther of setting sacred words to popular secular songs of the time. The familiar tune known as "Innsbruck" is an example. It was originally a song voicing the homesickness of a German artisan, *Innsbruck, ich muss dich lassen*, 'Innsbruck, I now must leave thee.' This suggested the idea and provided the tune of a hymn in contemplation of eternity, *O Welt, ich muss dich lassen*, 'O world, I now must leave thee'—the hymn which inspired the lovely chorale-prelude written by Brahms on his death-bed. The same melody was later used for a number of other hymns, including Paul Gerhardt's *Nun ruhen alle Wälder*, so exquisitely rendered by Robert Bridges as 'The duteous day now closes' †278 ‡57; though it should be noted that only the first two verses are a translation, and a free one at that, the last two being Bridges's own.[196] (The version of the tune in *A.M.* 86, 276 is debased and spoilt.)

The name of Heinrich von Laufenburg, the chief and the most prolific of the German sacred poets of the fifteenth century, is prominently identified with this transformation of secular songs into religious hymns, and also with the translation of the great Latin hymns into German. He was a secular priest in Switzerland and later at Freiburg in Baden : but in 1445 he became a monk in the convent of the Knights of St. John at Strassburg. He was still living in 1458, but probably died soon after. His lovely little cradle-song of the Blessed Virgin, *Ach lieber Herre, Jesus Christ*, was translated by Miss Winkworth, 'Ah, Jesu Christ, my Lord most dear,' and appears in

E.H. †338 as a hymn for Holy Baptism. It is set there to the original melody accompanying the words in Laufenburg's MS. and presumably of his own composition.

II

Even before the appearance of Luther on the scene the use of an exclusively vernacular liturgy and hymnody had found a foothold (however slender) in central Europe. The great German Reformation movement of the sixteenth century had its precursor in the fifteenth in the movement associated with the name of the Bohemian John Hus, who was condemned as a heretic by the Council of Constance and publicly burned in 1415. The determination of the majority of the Bohemian people to defend Hus's orthodoxy and their own led to civil war, in which the Roman party sought to crush the opposition with foreign aid. But soon a division appeared in the ranks of the followers of Hus. The more moderate party were content to demand certain disciplinary changes, including the restoration of the Cup at Mass to the laity. But the more extreme section, the "Taborites", wanted a complete recasting of the traditional Church system on democratic lines, with public worship in their own Bohemian tongue. Eventually Rome and the moderates came to terms : and the Taborites were crushed and ceased to exist as a political force. But they maintained an obscure and hunted existence as a religious fellowship, and in 1467 united with other rebels against Catholic orthodoxy to form a separate and organized church called the *Unitas Fratrum* or Bohemian Brethren. In their worship hymns played an important part. These hymns, old and new, were brought together in a number of successive collections culminating in the book of 1561, containing 744 hymns.[197]

A series of parallel collections in German began with the book called *Ein Neu Gesangbüchlein*, published in 1531 by Michael Weisse (*c.* 1480–1534).[198] Many of the hymns in these collections were subsequently embodied in the Lutheran books. Weisse was an ex-monk who, coming under the influence of Luther's writings, had joined the Bohemian Brethren and became the founder and leader of their German communities. Some of his hymns were translations from the Bohemian and Latin : others were of his own composition. Among the latter is *Christ ist erstanden*, familiar in Miss Winkworth's translation, 'Christ the LORD is risen again' *136 †129 ‡153. A later collection of 1566 contained Petrus Herbert's Sapphic hymn, *Die Nacht ist kommen*, 'Now GOD be with us, for the night is closing' ‡48. Besides these hymns a number of melodies have been taken over from the German books of the Bohemian Brethren ; four being found in *E.H.*, viz. †54, 121, 202, and the fine swinging melody of 604.

The hymns in Weisse's collection were well known to his great contemporary Martin Luther (1483–1546) and were much admired by him. By the time it appeared Luther had followed the example of the Bohemian Brethren in providing a vernacular public worship. A complete German liturgy was issued in 1526. In connection with this new psalms and hymns were needed to take the place of the old Latin hymns and Sequences. Luther had already set to work to provide them. The German hymns of the later Middle Ages were so steeped in what he believed to be false doctrine, and especially in an almost idolatrous veneration of the Blessed Virgin, as to be useless for his purpose. It was therefore a case of making new ones. Here Luther himself took the lead, at the same time inviting his friends and disciples to associate themselves with him in the task. To his friend Spalatin he wrote, at the close of 1523 :

It is my plan . . . to make vernacular psalms for the people. . . . We seek therefore everywhere for poets. And as you have such skill and practice in the German tongue, I entreat you to work with us in this matter and to turn one of the psalms into a hymn after the pattern of an effort of my own that I have sent you. But I desire that new-fangled and courtly expressions may be avoided and that the words may all be exceedingly simple and common, such as plain folk may understand, yet withal pure and skilfully handled [199]

—an excellent summary, by the way, of the *desiderata* of a good hymn.

Besides a number of such German versions of the psalms, etc. (including the *Te Deum* and the Lord's Prayer), and of translations from the Latin (e.g. of the *Veni Creator*), Luther remodelled certain of the earlier German hymns. But his most important contributions were entirely his own. Four of his hymns appeared in the first Lutheran hymn-book called *Achtliederbuch* and 18 in the *Erfurt Enchiridion*, both of which books were issued in 1524. Altogether 37 hymns may be with some confidence ascribed to him. Of these the most famous, and the only one that has come into fairly general use in English guise, is the great *Ein feste Burg*,[200] 'A safe stronghold our GOD is still' †362 ‡436=*678. It is inspired by the 46th Psalm, but is not a translation of it. The common account, popularized by Heine, is that it was written by Luther when on his way to the Diet of Worms in 1521, at the time when he uttered his famous words (echoed in v. 3): "If there were as many devils on the roofs as there are tiles in the roofs of Worms, I would go and would not be afraid." But it is now agreed that it was actually written at the time of the Diet of Speyer in 1529, when the German Princes made their great Protest and the name "Protestant" was born. A number of translations of it into English exist. Of these *E.H.* and *S.P.* use the magnificently rugged version by Thomas Carlyle, and *A.M.* one by Miss Elizabeth Wordsworth.

The tune of this grand hymn is not less glorious than the words, which it fits to perfection. There seems to be little doubt that it, too, is from Luther's pen. For the great Reformer was musician as well as poet. He did not merely see, like many religious leaders before and since, the value of music for propaganda purposes; he loved it for its own sake. He was wont to say: "He who despises music, as all fanatics do, will never be my friend." In his house after dinner he would take his lute and sing and play in the company of his intimates. He was no dour fanatic like Calvin and Knox, but a man whose intense humanity was at once his strength and his weakness. Thus it was only natural that he should pay special attention to the organization of church-song: for he said, "I would fain see all arts, specially music, in the service of Him Who made and created them." A large number of the old melodies set to Latin and German hymns were furbished afresh by him and his musical associates: and he wrote new tunes as well. Of these the *Ein feste Burg* tune is the only one that seems to be certainly his: though others have been attributed to him, including the tune associated with his own Christmas hymn (written for his children), *Vom Himmel hoch*; though on the hymn's first appearance in 1535 it was set to an old carol melody. (The tune is in *57, †17, ‡80 i.) The Advent hymn, 'Great GOD, what do I see and hear?', is often called "Luther's hymn": but there is no evidence that the tune was written by him, and it is certain that he had nothing whatever to do with the words (*see below*, p. 112).

Of the hymn-writers contemporary with Luther who contributed to the earliest Lutheran books, M. Weisse has been already spoken of. The following are also worthy of mention here: Justus Jonas, Paul Eber, Paul Speratus, Nicolas Decius, Nicolaus Hermann, and the shoemaker-poet of Nuremberg, Hans Sachs, the real hero of Wagner's *Die Meistersinger*. Of their hymns, as of those of Luther himself, it may be said that they are admirable examples of what really good popular hymns should be. being "neither didactic nor introspective, but natural, cordial and fearless, at once popular and churchly".[201] They express, as we have said, the spirit of the heroic period of the German Reformation on its best side : and there is nothing surprising in their continued popularity in their own country through centuries of use. They do not seem, however, to have borne transplantation to English soil. Each of these writers has had his translators : but no hymn of theirs has come into common use. On the other hand, a number of the melodies to which the hymns of this period were set figure in our hymnals, though it can hardly be said, despite their excellence, that any of them has won wide popularity. Besides those already mentioned, examples are the tunes to Luther's *Nun freut euch* *293 i, and his paraphrase of the Lord's Prayer *Vater unser* *644 †462 ‡566, to Speratus's *Es is das Heil* *293 ii †478 ‡156, and to Weisse's *Freuen wir uns* †314 ‡510. Of special interest is the tune used for Neale's translation of the Latin hymn (of uncertain origin), *Attolle paulum lumina*, 'O sinner, lift the eye of faith' *104 †103. It originally belonged to Decius's metrical German version of the *Gloria in excelsis*, *Allein Gott in der Höh' sei Ehr*, and is a transformation of the opening phrases of a mediaeval plainsong melody of the *Gloria* which had been already adapted to the prose German version of it in the Lutheran Massbook of 1524.[202] This may serve as an example of the reshaping of old material effected by Luther and his musical colleagues. The chief of these was Johann Walther, whom Luther summoned from Jorgau in 1524 to live with him for a time and help in the arrangement of church-song. Walther was responsible for the arrangement from melodies of an earlier date of the noble tune to Luther's version of St. Ambrose's *Veni Redemptor gentium*, *Nun komm, der Heiden Heiland* *89 †110 ‡295, and of the beautiful wistful one set to his own *Herzlich thut mich erfreuen* †284 ‡249 i.

The second period of German hymnody may be said to date from about 1570 to the close of the Thirty Years' War in 1648. It was something of a period of transition. The hymns produced retain for the most part the "objective, churchly" character of the period preceding, though their general level is by no means so high. But as time went on, and especially when Germany plunged headlong into the protracted agony of the terrible religious war that reduced much of her almost to a desert, the subjective and plaintive note began to creep in that was to be so marked a characteristic of the later Lutheran hymnody. Among the hymn-writers of the period the greatest name is that of Philipp Nicolai (1556–1608), author of the words, and probably of the tune as well, of *Wie schön leuchtet das Morgenstern*, 'How brightly beams the morning star' ‡90, and of the superb *Wachet auf*, 'Wake, O wake' †12=‡687; the latter written during a fearful visitation of the plague in the Westphalian town in which he was pastor. But the most celebrated hymn of the period is the splendid thanksgiving, *Nun danket alle Gott*, 'Now thank we all our GOD' *379 †533 ‡350, which has been called "the German *Te Deum*", and is almost the only Lutheran chorale that has really achieved the rank of a popular favourite in English-speaking countries. It has often been asserted that its author, Martin Rinkart (1586–1648), wrote it as a thanksgiving for the conclusion of the Peace of Westphalia that ended the Thirty Years' War. But it is probable that it appeared in the first edition of Rinkart's *Jesu Herz-Büchlein* in 1636, so that this can hardly be true.[203] Rinkart was a man of frail physique but heroic character, who distinguished himself by his selfless devotion to his flock at Eilenberg in Saxony during the war. He had only just finished burying over 4000 of them who had died of plague, when the town was faced with a demand from the Swedish forces for 30,000 thalers — a sum which through his intercession was reduced to 2000 florins. Two other hymn-writers may also be mentioned. First, Johann Heermann (1585–1647), author of the fine Sapphic Passion hymn, *Herzliebster Jesu*, translated by Robert Bridges as 'Ah, holy Jesu, how hast Thou offended' †70 ‡99. The tune of this was certainly, and the tune of *Nun danket* almost certainly, written by Johann Crüger, of whom more will be said in the next section. The other is Matthäus Apelles von Löwenstern (1594–1648), who wrote the hymn (also in Sapphics) *Christe du Beistand*, on which Philip Pusey, Dr. Pusey's brother, based his well-known 'Lord of our life and GOD of our salvation' *214 †435 ‡349, written in 1834 to portray the state of the English Church at the time, "assailed from without, enfeebled and distracted within, but on the eve of a great awakening".[204] Löwenstern was also an accomplished musician, and himself wrote the melody of his hymn (used for Pusey's in *S.P.*), along with two others which appear with it in *S.P.* ‡236, 670.

Another earlier hymn-writer of the same period, Bartholomäus Ringwaldt (1532–97), has been credited with supplying the German original of "Luther's hymn" so-called, 'Great GOD, what do I see and hear?' *52 †4. The attribution, however, is without foundation.[205] It is true that there is a hymn of Ringwaldt's written in the same metre and dealing with the same subject of the Second Advent: but there the resemblance ends. The first stanza of the English hymn appeared anonymously in a hymn-book published at Sheffield in 1802, the second being added by Dr. W. B. Collyer in his *Hymns* of 1812, along with two others. In place of these last two, the existing verses 3–4 were supplied by T. Cotterill in the 9th edition of his *Selection* in 1820 (*see below* p. 194). Fine hymn though it be of its kind, it can hardly be denied that its extremely literal application of Scriptural eschatology is uncongenial to modern ears: and it is much to be wished that the solemn old tune might become permanently wedded to new and adequate words that would retain for it its Advent associations.[206]

III

The leading figure in the later classical Lutheran hymnody, as Luther is in the earlier, is Paulus Gerhardt (1607–76). It has been said of him by Miss Winkworth that in his hymns "the religious song of Germany finds its purest and sweetest expression" and that "he may be said to be the typical poet of the Lutheran Church as Herbert is of the English".[207] He is by far the most eminent representative of the third period of German hymnody — dating from 1648 to the outbreak of the Pietistic controversy in 1690. In the writers of this period the subjective and mystical element that had already begun to appear becomes more and more marked, and the "churchly, confessional" element sinks into the background. But fervour and tenderness have not yet degenerated into sentimentality.

Nearly two-thirds of Gerhardt's life were passed in the dark days of the Thirty Years' War, and at the age of forty-four he was still only a private tutor and candidate for orders. But in 1651 he received a post as pastor near Berlin, whence in 1657 he was called to the great Church of St. Nicholas in that city. Here he became a favourite preacher and won universal love and esteem. Unfortunately he became involved in the dispute between the Elector Frederick William I and the Lutheran clergy of Berlin, and in 1666 was deprived of his office. Two years later he was appointed Archidiaconus of Lubben in Saxony, where he died. He wrote 120 hymns in all, which appeared at different times from 1649 onwards. The most famous is the grand Passion hymn, *O Haupt voll Blut und Wunden*, 'O sacred Head, sore wounded' †102 ‡128= *111. This was based on a mediaeval Latin hymn beginning *Salve caput cruentatum*, one of the earliest of the many poems inspired by the great carved and painted roods that began to tower in the churches of Western Europe during the thirteenth century. The Latin hymn was formerly attributed to St. Bernard : but it belongs rather to the thirteenth century and may possibly be by Arnulf von Loewen (1200–51).[208] Extraordinary to relate, the tragic "Passion-Chorale" indissolubly wedded to Gerhardt's hymn, in England as in Germany, was originally a love-song composed by the eminent musician H. L. Hassler (1564–1612) [209] — a further proof that tunes are adaptable things !

Another hymn of Gerhardt's has been already mentioned, the beautiful *Nun ruhen alle Wälder* (*see* p. 105). A third, *Befiehl du deine Weg'*, which well expresses the spirit of simple trust in GOD that supported Gerhardt through his troubled life, was freely translated by John Wesley. Of this translation two centos are in use : one in *A.M.*, 'Put thou thy trust in GOD' *692 (set to a fine manly tune by Wesley's nephew, Samuel), and another in *S.P.*, 'Commit thou all thy griefs' ‡479. *S.P.* adds two other hymns by Gerhardt : *Auf den Nebel folgt die Sonn'*, 'Cometh sunshine after rain' ‡478, and a 'modern' version of *Fröhlich soll*, 'Hearts at Christmas-time' ‡89. The latter appears in some collections in Miss Winkworth's translation, 'All my heart this night rejoices.'

Contemporary with Gerhardt and closely related to him is Johann Franck (1618–77). He was Burgomaster at Guben in Brandenburg and enjoyed in his day a high reputation as a poet, both secular and religious. His favourite theme is the mystical union of the soul with Christ. This is exemplified in the two best known of his hymns : *Jesu meine Freude*, 'Jesu, priceless treasure' ‡544, and the Communion hymn, *Schmücke dich*, 'Deck thyself, my soul' †306 ‡267. We may mention, too, Tobias Clausnitzer (1619–84), author of another Communion hymn, *Liebster Jesu*, 'Dearest Jesu, we are here' *713, with its beautiful tune by J. R. Ahle (1625–73), who also wrote the even more beautiful one set to George Herbert's 'King of glory' at *665.

In connection with Gerhardt and Franck it is fitting to mention the man who wrote the tunes for a number of their hymns, Johann Crüger (1598–1662). Crüger was a distinguished organist and composer who became Cantor of the cathedral at Berlin. In 1644 he published the first issue of his *Praxis pietatis melica*, a collection of tunes which ran into innumerable editions. To have written the melodies of *Nun danket* and *Herzliebster Jesu* would be title enough for fame : but Crüger wrote many other fine tunes as well, including those to Franck's *Schmücke dich* and *Jesu, meine Freude* (the latter treated with such ornate magnificence by Bach) and the melodies on which are founded the well-known tunes to 'Hail to the Lord's Anointed' *219 †45 ‡87 and 'Christ, Whose glory fills the skies' *7—the last better represented in †282 ‡24.

The same period, 1648–90, also witnessed the emergence, in Johann Neander (1650–80), of the first prominent name in the hymnody of the Church which divided with the Lutheran the allegiance of Protestant Germany, the so-called 'Reformed' Church. For a long time this Church, like the other more extreme Protestant bodies in Europe, frowned upon the use of anything save metrical versions of the Psalms in public worship. As time went on, however, the prejudice died down. Neander (the name is a Graecized form of Neumann) was, like Luther, both poet and musician. In his student days he came under the influence of Pietism : and after his appointment in 1674 as Rector of the Latin School at Düsseldorf his unconventional zeal brought him into conflict with the authorities of the Reformed Church there. He found comfort for the rest of his short life in writing hymns. These were published in 1680 in a volume called *A and Ω*, and many of them quickly found their way into the Lutheran books.

His finest and best-known hymn is the splendid *Lobe den Herrn*, 'Praise to the Lord, the Almighty, the King of creation' *657 †536 ‡626. The tune of this is an adaptation, probably by Neander himself, of an earlier chorale. Another hymn is *Meine Hoffnung stehet fest*, 'All my hope in GOD is founded' ‡442, the tune of which is also an adaptation (it appears in slightly altered form in *102 ii). But Neander's best-known tune is an original composition and is indissolubly joined in England to Neale's 'Come, ye faithful, raise the anthem' *302 †380 ‡477.

One interesting but rather isolated figure of the period remains to be mentioned, Johann Scheffler (1624–77). Brought up a Lutheran, he fell under the influence of Böhme and the mystics and finally found his way into the Church of Rome in 1653, taking the name of "Angelus Silesius". His hymns enjoy a high reputation; and he figures in our hymn-books as the author of *Liebe die du mich zum Bilde*, 'O Love, Who formedst me to wear' *192 †460 ‡608. The tune to which it is set in *A.M.* is a debased form of a very fine one by another hymn-writer of the period, Georg Neumark (1621–81), who wrote it for his own hymn, *Wer nur den lieben Gott lässt walten*. The original version is given in †458 ‡606. It appears in Mendelssohn's *St. Paul* set to the words 'To Thee, O Lord, I yield my spirit.'

The close of the seventeenth century was a bad time for Germany. The country had not yet recovered from the ravages of the Thirty Years' War: agriculture, trade and industry alike languished. Even religion had largely lost its power to help: for official Lutheranism had become arid and fossilized, concerned mainly with barren controversies. But already a movement had begun which was to inaugurate a kind of second Reformation. It was called "Pietism", and its founder was a Lutheran pastor, Philip Jacob Spener (1635–1705). In many ways Pietism resembled our own Methodism, being puritan in morality and at once emotional and practical in its religious outlook. At first it had to endure persecution : but eventually it won for itself a recognized place within the Lutheran fold. To this school of thought belonged nearly all the hymn-writers of the fourth period of German hymnody, which may be roughly dated 1690–1757. Spener himself wrote hymns : and an intimate friend of his, Johann Jakob Schütz (1640–90), was the author of *Sei Lob' und Ehr*, 'Sing praise to GOD' *293. But the chief singer of Lutheran Pietism was Johann Anastastius Freylinghausen (1670–1739). He wrote 44 hymns : but his importance for English hymnody lies in the sphere of music, not of words. His *Geistreiches Gesangbuch* (1704) is described by Dr. Frere as "the only book which can as a collection be set alongside with the *Praxis Pietatis Melica*".[210] Five tunes from it appear in *S.P.*, viz. ‡27 (a lovely tune here set to a translation of its own hymn, *Morgenglanz in Ewigkeit*, by Christian Knorr Baron von Rosenroth) ‡77, 139, 292, 645. The tune to 'On this day, the first of days' *34 is an adaptation of the last of these tunes. Another Pietist hymn-writer was Adam Drese (1620–1701) : but he, too, figures in English hymnals only as musician — as composer of the tune to his own hymn, *Seelenbräutigam*, set in *A.M.* to Zinzendorf's 'Jesus, still lead on' *669, and in *E.H.* and *S.P.* to W. Romanis's 'Round me falls the night' †272 ‡52. The great J. S. Bach (1685–1750) flourished at this period : but he was rather a harmonizer in his own matchless fashion of other men's chorales than a composer of new ones, though the lovely tune *Nicht so traurig* *318 ii †100 ‡264 is his. In addition *S.P.* has utilized a number of the melodies that he wrote or arranged for the Schemelli *Gesangbuch* and the *Anna Magdalena Notenbuch*.[211]

Besides J. J. Schütz only two hymn-writers of this period are represented in our hymnals. One is Heinrich Schenk (1656–1727), who wrote only a single hymn, but that one which in England is, perhaps, the German hymn next in popularity to *Nun danket*, viz. *Wer sind die vor Gottes Throne*,

'Who are these like stars appearing?' *427 †204 ‡210. The other is Benjamin Schmolck (1672–1737), a Silesian pastor who was the most popular and prolific hymn-writer of his time. His hymn for Baptism, *Liebster Jesu* (not to be confused with Clausnitzer's), 'Blessed Jesu, here we stand', is at †336.

The bulk of the Pietists, as we have said, remained within the Lutheran Church to leaven it. But a section of them broke off into the separatist body called the Moravians. We have already spoken of the *Unitas Fratrum* or Bohemian Brethren. Driven from Bohemia by persecution in 1547, they found a refuge in Moravia, only to be suppressed there too after the Catholic triumph at the Battle of the White Mountain in 1620. A remnant, however, lived on in secret, who called themselves the "hidden seed". Early in the eighteenth century Nicolaus, Count Zinzendorf (1700–60), a Saxon nobleman who had been brought up under Pietist influence (he was Spener's god-son), gave them a refuge on his ancestral estate, where they formed a colony called Herrnhut. Under Zinzendorf's auspices the old Moravian Church was virtually refounded in 1727, and spread to different parts of Germany and much more widely still. More will be said concerning Zinzendorf and the Moravians when we come to speak of their influence on the Methodism of John Wesley and its hymnody. All that concerns us now is that Zinzendorf himself was a hymn-writer and editor of hymn-books. His hymns number over 2000 and are of very varying merit. Two are represented in *A.M.*: *Jesu geh' voran*, 'Jesus, still lead on' *669 and *Deiner Kinder Sammelplatz*, 'Christ will gather in His own' *400.

Of far greater importance, however, than Zinzendorf is another figure who held aloof from the organized Lutheranism of his time, but in this case without founding a sect of his own. Gerard Tersteegen (1697–1769) was a pure mystic, influenced by the teachings of Jacob Böhme even more than by Pietism. Like many others of his kind, he was in no way a schismatic : it was merely that institutional religion did not interest him much. Brought up in the Reformed Church, he left a well-to-do home in early life to live in a little cottage near Mühlheim, where he practised ribbon-weaving and devoted his leisure to prayer, writing and addressing private religious gatherings. As the claims upon him increased, he devoted himself exclusively to this informal ministry and was much sought after from all quarters, both personally and by correspondence. As hymn-writer Tersteegen, alike in his mystical cast of mind and his poetic manner, more nearly resembles Johann Scheffler than anyone else. He deeply influenced John Wesley, who translated two of his finest hymns : *Gott ist gegenwärtig*, 'Lo ! GOD is here' *526 †637 ‡191, and *Verborgen Gottesliebe*, 'Thou hidden love of GOD' *600 ‡671.

By the middle of the eighteenth century the impulse of Pietism was in turn becoming exhausted. Like all similar movements it was weak on the intellectual side : and its emotionalism degenerated easily into sentimentality and the dreary *clichés* that are the despair of translators of those terrible *libretti* from which Bach's incredible genius contrived somehow to wring the inspiration of his Church-cantatas. In the sphere of religion, as elsewhere, the law of action and reaction largely holds sway : it was, too, the age of the "Enlightenment" in Europe. It was only natural, then, that the religious life of Germany should be penetrated by the ideas that were in the air : and that, there as in other countries, the particular brand of religion should prevail which we associate with the eighteenth century — cold, rational, theistic rather than Christian. The hymnody of the period (1750–1830) necessarily reflects the change. The old hymns were watered down to suit the new spirit : the new ones were lyrics and odes rather than hymns in the old sense. The chief representative of this school was Christian Fürchtegott Gellert (1715–69), a professor at Leipzig. He enjoyed a great reputation in his day, but is less admired now. We must not forget, however, that it is to him we owe the original of one of the best and best-loved of our hymns, *Jesus lebt*, 'Jesus lives !' *140=†134 ‡155. Another very popular hymn dates from the same period, 'We plough the fields and scatter' *383 †293 ‡14. It is a translation of three verses of a hymn by Matthias Claudius (1740–1815). The "German Milton", Klopstock, author of *Messiah*, was a hymn-writer of this school : but none of his hymns is used in England.

Among the tunes of German origin belonging to this period four are particularly popular. One is 'Austria', set to 'Glorious things of thee are spoken' *545 †393 ‡500. This was the work of the great Franz Joseph Haydn (1732–1809), and was originally written as a setting of a national hymn sung on the Emperor's birthday in 1797, being afterwards used by the composer as the theme of the splendid variations that form part of his "Emperor" quartet.[212] The second is the lusty tune to 'We plough the fields' *383 †293 ‡14, written by J. A. P. Schulz and set to Claudius's hymn in a collection of 1800 : and the two last those to 'O happy band of pilgrims' *224 and 'Blest Creator of the light' *38 — both by J. H. Knecht (1752–1817). A tune by Haydn's younger brother Michael appears at *666. In the tunes of this period, as we might expect, the starkness of the old chorales gives way to a lighter style, more flowing in melody, more luscious in harmony — a style which undoubtedly was one of the major factors that went to the making of the characteristic "Victorian" hymn-tune. Two later German examples of this style are the two chorales by F. Filitz (1804–76), from which are adapted the popular tunes 'Capetown' *163 †501 ‡507 and 'Mannheim' *196 †426 ‡555 ii. Apart from this musical influence, the debt of our hymnals to nineteenth-century German hymnody is negligible. Lutheranism went on producing its sacred poets as before : but none of their work has found a permanent welcome within our shores.

IV

Before closing this chapter something must be said concerning our debt to the Catholic hymnody of Germany — a debt (in respect of tunes rather than words) that has been considerably increased of late years. It is a curious fact that while Lutheran musicians were busy remoulding not a few of the old religious melodies of pre-Reformation Germany into chorales, the German Catholics appear to have been at small pains to guard their inheritance in its original form. Indeed, the earliest printed source of mediaeval German song is not of Catholic but of Swedish-Lutheran origin. In 1582 Theodoricus Petri published *Piae Cantiones*, a collection of such melodies, sacred and secular, most of them probably Swedish but a minority German.[213] This book has been a gold mine to editors of carol-collections, particularly to Neale and to Dr. G. R. Woodward. Some of its contents appear, too, in our hymn-books. The thirteenth-century melody ordinarily used for the Christmas hymn, 'Of the Father's love begotten', probably reached the *Hymnal Noted* (in which it first appeared) from this source ; though it has been found in MSS. of earlier date. It was originally set to a Trope on the *Sanctus* beginning *Divinum mysterium*.[214] The correct form is the "alternative version" in *A.M.* 56, which also appears at †613 ‡387. The second tune to *498, 'The foe behind', is also from *Piae Cantiones*, where it is set to a hymn on the Passion : Neale's words were written to "carry" it. *S.P.* has four more tunes from the same source, viz. ‡4, 272, 385, 502. Of these the first is our old friend, 'Good King Wenceslas' (a charming figment of Neale's imagination, by the way) ; the melody being set in *S.P.* to a translation of the springtide carol to which it belongs in *Piae Cantiones*.

The explanation of Catholic indifference to such things is doubtless that the Counter-Reformation, unlike the Reformation, was not encouraging to popular hymnody. But, as time went on, it was discovered that vernacular hymns could not be dispensed with : and from the closing decades of the sixteenth century onwards a series of collections of hymns, German as well as Latin, made their appearance. The earliest of these were the three collections by Leisentritt, the last of which (1584) contained the melody *Ave Virgo Virginum* already mentioned, along with another on which the well-known tune 'Narenza' *268 †518 is founded. In the Andernach *Geistliche Gesänge* (1608) the plainsong tunes of the Latin hymns were largely supplanted by melodies of the chorale type. *S.P.* has three tunes from this source, ‡130 ii, 305, 478, and *A.M.* one, *754 i. The Cologne *Gesangbuch* of 1623 contained the splendid Easter melody *Lasst uns erfreuen*, which has become so well known in connection with Mr. Riley's fine hymn, 'Ye watchers and ye holy ones' †519. In *A.M.* it is appropriately set (in a more exact version) to 'Light's glittering morn' *126 ; while the compilers of *S.P.* have rather rashly dared to mate its magnificence with a new Easter hymn, 'Let us rejoice' ‡157. *S.P.* has three other tunes from the 1619 and 1623 editions of this book, ‡163, 167, 549 ii. Lastly we may mention the collection called *Heilige Seelenlust*, first published in 1657. The author of it was Johann Scheffler, who has been dealt with above in connection with Lutheran hymnody because most of his hymns were written before his conversion to Rome. The musical editor of his book was Georg Joseph, who wrote or adapted the tune that forms the basis of the popular one to 'At even, ere the sun was set' *20 †266, 42 ii. Other tunes from the same source are that of the New Year's hymn 'For thy mercy' *73 †286 and the pretty lilting melody at ‡559.

CHAPTER VI

THE METRICAL PSALTERS

FROM the moment of its inception the Reformation movement of the sixteenth century showed the signs of division into two camps — a Right and a Left, to borrow the phraseology of continental politics. The Right is represented by Lutheranism and (in a still more marked degree) by our own Church of England; the Left by the various bodies that are grouped together as 'Reformed' or 'Calvinistic'. Calvin himself at this period had not yet appeared upon the scene. But even while Luther was initiating his own movement in Germany, a parallel revolt against Rome was being undertaken by Zwingli in Switzerland, but on more drastic lines. In Zwingli the mystical and emotional elements that were so marked a feature of Luther's make-up were lacking. He was essentially a humanist and an intellectualist; a man, too, devoid of any sentimental feeling for the past and always ready to push his principles to their logical issue. This mentality was reflected in his attitude towards public worship in general and the Mass in particular. The outward observances of religion were to be reduced to a minimum and nothing tolerated that was not authorized by the plain letter of Holy Scripture : the Sacrament was to be regarded as a "bare memorial" of Christ's Death. Zwingli himself perished in battle in 1531 : but his trenchant spirit was inherited and his work carried on by the Frenchman Jean Calvin, who proceeded to erect on the foundation laid by him a rigid and highly organized system of doctrine and discipline, which from its focus at Geneva was to spread over large parts of Western Europe and into the New World as well. In Germany it was never to win more than a minority-support (and even then only in a modified form) as against its rival Lutheranism. But in Protestant Switzerland, in Holland and in Scotland it was to be triumphant; in France it was for a long time to constitute a formidable menace to Catholicism; while in England it not only left its mark on the formularies of the national Church at the close of the sixteenth century, but also inspired the great Puritan revolt against the Elizabethan religious settlement.

The difference between Lutheranism and Calvinism is to be seen in their respective attitudes towards hymnody as well as in major matters. The former, while encouraging the use of German metrical translations of the Psalms, was willing at the same time to give free play to the poetic gifts of its members in the production of original hymns, and even to permit the adaptation of Catholic material for a similar purpose. Zwingli and Calvin, on the other hand, with their rigid insistence on "The Bible and nothing but the Bible", frowned on anything save the metrical psalms. Thus the hymn-singing of the "Reformed" Churches was for a long time virtually confined to these. The metrical psalters of these various Churches were naturally closely interconnected, despite their differences of language; so that in dealing with them we shall have to consider them as a single whole. It should be added that, while in doctrine, organization and ritual the Church of England was more Catholic than the Lutheran, in the sphere of hymnody it followed for a long time the Calvinistic churches in its preference for metrical psalms over hymns. Thus the French-Swiss (Genevan), the German, the English and the Scottish Psalters in their mutual inter-relations form the subject of the present chapter.

The beginnings of Protestant metrical psalmody arose in the rather surprising *milieu* of the frivolous and corrupt French Court of the Valois.[215] The sister of Francis I, Marguerite, married to the dispossessed King of Navarre, was a friend to Humanism and to the reforming doctrine that was so closely connected with it. Herself a contributor (at least) to the celebrated *Heptameron* that bears her name, she was the patroness of many of the leading literary figures of the time. Among them was a gentleman of her suite, the French poet Clément Marot (1497–1544), who later became *valet de chambre* to Francis I. Marot's poetic evolution was not unlike that of Venantius Fortunatus a thousand years before. He had won fame as a satirist and writer of exquisite lyrics, amatory and otherwise : but having come under the influence of the Reformation he turned his muse to sacred subjects and began to translate the Psalms into French verse.[216] The first of these translations (of ps. 6) was included in a volume of poems which he dedicated to his patroness in 1533. He went on to translate other psalms as well : and his versions, which could be sung to popular tunes of the time, created quite a *furore* at Court. In his charming book, *The Psalms in Human Life*, Lord Ernle writes of them as follows :

No one delighted in the *sanctes chansonnettes* more passionately than the Dauphin (afterwards Henry II). . . . He sang them himself with musicians who accompanied his voice on the viol or lute. To win his favour gentlemen of the Court begged him to choose for each a psalm. Courtiers adopted their special psalms, just as they adopted their particular arms, mottoes or liveries. . . . Diane de Poitiers [the king's mistress] sang the *De profundis* (ps. 130) to the air *Baisez-moi donc, beau Sire*.[217]

From the Court they spread to the city and the country generally ; and were unquestionably a considerable factor in winning support for the Reformed doctrine and worship.

In 1542 Marot published 30 of these psalms in a single volume. The book brought down the wrath of the authorities on the poet. He fled to Geneva, where a new collection, now containing 50 psalms, was published in 1543. Marot died next year, leaving the rest of the psalms to be translated by the great Huguenot divine, Theodore Beza, who published them at intervals between 1551 and 1562. In the latter year the complete collection appeared with the title *Les Psaumes mis en rime françoise par Clément Marot et Théodore de Bèze*. This was the famous "Genevan Psalter", which for a while was used even in Catholic circles. Henri II, we are told,

carolled ps. 42, 'Like as the hart,' as he hunted the stag in the forest of Fontainebleau, riding by the side of Diane, for the motto of whose portrait he chose the first verse of his favourite psalm.[218]

In the Protestant world it was used not only in France and Switzerland, but in translated form in Germany, Holland and Denmark.

For our present purpose the Genevan Psalter is less interesting from the point of view of its words than of its music. The English metrical versions of the Psalms were home-grown products and framed on other lines. The difference of metres, too, made it difficult (as we shall see) to adapt the Genevan melodies to the English versions. Thus even on the musical side the contemporary influence of the Swiss psalter on English psalmody was with a few exceptions transient and unimportant. It is only in the last forty years that the magnificence of the best of the Genevan melodies has forced compilers to find — or rather to create — a place for them in our hymnals. But in their new surroundings they are becoming so well known that it is necessary to say something here concerning their origin.

The 30 psalms published by Marot in 1542 were without music. But even before that date, a partial metrical psalter with melodies attached had been published by Calvin at Strasburg in 1539. Of the 18 psalms included 12 were by Marot, but in a form different from that in which they appeared in his own edition three years later: the rest were presumably by Calvin himself. Of this book — "Calvin's First Psalter", as it has been called — no copy was for a long time known to exist. But in 1878 M. Douen, in his work on the Huguenot Psalter, announced that he had discovered an exemplar of it in the Royal Library at Munich. Not till 1919, however, was a facsimile of it published. This was followed in 1932 by an edition by Sir Richard Terry,[219] with an introduction, harmonizations and English translations of the psalms included in their original metres. The tunes in this Strasburg Psalter would appear to be mostly of German origin — adaptations, like many of the German chorales, of mediaeval German melodies, religious and secular. The only tune in it that figures in our hymn-books is that of ps. 36 — the splendid sweeping melody to "carry" which Dr. T. A. Lacey wrote his hymn, 'O Faith of England' †544 ‡246. It also appears in *A.M.* set to the words 'From highest heaven' *171. It was set in the Anglo-Genevan Psalter of 1561 (*see below*, p. 146) to the 113th psalm — hence its English title of 'Old 113th'.

Between 1541 and 1562 the Genevan Psalter gradually grew towards completeness, and tunes were provided for the new psalms as they appeared in successive editions. The musical editor of all these except the first and the last was Louis Bourgeois (*c.* 1510–?), one of the most illustrious names in Christian hymnody. In the edition of 1542 he altered some of the earlier tunes and substituted new tunes for others. By the time he had finished his editorship he had enlarged a psalter with some 30 tunes into one containing 85 — 83 for the psalms and 2 for metrical versions of the Commandments and the *Nunc dimittis* respectively. Of these 10 survived from the Strasburg Psalter of 1539, while for the rest Bourgeois himself was responsible, and many of them no doubt were composed by him. His relations with the Genevan Consistory had, however, long been uneasy: and at last, failing to win permission for the introduction of part-singing into the services, he quitted Geneva and went to Paris. Thus he had nothing to do with the 40 new tunes accompanying the 60 new psalms that went to make up the completed Genevan Psalter of 1562: and we have no clue to the authorship of these.

Concerning Bourgeois's work, Dr. Bridges has said: "Historians who wish to give a true philosophical account of Calvin's influence at Geneva ought probably to refer a great part of it to the enthusiasm attendant on the singing of Bourgeois's melodies." [220] As is only natural, some of the psalm-tunes written or adapted by him are superior to others: but the best of them include some of the most beautiful tunes in our hymnals. Their rather unusual metrical structure has made it necessary in a number of cases to provide words specially written to fit them: and with this object Dr. Bridges himself in the *Yattendon Hymnal* made some of his most precious contributions to English hymnody. The following appear in *E.H.* and *S.P.*: 'Joy and triumph everlasting' †200 ‡291 (to ps. 42); 'O gladsome Light' †269 ‡50 (to *Nunc dimittis*): 'The King, O GOD, his heart to Thee upraiseth' †564 ‡324 (to ps. 12). The two former are translations, one from Adam of St. Victor, the other of the very early Greek hymn $\Phi\hat{\omega}s$ $i\lambda\alpha\rho\grave{o}\nu$: the last is stated to be "based on F. R. Tailour", but the resemblances to Tailour's 1615 version of ps. 21 are so slight that it should be regarded as an original composition. The tune of ps. 12 appears in *A.M.* at *494. Other psalm-tunes by Bourgeois have been utilized as follows: 'The day Thou gavest' †277 ‡56 i

(The Ten Commandments); 'Bread of the world' †305 ‡265=*484 (ps. 118); 'Virgin-born, we bow before Thee' †640=‡121 (ps. 86); 'Lord, through this Holy Week' *647=†538 ‡347 (ps. 110). The tunes by Bourgeois that found their way into use in England through the metrical psalters (including the 'Old 100th') will be dealt with in the next section. Their number was unfortunately very limited: for, in contrast to the rich metrical variety of the Genevan Psalter, the English in its early stages was almost entirely in D.C.M. For another tune from the Genevan Psalter (not by Bourgeois) Bridges wrote the words of ‡661, 'Thee will I love, my God and King' (ps. 138).

It should be added that for many of the Genevan psalm-tunes harmonies were provided by another eminent Protestant musician, Claude Goudimel, who perished in the massacre of St. Bartholomew in 1572. His arrangements are used in a number of the settings indicated above.

II

The history of the English metrical Psalter known as the "Old Version" is even more complicated than that of the French. Those who would study its intricacies more closely are referred to Dr. Frere's authoritative treatment of it in the *Historical Introductions to Hymns A. and M.* and to the articles on the "Old Version" in Julian's *Dictionary of Hymnology* and on "Psalter (English Metrical)" in Grove's *Dictionary of Music* — the latter by H. E. Woolridge. It must suffice here to give a bare outline of the subject.

The first stage in the production of English metrical versions of the Psalms is a little later in date than Marot's corresponding efforts in French. It is associated with the name of Thomas Sternhold (?-1549), who was groom of the robes to Henry VIII, even as Marot was *valet de chambre* to Francis I. Apart from this and their common Protestantism, however, there is small similarity between

the two. Marot was a brilliant French Court poet : Sternhold was a plain, pious Englishman who wrote to edify,
not to charm. His aim seems to have been to make sacred
songs for the people in place of the "amorous and obscene
songs" in which they delighted : and for this reason he
cast his versions in the familiar ballad-metre, called
"Common Measure" (C.M.) or "Double Common
Measure" (D.C.M.), when used for hymns. At first,
according to Strype, he wrote for his own "godly solace" :
and would sing his versions to his own accompaniment on
the organ. But, soon after the accession of Edward VI, the
young king chanced to overhear them and insisted on
their being repeated in his presence. A collection of 19
psalms was published : and in a second edition issued in
1549, after Sternhold's death, this number rose to 37 —
i.e. psalms 1–17, 19–21, with 17 others. All were in D.C.M.
except the 25th (D.S.M.) and the 120th (6.6.6.6.6.6.).
Besides these Sternhold would seem to have written
others, for in later editions of the English Psalter versions
additional to those issued in 1549 are attributed to him.

His work was carried on by his principal colleague in
framing the "Old Version", John Hopkins (d. ?1570). In
1551 Hopkins added 7 new versions to Sternhold's 37.
The book was several times reissued during Edward's
reign. But on the accession of Mary the Reformers had to
flee the country : and the next stages in the evolution of
the English Psalter have their scene at Geneva.

By this time (1553) the Genevan Psalter had come to
include 83 psalms and was still growing. Moreover, the
melodies of Bourgeois were ready to hand. The result was
the issue in 1556 of an enlarged English psalter with tunes.
This formed the central portion of a *Forme of prayer and
ministration of the Sacraments, etc.* . . . put forward as a rival
to the Book of Common Prayer, which the extremist
exiles assembled at Geneva detested. The number of
psalms had now risen to 51 by the addition of 7 new

versions, to which was added a version of the Ten Commandments. All these were from the hand of William Whittingham (?1524–1579), later Dean of Durham, who had married Calvin's sister and was pastor of the Genevan refugees. The bulk of them were still in D.C.M.: but ps. 51 and the Commandments introduced L.M., ps. 115 was in D.S.M. and ps. 130 introduced 7.6.7.6 D. Each item had its own tune. The great majority of these presumably came with the versions themselves from England: but the D.C.M. of Sternhold's version of ps. 128 and Whittingham's versions of the Commandments and ps. 130 are fitted to the tunes of the corresponding Genevan versions. The last of these adaptations is particularly clumsy, as will be seen by a comparison:

This example serves to illustrate the difficulties in the way of using the Genevan tunes for the English versions, due not only to metrical differences but to the predominance in the French versions of the "feminine" double-rhymed ending, ‾ ‿, which English verse did not favour.

Of the tunes in this book few, as we shall see, were to survive for long at all, and only three are familiar to-day. These are 'Old 44th', 'Old 137th' and the well-known 'Commandments', which last eventually assumed the dull and debased form represented in *3. In the case of this tune the use of Bourgeois's original version in †277 is made possible by the "feminine" ending in lines 1 and 3 of the words.

In later editions of the English Psalter the principle of a different tune for every psalm was abandoned. In 1558 22 tunes disappeared, and 5 more gave way to others. The English edition of 1560 and the Genevan edition of

1561 left the residue untouched : but the English edition of 1561 still further reduced it, as we shall see.

Meantime, while the tunes decreased, the psalm-versions increased, in number. The 1558 edition contained 11 new ones, to each of which was attached a new tune. These psalms and their tunes alike showed signs of Genevan influence : the former in the use of new metres, the latter in the adaptation of Genevan melodies. Including the 6 new tunes to the older psalm-versions, the total of new tunes in this edition was 17. Of these 9 found a place in the completed Psalter of 1562, 5 of them being of Genevan origin.

At this point the history of the English Psalter bifurcates into two streams. On the accession of Elizabeth the English exiles at Geneva flocked back to their own country, taking the Psalter with them. For a time there was doubt as to its legality : but the question was quickly settled in its favour, and the use of it was regarded as being covered by the 49th of the Royal Injunctions of 1559 (*see below*, p. 153). "After this," says Dr. Frere, "it was natural to regard the book as the ally and colleague of the Prayer Book." [221]

In a new edition issued in 1560 few new psalms were added : but there were considerable additions to the appendix, which had hitherto comprised only versions of the Commandments (1556) and *Nunc dimittis* (1558). The former was now companioned by versions of *Benedictus* and *Magnificat*, the Apostles' Creed and the Lord's Prayer ; while a new version of *Nunc dimittis* was substituted for the old. Further, the book showed signs of a new influence — not French this time, but German, and hailing from Strasburg. Two tunes from the Strasburg books are used for psalms 67 and 125 ; while the version of the Lord's Prayer (by Bishop Cox) is set to Luther's *Vater unser*. The two former were to disappear : but the last was to remain associated not only with the Lord's Prayer but also with ps. 112 — for which reason it is known as 'Old 112th'. It is to be found in *644 †462 ‡566.

The year 1561 produced two new books — one issued at Geneva, the other in London. The former, edited by William Kethe, is the parent of the Scottish Psalter : and more will be said about it in that connection. It is only necessary to note here that it and its English fellow alike included for the first time both words and music of the 'Old 100th' — the words written presumably by Kethe himself,[222] and the tune one of Bourgeois's. In the English edition we see Hopkins back at his old task of supplementing Sternhold and adding 14 new psalm-versions : to which must be added 3 posthumous ones by Sternhold and 4 by other hands, making now 83 psalms in all. The appendix was further enlarged and now became a prefix and appendix. The former included versions of the *Venite* and *Te Deum* ; while the latter included certain poetical oddments which justify Dr. Frere's comment that "the Psalter was by slow degrees becoming the nucleus of a hymn-book as well".[223] Here again we may probably see signs of Lutheran influence.

The slaughter of tunes in this edition has been already alluded to. Of the tunes of 1556 spared in 1558 9 more disappeared, along with 7 of the new ones of 1558 and 2 of those of 1560. As against this must be set the introduction of 18 new tunes both for the psalms and for the prefix and appendix.

Next year (1562), with the issue of the book bearing the title *The Whole Booke of Psalmes collected into Englysh metre, by T. Starnhold, I. Hopkins and others* . . . , the long business of producing a complete English Psalter was at last brought to an end : and the "Old Version" reached its final and standard form. In regard to pss. 1—104, Hopkins was mainly responsible for filling the gaps in the earlier psalms, and his colleague, Thomas Norton (described by Wood as "a forward and busy Calvinist"), for filling those in the later. After ps. 104 Kethe's versions made at Geneva were for the most part adopted where they existed. At the same time the appendix received 4 further additions. A considerable number of new tunes were also added and no further excisions were made. But the poverty of the book on its musical side may be gauged by the fact that of the 150 psalms only 47 had tunes of their own, while the remainder had to dress in borrowed plumes.

This musical poverty is revealed not only in the quantity but also in the quality of the tunes provided. Here, it must be confessed, the music only matched the text. Fuller's quaint and caustic verdict on the "Old Version" has often been quoted:

"Their piety was better than their poetry; they had drank more of Jordan than of Helicon. . . . Sometimes they make the Maker of the tongue speak little better than barbarism, and have in many verses such poor rhyme that two hammers on a smith's anvil would make better music."[224]

Even less complimentary is Lord Rochester's epigram on a parish clerk singing the psalms:

"Sternhold and Hopkins had great Qualms,
  When they translated David's Psalms,
    To make the heart full glad:
  But had it been poor David's Fate
  To hear thee sing, and them Translate,
    By G—, 'twould have made him mad."[225]

Not only were the words for the most part halting and uninspiring in themselves, but in place of the rich variety of the Genevan metres we have a continual repetition of the dreary jog-trot of D.C.M. Thus it is hardly surprising that, musically as verbally, the English Psalter is a poor affair, or that most of its tunes find no place in most of our hymnals, and few of those that do are very popular. The D.C.M. tunes are dull and diatonic; the modal character of the more interesting of the earlier ones having condemned them to ejection. 'Old 44th' *216 †211 ‡655, 'Old 81st' *439 †461 ‡216 and 'Old 137th' *375 †404 ‡526 have managed to survive, and 'Old 18th' ‡43 and 'Old 22nd' †163 ‡176 to be revived : but one can hardly say that their vocal "line" is very exciting. The popular tune, 'St Flavian' *162 †161 ‡188, is the first half of the D.C.M. tune to ps. 132. The tunes written in other metres are better : and the best of them are admirable. Besides those already mentioned there are : the wistful 'Old 25th' *149 †149 ‡195 ; 'Old 50th' *660 ; the splendid 'Old 100th' *166 †365 ‡443 ; and 'Old 122nd' *303 †512 ‡696— the two last by Bourgeois. The well-known S.M. tune, St. Michael, *70 †27 ‡702, is an adaptation of 'Old 134th', also taken from Bourgeois. There remains to be added another Bourgeois tune, 'Old 124th'. This has always enjoyed immense popularity in Scotland as wedded to Whittingham's finely-rugged version of the psalm to which Bourgeois set it, "Now Isräel may say and that truly." To bring it back into use in England E.H. provided two hymns written ad hoc, †114, 352. But it is best known in connection with Clifford Bax's fine poem, 'Turn back, O man, forswear they foolish ways' ‡329, which was written for Gustav Holst's motet on the tune. The version of the melody in *715 reduces its 5 lines to 4 and so spoils it.

Fortunately the bare cupboard of the 1562 book was to be restocked in the various collections of psalm-tunes that for more than half a century were to issue at intervals from the press as purely private undertakings. Up to 1562 inclusive the music of the metrical psalms was in the form of melodies only. But in 1563 harmonized settings appeared in the shape of four part-books with the title *The Whole Psalmes, in four partes, which may be song to al musicall instrumentes*, published by John Day, the well-known music printer. It would appear to have been edited by W. Parsons ; for he did most of the settings. This book contained not only all the tunes of 1562, in the majority of cases in two or three alternative settings, but additional tunes as well, some of them "throw-outs" from earlier editions of the Psalter, others entirely new. Only one verse of the words was printed in each case, and the vocal parts were issued in separate volumes; for, here as elsewhere, nothing of the nature of our "scores" was for a long time to exist. The melody is usually given to the Tenor, but sometimes to one of the other parts.

This "Day's Psalter" was succeeded in 1579 by another bearing the name of William Damon, "one of Her Maiesties Musitions". Damon, however, seems to have disclaimed responsibility for its settings: and the book was withdrawn. Only after his death was a new edition published (in 1591), in which his settings appeared in an authentic form. In these and other contemporary collections still to be mentioned we get the first of the four-line single C.M. tunes, sometimes called "Church tunes", which were to supplant the majority of the old D.C.M. tunes. These new tunes were often quarried from the latter, which lent themselves easily to the purpose. A similar use was made to some extent of the settings made by Dr. Christopher Tye for his quite comically doggerel metrical translation of the first chapters of the Acts of the Apostles, published in 1553. It is from this source that the tune 'Windsor' *267 †332 ‡547 ii is probably derived. The tune 'Southwell' *205 †77 ‡106 first appears in Damon's 1579 book: and the fine 'Old 120th' *770 †464 ‡615, which was not in the earlier Psalters, is also found there.

Between the two editions of Damon came another Psalter by John Cosyn (1585): but it need only be mentioned here. Of greater interest is Este's Psalter of 1592, in which the settings were the work of ten leading musicians of the day: 9 of the new four-line tunes are found here, of which 5 had been in Damon. Of the remainder two are still in common use: 'Winchester Old' *62 †30 ‡82 i, and 'Cheshire' *272 †109 ‡105. Barley's Psalter (undated) followed Este closely, but with a larger variety of settings. In Allison's Psalter of 1599 the 9 "short tunnes" of Este reappear with 1 new one. In the settings in this last psalter the melody is usually in the upper part.

Far more important than any of these is Thomas Ravenscroft's *Whole Booke of Psalmes* of 1621. This carries on the work of Este and Barley, but contains besides a large number of new four-line tunes. Hitherto D.C.M. tunes had preponderated : but now the balance swings over heavily to the side of the single ones. Este's practice of giving local names to these is followed, and extended to all. Here are 'Bristol' *53 †6 ‡62, 'Lincoln' *143 †140 ‡171, and 'Salisbury' *710, in the "English" category : and 'St. David' *352 †166 ‡301, in the "Welsh". The "Scottish" tunes (which include 'Dundee') are taken from the Scottish Psalter of 1615 and will be dealt with below. To ps. 104 is given, in place of the Genevan tune in use since 1561, a new English one, the splendid 'Old 104th' *167 †178 ‡211. Some twenty-four musicians contributed, but the bulk of the work was done by Ravenscroft himself, who reset many of the old tunes and set many of the new short ones. His resetting of the "Old 100th" (to serve for the "Psalme before Evening Prayer") is given in *166d †365b ‡443b. The Dowland setting in Este *166c †365c ‡443c kept its place for the psalm itself, but in a modified form.

"Ravenscroft's Psalter," says Dr. Frere, "thus represented the last term in a long development, and the most popular, though not in all respects the best, application of the English art in its heyday to the psalmody of the Church. It was several times republished and was the medium through which the tradition was principally handed on to the later generations." [226] Like the Prayer Book and the Old Version itself, it went down before the storm of the triumphant Puritan assault on the Church : but its influence was to reappear when the old Church life was built up again after the Restoration.

It was to help to revive this on its musical side that the music-publisher John Playford put forth in 1671 his *Psalms and Hymns in Solemn Musick of Foure Parts on the Common Tunes to the Psalms in Metre : Used in Parish-Churches*. In the preface he complains thus of the decay of psalmody :

At this day the Best, and almost all the Choice Tunes are lost, and out of use in our Churches : nor must we expect it otherwayes, when in and about this great City, in above One hundred Parishes, there is but few Parish Clerks to be found that have either Ear or Understanding to set one of these Tunes Musically as it ought to be.

By way of amending this situation Playford supplied 47 tunes of all sorts, with psalm-versions taken not from the Old Version only but from other translations as well. The melody of these is always in the Tenor : the other parts are two Counter-Tenors and Bass. If trebles are available they are to sing the melody with the Tenors. In this collection Playford seems to have worked in independence of Ravenscroft : and the confusing practice is adopted of assigning new names to several of the four-line tunes. In addition to the psalms that form the body of the book 17 hymns are given : but these will be more conveniently dealt with in the next chapter.

This first effort of Playford's was not a success. It was, in fact, too good for the taste and resources of its time. So six years later he made another attempt on a much less ambitious scale — a small book instead of a stately folio, with tunes in only three parts and the melody given to the Treble instead of the Tenor : for he realizes that often only trebles and basses will be available. Alternative tunes and versions, too, are provided where the others are too difficult. In this *Whole Book of Psalms* both the tunes and their nomenclature are much closer to Ravenscroft's : but Playford rejects most of his Scottish and Welsh tunes as "outlandish". He includes, however, the fine tune 'St. Mary' *93 †84 ‡116, which had appeared in Archdeacon

Prys's Welsh metrical psalter of 1621 and now found a place in an English Psalter for the first time. In this form Playford's book became the standard one in England for as long as the Old Version held the field.

Before leaving the subject of these psalm-tunes of the Old Version it may be well to say something concerning the manner in which they are set out in the early Psalters. A criticism frequently directed against nineteenth-century hymnals is that their versions of these tunes "iron them out" in such a way as to substitute a monotonous "equal-note" rhythm for the varied rhythm of the original forms : and the more recent hymnals take great credit to themselves for having "restored" the latter. But the question is not quite so simple as it appears. Dr. Frere has made careful researches into the subject and expresses his conclusion thus : "These hymn-tunes, as a rule, in their early form began each odd line with a long note, and each even line either with a corresponding long note or else with a syncopation ; but apart from this there was no uniformity of rhythm : minims and semibreves alternated in the freest possible way, and there was evidently nothing very settled in this respect, since in most tunes variations occur with every successive edition." [227] Thus it is hard to say that there is a "correct" version of any tune. Even in regard to the long note at the beginning of any line, it should be remembered that this was primarily intended as a "gathering-note" to help the congregation to get a grip on the melody of that particular line ; and that the proper degree of the observance of these notes will depend on the accentuation of the words. The first foot of an iambic line may be in practice either an iambus, ‿ ‒, or a trochee, ‒ ‿ ; in the former case a shorter note is indicated, in the latter a longer. The truth of the whole matter appears to be well summed up by Dr. S. H. Nicholson, when he says that "it would seem that the psalm-tune in its rhythm should be regarded (just as the Anglican chant) rather as a kind of musical formula, applicable to different verses, than as a set composition of unalterable accent : and as it seldom happens that all the verses of a hymn are exactly the same in the arrangement of the accents, it seems reasonable to give the tune in a form which most nearly matches in its rhythmic structure the normal form of the line. As the normal beginning is iambic and not trochaic, it seems more natural to begin with a short note than a long".[228]

Though the Old Version was the principal, it was far from being the only, metrical psalter that existed in the period which we have just reviewed. Two may be mentioned here on account of the traces that they have left in the music of our hymn-books. Archbishop Parker, while lying *perdu* in Mary's reign, translated the whole Psalter into various metres, along with the Canticles and the *Veni Creator*. This was printed for him in 1567 by Day. Its main interest for us lies in the 9 tunes by Thomas Tallis (*c.* 1510–85) set out at the end of it to provide settings for Parker's versions. The first 8 form a group, of which each is in one of the 8 "modes". 4 of these are in D.C.M., 2 in D.L.M., while the other 2 are in D.S.M. and 6.6.6.6.D respectively. The set is preceded by the following quaint description of "The nature of the eyght tunes" :

1. The first is meeke : devout to see,
2. The second sad : in maiesty,
3. The third doth rage : and roughly brayth,
4. The fourth doth fayne : and flattery playth,
5. The fifth delight : and laugheth the more,
6. The sixth bewayleth : and weepeth full sore,
7. The seventh tredeth stoute : in froward race,
8. The eyghte goeth milde : in modest pace.

The ninth tune is an "extra" and is in 4-line C.M., being set to the translation of *Veni Creator*. It is the well-known 'Tallis's Ordinal' *508 †453 ‡664. Even more familiar is the celebrated "Tallis's Canon" *23 †267 ‡45, which is a cutting down of the 8th tune from 8 lines to 4. Five of the others have recently been revived — those in the 1st, 2nd,

3rd, 5th and 7th modes respectively, †78 ‡625; †3; †92 ‡675; ‡483; †496. It may be added that the 3rd mode melody is the "theme of Thomas Tallis" on which Vaughan Williams has founded his solemn and moving 'Fantasia' for strings.

These modal tunes of Tallis are beautiful things of their kind: but it is doubtful whether they can be really said to come within the category of "hymn-tunes" in the modern popular sense. They are more appropriate for singing as little anthems than for congregational use. A note which Tallis has set at the head of them states that "the Tenor of these partes be for the people when they will sing alone, the other parts, put for greater queers [choirs], or to such as will syng or play them privatelye". In point of fact, the treble part of the original is often more attractive *as melody* than the tenor: but as Dr. E. H. Fellowes, the leading authority on Tudor music, says in a letter to the present writer which he has kindly given him leave to quote, "these great composers, writing in four parts, could make every one of them a melody". He adds: "Tallis states clearly that both the tenor and the treble parts are to be regarded as melody for alternative purposes. But in both uses the score *must* be kept *as Tallis wrote it*. It is pedantic and wrong to print these tunes, as has been done, with the tenor on the top and the treble part put into the tenor position."

A later metrical psalter which, like Parker's, was for private use was George Sandys's, of which the 2nd edition (1638), called *A Paraphrase upon the Divine Poems*, contained 24 "new tunes for private devotion" by Henry Lawes (1596–1662) — the musician to whom Milton addressed his sonnet beginning:

> Harry, whose tuneful and well measur'd song
> First taught our English music how to span
> Words with just note and accent, not to scan
> With Midas' ears, committing short and long.

4 of these find a place in both *E.H.* and *S.P.* : †217, 219, 234, 432 ; ‡22, 227, 589, 290. *E.H.* has also a fifth :†505.

III

The ever-growing multitude of rival metrical translations of the Psalter side by side with the Old Version was
for a long time without effect in challenging its supremacy.
But meanwhile the dissatisfaction of the polite and educated world at its patent crudities was steadily growing :
and at the end of the seventeenth century an opportunity
at last came of giving it an authorized successor. This was
the appearance of a new translation from the hands of
two Irishmen — the then Poet Laureate, Nahum Tate
(1652–1715) and Dr. Nicholas Brady (1659–?1726). It was
first published in 1696. William III accepted the dedication : and it was immediately "allowed" by order of the
King in Council. It should be understood that this "New
Version", as it came to be called, was no more than an
authorized alternative to the Old, "permitted to be used
in all churches, etc., as shall think fit to receive it". The
two rival versions were to go on side by side till the end,
though the popularity of the elder steadily declined, at
least later on.

At first there were few signs that this was to be the case.
The New Version was recommended by the Archbishop
of Canterbury and the Bishop of London. Dr. Bray,
founder of the Society for Promoting Christian Knowledge, maintained that the Old was the chief cause of the
decay of psalmody. But the learned Bishop Beveridge
launched a trenchant attack upon the intruder, not only
complaining of the inconvenience of having two versions,
but stressing the superiority of the Old in its fidelity to the
Hebrew and its capacity to be understood by the people,
and denouncing the "fine and modish" character,

142

"flourished with wit and fancy", of the New. It was at first used only in a few churches in London : and even there Brady's own church, St. Catharine Cree, cast it out as "an innovation not to be endured". Dr. Samuel Wesley, father of John and Charles, while considering it much superior to the Old, told his curate at Epworth that "they must be content with their grandsire Sternhold" for the sake of the people, "who have a strange genius at understanding nonsense".[229] The common people certainly did their best to justify this estimate of their capacities. The Old Version was regarded by many of them as possessing not less than a Divine authority. Tate himself tells us how a maid in his brother's house, refusing to join in family prayers, explained : "If you must know the plain truth, Sir : as long as you sung Jesus Christ's psalms, I sung along with ye : but now that you sing psalms of your own invention, ye may sing by yourselves." [230]

The new book was followed in 1700 by a separate *Supplement* (designed to be "bound up with the Volume"), which provided not only additions to the words in the shape of alternative versions and hymns, but also tunes which could be used either for the New Version or the Old. The alternative versions were intended to be used with the tunes in "peculiar" metre which had become familiar in connection with the Old Version : the "hymns", which included the famous Christmas hymn, 'While shepherds watched', will be spoken of later. The psalms of the New Version were almost all in the ordinary metres : and these metres were to be served by a collection of what were called "the Usuall tunes", which were all those of the earlier metrical Psalters, though sometimes differently named.

In the 3rd edition (1702) and the 4th (1704) this selection of tunes was enlarged : and in the 6th edition (1708) many new tunes were provided and all the tunes arranged in two parts. This edition is noteworthy for including a number of tunes that have attained to classic rank : 'St. Anne' *165 †450 ‡598, 'Hanover' *431 †466 ‡618, 'St. Matthew' *369 †526 ‡287 and 'Alfreton' *71 †240 ‡237. Its editor is said to have been the eminent Dr. William Croft (1678–1727), organist of Westminster Abbey : and there is every reason to believe that the four tunes in question are from his pen. Later editions followed this of 1708 closely.

From a literary point of view "Tate and Brady" was generally regarded by contemporary taste as an improvement on " Sternhold and Hopkins"— "Ye scoundrel old bards and a brace of dull knaves", as a satirist of the time retrospectively addressed the latter.[231] The "wit and fancy" with which Bishop Beveridge found fault are not too conspicuous to our eyes : and a modern taste may even find not very much to choose between the roughness of the Old Version and the tame smoothness of the New. The story goes that once Queen Victoria asked Bishop Wilberforce, "What is a drysalter ? " : to which the Bishop replied "Tate and Brady, Madam". Yet it is not to be denied that whereas the Old Version has left nothing behind in our hymnals, to the New we are indebted for two of our most popular hymns, 'Through all the changing scenes of life' *290 †502 ‡677, and 'As pants the hart' *238 †367 ‡449, as well as for three others : 'Thou, Lord, by strictest search' *658, 'Have mercy, Lord, on me' *249 †74 and 'O God of hosts' *237.

In addition to the *Supplement* a number of private collections of psalms and tunes were issued about the same period. A collection of 1697 for use in St. James', Westminster, contained the familiar tune, 'St. James' *199 †341 ‡96, probably by Ralph Courteville, organist of that church. But by far the most important of these collections was another Playford publication. In 1701 Henry Playford, son of John, first issued his celebrated *The Divine Companion, or David's Harp New Tun'd, being a choice collec-*

tion of New and Easy Psalms and Anthems. . . . The significance of this volume in its hymnal aspect will be dealt
with in the next chapter. Here we may mention that
among the new tunes (including 6 by Dr. Blow) appears
for the first time 'Uffingham' *658 †434 ‡564, by Jeremiah
Clarke (*c.* 1670–1707). The enlarged 2nd edition of 1709
included three more tunes by Croft, 'Croft's 148th' (or
136th) *414 †565 ‡657, 'Binchester' †398 ‡509 and
'Eatington' †639 ‡192, together with 'Brockham' *723
†220 ‡228, 'Tunbridge' *645 †88 ‡474, and the familiar
'St. Magnus' *301 †147 ‡175—the two former certainly,
and the last presumably, by Jeremiah Clarke. Concerning the tunes written by Clarke, who became organist of
St. Paul's in 1695 and died by his own hand in 1707,
Dr. Bridges has said that "they are the first in merit of
their kind, as they were the first in time ; and they are
truly national and popular in style." About a generation
later William Knapp (1690–1768), Parish Clerk of
Wareham, Dorset, published his *Sett of New Psalm
Tunes and Anthems* (1738). This contained the well-known
'Wareham' *63 †475 ‡631, and the even finer 'Spetis-
bury', so well wedded in *A.M.* to Bridges's splendid
hymn on the Holy Angels (originally written for the
Yattendon Hymnal to fit another tune), 'All praise be to
GOD' *753.

The publication of the New Version may thus be said
to mark the beginning of a new advance in the music of
the English Church. With regard to the manner of psalm-
singing at this period two points may be noted. First, the
psalms seem to have been sung at a pace in comparison
with which "the slowest singing of to-day would have
seemed fast".[232] Further, it was usual to interpolate
between the lines of a psalm organ-interludes often of
considerable elaboration. This custom continued till comparatively recent times, like the use of the psalm versions
themselves.[233]

IV

A detailed account of the Scottish Psalter lies outside the scope of the present book. But before concluding this chapter something may be said about its evolution, both for the sake of completeness and also on account of the musical legacies it has left to Anglican hymnals.

The English and the Scottish Psalters, as we have said, derive from the same parent-stem, and up to the year 1558 their history is identical. From that point, however, the two diverged, and developed in quite different ways while retaining a common nucleus.[234] We have already spoken of the English editions of 1560 and 1561, the two penultimate stages towards the completed Psalter of 1562. Concurrently with that of 1561 an "Anglo-Genevan" Psalter appeared at Geneva intended for the use of the exiles left behind, and still linked with the Genevan *Form of Prayer*. This contained 25 new psalm-versions in addition to the 62 of 1558, probably all written by William Kethe (who was presumably a Scot), and most of them written in metres to fit the Genevan tunes. Some 20 new tunes were given, all Genevan except for the 'Vater unser' used for Cox's Lord's Prayer. The Scottish Reformers adopted this book for their own : and in 1564 a complete Psalter, *The Whole Psalmes of David*, was issued as part of the Presbyterian *Book of Common Order*. Besides the 87 versions of 1561, 42 were taken from the English Psalter of 1562 and 21 were contributed by two Scots, Robert Pont and John Craig. The tunes numbered 105 in all, many of them Genevan — a far richer collection than that in the complete English Psalter.

The Scottish Psalter had no influence on the English save in one respect — the four-line C.M. tunes.[235] In 1615 an edition of the Psalter was published by Andro Hart in Edinburgh containing a supplement of these tunes (called "Common Tunes"), similar to those given by Este,

Barley and Allison. They numbered 12 and included some of those in the English books and some others: among them the 'French Tune', which was rechristened 'Dundee' by Ravenscroft and has become one of our best-known tunes, *221 †428 ‡557; 'The Stilt' (Ravenscroft's 'York') *237 †472 ‡628; and the splendid 'Old Martyrs' †449 ‡597, Burns's "plaintive Martyrs, worthy of the name" — most worthy, but in truth far more for its heroic than for its plaintive quality. All of these were incorporated by Ravenscroft. Playford for the most part rejected them: but through Ravenscroft's influence the three that we have particularized won their way to popularity in England.

In another book published by Hart's heirs in 1635 the number of 4-line tunes was increased to 31. One of these was adopted by Playford in his 1671 collection and renamed by him 'London New' *373 †394 ‡503. Another is 'Caithness' *630 ii, †445 i, ‡112.

From what has been said in this chapter it will appear that our debt to the metrical psalters of all lands lies much more in the department of music than of words. On the other hand, a far larger proportion of our current hymns than is generally realized by those who sing them is taken more or less direct from the psalms. If "Tate and Brady" have given us few hymns and "Sternhold and Hopkins" none at all (except the Old Hundredth, which is by somebody else), Christian poets of all ages since the Reformation have been successful in transforming the biblical psalms into English hymns of wide popular appeal. An attempt is made to give a list of these in Appendix D at the end of the volume. A glance at this list will suffice to show how even in the vast and various field of modern hymn-singing the old-fashioned ideal of "metrical psalmody" can still find a place.

CHAPTER VII

ENGLISH HYMNODY UP TO THE TIME OF WATTS

I

IN England as in other countries a vernacular hymnody grew up during the Middle Ages side by side with the Latin hymnody of the liturgical services. The first beginnings of this go back far into Anglo-Saxon times. Bede's charming story [236] is well known, telling how Caedmon, a lay brother in St. Hilda's monastery at Whitby, leaving the festive board one night because of his inability to take his turn at singing and withdrawing to the stable to watch the horses, heard in a dream the command, "Caedmon, sing," and was at once inspired to compose a hymn "to the praise of GOD" which he recited to the Abbess and his brethren next morning. Bede goes on to relate how afterwards in the exercise of his new gift Caedmon turned into verse "the whole series of sacred history". Another story [237] concerns a contemporary of Caedmon, St. Aldhelm, Bishop of Sherborne (d. 709). Being distressed, when Abbot of Malmesbury, by the unwillingness of the Wessex folk to hear sermons, he took his station on the bridge over the Avon, and there, minstrelwise, sang to the people lively songs of his own making until a crowd collected, whereupon he changed his strain to a graver and religious note. Lays attributed to Aldhelm were still sung in the days of King Alfred, who deemed him superior to any other native poet. Like Aldhelm, Alfred himself was poet and scholar : and to him is attributed the Anglo-Saxon original of a hymn in *A.M.*, 'O GOD our Maker, throned on high' *664.

The closing centuries of the Middle Ages produced in our country a remarkable efflorescence of sacred poetry marked by a tender and passionate piety that we hardly find it easy in these days to associate with the English character. Its most salient feature is an intense personal love of our Lord, which delights to contemplate Him as Lover of men and Redeemer and to dwell on the details of His Passion. Side by side with this goes a no less fervent devotion to His Mother. The leading figure in this school is the fourteenth-century Yorkshire hermit and mystic, Richard Rolle of Hampole (1290–1349), of whom it has been said that "Jesus is to him the one passion". His voluminous writings include both prose and verse. Of the poems of Rolle and his like no complete collection as yet exists : but a large number of them have been printed in various scholarly editions. The cream of them is collected and reproduced — with just enough of modernization in the language to make them easily intelligible to the ordinary reader — in Miss Frances Comper's beautiful volume recently published with the title *Spiritual Songs from English MSS. of Fourteenth to Sixteenth Centuries*. Two short examples taken from this collection may be set down here as illustrative of the general character of these poems. The first is a little song by Richard Rolle :

> Jhesu that died on the rood
> for the love of me,
> and bought me with thy precious blood,
> thou have mercy of me.
>
> What me lets of any thing
> for to love thee,
> be it me lief, be it me loth,
> do it away from me.

The second example consists of three of the eight verses

of a *Prayer to Jesus* that bears the name of Richard de
Caistre, a Norwich priest who died in 1420:

. . . . . .

Jhesu, for thy woundis smart
   Of thy feet and handen two,
Make me meek and low of heart
   And thee to love as I should do.

. . . . . .

Jhesu, Lord that madest me
   And with thy blessed blood me bought,
Forgive that I have grieved thee
   With wordë, workë, will and thought.

Jhesu, in whom is all my trust,
   That died upon the rood-tree,
Withdraw my heart fro fleshly lust,
   From covetise and vanity.[238]

. . . . . .

Concerning such poems Miss Comper says that "many
were set to music, and others, judging by their lilt and
rhythm, may have been sung. For friars and monks, and
no doubt anchoresses and nuns also, as well as trouba-
dours, sang their spiritual love ditties to simple instruments of their own devising".[239] But we have no proof
that they were used as "hymns" in the sense of being sung
in church. They were apparently intended in many cases
to be used as silent devotions at Mass. The case is otherwise with the carols for Christmas and other sacred seasons
which England, like the other countries of Western
Europe, produced in abundance in the later Middle
Ages. Here, too, not only the words have survived, but
in many cases the music also. We cannot deal with these
carols here beyond saying that they often breathe the
same tender fervour as the poems mentioned above, and
that their rediscovery and publication in many collections
of carols of the last generation have brought a wonderful
enrichment of our native sacred song, and resulted in a
large-scale eviction of the faded sentimentalities that

masqueraded under the title of carol in the Victorian age. But we may cite as examples the exquisite poem 'I sing of a maiden that is makeles' (dating from the fifteenth century), and the two lovely carols in the Coventry Nativity Play, 'This endris night' and 'Lullay, lullay, thou little tiny child'. The contemporary tune of the second of these three is used in †20 ‡72.

II

During the two centuries that followed the Reformation the Church of England had practically nothing to show in the way of congregational hymnody apart from metrical versions of the Psalter. In the first stage of the reforming movement there seemed a momentary possibility of its developing a hymnody on the Lutheran model. Evidence of this is the volume called *Goostly Psalmes and Spiritualle Songs*,[240] of which an unique copy exists in the library of Queen's College, Oxford. It is the work of the translator of the Bible, Miles Coverdale, who was made Bishop of Exeter in 1551. It was published in the reign of Henry VIII: but the exact date is uncertain. The preface thus indicates its object:

Would GOD our carters and ploughmen (had none) other thing to whistle upon save psalms . . . and if women . . . spinning at the wheels had none other songs . . . they should be better occupied than with hey nony nony, hey troly loly.

— a characteristic anticipation of the later Puritan attitude towards secular folk-song. The 41 items contained in it include 15 versions of the psalms, together with paraphrases of the Commandments, Creed, Lord's Prayer, *Media vita* ('In the midst of life'), *Gloria in excelsis, Magnificat, Nunc dimittis, Christe qui lux* and *Veni Creator* — sometimes more than one of a single original. Of the remaining 15 items, 13 are English translations of German hymns of the Reformation. The first verse of one of these, 'Crist is now risen agayne', was quoted in an earlier chapter. The other two of the 15 "hymns" would seem to be of native origin — viz. a hymn to the Holy Spirit (based on the *Veni Creator*), and one that begins with the uncompromising sentiment, 'Let go the whore of Babilon'! Apart from these two it would appear that not the hymns only but all the contents of the volume are translated from German originals.

A further proof that the pioneers of the English Reformation intended to make hymns a part of Divine Service is supplied by the well-known letter of Cranmer to Henry VIII, dated Oct. 7, 1544 (or 1545). The Archbishop writes:

> I have translated into the English Tongue, so well as I could in so short time, certain processions, to be used upon festival days. . . . If your grace command some devout and solemn note to be made thereunto . . . I trust it will much excitate and stir the hearts of all men unto devotion and godliness. But in mine opinion the song that shall be made thereunto would not be full of notes, but, as near as may be, for every syllable a note, so that it may be sung distinctly and devoutly. . . . As concerning the *Salve festa dies* the Latin note, as I think, is sober and distinct enough: wherefore I have travailed to make the verses in English and have put the Latin note unto the same. Nevertheless they that be cunning in singing can make a much more solemn note thereto. I made them only for proof to see how English would do in song. But, by cause mine English verses want the grace and facility that I could wish they had, your majesty may cause some other to make them again that can do the same in more pleasant English and phrase.[241]

For some reason, however (we may conjecture that the influence of Calvin had something to do with it), nothing more came of the matter: and in the successive editions of the Book of Common Prayer the only hymns that appear are the translations of the *Veni Creator* in the Ordinal (*see* pp. 81, 159). On the other hand, the Primers issued for private devotion did include hymns. Rough versions of Latin hymns had already figured in the pre-Reformation Sarum Primers: and they are also to be found in the Primers of Henry VIII, which doubtless passed through Cranmer's hands. In Edward VI's Primer of 1553 they are excluded, no doubt deliberately : but they reappear in Elizabeth's Primer of 1559, which was based on those of Henry VIII. The use of hymns, whether translations from the Latin or otherwise, is envisaged by the 49th of the Royal Injunctions of 1559, which permits

> that in the beginning, or in the end of common prayers, either at morning or evening, there may be sung a hymn, or such-like song . . . in the best sort of melody and music that may be conveniently devised, having regard that the sentence of the hymn may be understood and perceived.[242]

But by this time the people had taken a fancy for singing metrical psalms : and no doubt the influence of the Reformers newly come back from Geneva was adverse to the use of anything else. The Old Version of Sternhold and Hopkins quickly acquired an almost canonical authority ; and held the field to the virtual exclusion of the experiments on Latin or Lutheran models which a decade or two earlier had seemed to have a future before them.

Only through the back-door of the appendices to the successive editions of the Psalter was it possible for a few hymns to make a shy and tentative re-entry in that psalm-ridden age. In that of 1561 appears the "Humble Suit of a Sinner", 'O Lord, turn not away Thy face' *93 †84 ‡116, which still holds its place in our hymn-books ; along with five other hymns (two of them translations of Lutheran originals) that have sunk beneath the stream of time. In 1562 the "Humble Suit" reappears, now rechristened "The Lamentation of a Sinner" and with the name of J. Marckant attached to it, together with two more hymns in a similar penitential key.

For a long time no addition was to be made to this beggarly repertory. The Church of England had to rest content with the Old Version and its meagre doggerel

Supplement. It may seem strange that a Church that possessed so magnificent a prose liturgy as the Book of Common Prayer should have been satisfied to be so poorly equipped on the poetical side of its worship. But here the Genevan influence reigned supreme. The Prayer Book it had to accept as a *fait accompli*, along with the noble buildings inherited from the Middle Ages, while at the same time doing its best to reduce to a minimum the appeal of both to the aesthetic sensibilities of its victims. But so far as Church song was concerned, its pet principle of "The Bible and the Bible only" held the field. Thus the superb poetical outburst of the Elizabethan Age expressed such religious aspiration as it could show in elaborate forms unintended and unsuitable for Church use. For Spenser, as for Milton more than a generation later, a "Hymn" is simply a religious ode. The only trace that the age has left in our hymn-books consists of a few treasures that have recently been made to serve a purpose for which they were not designed and are not always well-fitted. The Sunday hymn 'Most glorious Lord of life' †283 ‡22 is a sonnet of Spenser's : and *S.P.* has made similar but far less appropriate use of one of Shakespeare's sonnets, 'Poor soul, the centre of my sinful earth' ‡622, and of the exquisite song of Edmund Campion, 'Never weather-beaten sail' ‡587. More suitable for use as hymns are three other poems in the same collection : a second song of Campion's, 'Sing a song of joy' ‡639, Thomas Gascoigne's 'You that have spent the silent night' ‡38, and Sir H. Wotton's 'How happy is he born and taught' ‡524, with Sir Philip Sidney's beautiful paraphrase of ps. 139, 'O Lord, in me there lieth naught' ‡605.

Apart from these the only Elizabethan hymn in our collections — and the only one of them all that has as yet come into common use — is of Roman Catholic origin : 'Jerusalem my happy home.' [243] The version of it in *A.M.* *236 is a rewritten fragment. The whole is given in †638

‡395, and is exquisitely quaint and charming. Its author-ship is more or less a mystery, as to which there has been much conjecture but can be no certainty. It is found in a MS. book in the British Museum. The MS. is undated ; but appears to belong to the end of the sixteenth or be-ginning of the seventeenth century. The poem is headed, 'A song made by F.B.P. to the tune of Diana'. It was first printed in 1601 in a volume entitled *The Song of Mary the Mother of Christ . . . with the Description of Heavenly Jerusalem*. In this version the number of stanzas is reduced from 26 to 19, and there are many variants from the original MS. text — if it be the original and not another form of a still earlier version. Inasmuch as the British Museum MS. con-tains several other pieces of poetry evidently written by Roman Catholics, it has been suggested that F.B.P. was a victim of the persecution of Roman Catholics under Elizabeth or James I. The further suggestion has been made that the initials stand for Francis Baker, Pater (or Priest) : but there seems to be no proof of this whatever. The writer was presumably a Roman Catholic and possibly a priest — that is all that we can say. There is a striking general resemblance between his poem and another on the same subject of the Heavenly Jerusalem by W. Prid (first published in 1585), a cento from which appears in *S.P.* ‡393. The likeness may be due to the fact that both are apparently based on a passage describing the joys of heaven in a book of *Meditations* ascribed to St. Augustine which was very popular in the sixteenth century.

The Jacobean and Caroline periods were hardly less barren in the sphere of hymnody than the Elizabethan : for the tyranny of the Genevan principle still held firm. It is true that our modern hymnals contain a certain number of hymns of this date : but the poets whose names they bear wrote these lyrics for their own satisfaction and that of the literary public, not with an eye to liturgical use. This, for example, is the case with George Herbert (1593–1633). Not only were his poems not written to be sung in church, but most of them are quite unsuited to the purpose by reason of the elaborate and fantastic imagery which Herbert shared with the other poets of his time, and also on account of their peculiar metres. One could wish that this were not so : for no poet quite so perfectly expresses the characteristic Anglican mentality at its best as this exquisite combination of the poet, the scholar, the gentleman and the saint — the scion of a great house who after a brilliant career at Cambridge, where he was Public Orator, retired to the little village of Bemerton near Salisbury to end his short life as a model parish priest. On the other hand, the few poems of his that have come into use as hymns are in every way worthy of their place, and three of them at least have won wide popularity. They include the splendid 'Antiphon', 'Let all the world in every corner sing' *548 †427 ‡556, 'King of glory, King of peace' *665 †424 ‡553, 'Teach me, my GOD and King', †485 ‡652, 'Come, my Way, my Truth, my Life' ‡474, and the lovely paraphrase of the 23rd psalm, 'The GOD of love my Shepherd is' †93 ‡653.

A senior contemporary of Herbert was John Donne (1573–1631), the famous Dean of St. Paul's. His poem (written during the illness which was the occasion of his volume of *Devotions*), 'Wilt Thou forgive that sin where I begun' ‡123 = †515, has been of late years turned to use as a hymn. Concerning it Izaak Walton tells us in his *Life* of the author that after his recovery "he caused it to be set to a most grave and solemn tune, and to be often sung by the Choristers of St. Paul's Church, in his own hearing ; especially at the Evening Service" [244] — as a kind of anthem, we may assume. Fine and deeply felt poem though it be, it can hardly be regarded as entirely suitable for general congregational use.

Other poets of the time whose poems have been used as

hymns include Robert Herrick ('In the hour of my distress' †410) ; Phineas Fletcher ('Drop, drop, slow tears' †98 ‡125) ; Henry Vaughan the Silurist ('My soul, there is a country' ‡585) ; Thomas Pestel, Charles I's Chaplain in Ordinary, evicted by the Roundheads in 1646 ('Behold, the great Creator makes' †20 ‡72) ; and Sir Thomas Browne ('The night is come like to the day' ‡58). The similarity of the last-named hymn to Ken's Evening Hymn will be referred to later. The 19 psalm-paraphrases by the great John Milton (1608–74), of which 'Let us with a gladsome mind' † 532 ‡12, and 'The Lord will come and not be slow' †492 ‡658, are two specimens, may have been in part written with a view to a new Puritan psalter. Sir H. W. Baker's harvest hymn, 'Praise, O praise our GOD and King' *381, is based upon the former, which was written by the poet at the age of fifteen.

For a brief moment in the first half of the seventeenth century the monopoly of the Old Version seemed to be threatened and the possibility of a large development of hymnody proper appeared on the horizon, only to be quickly eclipsed. In 1623 George Wither (1588–1667) published his *Hymns and Songs of the Church*,[245] a book which has been described as "the earliest attempt at an English hymn-book". It was accompanied by a number of tunes by the foremost English musician of the age, Orlando Gibbons (1583–1625). These tunes, which are in various metres and are set out in two parts, treble and bass, number 16 in all : but some of them are only different versions of a single tune. The book was at first received with high favour at Court and elsewhere : and the author obtained a patent from the King, ordering it to be bound up with the Old Version wherever this was in use. The first part consisted of metrical paraphrases o Scripture ; the second of hymns for the Festivals, Seasons and Holy Days of the Prayer Book, and also for Special Occasions, together with a long hymn for use at the administration of

Holy Communion. But despite the approval of the King and of leading Churchmen, Wither's book aroused bitter opposition. The Stationers' Company, which had a monopoly of the Old Version, contrived to make the patent nugatory : and it was withdrawn by the Council in 1634. Later Wither went over to the Parliament side and eventually became one of Cromwell's Major-Generals. The story goes that, when he was taken prisoner by the Royalists, Sir John Denham saved his life by pleading that "his Majesty must not hang George Wither, for so long as he lives no one will account me the worst poet in England". This anecdote and Pope's name for him "wretched Withers (*sic*)" hardly suggest for him a high rank as poet : but his writings contain good stuff as well as bad. "Wither," said Lord Selborne, "wrote, generally, in a pure nervous English idiom, and preferred the reputation of 'rusticity' (an epithet applied to him even by Baxter) to the tricks and artifices of poetical style which were then in favour." [246] *S.P.* contains three of his hymns : the "Sunset Hymn", 'Behold the sun that seem'd but now' ‡43 (also *476), 'To GOD with heart and cheerful voice' ‡176 and 'The Lord of heaven confess' ‡657. It should be added that Gibbons's tunes shared the fate of the hymns they companioned and were entirely neglected for many generations, apart from 'Angels' or 'Angel's Song' †259 ‡29 (the version in *8 is spoilt) — so called because originally set to a song beginning 'Thus angels sung, and thus sing we' — which got into general use through its inclusion in Playford's collection of 1671. But in recent years they have won wide admiration and currency, and assuredly may take rank among the most beautiful, not of English hymn-tunes only, but of those of all lands. *S.P.* gives no less than 11 of them : ‡29, 103, 125, 134, 204, 261, 485, 574, 584, 604 (i), 648.

In 1627 the saintly John Cosin (1564–1672), who was to become Bishop of Durham at the Restoration, first published his *Collection of Private Devotions in the Practice of the Ancient Church called the Hours of Prayer*. This (as its name indicates) was intended for private use, like the old Primers, the successor of which it claimed to be. Its extensive employment of patristic and mediaeval material (including translations of old Latin Office hymns) brought down upon it the virulent attacks of the Puritan party — Prynne nicknamed it "Mr. Cozens His Couzening Devotions": and even after the Restoration its vogue and influence were limited. But one of its translations won the signal honour of being included in the Ordinal of the Prayer Book of 1661 — the version (or, rather, paraphrase) of the "Hymn for the Third Hour", *Veni Creator Spiritus*, which was then provided in addition to the dull C.M. version that had done duty alone since 1549 (p. 81).

This, however, was merely a matter of supplying an alternative for something that was already there. The Church's triumph over Puritanism at the Restoration brought with it no extension of the province of hymnody in Anglican worship. The Old Version still provided all that was deemed necessary in this respect. On the other hand, it was during the Restoration period that the first tentative steps were taken towards the evolution of the "English hymn" in the sense in which we now understand the phrase. This process manifested itself in two directions.

1. The first of these is the extension of the principle of metrical translation or paraphrase from the Psalter to other portions of Scripture. The appendix to the Old Version had already done this in regard to the Gospel Canticles: and during the Commonwealth period attempts were made both in England and in Scotland to apply the same principle more widely. Of the English attempts the most notable is connected with the name of William Barton (*c.* 1603–1678), a Puritan divine who conformed to the Anglican settlement after the Restoration. Of him Dr. Louis Benson has remarked that "he stands at,

and it must be said, he crosses the dividing line between the old Psalmody and the new Hymnody".[247] His contribution took the form of a collection of hymns, each of which consisted of selected texts and passages of Scripture turned into verse and woven into a single whole. Barton's first *Century of select hymns* framed on these lines was published in 1659. In 1670 this had expanded into *Two Centuries*, and in 1688 (after his death) the whole collection was published as *Six Centuries*. In the Anglican Church Barton's experiment had small success : but it was widely taken up by the Independents and undoubtedly prepared the way for the later epoch-making achievement of Dr. Watts. Indeed, to quote Dr. Benson again, "there was no essential difference between Barton's hymns collected out of Scripture and the succeeding hymns based upon Scripture".[248]

2. A parallel and more permanently important development is seen in the appearance during the Restoration period of a number of works by various authors which, though originally designed for private use only, did much to fix the type of the English hymn as it ultimately established itself, and have in fact made important contributions to our current hymnody. The earliest of these was a little volume published in 1664 with the title *The Young Man's Meditation, or some few Sacred Poems upon Select Subjects and Scriptures*. This was the work of Samuel Crossman, a divine concerning whom our chief information comes from a passage in Wood's *Athenae Oxonienses*.[249] He was born in 1623–4 in Suffolk, and was a Bachelor of Divinity of Cambridge University. He was appointed Prebendary of Bristol Cathedral and died, aged 59, on Feb. 4, 1683, a few weeks after his appointment as Dean. Among the poems in his book is the deservedly popular hymn 'Jerusalem on high' *233 †411 ‡197, which forms the second part of a poem on Heaven of which the first part begins, 'Sweet place, sweet place alone'. Another hymn in the

same collection and written in the same fine striding metre (already employed in some of the old psalm-versions) is 'My song is love unknown' ‡127. This is a hymn of remarkable beauty and breathing real religious passion : and it thoroughly deserves to share the popularity of its better-known companion. Taken over by *S.P.* from the *Public School H.B.*, where (with John Ireland's fine tune) it first appeared, it ranks as one of the most precious additions to our hymnody.

Another of these welcome contributions comes from a book, *Divine Dialogues with Divine Hymns*, published in 1668 by Dr. Henry More (1614–?87), the Cambridge Platonist who figures as one of the characters in *John Inglesant*. John Wesley was an admirer of More's book. He took it with him on his visit to Georgia in 1735, and later made one of its hymns into two for congregational use. The beautiful Christmas hymn in *S.P.*, 'The holy Son of GOD most high' ‡80, consists of 4 of the 10 stanzas of More's first *Hymn*.

The same year, 1668, saw the publication in Paris of a book by a Roman Catholic convert, John Austin (1613–69), bearing the title *Devotions in the Antient Way of Offices*. It was to have considerable influence in Anglican circles; for more than one adaptation of it was made for the use of English Churchmen. Even before this was done Playford had taken the rather surprising step of including a number of its contents in his first book of 1671. Probably this had something to do with the failure of his venture. In any case it is only recently that Austin's hymns have come into public use. Two of them appear in *S.P.* — the charming 'Hark, my soul, how everything' ‡19 (also †296) and 'Hail, glorious spirits, heirs of light' ‡205.

Far more famous than any of the hymns derived from these Restoration collections are two that were presumably written about the same time — the "Morning" and "Evening Hymns" of Thomas Ken (1637–1711), the admirable divine who was appointed Bishop of Bath and

Wells in 1685 and resigned his see four years later rather than acknowledge the "usurper" William III. They are: 'Awake, my soul, and with the sun' *3 †257 ‡25, and 'Glory to Thee, my GOD, this night' *23 †267 ‡45. The exact date when they made their first appearance is uncertain: 250 but they would seem to have been in limited use in 1674, for they are apparently referred to in a *Manual of Prayers for the Use of the Scholars of Winchester College* which Ken, then Prebendary of Winchester, published in that year, and in which he says: "Be sure to sing the Morning and Evening Hymn in your chamber devoutly." The hymns themselves are not given in the 1674 Manual nor in successive editions until that of 1695, when they were added as an appendix along with a third, less well-known, called a "Midnight Hymn." The question of their date and exact text is complicated, and need not be dealt with here except in so far as it affects that of Ken's alleged "plagiarism." There are (as we have said) indisputable resemblances between the Evening Hymn and Sir Thomas Browne's "dormitive" in *Religio Medici* (1643)251; as also between the Morning Hymn and a poem by Thomas Flatman published in 1674. It may well be, however, that each of the three authors (all Wykehamists) were no more than harking back, consciously or unconsciously, to the Latin hymns for Prime and Compline then still in use at College Prayers at Winchester. Even more striking is the resemblance between Ken's hymns and two metrical prayers given at the end of a little book, *Verbum Sempiternum*, published in 1693. This book was a reprint of a poem by John Taylor, originally published in 1614; but the two prayers do not appear till 1693 and there is no reason to think that they are by Taylor. On the other hand, there seems to be no doubt that Ken's hymns were written and circulated long before they were included in the 1695 *Manual*. It was indeed the existence of pirated editions that led Ken to publish an authorized text.[252] Once put into general currency Ken's Morning and Evening Hymns became immensely popular and eventually came to be inserted in the *Supplement* to the New Version. No hymns are more familiar to Christians of all denominations throughout the English-speaking world : and none more deserve their popularity. No one would call them great poetry : but they have the simple yet dignified eloquence that belongs to the best popular hymns.

Ken's famous hymns, written by an Anglican for Anglicans, have always been not less favoured by Nonconformists. In the case of two writers who were his contemporaries the borrowing is the other way. No hymn has more quickly achieved popularity in our generation than the 'Pilgrim's Song' of the great-hearted Baptist tinker John Bunyan (1628–88), taken from the concluding portion of the second part of the *Pilgrim's Progress*. It is best known in the form in which it appears in *E.H.*, which first gave it currency : 'He who would valiant be' †402 (also ‡515). But this version departs considerably from Bunyan's own, which is given in *A.M.*, 'Who would true valour see ? ' *676. Whether the changes were either necessary or an improvement is a matter on which each man must form his own opinion. The rapid popularity won by the hymn is of course not a little due to the singularly happy folk-tune that has come to be usually associated with it — a discovery of Vaughan Williams.[253] In *A.M.* Bunyan's hymn is set to a tune to the words 'Remember, O thou man' from Ravenscroft's *Melismata*, which may have been in Bunyan's mind when he wrote the hymn and have suggested its metre. *S.P.* contains also a second hymn by Bunyan — the song sung by the shepherd boy "in very mean Cloaths but of a very fresh and well-favoured Countenance" in the same part of the *Pilgrim's Progress*, 'He that is down needs fear no fall' ‡513.

Another Nonconformist writer of the Restoration period

who has helped to enrich our Anglican hymnals is Richard
Baxter (1615–91), the saintly author of the once famous
work of piety, *The Saints' Everlasting Rest*. Formerly chaplain to one of Cromwell's regiments, he became at the
Restoration Chaplain to Charles II and refused the see of
Hereford. But on the passing of the Act of Uniformity he
left the Church of England and became a Nonconformist
Minister. His hymns include : 'Lord, it belongs not to my
care' *535 †433 ‡105, 'He wants not friends that hath
Thy love' †401 ‡514 and 'Christ who knows all His sheep'
‡288. His most famous hymn, however, 'Ye holy angels
bright' *546 †517 ‡701, is only partly his. It was rewritten by J. Hampden Gurney in his *Church Psalmody*
(1838), and the two last verses seem to be by him.[254] Its
fine tune, "Darwall's 148th", is one of the 150 tunes composed by the Rev. H. Darwall for the complete metrical
psalter, and was first published in 1770.

One more hymn-writer of the Restoration deserves to
be mentioned, not only because of what he wrote but even
more because he seems to have been one of the first
Anglican clergymen to favour the practice of hymn-singing
in Church, as distinct from the use of metrical psalms.
This is John Mason (*c.* 1645–94),[255] the son of a Nonconformist minister, who became Vicar of Stantonbury,
Bucks, in 1668, and later Rector of Water Stratford in the
same county. He was described as "a light in the pulpit
and a pattern out of it". His *Spiritual Songs, or Songs of
Praise to Almighty God* were first published in 1683. The
noble hymn, 'How shall I sing that majesty' †404 ‡526, is
by him. *S.P.* also includes a second : 'Thou wast, O GOD,
and Thou wast blest' ‡675. Another of his hymns appears
to supply the basis of Keble's, 'A living stream of crystal
clear' *213.

Our account of the sacred poets of the Restoration
period makes it clear that the debt of our modern hymnals
to them is considerable : nor should we omit to mention

in addition the four fine hymns first published in the *Spectator* a generation later (1712) by the poet and essayist Joseph Addison (1672–1719): 'When all Thy mercies, O my GOD' *517 †511 ‡694, 'The spacious firmament on high' *662 †297 ‡659, 'How are Thy servants blest, O Lord' †542 ‡522, and the beautiful "classically-embroidered" version of ps. 23, 'The Lord my pasture shall prepare' †491 ‡656. But it must be repeated that nearly all these hymns, at the time when they were produced, were neither intended nor employed for use in public worship. The official provision of "hymns" proper, as apart from metrical psalms, was still confined to the meagre contents of the appendices of the Old and (when it arrived) the New Versions. The first *Supplement* to the latter, issued in 1700, contained, in addition to versions of the Canticles, Commandments, etc., and the *Veni Creator*, six hymns, one for Christmas, two for Easter and three for Holy Communion. The Christmas hymn is the favourite 'While shepherds watched' *62 †30 ‡82 — a versification of St. Luke ii. 8–14. To these the 6th edition (1708) added three more, including a revised text of Marckant's "Lamentation." A rather richer hymnody was included in Henry Playford's *The Divine Companion*, issued in 1701, which contained 12 hymns taken from Crashaw, George Herbert, Austin and William Drummond. These 12 were increased to 17 in the second edition of 1709, along with 4 hymns for Christmas Day, Good Friday, Easter Day and Whitsunday. But the day of hymn-singing in Church on a large scale was still far off. In this department of religious life it was not the Church of England but the bodies separated from her that were to be the effective pioneers.

III

"The English Independents, as represented by Dr. Watts," wrote Lord Selborne nearly 60 years ago, "have a just claim to be considered the real founders of modern English hymnody. Watts was the first to understand the nature of the want ; and . . . he led the way in providing for it." 256 This statement needs a certain amount of qualification in the light of fuller knowledge. We have already mentioned Barton and Mason, both of whom were clergymen of the Established Church, though the use of their hymns was practically confined to the Nonconformists. Among the Baptists, too, a sectional movement in favour of hymn-singing began about 1675, associated with the name of Benjamin Keach, who, in a pamphlet published in 1691, undertook the defence of a practice which for a time seriously divided the Baptist body. A similar practice arose about the same time among the Independents (the ancestors of the Congregationalists of to-day), whose earliest hymn-collections date from the last decade of the seventeenth century. But these early efforts only have significance for us in that they helped to prepare the way for the success of Watts's "System of Praise".257 For him it was reserved to overthrow the tyranny of Psalmody by the practical and obvious method of putting something better in its place — "a Hymnody", to quote Dr. Louis Benson, "that satisfied the religious sentiment more completely, and yet retained a sufficiency of the familiar form and tone of the accustomed psalm".258 It is indeed hardly an exaggeration to compare Watts with St. Ambrose. Like his illustrious prototype, he at the same time secured the triumph of Hymnody, made important and imperishable contributions to it and permanently influenced the form which it was to assume in the generations that followed.

It is easy to poke fun at Watts : and he is in fact rather a favourite target for our contemporary sense of humour. But we shall resist the temptation to enliven our pages by quoting his more absurd and repellent lines, which are specially abundant, unfortunately, in his *Hymns for Little*

Children. A man's genius is assessed not by his worst work but by his best. Watts shared the weaknesses of his time not only in its theology, with its over-insistence on the motive of self-regarding fear, but even more in its taste for an artificial and bombastic literary style. What is not sufficiently recognized is how often in both respects he rose above it. One of his main objections to the exclusive use of metrical psalms is precisely that, representing as they do the products of a pre-Christian era, they cannot voice the Christian spirit. Concerning them he declares roundly in an *Essay* printed in the 1707 volume of his *Hymns* :

> Some of 'em are almost opposite to the Spirit of the Gospel : Many of them foreign to the State of the New-Testament, and widely different from the present Circumstances of Christians. . . . Thus by keeping too close to David in the House of GOD, the vail of Moses is thrown over our Hearts.[259]

The hymns of Christians should freely express their own spiritual experience, not "the thoughts of David or Asaph". Thus the tyranny of the Genevan principle of "The Bible and the Bible only" was swept away. Again, in the matter of literary style Watts was capable of an admirable simplicity of expression when his purpose was to edify the simple (always in reality his chief preoccupation) rather than to charm the polite. "It will be found," it has been acutely remarked, "that just in those pieces where he is conscious of a refined audience on one side and the unlettered congregation on the other, Watts's best work appears." [260] In his hymns he adheres for the most part to the old metres that had been consecrated by the psalm-versions, while often protesting against the "fetter" of them. But at his best he wielded them with an altogether new grace and dignity : and his hymns have a compact and balanced structure which those of his predecessors lacked and which was to be deliberately aimed at as a prime requisite of good hymn-writing by his successors.

In view of Watts's pre-eminent position in English hymnody it is desirable to give here a brief account of his life.[261] He was born in 1674, the son of a Nonconformist schoolmaster who had twice suffered imprisonment for his religious convictions. Being a brilliantly clever boy, he was offered the chance of education at one of the Universities with a view to ordination to the Anglican ministry. But he preferred to enter one of the rising Nonconformist Academies situated at Stoke Newington. On leaving this at the age of twenty he spent two years at home : and it was then that he wrote many of the pieces contained in his first collection of hymns, *Hymns and Spiritual Songs*, though this was not published till 1707, with a second and enlarged edition in 1709. It is necessary to lay stress on this : for the name "Dr. Watts" suggests to most of us a venerable and rather grim divine, not a young enthusiast with giants of conventional routine and prejudice to fight. Dr. Dearmer well speaks of his "magnificent youthful aggression".[262] The next six years he spent in tutoring the son of a Nonconformist knight and in studying with an ardour for which he was to pay heavily in the sequel. In 1702 he was ordained pastor of the important Independent congregation in Mark Lane : but at the end of a year his health failed and an assistant pastor had to be provided, who after another severe illness of Watts in 1712 was appointed co-pastor. For the rest of his life Watts was the guest of Sir Thomas Abney and later of his widow. He received the degree of D.D. from the University of Edinburgh in 1728. Twenty years later his suffering life came to an end.

Watts's hymns number about 600 in all. Besides the collection already mentioned he published *Horae Lyricae* (1706–9), in which hymns were mingled among the poems ; *Divine and Moral Songs for the Use of Children* (1715) ; and *The Psalms of David* (1719) — the last containing not translations of the psalms in the strict sense, but rather poems based upon them. From this collection is taken Watts's finest and most famous hymn, 'O GOD, our help in ages past' *165 †450 ‡598 — based on ps. xc. Watts's own version began '*Our* GOD . . . ' : but this was altered by John Wesley in his collection of 1737 to its present form. In the current version the original 9 stanzas are reduced to 6. The story is told that Jowett once asked a number of Oxford dons to jot down a small list of the best hymns. All returned with only one hymn, 'O GOD, our help', which each regarded as fulfilling all the requisites of a perfect hymn.[263] Of it Mr. F. J. Gillman has said with truth that it "has become the great ceremonial hymn of the English nation, and if nothing else had come from his pen it justifies its author's memorial in Westminster Abbey".[264]

Another of Watts's hymns is only less celebrated, and breathes a spiritual ardour that 'O GOD, our help' necessarily lacks — the splendid Passion hymn, first of all English hymns on that subject, 'When I survey the wondrous Cross' *108 †107 ‡133, which originally appeared in the 1707 collection. To these masterpieces may be added several more hymns in well-nigh universal use which give further proof of the extent to which the genius of Watts has enriched the hymnody of the English-speaking race : 'How bright those glorious spirits shine' *438 †199 ‡207, 'Give me the wings of faith to rise' *623 †197 ‡204, 'Come, let us join our cheerful songs' *299 †376 ‡472, 'Jesus shall reign where'er the sun' *220 †420 ‡545, 'This is the day the Lord hath made' *478 ‡23 and 'There is a land of pure delight' *536 †498 ‡201. Tradition says that the last-named came upon him one summer day, while he was gazing across Southampton Water ; and the pleasant meadows near Netley are said to have suggested the phrase, "Sweet fields beyond the swelling flood".[265] Other hymns that are less well known are 'Awake, our souls ! away, our fears' *682 ‡451 and 'Christ hath a garden walled around' ‡245. Robert Bridges's fine hymn, 'My Lord, my Life, my Love' †442 ‡584, is based on an original by Watts.

Of those who followed in the trail blazed by Watts the most important name is that of one of his friends, another eminent Nonconformist divine, Dr. Philip Doddridge (1702–51). Like Watts he was offered the chance of being educated for ordination in the Church of England, but preferred to become a Nonconformist minister. He held various charges in the Midlands and died of consumption at Lisbon at the age of 49. His hymns were published by his friend Job Orton in 1755 after his death. The best known are the following: 'Hark, the glad sound' *47 †6 ‡62, 'Ye servants of the Lord' *268 †518 ‡702, 'My GOD, and is Thy table spread' *317 †320 and 'O GOD of Bethel' †447 ‡596. The last was published by Orton with the variant first line adopted in *A.M.*, 'O GOD of Jacob' *512. The current form of it is a drastic recast by a Scotsman called Logan (1781). It became immensely popular in Scotland, where "it holds a place in the affection of all Scotsmen second only to 'The Lord's my Shepherd' ".[266] Of hymns for national occasions it and 'O GOD, our help' easily stand first.

CHAPTER VIII

THE METHODIST AND EVANGELICAL MOVEMENTS

IN a letter written to a correspondent at Truro in 1757 John Wesley made a comparison between the worship of the Established Church and that of the young Methodist societies, very much to the advantage of the latter. Having commented on the superior reverence in their case of both congregation and officiant he went on as follows:

> Nor are their solemn addresses to GOD interrupted either by the formal drawl of a parish clerk, the screaming of boys who bawl out what they neither feel or understand, or the unreasonable and unmeaning impertinence of a voluntary on the organ. When it is seasonable to sing praise to GOD they do it with the spirit and with the understanding also; not in the miserable, scandalous doggerel of Hopkins and Sternhold, but in psalms and hymns which are both sense and poetry, such as would sooner dispose a critic to turn Christian than a Christian to turn critic. What they sing is therefore a proper continuation of the spiritual and reasonable service; being selected for that end, not by a poor humdrum wretch who can scarce read what he drones out with such an air of importance, but by one who knows what he is about and how to connect the preceding with the following part of the service. Nor does he take just "two staves", but more or less, as may best raise the soul to GOD; especially when sung in well-composed and well-adapted tunes, not by an handful of unawakened striplings, but by a whole serious congregation; and these not lolling at ease, or in the indecent posture of sitting, drawling out one word after another, but all standing before GOD and praising Him lustily and with a good courage.[267]

The animus in all this can hardly be disputed: Wesley is certainly making the worst of what he criticizes. Yet it is

a simple historical fact that an enormous part of the
attraction of the movement that he created and led consisted in the warmer and more enthusiastic conception of
worship for which it stood, and especially in the free,
heartfelt participation of the whole congregation in that
worship by means of a new, intimately personal type of
hymnody. In the days when the old metrical psalmody
was new, it, too, had been an intensely popular and
personal thing — indeed these psalms had been the war-
songs of the rebel army in its fight against Rome. But, like
the Office Hymns of an earlier day, they had in course of
time lost their power to stir men's hearts and had become
for most people nothing but a humdrum part of the liturgical routine. As against their monopoly Watts had successfully vindicated the claim of hymns to be a part of
congregational worship. But his success had been won
outside the National Church : and even so the movement
inaugurated by him was "purely liturgical, a sober and
deliberate undertaking for the 'Renovation of psalmody'
in the ordinary worship of the Church".[268] The revivalist
methods of Wesley and his associates called for something different. What was wanted was a hymnody that
would reflect the new kind of preaching initiated by them
— a preaching that meant, not the reading from the pulpit
of an elaborately phrased and long-winded dissertation on
morality or attentuated doctrine, but a bold impromptu
appeal to each man's heart and conscience couched in
popular language. The feelings aroused by the preacher
must be given an outlet on the lips of his hearers in accordance with the principle that modern educationalists sum
up in the phrase, "Expression must follow impression".
When men's hearts are full their emotions clamour for
utterance in speech and song : and it was to their recognition of this simple psychological fact that a great part
of the success of the pioneers of Methodism was due.

The need of a new type of hymnody framed on such

lines would no doubt have led in any case to attempts to supply it. But by a superb stroke of good fortune the prime leaders of the movement themselves were able and ready to show the way. A comparison has often been made between John Wesley and General Booth : but while both were great preachers and great organizers, Wesley, unlike Booth, was a sacred poet as well. And his brother and constant associate, Charles Wesley, ranks with Isaac Watts as one of the two greatest names in English hymnody. A taste for writing religious poetry seems indeed to have been a hereditary trait in the Wesley family. The father of John and Charles, Samuel Wesley, Rector of Epworth, Lincs., wrote a number of poems, including a *Heroic Poem* on the life of our Lord that was much admired in its day. His eldest son, Samuel Wesley the younger, wrote along with other religious verses a number of hymns that still survive in Wesleyan hymn-books : one of them appears, too, in *A.M.* *510. His daughter Mehetabel (the "Hetty Wesley" of Sir Arthur Quiller-Couch's novel) was a poetess of talent, though she wrote no hymns. It is, however, upon the achievement of the second and the youngest sons of the elder Samuel, John and Charles, that the fame of the family rests, in hymnody as in other directions.[269]

From start to finish the two brothers were united by the closest bond of affection and also by a profound community of ideas, aims and work ; even though towards the end of his life Charles, always a staunch Church of England man, viewed with grave misgivings his brother's tendency to encourage the schismatic tendencies which, after the death of both, were to cut Methodism away altogether from the Church that had given it birth. John was born in 1703, Charles in 1707 ; the former being educated at Charterhouse, the latter at Westminster. John went up to Christ Church, Oxford, in 1720, and six years after was elected Fellow of Lincoln. In the same year, 1726, Charles, too, went to Christ Church, where he later became a Tutor. At Oxford (whither John returned in 1729 after serving for a time as his father's curate at Epworth) the two brothers became the leading figures in a small group of devout members of the University nicknamed "Methodists" on account of their strictly disciplined life and zeal in observing the fast days and frequenting the sacraments of the Church. Other opprobrious names for them were "Sacramentarians", "Bible-bigots" and "The Holy Club". To the same group belonged James Hervey, author of the once celebrated *Meditations among the Tombs*, and another figure hardly less significant than the Wesleys themselves, George Whitefield, destined to be closely associated with them in the earliest phase of Methodism. Whitefield, the son of an innkeeper at Gloucester, went up to Oxford in 1732 as servitor of Pembroke: he was thus the junior of the Wesleys in age and standing.

In 1735 John Wesley received an invitation to evangelize the settlers and the Indians in the newly planted American colony of Georgia. After some hesitation he accepted, and Charles decided to accompany him. On their voyage out they were much impressed by the piety of some German Moravians who were their fellow-passengers. One result of this contact was to confirm the brothers in an already pronounced taste for the singing of hymns. On arriving in America they introduced the practice to the congregations to which they ministered, not without exciting opposition: and in 1737 John Wesley, described as "Missioner of Georgia", published at Charlestown a *Collection of Psalms and Hymns*. This book, like the *Divine Companion*, included in its 70 items adaptations from Herbert, Austin and Addison; half of its contents were by Watts; while the remainder consisted of 5 hymns by each of the two Samuel Wesleys (Charles was not a contributor) and 5 translations from the German by John

Wesley himself, who had recently been a diligent student of German pietistic hymnody. Much of the book was reproduced in a volume with the same title which John published on his return to England in 1738.

This return was accompanied by a deep discouragement at the scant success of his labours, which he was inclined to attribute to the fact that he himself was not yet converted. He consorted closely once more with the Moravians and their leader, Peter Böhler. On May 24, 1738, he went to a meeting in Aldersgate Street, at which someone was reading Luther's Preface to the Epistle to the Romans. His *Journal* narrates the experience which followed:

> About a quarter before nine, while he was describing the change which GOD works in the heart through faith in Christ, I felt my heart strangely warmed. I felt I did trust in Christ, Christ alone for salvation; and an assurance was given me that He had taken away my sins, even mine, and saved me from the law of sin and death.[270]

Henceforth, he believed, his conversion was an accomplished fact: and for him this could only mean the call to a lifelong task of helping others to share the blessings of which he himself was so richly conscious. The following month he paid a visit to the headquarters of the Moravians at Herrnhut, where he met their patron, Count Zinzendorf, and had further opportunity of becoming acquainted with their hymnody. On Aug. 1, he records,

> About eight we went to the public service, at which they frequently use other instruments with their organ. They began (as usual) with singing. Then followed the expounding, closed by a second hymn. Prayer followed this; and then a few verses of a third hymn, which concluded the service.[271]

The effect of this was still further to increase his enthusiasm for hymn-singing of the emotional type affected by the Moravians.

Returning to England in September, "I began again," he says, "to declare in my own country the glad tidings of salvation".[272] His brother, who had himself experienced conversion a short while before, associated himself with his labours. Soon, following the example already set by Whitefield, John began that practice of "field-preaching" which he was to pursue with such enormous success for the rest of his long life, travelling immense distances over the length and breadth of England. His converts were organized into bands or societies on the model of the Moravians : and, after Wesley had parted company with the latter on account of the alleged Antinomian tendencies that they had developed, he formed his own societies into a separate organization, with its headquarters at a disused foundry in Moorfields, which he converted into the first Methodist meeting-house in London (1739).

With the further development of Methodism we need not concern ourselves here apart from its bearing on English hymnody. "The English Hymn," (to quote Dr. Louis Benson's apt remark), "that had found so capable a tutor as Watts, had been waiting for so devoted a lover as Wesley." [273] To the practice of hymn-singing John Wesley, like Luther, attached the utmost importance, not only for its value in exciting and voicing religious emotion but also as a means of instruction and edification. The Methodist hymns were to be "a body of experimental and practical divinity". In his preface to the *Wesleyan Hymn-book* of 1780 Wesley asks :

In what other publication have you so distinct and full an account of Scriptural Christianity : such a declaration of the heights and depths of religion, speculative and practical : so strong cautions against the most plausible errors, particularly those now most prevalent : and so clear directions for making your calling and election sure ; for perfecting holiness in the fear of GOD ?

He himself was continually active in providing what was needed. It is a mistake to separate off the two brothers into John the preacher and Charles the hymn-writer.

Both were preachers, both were hymn-writers; though the one was more gifted in the first direction, the other in the second. And, despite his inferior poetic endowment, it was John, not Charles, who took the lead in hymnody, as in everything else. His was the brain that planned the Methodist hymnody, gave it its shape, made provision for and encouraged its use and recalled it to more sober paths when it degenerated into extravagance. In the hymnal publications which bear the name of the two brothers it is impossible to say which of them was the author of a particular hymn. The common view assigns to John all those hymns that are translated from the German (a language unknown to Charles) and to Charles all the original hymns. But a conviction is growing that John's share in the latter was considerably greater than has been commonly supposed.[274]

The first collection of hymns published jointly by the brothers appeared in 1739 with the title *Hymns and Sacred Poems. Published by John and Charles Wesley*. This contained the earliest versions of the two hymns which, having undergone not a few alterations, have emerged as 'Hark! the herald angels sing' *60 †24 ‡74 (originally 'Hark, how all the welkin rings') and 'Hail the day that sees Him rise' *147 †143 ‡172. An entirely new book with the same title was issued in 1740; its contents including, 'Jesu, Lover of my soul' *193 †414 ‡542, 'O for a thousand tongues to sing' *522 †446 ‡595 and 'Christ, Whose glory fills the skies' *7 †258 ‡26. Next year came a *Collection of Psalms and Hymns*, and in 1742 still another volume of *Hymns and Sacred Poems*. In the latter year, too, appeared the first Methodist tune-book with the title *A Collection of Tunes Set to music as they are commonly sung at the Foundery*. This contained over 40 tunes intended to supplement the psalm-tunes already in use. From this "Foundery Collection" comes the well-known tune 'Savannah' (or 'Herrn-hut') †135 ‡160. Another book with tunes followed in

177

1746 entitled *Hymns on the Great Festivals and Other Occasions*, and containing 24 hymns written by Charles Wesley, along with the same number of tunes by a German bassoon-player called Lampe, a friend of a convert of John's. (The tune 'Devonshire' *682 = 'Kent' ‡524, is from this book: its solid simplicity is in wholesome contrast to Lampe's usually over-florid style, of which 'Dying Stephen' *674 is a mild specimen.) This collection was in turn followed in 1753 by a volume issued by Thomas Butts, a friend of the Wesleys, and called *Harmonia Sacra*, containing, together with the tunes, words written by the Wesleys and others.

Meanwhile various new collections of words had made their appearance, of which one, *Hymns on the Lord's Supper*, issued in 1745, deserves special mention, alike on literary grounds and for its careful and profound theology. From this come the 7 Eucharistic hymns in *A.M.*: 'Author of life divine' *319 †303 ‡263, 'O Thou, before the world began' *554, 'Victim Divine' *556 †333, 'Saviour, and can it be' *718, 'With solemn faith we offer up' *720, 'How glorious is the life above' *723 and the exultant 'Hosanna in the highest' *724; the last of which, in particular, as set to Dr. S. H. Nicholson's fine tune, deserves to be far better known than it is. A collection of 1744 contains 'Rejoice ! The Lord is King' *202 †476 ‡632, for which Handel wrote his grand tune 'Gopsal': and another of 1747 the beautiful 'Love Divine, all loves excelling' *520 †437 ‡573, not less worthily set by Stanford in our own day. On his marriage in 1749 Charles Wesley raised the money required for furnishing his house by issuing his unpublished compositions in two volumes and selling them by subscription through the Methodist preachers. It is gratifying to add that the proceeds were fully adequate for the purpose in view.

A further collection of 1758 contained the Advent hymn, 'Lo ! He comes with clouds descending' *51 †7

178

‡65. The history of this hymn is almost as complicated as its fame is great.[275] The genesis of it is due to one of Wesley's early associates, John Cennick (*see below*, p. 185), who published in 1752 a hymn beginning:

> Lo ! He cometh, countless trumpets
> Blow before His bloody sign. . . .

It won the notice of Charles Wesley, who appears to have been at the same time attracted by its ideas and form and repelled by Cennick's rather revolting manipulation of them. He therefore remodelled it, reducing the original 6 stanzas to 4. In 1760 Martin Madan (of whom later) combined these 4 stanzas with 2 of Cennick's to produce a cento which has been in wide use in English-speaking countries. The form of the hymn, however, as given in *A.M.*, *E.H.* and *S.P.* omits the Cennick verses and reproduces Wesley's version in a slightly altered form. The famous tune, 'Helmsley', which has become inextricably associated with it, is attributed to the early Wesleyan preacher, Thomas Olivers, who apparently adapted it from a song by the Irish composer, Charles Thomas Carter, 'Gracious angels, now protect me', which enjoyed great vogue at the period.[276]

The collection of 1758 was followed in 1759 by three more, including a set of *Funeral Hymns*, one of which, 'Come let us join our friends above', is the source from which after many cuts and changes is derived 'Let saints on earth in concert sing' *221 †428 ‡557. By this time the total number of hymns sponsored by the Wesleys had reached such proportions that it was felt that the time was come to submit them to a process of selection. Further, John Wesley was not wholly satisfied with the tunes in use, erring as they did more and more on the florid side as time went on, and desired to have a collection of them authorized by himself. In 1761, therefore, he published a volume of *Select Hymns for the use of Christians of all*

Denominations, for which was provided a selection of *Tunes Annext*. With these appeared Wesley's "Directions for Singing", containing seven rules, which are as follows:

> Learn *these* tunes before any others; sing them exactly as printed; sing all of them; sing lustily; sing modestly; sing in tune; above all sing spiritually, with an eye to GOD in every word.

Several editions of this book were issued at intervals. Concerning them Dr. Frere remarks: "In these volumes it is possible to trace the development of Methodist hymn-singing as the Wesleys wished it to be. About one-third of the tunes and compositions in Butts's *Harmonia Sacra* find no place here: on the whole it is the more solid and congregational melodies that are included. Wesley, as a musician and revivalist, seems to have used his influence to exclude the worst of the bad specimens of hymnody which were everywhere in growing favour. But even so some of the things that remain are surprising." [277]

Meanwhile Charles Wesley's torrential spate of sacred song continued unabated. In 1762 he published two volumes of *Short Hymns on Selected Passages of Holy Scripture*, containing the staggering total of 2030 new compositions ! *Hymns for Children* appeared in 1763, including 'Gentle Jesus, meek and mild' †591 ‡356: and a number of other collections were still to come. It was only in the last years of his long life that the source began to dry up. He died in 1788 with the words on his lips: "I have lived, and I die, in the Communion of the Church of England." A fortnight after his death John Wesley gave out before preaching his brother's hymn, 'Come, O Thou Traveller unknown' *774 †378 ‡476, first published in the 1742 collection and deemed by many the finest thing he ever wrote, though its almost agonized note of spiritual passion makes it unsuitable for common use. When he reached the words, "My company before is gone, And I am left alone with Thee," the old man burst into tears and covered his

face with his hands, while the congregation wept too.[278]
Less than three years later (on March 2, 1792) he himself
passed to fresh fields of service (the word 'rest' is unthink-
able in connection with John Wesley), at the great age of
87. Like many other great men (and even great saints) he
was not always easy to get on with. But in spiritual ardour
and zeal for souls he has had few equals in the Christian
centuries : and it is hardly possible to exaggerate the work
he did for the toiling and neglected masses of his time in
an age when the so-called National Church had largely
gone to sleep. Indeed, it has been maintained that he
more than any other individual man saved England from
sharing the horrors and excesses of the French Revolution, by turning the aspirations of the common people to
spiritual rather than temporal satisfactions. Nor, one may
believe, would he have been unwilling to admit that the
sweet serenity of his beloved inseparable Charles displayed
an aspect of Christian holiness which his own fiery auto-
cratic nature was unable to achieve.

Concerning the hymns written by the Wesleys it is no
exaggeration to say that for a long time they occupied the
whole field of Methodist hymnody to the virtual exclusion
of anything else. Of their Methodist contemporaries only
two made any mark — Thomas Olivers (1725–99) and
John Bakewell ; while in the generation following there
were practically no Methodist hymn-writers at all. It was
Olivers who wrote the stately hymn 'The GOD of Abraham
praise' *601 †646 ‡398, based on the Hebrew 'Yigdal'.
The tune, a "synagogue melody" supplied to the poet
by the Jewish singer Leoni (Lyons), has a suspicious likeness to a song 'Why, soldiers, why' sung at the Haymarket
Theatre in 1729.[279]

The indisputable contributions of John Wesley to our
Anglican hymn-books are not many : but they well
deserve their place. All are translations from the German,
and have been already spoken of in an earlier chapter in

connection with their originals. Two are taken from Gerald Tersteegen, 'Lo ! God is here' *526 †637 ‡191, and 'Thou hidden love of God' *600 ‡671 ; one (the best of all) from Paul Gerhardt, 'Put thou thy trust in God' *692 (*S.P.* supplies an alternative cento, 'Commit thou all thy griefs' ‡479). The Communion hymn, 'Author of life divine' *319 †303 ‡263, is sometimes attributed to John : but in the collection of 1745 in which it first appeared the authorship is not stated and it is more likely to be his brother's.

The contribution of Charles is much more extensive : and it is one of the chief merits of *A.M.* that it gives him such copious and admirable representation. The great bulk of his hymns have of course sunk beneath the stream of time beyond possibility of rescue. It is estimated that his compositions totalled 6500 in all — an appalling thought. Obviously he could hardly have spent much time in polishing them up — nor would he himself have thought it necessary or even desirable to do so, for they were written to serve the turn of an active and incessant evangelism and also to relieve his own glowing heart. Many were probably written in order to drive home a particular sermon. But, as Dr. Dearmer has justly observed, "his masterpieces would have been more if he had had more of the craftsman's conscience":[280] and even those of his hymns that have won a perennial fame have often needed a good deal of emendation before they could fully deserve it. He himself deprecated any tampering with his work. In the preface to the 1780 *Collection* he gives leave to all to print his hymns "provided they print them as they are. But I desire they would not attempt to mend them, for they really are not able".[281] His editors, however, have judged otherwise : and no doubt they are right. But his incredible abundance has at least had the advantage of providing a wider range of selection for time and taste to ply their winnowing-fan upon. After all, with

Wesley as with Watts (and with far greater poets than either for that matter) it signifies little to posterity how much chaff they produced so long as the good grain is there. And who shall deny that the man who wrote the hymns of which mention has been made in this chapter was anything less than one of the greatest hymn-writers of all time ? Some have even called him the greatest of all. Of many of his hymns the ardent personal emotion is not for all tastes, nor perhaps in any case for all congregations or all occasions. In the ears of an undogmatic age their unashamed accent of evangelical Christianity may even sound tiresome and out-of-date. Yet none the less the religion they express has the authentic note of the Gospels and Epistles of the New Testament in which their author was saturated : and if ever the glow of the early Methodism comes back to the English-speaking world, men will find no hymns more fitted to express it than the best of what Charles Wesley has bequeathed to them.

II

We have seen how at the very outset of his evangelistic career Wesley felt compelled to sever himself from his spiritual parents, the Moravians. Not long after (*c.* 1740) the abysmal issue of Predestination and Freewill clove a gulf between him and his most gifted co-operator Whitefield. Wesley declared for the Arminian view of the operation of Divine grace, Whitefield for the Calvinist. The personal difference was soon healed : but henceforth the ways of the two friends lay apart. As a preacher Whitefield was perhaps even more remarkable than Wesley : but he possessed none of the latter's gifts of leadership and organizing power. However, his association with that masterful exemplar of high-born feminine piety, Selina, Countess of Huntingdon, helped considerably to make up for his own deficiency in these respects. He himself made no attempt to found a new denomination : and the societies that he formed did not last long. The Countess's work was to be more enduring. Her original intention was not to break with the Church of England but to uplift it. With this object she built proprietary chapels and appointed clergymen as her chaplains to officiate in them. But opposition to the opening of a new chapel in Spa Fields in 1779 compelled her to register her chapels as dissenting conventicles: and a new denomination thus came into existence called "The Countess of Huntingdon's Connexion". Meanwhile Wesley steadily pursued his own path, which in spite of his repeated professions of devotion to the Church of England led him further and further away from her. Yet even the torpid National Church could not remain wholly unaffected by the religious impetus that he had set in motion, however much its prelates might frown upon "enthusiasm" and many of the parochial clergy resent the incursions of Wesley and his preachers upon their preserves. The Evangelical movement in the Church of England was just as much Wesley's child as the Methodism that bears his name ; even though on the doctrinal side it preferred the Calvinism of White-field and Lady Huntingdon to the Arminianism of Wesley himself.

Each of these movements, Moravian, Huntingdonian and Evangelical, was to develop its own hymnody. Outside the charmed circle of Methodism itself the character-istic hymnody of the Wesleys had little popularity or currency for a long time. Its unusual metres, its theology, its emotionalism and spiritual elevation, were alike un-congenial. The great name was still Dr. Watts, who (as Dr. Benson says) "embodied the theology of his surround-ings, and kept well within the average range of spiritual experience".[282]

i. The one exception to this sober preference was fur-nished by the Moravians. Their hymnody was not less emotional than the Methodist, but more so. In fact its extravagant and often repulsive imagery so shocked John Wesley that he repudiated it and even held it up to public obloquy. The earlier Moravian hymns were for the most part translated from those of the German Pietistic school: and their bizarre foreignness was increased by the clumsiness and illiteracy of the versions. Later on, however, the Moravian hymnody sobered down, and its products were drastically pruned and remodelled.[283] Of English hymnwriters two belonged to the Moravian persuasion: John Cennick (1718–55) and James Montgomery (1771–1854). The former, however, was but slightly represented in the first Moravian books: and his earlier hymns were written in the days of his association with Wesley and (after 1740) with Whitefield, before he finally joined the Moravians in 1745. Of his hymns only one is well known, 'Children of the heavenly King' *547 †373 ‡463. His part in the evolution of 'Lo! He comes' has already been spoken of. Montgomery belongs to a considerably later period: and his catholic connections, and particularly his association with the Evangelical Cotterill (concerning which more will be said later), give him a far more than sectarian significance. The son of a Moravian minister, he became a journalist, and in 1796 editor of the *Sheffield Reporter*. Twice in the next two years he suffered imprisonment for his advanced Liberal opinions: but he lived to receive a royal pension in 1833. A list of his best-known hymns will suffice to indicate the debt of posterity to his poetic gift: 'Hail to the Lord's Anointed' *219 †45 ‡87, 'For ever with the Lord' *231 †391 ‡195, 'Angels, from the realms of glory' *482 ‡71, 'Stand up and bless the Lord' *706, 'Songs of praise the angels sang' *297 †481 ‡644, 'Palms of glory' *445 †201, and the two fine missionary hymns (Montgomery was an enthusiast for foreign missions), 'O Spirit of the living GOD' *585 and 'Lift up your heads, ye gates of brass' *586 †549.

ii. In the evolution of the hymnody of the Countess of

Huntingdon's Connexion the "noble and elect lady" (as her votaries styled her) played the leading part, as we might expect. She is even said by tradition to have been a hymn-writer herself: but there is no satisfactory evidence of this. After various experiments a definitive hymn-book for the use of the whole Connexion was issued in 1780. Lady Huntingdon herself made the selection, with the assistance of her cousin, the Honourable and Reverend Walter Shirley (1725–86). The book had a pronounced Calvinist flavour, and held its place till 1854. Three names represented in Anglican hymnals belonged to the Huntingdon *entourage*. One was Shirley himself, who besides hymns of his own was responsible for the popular Good Friday hymn, 'Sweet the moments rich in blessing' *109 †105. This was a very drastic recast of an earlier hymn that appeared in 1757 in an "Inghamite" collection usually known as the *Kendal Hymn Book*. Still more famous is 'All hail, the power of Jesus' name' *300 †364 ‡440, the writer of which, Edward Perronet (? 1726–92), offici-ated at Canterbury as one of her ladyship's "ministers" until he quarrelled with her. The third name is Thomas Haweis (1734–1820), author of the hymn 'O Thou from Whom all goodness flows' *283 †85 ‡117, and also of the fine tune to which it was originally set, known as 'Rich-mond' *172 ii †375 ‡468.

iii. The permanent contribution to hymnody of the Evangelical movement within the Church of England is far more important than that of any other outcome of Wesley's initial impulse except Methodism itself, with which it may fairly challenge comparison in this respect. The first of the Evangelical leaders, William Romaine, was indeed an irreconcilable opponent of the practice of hymn-singing and adhered to Calvin's principle of "The Bible and the Bible only" in Church song. But even in attacking the new Hymnody he was compelled to bear an unwilling testimony to its success. "The singing of the psalms," he wrote in 1775, "is now almost as despicable among the modern religions as it was some time ago among the prophane." [284] He is, of course, speaking of Evangelical circles only : elsewhere the old Psalmody still reigned more or less supreme. The opposite view to Romaine's was championed by Martin Madan, a clergyman who had founded with the assistance of his friends the Lock Hospital, near Hyde Park Corner, where he officiated as chaplain and won considerable repute as a preacher. For its use he published in 1760 a *Collection of Psalms and Hymns* (usually called the "Lock Hospital Collection") to which reference has already been made. Other collections from various hands followed Madan's, of which that issued by Richard Conyers (1767) is worthy of mention in that in its second edition (1772) Cowper's two famous hymns, 'There is a fountain filled with blood' and 'O for a closer walk with God', first saw the light. More important, however, than any of these is *Psalms and Hymns for Public and Private worship*, put forth in 1776 by Augustus Toplady (1740–78). Toplady was a consumptive graduate of Dublin University who became Vicar of Broadhembury in Devon. He was a popular preacher and withal a fanatical Calvinist. From this standpoint he made sustained and bitter attacks on John Wesley, who held his tongue on the ground that he "did not fight with chimney-sweeps". Toplady's controversial fury, however, reveals only the less attractive side of an odd and unbalanced character that had many compensating qualities. In his collection he included a number of Charles Wesley's hymns, but emended from his own Calvinist standpoint. It also contained six hymns by himself, one of them the celebrated 'Rock of ages, cleft for me' *184 †477 ‡636. It has been frequently criticized, and is perhaps hardly as popular to-day as it was : but it has an intense and profoundly moving quality that is all its own. It was a great favourite of the High Churchman Gladstone, and was sung at his funeral. The form in which it is familiar is the author's own, apart from a well-justified alteration of the line 'When my eye-strings break in death'. It may be added that the story that Toplady wrote it when sheltering from a storm in a cleft rock in the Mendips is without any foundation in fact.[285]

Three years after Toplady's collection, in 1779, appeared the most remarkable product of the Evangelical movement in the sphere of hymnody, the book which may be said to have definitely fixed the type of the "Evangelical" hymn. This was the volume entitled *Olney Hymns*,[286] arranged in three books and containing 280 hymns by John Newton (1725–1807), Vicar of Olney, Bucks, and 68 by his friend, the poet William Cowper (1731–1800). The project was begun at the latter's suggestion and was undertaken (as Newton informs us in his preface) partly from "a desire of promoting the faith and comfort of sincere Christians", partly "as a monument, to perpetuate the remembrance of an intimate and endeared friendship". But it had not proceeded far when Cowper was stricken with mental breakdown (1773) ; and Newton had to complete it by himself. To prevent misapprehension he appended the letter C to his friend's hymns in the published volume.

The close friendship of Newton and Cowper is a striking proof of the power of a common religious interest to unite men as widely sundered as possible in temperament and in life-history. John Newton, like many of Wesley's early preachers (including Olivers), was a "brand plucked from the burning". Whether either he or they were quite as bad in their unregenerate days as they afterwards believed is perhaps open to doubt: but Newton's early life was at least sufficiently adventurous. He went to sea at the age of eleven, was flogged as a deserter from the Navy and for fifteen months was servant to a slave-dealer in Africa. The one anchor of his existence in these years was his love for his future wife, Mary Catlett. His conversion was begun by a chance reading of Thomas à Kempis and sealed by the experiences of a terrible night at sea. For six years he was the pious captain of a slave-ship. After nine more years, during which he consorted with Wesley and Whitefield and struggled hard to make good his lack of education, he was ordained as curate of Olney (1764). It was here that he formed his friendship with Cowper, who assisted him as a sort of unpaid lay curate. He left Olney in 1780 to be Rector of St. Mary Woolnoth in the city of London, where he became a notable pillar of Evangelicalism and remained till his death.

The tragic story of Cowper's life is too well known to need retelling in these pages. It was as lacking in external incident as Newton's was the reverse. The interest of it lies partly in its revelation of a character as gentle and humorous as it was exquisitely gifted, partly in the appalling religious melancholia which overshadowed by far the greater part of it and issued three times in definite bouts of insanity, from the last of which he never emerged. It was after his recovery from the first of these attacks that he formed his friendship with his guardian-angel, Mrs. Unwin ("My Mary"), in whose home he lived, first at Huntingdon and then from 1768 to 1786 at Olney. Opinions vary as to the effect of Newton's influence on the poet. Perhaps the truth is fairly accurately summed up by Sir Leslie Stephen: "The friendship was durable. Newton, if stern, was a man of sense and feeling. It seems probable, however, that he was insufficiently alive to the danger of exciting Cowper's nerves." [287] The "old African blasphemer" (as Newton called himself in later years) was hardly an ideal companion for one of Cowper's sensitive, shrinking temperament: and his fiery emotional type of religion cannot have had a precisely soothing effect. It seems undeniable that when Newton left Olney Cowper's health improved and his spirits became more equable. On the other hand, it is most unfair to regard Cowper's madness as due to religion. His belief that he was a lost soul was the effect of his insanity, not *vice versa*. Indeed, so long as he was not pressed too hard, his religion seems to have been the ultimate source of whatever inward peace and happiness he ever knew.[288]

Remembering the fierce furnace of spiritual experience through which in their different ways the two friends were called to pass, we shall scarcely be surprised at the emotionalism that characterizes their hymns. The inspiration of both was essentially autobiographical: and this is always perilous in a hymn-writer. It is hard to say how far the *Olney Hymns* were designed for congregational use as a whole. Many of them are indubitably quite unsuited for the purpose, voicing as they do a kind of religious experience to which the average worshipper is a stranger. But the contents of the book were quickly laid hold of by hymnal-compilers: and many of its hymns achieved great popularity in all denominations. The effect of this was by no means wholly beneficial, encouraging as it did that tendency to force emotion and to invite to self-deception in regard to it which is the great danger of Revivalist religion. But not all the *Olney Hymns* are tarred with this brush: and their excessively gloomy view of man's fallen nature is normally offset by an exultant sense of his escape from it into the paths of salvation. Those of them that have survived in common use are for the most part remarkably free from the morbidity that we usually associate with Evangelical hymnody. Of Newton's we may mention: 'Glorious things of thee are spoken' *545 †393 ‡500; 'Great Shepherd of Thy people, hear' *690; 'How sweet the name of Jesus sounds' *176 †405 ‡527; and 'Come, my soul, thy suit prepare' *527 †377 ‡473; to which may be added the gay, lilting spring-song, 'Kindly spring again is here' †287 ‡2. Cowper's hymns include the noble 'GOD moves in a mysterious way' *373 †394 ‡503 (a hymn that has helped to save many a tried and tormented spirit from the poet's own despair) and the lovely 'O for a closer walk with GOD' *630 †445 ‡112, together with 'Hark, my soul, it is the Lord' *260 †400 ‡510, 'Jesus, where'er Thy people meet' *529 †422 ‡551 and 'There is a fountain filled with blood' *633 †332 ; of which only the last has "dated" through its use of the old-fashioned Evangelical imagery.

III

With the appearance of the *Olney Hymns* the earlier type of Evangelical hymn-book, arranged according to a purely subjective classification and ignoring entirely the Prayer Book scheme of worship, may be said to come to an end. In the succeeding period there emerged a new type of book, which sought "to adapt the new Hymnody to the methods and manners of the Church".[289]

The inspiration of these books was still Evangelical : but their emergence was assisted by a slow yet steady change that was taking place in the attitude of the National Church at large in regard to hymn-singing. The change was as yet far from universal. The more conservative still clung manfully to their "Tate and Brady" and "Sternhold and Hopkins". To do otherwise would be to bow the knee to Dissent. When Dr. Johnson saw a girl attending the Sacrament in a bedgown, "I gave her privately a crown," he says, "though I saw Hart's *Hymns* in her hand." [290] At the most it might be permissible to do what Bishop Gibson suggested,[291] and arrange the metrical psalms in such a way as to strike the keynote of the Church's times and seasons as they came round. Others would tolerate hymns on condition that they were not used in the liturgical services. On the other hand, there was a growing inclination to allow their use even here, so long as it was done in strict moderation and confined to the chief festivals. This attitude showed itself in an increased readiness to use the meagre collection of hymns provided in the *Supplement* to

191

the New Version. These hymns began to be printed in the prayer-books along with the psalm-versions themselves : and additions were even made to their number. It was in this way that about 1816 the Easter hymn, 'Jesus Christ is risen to-day' [292] *134 †133 ‡145 (of which both words and music are first found in a little collection of 1708 framed on German models and called *Lyra Davidica*) began to be included by the side of the products of Tate and Brady.

To the new movement in favour of hymn-singing a further impetus was given by the great popularity accorded to the vocal performances of the inmates of certain charitable institutions in London. In the later part of the eighteenth century the polite world loved to parade its "sensibility" : and it became the fashion to luxuriate in the emotion excited by the singing of "Magdalens" and "charity-children". For the institutions in question special compositions were written and hymn-books compiled. We have already mentioned Madan's collection of 1760, prepared for the use of the Lock Hospital with its choir of "female penitents". Similar collections were produced for the Magdalen Hospital at Streatham and the House of Refuge for Female Orphans near Westminster Bridge. The organist of the latter, Thomas Riley, set his face against the frivolous tunes of the Methodists, "which", he said, "mostly consist of what they call Fuges, or (more properly) Imitations, and are indeed fit to be sung only by those who made them". [293] As a counterpoise he issued in 1762 a collection of tunes in the old solid style, in which Dr. Samuel Howard's tune, 'St. Bride' *101 †74 ‡699 and Gilding's 'St. Edmund' *395 ii †171 ‡120 ii, first saw the light. A later collection by Riley's successor included the Frenchman François Barthélémon's 'Morning Hymn' *3 ii †257 ‡25. To these must be added the *Foundling Hospital Collection*, first issued in 1774, which contributed (*c.* 1801) one well-known hymn to our hymn-books, 'Praise the Lord, ye heavens adore Him' *292 †535 ‡624. A specimen of the sort of thing that the foundlings were sometimes expected to sing may be quoted :

> Obscured by mean and humble birth
>   In ignorance we lay,
> Till Christian bounty call'd us forth
>   And led us into day.[294]

In the parish churches, too, the children of the local charity schools were formed into a sort of choir to lead the singing. Once a year the "charity-children" of the metropolis, institutional and otherwise, were gathered together for a united service, held latterly in St. Paul's Cathedral and regarded as one of the sights of the town. The arrangement lasted till 1877, by which time public interest in the event no longer warranted the trouble and expense involved in installing the staging, etc., required for it.

While the prejudice against hymns on the part of Churchmen generally was thus dying down, the Evangelical movement which championed them was on its side ceasing to be a sort of ecclesiastical Ishmael, and was coming into close contact with the main body of the Church. It was no longer an affair of proprietary chapels and isolated centres of influence, but was becoming a definite party within the Establishment and was entrenching itself firmly in the parochial system. Thus on both sides, at the end of the eighteenth century, the time was ripe for the first beginnings of a movement towards a hymn-book that should be "the companion of the Book of Common Prayer".

The credit of initiating this development belongs to an Evangelical divine, the Reverend Basil Woodd (1760–1831), who was preacher and later Incumbent of Bentinck Chapel, Marylebone.[295] Woodd issued in 1794 a book entitled *The Psalms of David, and other portions of the Sacred Scriptures, arranged according to the order of the Church of*

England for every Sunday in the year ; also for the Saints' Days, Holy Communion and other services. In this a metrical psalm was indicated for each Sunday and Holy Day to serve as an Introit, along with one or more hymns adapted to the season or subject of the day. This section was followed by hymns for Communion, Baptism, etc., and a few for general use in worship.

During the next two or three decades numerous collections were published on more or less similar lines to Woodd's. Of course the resulting growth of hymnody was by no means welcomed everywhere. "The importance which in many places attaches to the Hymn Book," complained Bishop Marsh of Peterborough in a charge of 1820,[296] "is equal if not superior to the importance ascribed to the Prayer Book." Some bishops even prohibited the use of hymns in their dioceses altogether. The crisis came to a head when in 1819 Thomas Cotterill, Vicar of St. Paul's, Sheffield, issued the eighth edition of his *Selection of Psalms and Hymns for public and private use, adapted to the services of the Church of England.* In this edition he had the assistance of the Sheffield editor, the Moravian Montgomery, who not only printed the book and collaborated in it, but contributed some 50 of his own hymns. It was presumably at his suggestion, too, that the book introduced the Christmas hymn, 'Christians, awake' *61 †21 ‡73, in the familiar version — a reduction (further reduced in *E.H.* and *S.P.*) from 48 lines to 36 of the original written in 1749 as a Christmas gift for his daughter by John Byrom (1691–1763), a former Fellow of Trinity, Cambridge, who became a well-known teacher of shorthand and eventually settled in Manchester.[297] When Cotterill's book was put into use part of his congregation took umbrage : and a suit was brought against him in the York Consistory Court. Through the mediation of Archbishop Vernon-Harcourt, however, a compromise was effected. Cotterill withdrew his book : and in 1820 a revised and smaller edition was issued under the Archbishop's supervision and at his expense. The battle on behalf of hymnody was thus effectively won. Its enemies continued to attack it : but no further legal action was attempted. A further shower of hymnals followed, in which the influence of Cotterill's was very marked. The metrical psalms did not yet disappear : but they were only used in selections and were accompanied by hymns on the same footing. The usual title of these collections was "Psalms and Hymns".

Before leaving the period under review mention should be made of two pairs of hymn-writers who fall within it but lie off the main track of the movement, at once Evangelical and within the framework of the National Church, that we have been describing. The first pair were Evangelical clergymen who found themselves unable to accommodate themselves to the Church's system and pursued paths of their own — Rowland Hill (1744–1833) and Thomas Kelly (1769–1854). The former, the son of a Shropshire baronet, quitted his curacy to practise for twelve years an itinerant ministry and finally, in 1783, established himself at the Surrey Chapel in Blackfriars Road. He never renounced his Orders, but carried on a very successful ministry in London for fifty years without episcopal sanction. On opening his chapel he printed a *Collection of Psalms and Hymns*, for which his organist compiled a tune-book *c.* 1800. Hill was an enthusiast for Sunday Schools and popularized the idea of a children's hymnody. He wrote the hymn that has been recast as 'Lo ! round the throne a glorious band' *435.

Kelly was an Irishman who was ordained in 1792 and worked for a time in Dublin in collaboration with Hill. Both were inhibited by the Archbishop, who disapproved of their evangelistic methods. Thereupon Kelly began to preach in unconsecrated buildings, and finally, unlike his friend, seceded from the Church altogether to found a sect of his own, now extinct. He was an extremely prolific writer, his hymns totalling 751 in all. Three of them are very well known : 'The Head that once was crowned with thorns' *301 †147 ‡175, 'We sing the praise of Him who died' *200 †510 ‡132 and 'The Lord is risen indeed' *504 †627 : and two others are hardly less so : 'Through the day Thy love has spared us' *25 †281 and 'Come, see the place where Jesus lay' *139.

The personal link that united Hill and Kelly is reproduced in the case of the other pair of hymn-writers — Reginald Heber (1783–1826) and Henry Hart Milman (1791–1868). But whereas the two former diverged on one side from the main track of Evangelical Church hymnody, the latter two diverged from it on the opposite side. Heber and Milman were not Evangelicals, but High Churchmen in the sense of their time. Of the two Heber is the more important, as the initiator of a movement in which Milman only collaborated. The son of an old and wealthy family, he went up to Brasenose College, Oxford, where he won the Newdigate with a poem, *Palestine*, which is practically the only prize-poem that has secured more than an ephemeral fame. In 1807 he became Vicar of the family living of Hodnet, Salop. Here he combined a devoted ministry to his flock with the practice of literature, writing for the *Quarterly Review*, editing Jeremy Taylor and enjoying the friendship of some of the leading men of letters of his time. He had always been deeply interested in foreign missions, especially work in India : and when in 1823 he was offered the see of Calcutta he accepted it. For three years he laboured unceasingly, travelling immense distances and accomplishing a signal work. He died worn out at Trichinopoly in 1826.

As a hymn-writer Heber is important not only on account of his personal output but as inaugurating a new type of hymn — the "literary hymn", aiming not merely at the expression of religious feeling but also at deliberately controlling that expression by the canons of the poetic art.[298] At the same time he carried on the principle, already put into practice by Basil Woodd and others, of adapting hymnody to the requirements of the Church's year. On these lines he projected at Hodnet a Church hymn-book which should be at the same time "a collection of sacred poetry". For this he not only collected materials from earlier sources, but wrote hymns himself and asked his literary friends, including Scott, Southey and Milman, to write them too. Actually only Milman did so. An attempt was also made to secure for his hymnal the authorization of the Primate and the Bishop of London : but the cautious prelates, though sympathetic, shrank from so definite a step. Heber's collection travelled with him in manuscript to India, and was only published after his death, with the title *Hymns written and adapted to the Weekly Church Service of the Year* and a personal dedication to the Archbishop of Canterbury. Its contents consisted of 57 hymns by Heber himself, 12 by Milman and 29 by other writers. Of Heber's own hymns the best, as the most famous, is 'Holy, Holy, Holy, Lord GOD Almighty' *160 †162 ‡187. Others are : 'From Greenland's icy mountains' *358 †547, 'Brightest and best of the sons of the morning' *643 †41, ‡85, 'The Son of GOD goes forth to war' *439 †202 ‡216, 'Virgin-born, we bow before Thee' *622 †640, 'GOD that madest earth and heaven' (verse 1 only) *26 †268 ‡46, and the two beautiful Eucharistic hymns, 'Bread of the world' *714 †305 ‡265 and 'O most merciful' †323 ‡276. Of the hymns by Milman, who later became Dean of St. Paul's and the eminent historian of Latin Christianity, the best is the splendid Palm Sunday hymn, 'Ride on, ride on, in majesty' *99 †620 ‡137. Others are 'O help us, Lord ; each hour of need' *279 †83 ‡114 and 'When our heads are bowed with woe' *399 †513.

CHAPTER IX

THE OXFORD MOVEMENT AND AFTER

I

BISHOP HEBER'S attempt to provide a hymnal that should be at the same time "literary" and "liturgical" — unexceptionable as poetry and adapted to the varying requirements of the Church's year — was not destined to any great success, so far as actual use of his collection was concerned. Indeed, quite apart from anything else, the lack of suitable tunes was an insuperable difficulty. Yet it may rightly be regarded as a landmark in the process by which hymns came to achieve their present position in Anglican worship. In addition to the permanent contributions that it made to English hymnody in the shape of individual hymns, its significance lies in two directions — first, in its character as definitely a "hymn-book" with only a few psalms introduced that could be worked into its scheme, as opposed to the "psalms and hymns" on an equal footing of the contemporary Evangelical collections; and, secondly, in the work that it did in helping to break down the prejudice against hymns which still persisted in non-Evangelical circles.

In this latter respect, however, its influence was slight as compared with the truly revolutionary change that was to be set in motion soon afterwards by the coming of the Oxford Movement. In the same year (1827) in which Heber's *Hymns* first saw the light John Keble published his *Christian Year*. This was in no sense a hymnal, but a collection of pious meditations on the liturgical round of fast and festival. Its significance lay in the mild glow of "Catholic" sentiment — an inheritance from the Laudian divines of the seventeenth century — with which the poet contrived to invest his themes, and which unquestionably did much to prepare men's minds for the great Movement that was speedily to be inaugurated by his famous sermon on "National Apostasy" in 1833 and to be given shape and substance in the *Tracts for the Times*. The essence of the Tractarian position was the appeal to Catholic antiquity : and this was to have important results in hymnody as in weightier matters. Hitherto the Hymn, with its Methodist and Evangelical associations, had been deeply suspect to those who prided themselves on a loyal and conservative Churchmanship. Such men had constituted themselves the champions of Psalmody, despite the taint of its Genevan origin, because they disliked Hymnody far more. This view appears to have been shared at first by most of the Tractarians themselves. But soon the logic of facts began to operate irresistibly in favour of a practice which a study of ancient liturgical forms had revealed as no mere schismatic innovation, but as an integral part of the venerable Catholic order of worship. This being so, those who desired to restore to the Church of England its Catholic heritage must be careful not to neglect this part of it — both by using the old Catholic hymns in translated form and also by the production of new hymns that should share their spirit and atmosphere. Such new hymns, like the old, must be less an expression of personal experience and need than a reflection of the Church's order of doctrine and worship. In a word, they must be, first and foremost, "liturgical". In them should be heard the voice "not of the individual believer, but of the worshipping Church".[299]

So far as translation was concerned, Keble's pupil and friend, Isaac Williams (1802–65), Fellow of Trinity,

Oxford, and later Newman's curate at St. Mary's, had already made a start even before the formal inception of the Movement in 1833 ; although it would appear that his versions were not made with any idea of their being used in public worship, but simply for his "personal edification". Indeed he has told us that he chose for them "unrhythmical harsh metres" with the express object of excluding such use, which he regarded as "unauthorized".[300] Williams's translations were not made from the hymns in the mediaeval service-books, which at this period were virtually inaccessible, but from those in the "neo-Gallican" French breviaries of the later seventeenth and eighteenth centuries. He himself has related in his *Autobiography* how about 1829 he came across a copy of the Paris Breviary brought from France by a friend, and how he and Keble were "very much struck".[301] At once he set to work to make English versions of some of its contents, which were published in the *British Magazine* from 1833 onwards and were brought together in 1839 in a volume with the title *Hymns from the Parisian Breviary*. This included a number of hymns that have since become well known, including 'O Word of God above' *395 †171, 'O heavenly Jerusalem' *429 †251 and the splendid hymn for Apostles, Williams's masterpiece, 'Disposer supreme' *431 †178 — the last a translation from Santeuil. In the previous year he had published a volume of sacred poems, *The Cathedral*, in which he worked out the symbolism of the component parts of a great church : but the form of these poems makes them unsuitable for use as hymns. Williams's best-known original hymn, 'Be Thou my guardian and my guide' *282 †369 ‡100, appeared in 1842 in a little book called *Hymns on the Catechism*; and the Lenten hymn, 'Lord, in this Thy mercy's day' *94 †76, in a much more ambitious collection, *The Baptistery*, published in the same year.

Meanwhile side by side with Isaac Williams two other

translators had been at work. One of these, John Chandler (1806–76), who became Vicar of Witley, Surrey, in 1837, was directly inspired by Williams's efforts. For some time he had been anxious to see the ancient prayers of the Liturgy companioned by hymns of corresponding date instead of the hymns in current use, "many of which", he felt, were "from sources to which our Primitive Apostolic Church would not choose to be indebted". Having seen Williams's versions in the *British Magazine* he felt that many of them provided exactly what was required, and he decided to follow his example. "So," he tells us, "I got a copy of the Parisian Breviary [1736] and one or two other old books of Latin Hymns, especially one compiled by Georgius Cassander, printed at Cologne in the year 1556, and regularly applied myself to the work of selection and translation." [302] The result was seen in a collection issued in 1837, *The Hymns of the Primitive Church*. The title was hardly accurate, as most of the Latin originals dated from the seventeenth and eighteenth centuries: but presumably Chandler was not aware of this. His translations, which were very free but also very singable, speedily found their way into hymn-books: and a considerable number of them are familiar. The best known are: 'On Jordan's bank the Baptist's cry' *50 †9, 'Conquering kings their titles take' *175 †37, 'In stature grows the Heavenly Child' †46=*78, 'As now the sun's declining rays' *13 †265 and 'Christ is our corner-stone' *239.

The year in which Chandler's collection appeared saw also the publication of another, with the title *Ancient Hymns from the Roman Breviary, for Domestick Use. . . . To which are added Original Hymns*. The author of this, Richard Mant (1776–1848), was an English-born divine who after being Rector of St. Botolph's, Bishopsgate, held three Irish sees in succession — Killaloe (1820), Down and Connor (1823) and Dromore (1842). Here again the versions were very free: nor had the originals much better claim to be described as "ancient", being taken from the Roman Breviary of 1632, in which the mediaeval Office Hymns had been ruthlessly mangled to satisfy the classical taste of the Renaissance. However, in the then state of liturgical science no one knew or cared about such things. The hymns were "from the Latin" — that was enough. Indeed the elegant Latinity of Mant's and Chandler's originals appealed to men with a classical education far more than the really "ancient" hymns could have done, even if these had been available. Of Mant's versions one figures in most hymnals, viz. the hymn for Apostles, 'Let the round world with songs rejoice' †176=*754. His version of *Stabat mater* provides the basis (with many alterations) of that in *E.H.* †115. Another Passion hymn, 'See the destined day arise' *113 †110, is based on parts of Fortunatus's *Pange lingua*, but with such freedom that it can hardly be described as a translation. Mant's best and best-known hymn, however, is one of the "original" hymns included in the 1837 volume, 'Bright the vision that delighted' *161 †372 ‡460; another being 'For all Thy saints, O Lord' †196=*448.

The new interest in Latin hymns aroused by these productions was greatly strengthened when in 1838 John Henry Newman (1801–90), then the leading Tractarian of them all and destined after his conversion to Rome in 1845 to become an Oratorian, and finally (1879) Cardinal, published two volumes entitled *Hymni Ecclesiae*, which made the text of a large number of them for the first time easily accessible to the English reading public. Here again the hymns, or at least the great majority, were far from representing the authentic "ancient" hymnody of the Catholic Church. But at least Newman appears to have been aware of the limitations of his collection in this respect. The 199 hymns in the first volume were selected from the Paris Breviary; the 130 hymns in the second (which include some duplicates) from the Roman

Breviary and the English mediaeval Breviaries of Sarum and York. At the end were appended two collections of 'Proses', taken from the Paris Missal and the York Processional respectively. The purpose of Newman's work was to enrich private devotion, pending the time when the Church of England, condemned since the Reformation (at least officially) to the use of nothing but the metrical psalter, should again be found worthy to have a hymnody of her own. As the preface puts it, with the true Newman eloquence :

She waits for the majestic course [of Providence] to perfect in its own good time what she cannot extort from it ; for the gradual drifting of precious things upon her shores, now one and now another, out of which she may complete her rosary and enrich her beads — beads and rosary more pure and true than those which at the command of duty she flung away.

Meanwhile those who can make use of them will do well

to revert to the discarded collections of the ante-reform era, [which] are far more profitable to the Christian than the light and wanton effusions which are their present substitute among us.

Among the "precious things" spoken of in his preface Newman may well have contemplated such translations of the ancient Latin hymns as those to which Williams and Chandler had already set their hand. But his own experiments in this direction were neither numerous nor particularly successful : he was content to supply an abundance of materials for others to work upon. His single contribution (at least in his Tractarian days) appeared in *Tract* 75, 'On the Roman Breviary', which contained 14 translations taken from that source. Of these only two have survived in *A.M.* — the hymn for Terce, 'Come, Holy Ghost, Who ever One' *9 and the Compline hymn, 'Now that the daylight dies away' *16. Neither is much used : and neither has found a place in *E.H.*

Newman's reputation as a hymn-writer rests on quite other grounds. His two famous hymns were original compositions and were never intended for use as hymns at all. By a curious irony, indeed, one of them, 'Lead, kindly light' *266 †425 †554, represents, in the intense subjectivity of its mood, the very opposite of everything that Newman himself regarded as suitable to a hymn. Like many of the Evangelical hymns, it was originally written as an outlet for the author's own personal emotion. He has told the story in his *Apologia*. While travelling in Italy with Hurrell Froude early in 1833, he was weighed down by the thought of the peril threatening the Church of England from the triumphant Liberalism of the Reform era and became conscious of a "mission" to save her. At Leonforte in Sicily he was stricken down with fever:

> My servant thought that I was dying, and begged for my last directions. I gave them, as he wished; but I said, "I shall not die . . . for I have not sinned against light". . . . Towards the end of May I left for Palermo. . . . I was aching to get home; yet for want of a vessel I was kept at Palermo for three weeks. . . . At last I got off in an orange-boat, bound for Marseilles. Then it was that I wrote the lines, "Lead, kindly light", which have since become well known. We were becalmed a whole week in the Straits of Bonifacio. I was writing verses the whole time of my passage.[303]

Immediately after his return to England Keble preached his famous sermon, and the Oxford Movement began. The poem was published in the *British Magazine* in 1834 and again in *Lyra Apostolica* (1836). Newman's other famous hymn, 'Praise to the Holiest in the height' *172 †471 ‡625, belongs to a much later period, when he had been for many years a Roman Catholic. It is part of the 'Chorus of Angelicals' from his poem *The Dream of Gerontius*, written in 1865. Another excerpt from the same poem, 'Firmly I believe and truly', forming part of the dying Gerontius's profession of faith, appears as a hymn in *E.H.* †390.

If the Tractarian leaders inclined, at any rate at first, to share the general "High Church" objection of the time to the singing of hymns at all in public worship, a number of their followers were anxious, like Chandler, to introduce translations of Latin hymns as "Catholic" rivals to the hymns popularized by the Evangelicals. It was felt, too, that since it was impossible to substitute the Breviary Offices for those of the Prayer Book, the use of such hymns would at least serve to impart a Catholic atmosphere to the latter, and also help towards a more adequate observance of seasons and saints' days. This was the line adopted at Margaret Chapel (the forerunner of the present All Saints', Margaret Street), which had become the chief focus of Tractarian influence in London and sought to provide a model of what Tractarian worship should be. In 1837 its Incumbent, William Dodsworth, published a collection for use there entitled *A Selection of Psalms, to which are added Hymns chiefly ancient*. Four years later Chandler rearranged and expanded his original volume in the form of a hymnal with the title *The Hymns of the Church, mostly Primitive, Collected, Translated and Arranged for Public Use*. In 1849 a new collection of *Introits and Hymns* was printed for use in Margaret Chapel : and other collections appeared framed on similar lines.

Meanwhile other translators had been in the field, whose work was drawn upon in the later of these collections. Three may be mentioned here. The first, Frederick Oakeley (1802–80), has been spoken of earlier (p. 98) in connection with his translation of *Adeste fideles*. A former Fellow of Balliol, he succeeded Dodsworth in 1839 as Incumbent of Margaret Chapel, for the congregation of which he wrote his famous version in 1841. He became a Roman Catholic in 1845 — the same year as Newman. A second translator was W. J. Copeland (1804–85), who in 1848 published his *Hymns for the Week and Hymns for the Seasons, Translated from the Latin*. Copeland, a Fellow of

Trinity, Oxford, had been Newman's curate at Little-more, but remained faithful to the Church of his baptism and spent the last 36 years of his life as Rector of Farnham, Essex. He is represented in *A.M.* by his versions of three of the seasonal Compline hymns *63, 95, 141. Of these the Lenten one, 'O Christ, Who art the Light and Day', is also in *E.H.* †81. More important is Edward Caswall (1814–78), who in 1850 went over to Rome and joined Newman at the Birmingham Oratory. The year before his conversion he published *Lyra Catholica* (1849), containing 197 translations from the Roman Breviary and Missal and from other sources. A number of these have achieved wide currency, especially 'Hark! a thrilling voice is sounding' *47=†5, 'My GOD, I love Thee' *106 †80, 'Bethlehem, of noblest cities' †40=*76, 'All ye who seek a comfort sure' †71=*112, and the translation in C.M. of *Jesu dulcis memoria*, 'Jesu, the very thought of Thee' *178 †419.

None of the earlier Tractarian collections succeeded in winning more than a limited local use: nor did they deserve to do so. Their defects and the defects of the translators whose work they embodied were exposed with merciless rigour in an article on "English Hymnology" contributed by Neale to the *Christian Remembrancer* in its issue of October, 1849.[304] It was pointed out that in the majority of cases these translators had preferred the comparatively modern (and sometimes even heretical) products of the Paris Breviary to the really ancient hymns of the Church; that they had failed to reproduce the metres of the originals; and that (worst of all) their work betrayed "great carelessness, haste and slovenliness". No hymnal based on such material could be worthy of general acceptance.

Having thus performed the negative task of criticism Neale proceeded to the positive and practical one of showing a more excellent way — and not merely of showing it but of doing himself the bulk of the work involved.

Of the Tractarian hymn-writers he stands out as incomparably the first. Indeed, it is no exaggeration to say that, along with Isaac Watts and Charles Wesley, he stands at the head of all other English hymn-writers, even though his achievement lay in the field of translation rather than of original composition. The external side of his short life can be quickly told. John Mason Neale (1818–65) was the son of a clergyman of "pronounced Evangelical opinions" who had been Senior Wrangler and Fellow of St. John's, Cambridge. He went up in 1836 to Trinity College, Cambridge, where he obtained a Scholarship and was reputed the best classic of his year : but his lack of mathematical aptitude compelled him to take an ordinary degree. He was none the less elected Fellow of Downing College. At Cambridge he threw himself with enthusiasm into the Church movement and was one of the founders of the Cambridge Camden Society for the study of ecclesiology. After a stay in Madeira necessitated by lung trouble he was appointed in 1846 Warden of Sackville College, East Grinstead, where he remained without receiving further preferment to the end of his life. Yet from this insignificant centre — described by his friend Littledale as "an obscure almshouse with a salary of £27 a year" — and despite his physical frailty, Neale contrived to do a work on behalf of the Anglo-Catholic Revival of which it is hardly possible to exaggerate the extent or importance. Besides his achievement in the field of hymnody, he wrote *The History of the Eastern Church*, in 5 volumes (1847–73) — still a standard work ; *A History of the Jansenist Church in Holland* (1858) ; a 4-volume *Commentary on the Psalms* (1860–74) in collaboration with Littledale ; translations of the *Primitive Liturgies* of the East ; together with essays on liturgiology, articles, sermons and even stories. Nor was it only with his pen that he found an outlet for his zeal : he was also a man of action. An enthusiastic champion of the religious life for women, he successfully founded the well-known Sisterhood of St. Margaret at East Grinstead in the teeth of bitter popular prejudice and opposition, which on one occasion nearly cost him his life.

It is, however, with Neale's contribution to hymnody that we are here concerned. The ideas on which he worked in making a hymnal for Anglican use were rigid indeed, and thoroughly consonant with his almost incredibly mediaeval cast of mind. They amounted, in fact, to nothing less than the throwing overboard of English post-Reformation hymns altogether and the substitution of translations of the Latin hymns in use in England in the Middle Ages. Further, these hymns were to be sung to their own plainsong melodies, which of course made it necessary that the translations should be in the same metres as the originals. These were the principles embodied in the *Hymnal Noted*, of which the first part appeared in 1852, containing 46 hymns mostly from the Sarum books, and the second, containing 59 more hymns, in 1854. Of the 105 hymns 94 were by Neale himself. Another translator was one of Neale's co-editors, Benjamin Webb (1820–85), later Vicar of St. Andrew's, Wells Street, and Prebendary of St. Paul's, whose versions included 'O love how deep, how broad, how high' *173 †459, and 'Sing we triumphant hymns of praise' †146. The hymns were accompanied by their proper melodies, the musical side of the work being under the care of the Rev. Thomas Helmore.

Neale's experiment was courageous and interesting, and may be regarded as embodying the Tractarian ideal of a "Catholic" hymnal in its most uncompromising form. But in the nature of things it could not hope to win more than a very limited success: and in many quarters it merely excited ridicule. To ears attuned to the gushing rapture of Evangelical hymns the majority of Neale's versions must have sounded terribly grim and austere: yet his hymnal provided no jam to mingle with the powder. As for the "Gregorian" melodies accompanying them, the ordinary organist and choir were unable even to read the notation in which they were set out; while to the ordinary congregation their idiom sounded strange and unattractive, as indeed it largely continues to do to this day. The *Hymnal Noted*, in fact, appealed only to churches determined to be "Catholic" at any price.

None the less, it is of great importance, not only as expressing an ideal, but also on account of the large contributions it has made to subsequent hymnals, especially (but by no means exclusively) those of the "High Church" type. For example, Neale's versions bulk largely both in *A.M.* and *E.H.*, though the text of many has undergone not a little emendation. A considerable number of them are hardly of the kind to win great popularity: but others have achieved an almost universal fame. Neale's best-known hymns need not be dealt with here: for we have already spoken of them in an earlier chapter in connection with their originals.

Besides the translations in the *Hymnal Noted* Neale also produced many others. Already in 1851 he had put forth a volume of *Mediaeval Hymns and Sequences*, in which a number of hymns that figured in the *Hymnal Noted* were published for the first time, including his versions of *Pange lingua*, *Vexilla Regis* and *Urbs beata*. The Sequences in this collection were the first translations of this kind of hymn offered to the English public. Among them was the "Alleluiatic Sequence" *295 †494, and a number by (or attributed to) Adam of St. Victor, whom Neale esteemed as "to my mind the greatest Latin poet, not only of mediaeval, but of all ages"![305] Believers in transmigration might certainly put forward more absurd theories than that the soul of the French poet had taken up its abode in the nineteenth century English one — the resemblances between them are so striking, especially in their love of Scriptural typology. Neale's (partial) translation of the

Rhythm of Bernard de Morlaix followed in 1858, and was accompanied by a descriptive preface. This volume is the source of the quartet of hymns of which 'Jerusalem the golden' is the best known. A further collection of *Hymns on the Joys and Glories of Paradise* was published in 1865. In addition to these translations Neale also published two important and valuable collections of Latin hymnal texts — one of hymns from various Breviaries and Missals in 1851 and another of Sequences in 1852.

It is not only, however, by his translations from the Latin that Neale has put English Christianity under an undying obligation. What he did for the hymnody of the mediaeval Church of the West he also did, if less abundantly, for that of the East in his *Hymns of the Eastern Church* (1862). Here his task was more difficult : for (as he himself explains in his preface) he could neither reproduce the form of his originals nor present them in their entirety. [306] But even with these handicaps he managed to produce (as we have seen in an earlier chapter) a number of hymns that have become classical.

Besides his translations from Latin and Greek, Neale produced a considerable number of original hymns as well. Two small volumes of *Hymns for Children* were published in 1842 and 1844 : the first including 'Around the throne of GOD a band' *335 †243 ‡239 and the Embertide hymn, 'Christ is gone up' *352 †166 ; and the second the other Embertide hymn, 'The earth, O Lord, is one great field' †168=*354. The well known 'Come, ye faithful, raise the anthem' *302 †380 is a drastic recasting of a hymn by one Job Hupton, published in the *Gospel Magazine* in 1805. It appeared first in an article of Neale's in the *Christian Remembrancer*, July, 1863, as an illustration of how a crude original might be improved. (The version in *S.P.* has ventured in turn to "improve" on Neale's improvement, ‡477.) A final collection of *Sequences and Hymns* was published after the author's death (1866). Nor should we omit a passing tribute to Neale as a writer of carols. Some of those contained in his *Carols for Christmastide and Eastertide* (1852–3), and mostly based on mediaeval originals, have become classics of their kind. The best known of all is 'Good King Wenceslas' — in this case an original composition.

So vast an output, in addition to all his other literary work, is sufficient in itself to prove Neale's amazing facility. For this, of course, the usual price had to be paid. Compilers of hymnals have often resolved at the outset on "Neale pure and undefiled" : but they have seldom been able to maintain this attitude in practice. His versification is for the most part easy and graceful, at least when iambic measures are concerned : for when he attempts such metres as sapphics and elegiacs he is much less successful. His power of finding rhymes is nothing less than astounding, and may well be the despair of those who attempt a task similar to his own. But he is always liable to sudden lapses and can be banal and even absurd on occasion. Among his manifold gifts a sense of humour was hardly included, at least where what is Catholic and mediaeval was concerned. This mediaevalism of his made him a good deal of a portent even in his own romantic age : and it is even more unsympathetic to our own. The reader of his *Collected Hymns* will find not a little that will amuse rather than edify him. Yet if we judge him by his best work Neale's fame stands secure — and in his own line supreme.

II

Hitherto the two streams of Evangelical and Tractarian hymnody respectively have pursued their course apart. But we have now reached a period when they are to mingle in hymn-books of the modern "comprehensive" type. Here it was the High Churchmen who were to take the lead. So far as they were concerned, the fight for the recognition of hymnody had been won: and the New Version and the Old (apart from a few fragments of the former turned to other use) vanished henceforth into the limbo of things forgotten. All that remained was to solve the practical problem of evolving a scheme of hymnody which, while giving a due place to the ancient liturgical hymns of Christendom, should at the same time meet popular taste and requirements by including such elements from other sources as could be acclimatized in the "High Church" atmosphere. Even Neale himself was not so uncompromising as the plan of the *Hymnal Noted* might suggest. Not only did he add translations from the Greek service-books to those which he had already made from the Latin and compose hymns of his own, but in his article in the *Christian Remembrancer* of October, 1849, he expressly asserts that even the hymns of Dissenters are not to be entirely forbidden to Churchmen. It is true that he condemns most of them, and damns even the rest with faint praise. But their origin is not by itself to exclude them. Their acceptance or rejection must be determined "not on the bare simple ground that their authors did not hold the Catholic faith" but "by Convocation on their own merit or demerit" — with, of course, such emendation as might be made necessary by their often "heretical" character as they stood.[307]

As things turned out — and no doubt fortunately — Convocation had nothing to do with the matter. The immense development of hymnody in the second half of the nineteenth century was the result not of official action but of private enterprise. But the guiding idea behind it was very much the same as that suggested by Neale, only with a more generous treatment of non-Catholic material than Neale himself would probably have been prepared to endorse. Before, however, we attempt a sketch of "the spate of hymn-books" (to borrow Dr. Dearmer's phrase) which set in after 1850, it may be well to say something about certain elements included in them that have not yet been noticed in these pages.

1. It will be convenient to mention first certain further translators of Latin and Greek hymns — not so much because of their intrinsic importance as by way of completing what has been already said on the subject. Of these two figure here on the strength in each case of a well-known version of a single hymn — W. J. Irons (1812–83), Prebendary of St. Paul's, and J. R. Woodford (1820–85), Bishop of Ely, translators of the *Dies irae* and *Adoro te devote* respectively. Another name is Robert Campbell (1814–68), a Scots advocate who was born a Presbyterian, became a devout member of the Episcopal Church of Scotland, and finally joined the Church of Rome in 1852. Two years before he had published a collection of *Hymns and Anthems for use . . . in the diocese of St. Andrews*, containing a selection of his translations, along with a certain amount of other material. Of the translations the best known is the C.M. rendering of *Chorus novae Hierusalem*, 'Ye choirs of new Jerusalem' †139 *125. Others are a second Easter hymn, 'At the Lamb's high feast we sing' *127 †128 and the hymn for Evangelists (a cento from Adam of St. Victor), 'Come, pure hearts, in sweetest measure' *434 — though in the latter case only verses 1, 2 are his. The same collection also contained his beautiful hymn on the Angels, 'They come, GOD's messengers of love' *424 †246 — an original composition. Mention should also be made of Jackson Mason (1833–89) — not to be confused, by the way, with the seventeenth-century J[ohn] Mason, who wrote 'How shall I sing Thy majesty'. He is of rather later date ; but may be included here for the sake of convenience. He was Vicar of Settle, Yorks, and contributed, besides original hymns, several translations to the *A.M.* First Supplement of 1889, including two from Adam of St. Victor, 'Come sing, ye choirs exultant' *621 †179 and 'In royal robes of splendour' *620.

Among translators of Greek hymns Neale, of course, stands in a class entirely by himself. But we must not forget Keble's beautiful version of Φῶς ἱλαρὸν, 'Hail, gladdening Light' *18, which was first published in the *British Magazine* in 1834, nor omit a passing tribute to A. W. Chatfield, who wrote 'Lord Jesus, think on me' *185 †77, and R. M. Moorsom (*490, 641), though these are a little later than the date that we have reached.

2. It was not Latin and Greek hymnody only, however, that was to be laid under contribution in the new hymnals. We have seen that in the Reformation period an attempt had been made to acclimatize some of the contemporary Lutheran hymns, but without permanent result. Two centuries later John Wesley successfully transplanted a number of the later Lutheran hymns of the Pietist type. But apart from these German hymnody remained a sealed book to English worshippers. The credit of unlocking its treasures belongs in the main to two ladies : Frances Cox (1812–97) and Catherine Winkworth (1829–78). The former published in 1841 her *Sacred Hymns from the German*, containing 49 hymns with their original texts. In the second edition of 1864 27 of these reappeared along with 29 new ones. *A.M.* contains 4 of her versions, the best known being 'Jesus lives ! ' *140 †134 and 'Who are these like stars appearing' *427 †204. Concerning Miss Winkworth Dr. Julian has said that "her translations have had more to do with the modern revival of the English use of German hymns than the versions of any other writer".[308] She was a woman of remarkable ability, not only an excellent German scholar and a charming writer (her *Christian Singers of Germany* is a classic of its kind), but also an early pioneer on behalf of the higher education of women. Her translations were published in *Lyra Germanica*, of which the first series appeared in 1855 and the second in 1858. Of these translations *A.M.* contains 8 and *E.H.* 9. The best known are : 'Now thank we all our GOD' *379

†533, 'Christ the Lord is risen again' *136 †129 and 'Praise to the Lord, the Almighty' *657 †536.

Along with the words of the German hymns the chorale-melodies accompanying them also came into use — a process encouraged by the interest in the music of J. S. Bach, which had its beginning in the first decade of the nineteenth century (Samuel Wesley, Charles's musician son, acting as chief pioneer) and was further stimulated by the enthusiasm of Mendelssohn on his visits to England. W. H. Havergal included a good many in his *Old Church Psalmody* (1847) : and they were still more fully represented in Dr. Maurice's *Choral Harmony* of 1854 and (especially) in the *Church Psalter and Hymn Book* of the same year. The last book, edited (with Montgomery's assistance) by a Sheffield clergyman, William Mercer, had [Sir] John Goss (1800–80) as its musical editor and was used for the nave evening services at St. Paul's until supplanted by *A.M.* in 1871.[309] But the most comprehensive and scholarly adaptation of German chorales for English use is the *Chorale Book for England* (1863), in which Miss Winkworth collaborated with Sterndale Bennett and Otto Goldschmidt, the husband of the great Swedish singer Jenny Lind and founder of the Bach Choir. "This book," says Dr. Frere, "was for German hymnody what the *Hymnal Noted* was for old Latin hymnody. It was too much restricted in scope to become popular as a hymn-book ; but nevertheless it had great effect." [310]

3. When to these treasures of earlier centuries translated from various foreign tongues is added the vast mass of native material also inherited from the past, including the hymns of Watts, the Wesleys and the earlier Evangelicals, it is obvious that the compilers of the new hymnals had already a vast field from which to make their selection. But hymnody never stands still : and the generation that witnessed the rise of the Oxford Movement had had its own contribution to make to the stock of English

original hymns. Even the Tractarians had not confined themselves to translating old hymns, but had written new ones as well. Newman, Isaac Williams, Caswall and Neale have been already spoken of in this connection. But the outstanding figure is John Keble (1792–1866), the poet and saint who from his quiet Hampshire vicarage of Hursley set himself to rally what was left of the Tractarian party after the shattering defections of 1845 and 1850, and, along with his friend Pusey, did more than anyone else to save from utter shipwreck the Movement which he had inaugurated in 1833. It is true that, in exact analogy with the case of Prudentius, his most celebrated hymns are all fragments from the *Christian Year* torn from their context: but this has not prevented them from winning an immense popularity in all English-speaking lands. Few compilers of hymnals would dream of omitting 'New every morning is the love' *4 †260 ‡31, 'Sun of my soul' *24 †274 ‡55, 'Blest are the pure in heart' *261 †370 ‡455, 'When GOD of old came down from heaven' *154 †158, or even 'There is a book who runs may read' *168 †497 ‡664, with its fine treatment of the sacramental aspect of Nature. To the hymns from this source may be added, 'Ave Maria! blessèd Maid' †216. Besides the *Christian Year* Keble also wrote a metrical translation of the Psalms (1839) and *Lyra Innocentium* (1846) — the latter a book *about* children rather than a book *for* children: but neither of these has been used with success as a source for hymns. In his later years Keble turned to hymn-writing proper and contributed to the *Salisbury Hymn Book* of 1857, edited by Earl Nelson, great-nephew of the Admiral. But by this time his powers were waning: and none of these hymns has won the fame of those already mentioned. The best known are the Rogation hymn, 'Lord in Thy name Thy servants plead' *143 †140 ‡171 and the wedding hymn, 'The voice that breath'd o'er Eden' *350 †348.

Side by side with Keble and Newman as a writer of

original hymns stands Frederick William Faber (1814–63); though his first volumes of hymns only appeared in 1849, three years after he became a Roman Catholic. Like Newman, he became an Oratorian: and he founded the London branch of that congregation, which since 1854 has had its seat at the Brompton Oratory. Faber's Catholicism was of a far more emotional and full-blooded type than that of the austere and reserved Newman, who was often a good deal worried by his friend's "extravagances": but for that very reason it had a stronger popular appeal. His temperament is reflected in his hymns, which are a sort of Catholic counterpart of those of the Wesleys and of the *Olney Hymns*. Concerning the latter, Faber confessed in the preface to his Hymns that "they acted like a spell upon him for years, strong enough to be for long a counter-influence to very grave convictions, and even now to come back from time to time unbidden to the mind". His emotionalism not infrequently degenerates into sentimentality: and some of his hymns, like 'O Paradise, O Paradise' and 'Hark! hark, my soul', when taken from their personal context, seem positively nauseating to many people to-day. But the best of them, e.g. 'My GOD, how wonderful Thou art' *169 †441 ‡581 and 'O come and mourn with me awhile' *114 †111 ‡140 — are fine, moving hymns of their kind.

Two other hymn-writers who passed through Tractarianism to Roman Catholicism are Matthew Bridges (1800–93) and Henry Collins (1827–1919). The former, a layman, spent his later years in Canada. His best-known hymn is 'Crown Him with many crowns' *304 †381. The latter was a clergyman who became a Roman Catholic in 1857 and subsequently a Cistercian monk. In 1854 he published a collection of *Hymns for Missions* containing two contributions by himself — the well-known 'Jesu, meek and lowly' *188 †416 and 'Jesu, my Lord, my GOD, my All' *191 †417.

4. The Evangelical contribution to hymnody during the same period was not less important. Some of the best loved of English hymns, in fact, are from this source. Among them is what may almost certainly rank as the most popular hymn in the English language, 'Abide with me' *27 †363 ‡437. Its author, Henry Francis Lyte (1793–1847), was a former scholar of Trinity College, Dublin, who was ordained in 1815 and some years afterwards underwent the experience of Evangelical "conversion". He was appointed in 1823 Perpetual Curate of Lower Brixham, Devon, where he remained till his death. Like Toplady, the author of 'Rock of ages', he was a consumptive. In the last September of his life (as his daughter relates in the memoir prefaced to his Remains [311]) he was about to leave England for a more genial climate when

his family were surprised and almost alarmed at his announcing his intention of preaching once more to his people. His weakness, and the possible danger attending the effort, were urged to prevent it, but in vain. . . . He did preach, . . . amid the breathless attention of his hearers. . . . He afterwards assisted at the administration of the Holy Eucharist, and though necessarily much exhausted . . . yet his friends had no reason to believe it had been hurtful to him. In the evening of the same day he placed in the hands of a near and dear relative the little hymn, 'Abide with me', with an air of his own composing.

This has generally been regarded as implying that the hymn had been written just before, as an expression of the dying man's sense of helplessness and need of Divine strength. But there now seems reason to believe that it had actually been written many years previously. In the *Spectator* for Oct. 3, 1925, Dr. T. H. Bindley made the assertion that it was written in 1820 when

Lyte, as a young clergyman, was staying with the Hores at Pole Hore, near Wexford. He went out to see an old friend, William Augustus Le Hunte, who lay dying, and who kept repeating the phrase, "Abide with me". After leaving the bedside, Lyte wrote the hymn and gave a copy of it to Sir Francis Le Hunte, William's brother, among whose papers it remained. . . . These details were given me some years ago by Sir George Ruthven Le Hunte, grandson of William Augustus, and I have recently had them confirmed by members of his family.[312]

In any case the hymn was not originally intended as an evening hymn at all : the "eventide" in the first line clearly refers to the close of life's day, not to evening in the literal sense. Its immense popularity may be regarded as largely due to its melodious and eminently singable tune, written by W. H. Monk. It is often said to have been composed by him in ten minutes : [313] but this is probably only one of the innumerable legends that cluster round the origin of popular hymns.

In 1834 Lyte published a volume entitled *The Spirit of the Psalms*, containing over 280 free paraphrases of individual psalms. From this are taken three well-known hymns : 'GOD of mercy, GOD of grace' *218 †395 ‡170 (ps. lxv) ; 'Pleasant are Thy courts above' *240 †469 (ps. lxxxiv) ; and his masterpiece, 'Praise, my soul, the King of heaven' *298 †470 ‡623 (ps. ciii), so magnificently matched with Goss's great tune (first published in a minor collection of 1869). Another of his hymns is 'When at Thy footstool, Lord, I bend' *245—one of the most characteristically Evangelical of all Evangelical hymns.

A contemporary of Lyte was Sir Robert Grant (1785–1838), who died when Governor of Bombay. His splendid 'O worship the King' *167 †466 ‡618, based on Kethe's version of Ps. civ, was first published in 1833. Representative of a later and considerably different type of Evangelicalism was Henry Alford (1810–71), a Fellow of Trinity, Cambridge, who became Dean of Canterbury in 1857. He was a man of extraordinarily varied accomplishments and wrote a Commentary on the Bible that enjoyed immense reputation in its day. Opinion varies as to Alford's merits as a hymn-writer : but the man who wrote 'Come, ye thankful people, come' *382 †289 ‡9 and 'Ten thousand times ten thousand' *222 †486 may at least claim to have known how to suit the popular taste.

Side by side with these masculine names may be set two feminine ones — Harriet Auber (1771–1862), author of 'Our blest Redeemer, ere He breathed' *207 †157 ‡182, and Charlotte Elliott (1789–1871), an invalid who composed an *Invalid's Hymn Book*, in which first appeared 'Just as I am' *255 †316 ‡253 and 'Christian, seek not yet repose' *269 †374 ‡467.

III

The remarkable crop of new hymnals which marked the decade after 1850 emanated in the main, as we have said, from the High Church side. The Evangelicals already had their books ; though even here it was soon found necessary to discard some and to recast others. But for High Churchmen hymn-singing was a new luxury which could only be catered for by the production of entirely new books. At first, indeed, these were so numerous as to be positively an embarrassment. The year (1852) that saw the appearance of the first part of the *Hymnal Noted* gave birth as well to no less than three other hymn-books of a more comprehensive type. These were : *A Hymnal for Use in the English Church*, by the Rev. F. H. Murray, Rector of Chislehurst ; *Hymns and Introits compiled for the use of the Collegiate Church of Cumbrae*, by the Rev. G. Cosby White, then its Provost ; and *The Church Hymn and Tune Book*, edited by the Rev. W. J. Blew. The last had Dr. H. J. Gauntlett as its musical editor : and most of his well-known tunes first appeared in it. In 1853 followed the *Church Hymnal*, edited by the Rev. W. Cooke and the Rev. W. Denton, and in 1857 Earl Nelson's *Salisbury Hymn Book* already mentioned.

All these hymnals embodied the same ideal of a book that should combine the ancient hymns of the Catholic Church with the best products of more modern times. But for that very reason they could only be competitors and stand in one another's light. A project was therefore set on foot for pooling their resources and evolving a common book which, it was hoped, might not only secure the undivided support of churches of a definitely High Church type but also gradually win its way on its merits into other churches as well. Such was the genesis of the most celebrated and widely used of all Anglican hymnals, *Hymns Ancient and Modern*.[314]

The conceiver of the scheme was Mr Murray, who secured the co-operation of the Rev. Sir H. W. Baker, Vicar of Monkland, Herefordshire. Together they approached Mr. Cosby White, and towards the end of 1857 a small committee was formed to initiate the project. Next year the editors of several other hymn-books agreed to co-operate. In October an advertisement was inserted in the *Guardian*, intimating that "The Editors of several existing Hymnals, being engaged with others in the compilation of a Book which they hope may secure a more general acceptance from Churchmen, would be very thankful for any suggestions from persons interested in the matter." More than 200 clergymen replied: and a large committee was at once formed and held its first meeting in January, 1859, with Sir H. W. Baker in the chair. Keble did not actually join the Committee: but he took great interest in the project and gave the advice: "If you wish to make a Hymn Book for the use of the Church, make it comprehensive."

On Nov. 18, 1859, a small paper-covered book, containing 138 hymns, was issued "for temporary use and as a specimen still open to revision". The musical editor was Dr. William Henry Monk (1823–89), organist at King's College, London, who suggested the admirably appropriate title "Hymns Ancient and Modern". The completed book (known to-day as the "Original Edition") was published in 1861. Its significance has been thus characterized by Dr. Louis Benson, an American Congregationalist: "Its part in establishing, as it did, the type and tone of the representative Church of England Hymnody, and its influence on the Hymnody of other denominations, entitle its publication to rank as one of the great events in the Hymnody of the English-speaking Churches." [315]

The book contained 273 hymns, with accompanying tunes, and made full provision for the feasts and seasons of the Prayer Book. There were 132 translations of Latin hymns and 10 of German: the remainder were English hymns of all periods, nearly one-half being by living authors. These included Milman, Keble, Faber and Neale: but the largest contributor of all was the Chairman of the Committee, Sir Henry William Baker (1821–77), who was represented by 13 original hymns and 9 translations from the Latin. A good deal of Baker's work for the book, now and later, was of the nature of *pièces d'occasion* written to fill a gap, and is unlikely therefore to endure. But 'The King of love my Shepherd is' *197 †490 ‡654 and 'Lord, Thy word abideth' *243 †436 ‡570 appear to have established themselves firmly. 'O praise ye the Lord' *308 ‡351, too, deserves to survive, if only as a "carrier" for Sir Hubert Parry's noble tune, written for it much later as part of an anthem.

Of the tunes in the Original Edition the great majority were old, but there were a certain number of new ones too. The largest contributors here were Monk himself (17), the Rev. John Bacchus Dykes (1823–76), then Precentor of Durham and later Vicar of St. Oswald's in that city (7), and Sir Frederick A. Gore Ouseley (1825–89), Professor of Music at Oxford (5). Of these Ouseley represented on the whole the staid, solid manner inherited from the better products of the eighteenth century, while Monk stood midway between this and the new "Victorian" type of tune with its fluent, wistful melody and rather cloying harmony inspired by Mendelssohn and Spohr. In Dykes this new type stands forth full-blown. His style is to be seen at its best in the three famous tunes contributed by him to the 1861 book for 'Holy, Holy, Holy' *160, 'Jesu, Lover of my soul' *193 and 'Eternal Father, strong to save' *370; and at its weakest in two later insertions, 'How bright these glorious spirits shine' *438 and 'Hark, my soul, it is the Lord' *260. Its merits and its defects alike recommended it to contemporary taste : and in the 1875 edition of the book Dykes's contribution had significantly risen to 55 tunes. Not only so, but a host of imitators hastened to follow in his footsteps. It is the superabundance of this kind of tune that makes *Hymns Ancient and Modern* so characteristic of the epoch which produced it, and also renders it so vulnerable a target for contemporary criticism.   On this subject more will be said in a later chapter. But it should be added here in justice to Dykes and his school that there are already signs of a tendency among competent musicians to qualify the harsh judgments of a generation ago, at least in regard to their more defensible productions. As Sir Walford Davies and Dr. Harvey Grace have pointed out in their book *Music and Worship*, these "Victorian" tunes have at least the quality of "singableness" in an eminent degree, and if their rhythm is unenterprising, it is for that very reason a rhythm "without pitfalls for a congregation".[316]

That the book met a real need was shown by the remarkable success which it achieved from the beginning : 350,000 copies of it were sold in the first three years. This success encouraged the promoters to expand it : and in 1868 an Appendix was issued, raising the number of hymns to 386. In the additions "ancient" and "modern" were again mingled : but now the latter were by far the more numerous. The great bulk of the new hymns were by contemporaries. Newman's two famous hymns now appeared for the first time ; while Neale and Baker added largely to their share, the former's contribution including a number of his translations of Greek hymns. Of new writers the most important were Bishop Christopher Wordsworth of Lincoln (1807–85), who contributed 8 hymns from his *Holy Year* (1862), among them being 'Alleluia ! Alleluia! hearts to heaven and voices raise' *137 †127 ‡150 and 'Hark the sound of holy voices' *436 †198 ‡206 ; Professor William Bright (1824–1901), Canon of Christ Church, Oxford, author of 'Once, only once and once for all' *315 †327 and (later) of 'And now, O Father, mindful of the love' *316 †302 ‡261 ; and Cecil Frances Alexander (1823–95), who contributed three hymns for children, including 'Once in royal David's city' *329 †605 ‡368 and 'There is a green hill far away' *332 †106 ‡131. (Her other most notable hymn, 'All things bright and beautiful' *573 †587 ‡444, did not appear until the First Supplement of 1889.) Another important addition is 'The Church's one foundation' *215 †489 ‡249, by the Rev. S. J. Stone (1839–1900), later Vicar of St. Paul's, Haggerston. Its familiar tune, 'Aurelia', by Dr. S. S. Wesley, was originally written for another collection as a setting of 'Jerusalem the golden'. As regards the music of the book in general, the element of novelty was even more striking here than in the case of the words, half of the tunes being printed for the first time. Dykes's contribution was largely increased : and other composers represented were Henry Smart, John Stainer and Joseph Barnby.

The subsequent history of *Hymns Ancient and Modern* must be more briefly summarized. In 1875 the Original Edition with its Appendix was entirely recast, without, however, disturbing the fundamental basis of the book. There were a considerable number of omissions, many additions, and not a little revision and alteration of the existing material. Two names that now appear for the first time deserve mention : Frances Ridley Havergal (1836–79), a devout and accomplished Evangelical lady who wrote many hymns mostly of a highly subjective type, of which 'I could not do without Thee' *186 †572 may serve as a specimen, and William Walsham How (1823–97), Rector of Whittington, Salop, and later Bishop of Bedford and (1888) the first Bishop of Wakefield, whose contributions included his *chef d'oeuvre* 'For all the Saints' *437 †641 ‡202 and the Rogationtide intercession, 'To Thee, our GOD, we fly' *142 †565. Barnby's popular setting of the former first appeared in the 1889 Supplement. It is vigorous and extremely singable, but has the fatal defect (among others) of being in a different metre from the words! It is therefore being rightly supplanted more and more by Vaughan Williams's noble tune 'Sine nomine' †641 ‡202. Stanford's setting *437 iv is not less excellent, but perhaps less congregational.

Fourteen years after the publication of the "Revised Edition" of 1875 the so-called "First Supplement" was issued, which added 165 hymns. It is notable for the inclusion of a large number of the hymns of Charles Wesley and other eighteenth-century writers. But a good deal of the material included (and especially of the music) was of inferior quality : and it is on the whole the weakest part of the book as it stands. In this respect it offers a conspicuous contrast to the "Second Supplement" of 1916. But this will be spoken of in the next chapter.

Great as was the success of *Hymns Ancient and Modern* from the start, it was none the less regarded with suspicion and dislike in many quarters, quite apart from the Evangelicals, who naturally abhorred it both for its origin and for much of its contents. Nowadays it has become so much the "moderate" hymnal *par excellence* that it is difficult to realize that there was a time when its use was often regarded as a party-badge and an offence to sober Churchmanship, and in some cases even led to serious disturbances. For those who eyed it askance a less dubious and provoking alternative was forthcoming in *Church Hymns*, which had its origin in a small collection issued in 1852 and grew through successive revisions into the large book of 1871. Its leading compiler was John Ellerton (1826–93), a disciple of F. D. Maurice and from 1876 to 1884 Rector of Barnes. Ellerton was himself a hymn-writer of note. Among his hymns are two that are universally popular: 'Saviour, again to Thy dear name we raise' *31 †273 ‡53 and 'The day Thou gavest' *477 †277 ‡56. The musical edition of 1874 was under the care of Sir Arthur Sullivan, who contributed to it many tunes of his own, including the famous — and, as many think, exceedingly vulgar — 'St. Gertrude' for the Rev. S. Baring Gould's hearty processional (originally written in 1865 for a Sunday School feast at Horbury, Yorks), 'Onward, Christian soldiers' *391 †643 ‡397. Sullivan's share in the book combined with its "average" Church tone to win for it much success, and for a long time it was the only serious rival to *Hymns A. and M.* Another hymnal representing a similar moderate standpoint was the *Church of England Hymn Book* (1880), edited by Prebendary Godfrey Thring. It had considerable literary merits; but never attained to wide use.

But if for many *Hymns A. and M.* was too "Catholic", there were others for whom it was not "Catholic" enough. Hence the emergence of a number of hymnals framed on similar lines but in such a fashion as to obviate this reproach. The *Hymnal Noted* was gradually expanded by the addition of a large and very miscellaneous Appendix, and later of a Supplement as well. Another book was the *People's Hymnal* (1867), edited by Dr. Littledale. But the most complete collection of this kind was the *Hymnary* (1870), edited by Neale's old associate, Benjamin Webb, with the assistance of Canon W. Cooke. It is specially rich in translations from the Latin, with a preference for the hymns of Sarum Use. On the literary side it was rather an austere and forbidding affair : but this was to some extent compensated for by the floridity of its music, which was edited by [Sir] Joseph Barnby, who had made a great reputation through the excellence of the musical services at Webb's church, St. Andrew's, Wells Street. Among the musicians who contributed was Gounod : and Barnby himself, a keen disciple of the French musician, was copiously represented. His tunes were greatly admired in their day : but their luscious and chromatic character makes them displeasing now to critical ears. Along with these hymnals proper should be mentioned two books designed to make the fullest possible provision for Eucharistic worship — the *Eucharistic Hymnal* (1877) and the *Altar Hymnal* (1884).

At the opposite extreme to those who used these books stood the Evangelicals. These, for all their acute disapproval of *Hymns A. and M.*, were unable to resist the influence of the ideal for which it stood. More and more the old collections of "Psalms and Hymns" tended to disappear and to give place to "hymn-books" (in the strict sense) of the new comprehensive type. Of these the best and most important, destined increasingly to supplant the others, was the *Hymnal Companion*, first issued in 1870 under the editorship of Edward Henry Bickersteth (1825–1906), later Bishop of Exeter, and the author of 'Peace, perfect peace' *537 †468. It was based on a careful study of already existing hymnals, and, apart from its inevitable distrust of material from "Catholic" sources, represented a wide area of choice. Its texts, as Julian remarks, are admirably pure ; even though the editor had the temerity to add an extra verse to Newman's 'Lead, kindly light'. But its use to-day is almost entirely restricted to churches of the most marked Evangelical type.

In fact, just as *Hymns A. and M.* set the pattern of all the hymnals that have been mentioned, so in the long run it was to drive them almost entirely out of the field and to garner within itself most of their contents that had been found by experience to be worth keeping. For this reason, as well as for lack of space, it seems unnecessary to go into further details concerning these books, which in any case were only the most conspicuous and representative among the vast crowd of hymn-books of every kind in which the unexampled activity of what may be called the "experimental" period of English hymnal-making found expression.

CHAPTER X

NEW IDEAS IN THE TWENTIETH CENTURY

THE close of the nineteenth century saw the success of *Hymns Ancient and Modern* at its apogee. It had to a large extent vanquished its older rivals; while the younger rivals that were soon to challenge, without destroying, its supremacy had not yet appeared upon the field. It is indeed appropriate that the end of the Victorian age should be specially associated in English hymnody with a book so intensely characteristic of that age — alike in its strength and in its weakness — as the Revised Edition with the Supplement of 1889. In its combination of the sober yet definite Churchmanship of the Tractarians with the individualistic and somewhat sentimental type of personal religion that was favoured by Churchmen and Nonconformists alike in the Victorian age, it reflected faithfully the Anglican *ethos* at a period when the Established Church was perhaps a more influential spiritual force in the life of the nation than it has ever been. Its music, or at least the contemporary element in it, was not less characteristic. Someone has described the music of Elgar, the supreme English composer of the turn of the century, as "the sublimation of an *Ancient and Modern* hymn-tune": and there is at least a measure of truth in the epigram.

But already for some time there had been signs that the maintenance of the book's proud position could not be taken for granted. The general public might cling to its favourite, as indeed it largely continues to do to this day. But in circles less dominated by custom and association a more critical spirit was at work. It was not denied that both the general scheme of the book and much of its contents were excellent. But it was felt no less that it contained a good deal of "dead wood" that had failed to justify itself in practice. This criticism applied more particularly to the work of contemporary writers, much of which bore signs of having been "written to order" because no suitable material of the kind required was already in existence. On the other hand, the compilers (it was objected) had failed to explore thoroughly the sources of English hymnody: and many hymns that deserved to be included were absent. In some ways, too, the book had failed to keep pace with the best religious thought of the age. Certain aspects of Christianity were over-emphasized; while others which were assuming a growing importance were hardly represented at all. In particular, there seemed to be little reference to those social aspects of the Christian message which such great teachers as Maurice, Kingsley and Westcott had emphasized as against the excessive individualism of the old-fashioned conception of it.

The music was even more criticized than the words. In the decades before 1890 creative music in England had been at a low ebb. But now the "Renaissance of English music" had begun under the leadership of such gifted and scholarly musicians as Parry and Stanford: and with it came a change in the standards of educated musical taste. Mendelssohn, Spohr and Gounod toppled from their thrones, and a more austere and intellectual style came to be preferred. Thus the musical atmosphere that had engendered the Victorian hymn-tune had grown stale: and those who had emancipated themselves from it eyed its products askance. Moreover, the classical hymn-melodies were becoming better known to musicians: and by comparison Dykes and Stainer and Barnby seemed to be very "small beer". This new critical attitude found distinguished expression in Robert Bridges's essay, *A Practical*

Discourse on some Principles of Hymn-singing, which appeared in 1899. The publication in the same year of his *Yattendon Hymnal*, containing "100 hymns with their music, chosen for a village choir" and designed to "show what sort of a hymnal might be made on my principles", [317] added example to precept.

These various considerations would in any case have led those responsible for *Hymns A. and M.* to face the necessity of thoroughly overhauling it — at least in time. The history of the book proves that they had never claimed finality for their work. But, quite apart from this, a situation had already arisen that appeared to leave them no option in the matter. [318] In 1892 a committee of the Convocation of Canterbury made the formal suggestion that the next revision of *Hymns A. and M.* should be undertaken, not by the Proprietors alone, but by two committees appointed by the Convocations of Canterbury and York respectively, acting in consultation with them. The book was to retain its existing title : but after the revision it should become the property of the Convocations or of some body which they approved. The Proprietors very naturally refused to accept these sweeping suggestions ; though they expressed their willingness to allow their book to be used in drawing up any hymnal which the Convocations should put forth by authority. Eventually the idea of a hymnal authorized by Convocation was dropped : but the Proprietors felt themselves pledged to undertake the revision of their book themselves. The work went on for ten years — from 1894 to 1904.

The "New Edition" (as it is called) which made its appearance in the latter year was in every way a great advance on the Old. Behind it lay an immense amount of research, bringing to light a large amount of material that had hitherto been hidden from view. Some idea of the learning and scholarship involved in this research may be gauged from the *Historical Edition of Hymns Ancient and*

Q 231

Modern, which (it should be noted) takes as its text for commentary the 1904 book and not that generally used. It was published in 1909; and though issued anonymously was the work of Dr. Frere. It is invaluable to all serious students of hymnody, and its stores have been freely drawn upon by subsequent compilers of hymnals, like the 1904 book itself. In the latter many new hymns and tunes of all periods were included : and the texts of those that had already appeared were brought much closer to those of the originals. A considerable number of the hymns in the earlier edition were omitted : and in introducing new material the compilers (among whom that accomplished scholar and theologian, Dr. A. J. Mason, was specially prominent) showed themselves considerably more exacting than their predecessors had been. On the musical side much assistance was received from [Sir] Charles Stanford (1852–1924)and Sir Hubert Parry (1848–1918). Both made several valuable contributions, some of which have been already mentioned. A feature of the book was a full complement of the ancient Sarum Office Hymns for the seasons and most important festivals with their proper tunes ; while among the melodies introduced for the first time were not a few fine examples by Bourgeois and Gibbons and some of the best of the English eighteenth-century tunes which had passed into disuse. Many of these melodies have achieved wide use and popularity since.

Unhappily the fortune of the new book was not equal to its deserts. It was, in fact, a colossal failure : and the unfortunate Proprietors, in addition to an immense loss of time and trouble, found themselves saddled with a huge financial loss as well. The 1904 *Hymns A. and M.* has never been permanently taken up anywhere. The great mass of Churchgoers clung to the book to which they had become accustomed, and especially resented the idea that they should provide themselves with substitutes for the hymn-books which they already possessed. It was found, too, on examination that not a few of their "favourites" had been omitted : and the changing of the familiar numeration was also very unpopular. To discover that 'Abide with me' was no longer 'Hymn 27' or 'Jesu, Lover of my soul' 'Hymn 193' was desolating ! In addition, the book had a thoroughly bad "press" in the more widely read journals. The most widely read of all leaped in particular on the compilers' conscientious but not very prudent restoration of Charles Wesley's own text in line 1 of 'Hymn 60', 'Hark, how all the welkin rings'. The public laughed long and loud : and it is hardly an exaggeration to say that 'the welkin' gave the final death-blow to the 1904 book.

In the face of so disastrous a shipwreck all that could be done was to gather up the fragments and use them in another way. Such was the object of the "Second Supplement" appended to the old book in 1916. The obvious drawback to this expedient was that it meant that the latter remained *in statu quo*, burdened with all the inferior stuff which the compilers had sought to get rid of. But it was the best that could be done in the circumstances. The Second Supplement as originally issued was a separate volume and fell into two sections. The first section added 161 new hymns with accompanying tunes, making 779 in all. The second provided better tunes (mostly old ones) as alternatives to those in the old book which were felt to be unworthy of their place. The material in both parts was largely drawn from the 1904 book : but there was a good deal of entirely new material as well — both words and music. On its musical side the standard is particularly high. In addition to many fine melodies drawn from earlier periods, considerable use was made of the beautiful and hitherto strangely neglected tunes by the eminent Church musician, Samuel Sebastian Wesley (1810–76), included by him in a collection published in 1872 with the title of *The European Psalmist*. Several of the

233

tunes inserted were settings of hymns by the composer's grandfather, Charles Wesley.

The original form of the Second Supplement was an inconvenient arrangement that could obviously only be temporary. In 1922 it was incorporated with the main body of the book and the whole collection was reset in a single volume. The alternative tunes provided for the sections of 1875 and 1889 were inserted in their proper places with the hymns to which they belonged : and the new hymns and tunes added in 1916 were bound in at the end. This is the "Standard Edition" — the sole current form of *Hymns A. and M.* But the Second Supplement, which undeniably adds so much to the worth of the book, is still strangely neglected in many churches that use it. It is there ready to hand : but its contents are little known. It is this situation which may partly explain the curious persistence with which most critics of *Hymns A. and M.* ignore the existence of the Second Supplement and denounce it as a purely "Victorian hymn-book" that has never shown signs of repentance.

Before leaving the subject of *Hymns A. and M.* mention should be made of a further venture of those responsible for it — the *Plainsong Hymn Book*, issued in 1932. This contains 164 hymns accompanied by a rather larger number of plainsong melodies, and including a complete cycle of representative Sarum Office Hymns. Much of the material is new, both words and tunes. The latter are specially important and interesting, and represent the fruits of a life-time's study and research by the compiler, Dr. Frere. About half of the tunes had appeared in his *Plainsong Hymn Melodies and Sequences*, first published by the Plainsong and Mediaeval Music Society in 1896 (4th edn. 1920) : the rest had not been published before. They are of all dates down to the eighteenth century : and many of them are culled direct from MSS. in the libraries of England and the Continent. Like the 1904 *Hymns A. and M.*, the book has failed to win the attention and use that it deserves, at least as yet. But it is, and is likely to remain, by far the largest and most comprehensive collection of plainsong hymns available for English Churchpeople.

II

The failure of the 1904 revision was the price paid for the popularity of the old *Hymns A. and M.* The great mass of Churchpeople had turned a deaf ear to the criticisms of the minority and shown that they "hated to be reformed". But the minority was still there, as were the patent weaknesses of *Hymns A. and M.* in its unreformed state still in general use. It seemed likely, too, that the future would lie with the critics rather than with the conservatives. The twentieth century had arrived : and with it the reaction against "Victorianism" had begun and new ideas were everywhere in the air. Thus the times were propitious for the appearance of a new hymn-book that should correspond with the ideals and taste of the new age. Such a book must expect to make its way slowly, in view of the *vis inertiae* which always plays so great a part in Church affairs and had already defeated the revisers of *Hymns A. and M.* But it would have influential backing, which might be relied upon to grow still stronger in process of time.

Even before the revised *Hymns A. and M.* made its appearance a potential candidate had arrived in the shape of the revised edition of the S.P.C.K. *Church Hymns* (1903). Here, too, there was a notable advance both in the selection of hymns and tunes and in the purity of the texts. But the book was, after all, only a new form of an old book which had always been overshadowed by a more successful rival : and in this and other ways it lacked the charm of novelty. Moreover, its very moderate tone made

235

little appeal to Anglo-Catholics, who were growing rapidly in numbers and importance and, so far at least as a large and active section of them was concerned, were adopting a "progressive" outlook on things in general very different from the cautious traditionalism of the old Tractarians and their successors.

It was from this section of the Anglo-Catholics that the *English Hymnal* (1906) was to proceed — the most formidable rival that *Hymns A. and M.* has as yet had to face. At the same time its compilers were careful to deny any propagandist intent. Its preface states expressly that "it is not a party book . . . but an attempt to combine . . . the worthiest expressions of all that lies within the Christian Creed, from those 'ancient Fathers' who were the earliest hymn-writers down to contemporary exponents of modern aspirations and ideals". The book is "offered to all broadminded men". These disclaimers, however, did not wholly succeed in carrying conviction in view of the decidedly "Catholic" tone of many of the contents of the book, with their high sacramental doctrine and bold resort to prayers for the dead and even the "invocation of saints". Certain leading bishops frowned on the *English Hymnal*, and even forbade its use in their dioceses. Objection was particularly taken to certain appeals for the intercession of the Blessed Virgin. The difficulty was solved in 1907 by an "abridged edition" in which 5 hymns were altered and 4 omitted altogether.

If the *English Hymnal* was and remains too "Catholic" for many tastes, it is admirably "catholic" in the other sense of that obliging word. There is a complete set of the Sarum Office Hymns for the seasons, for the Common of Saints and for the Proper of the most important individual saints. Many of the translations of these hymns were specially made for the book and are a great improvement on those which had appeared in the earlier Anglo-Catholic hymnals. Greek hymnody and German contribute not a few examples, along with the seventeenth century Latin hymns from the French Breviaries. As regards hymns of English origin, all periods are well and worthily represented. To a large extent the selection is identical with that found in *Hymns A. and M.*: but the compilers were free to get rid of most of the inferior Victorian hymns which still unduly cumber the older book, and at the same time added a large number of English hymns of all periods that had not found a place there. Many of these additions have been already commented on in earlier chapters. They include two classes that are specially worthy of note. The first of these consists of 10 of the fine versions of Latin and Greek and German originals made by the late Poet Laureate Robert Bridges (1844–1930) for the *Yattendon Hymnal*, together with 3 more or less original compositions from the same accomplished hand. The second is a group of hymns of American origin, some of which have already won wide and deserved popularity. We may specially mention 'Once to every man and nation' †563, an extensively altered cento (the 5 long lines in each verse of the original are even reduced to 8 half-lines) of a poem by the distinguished American man of letters, James Russell Lowell (1819–91), written in 1845 in the anti-slavery interest at the time of the war between the United States and Mexico; 'City of GOD, how broad and fair' †375, by Samuel Johnson (1822–82); 'Thy kingdom come! on bended knee' †504 and 'O Thou in all Thy might so far' †463, by Frederick L. Hosmer (1840–1929); 'Lord of all being, throned afar' †434, by the essayist and poet, Oliver Wendell Holmes (1809–94); and 'Jesus, these eyes have never seen' †421, by Ray Palmer (1808–87). The first four of these authors were Unitarians, the last a Congregationalist. Their hymns thus exhibit a broadly theistic and "non-ecclesiastical" religious outlook which is no doubt partly the secret of the strong appeal that they make to many minds in the present age. In addition, the first three of the hymns that we have mentioned emphasize the national and social bearings of the Christian message that had been inadequately represented in previous Church hymnals. Three other hymns in *E.H.* are notable as having a similar significance: the "Recessional" of Rudyard Kipling (1865–1936), written on the occasion of Queen Victoria's Diamond Jubilee in 1897, 'GOD of our fathers, known of old' †558; 'O GOD of earth and altar' †562, by Gilbert K. Chesterton (1874–1936); and 'Judge eternal, throned in splendour' †423, by the celebrated preacher, Henry Scott Holland (1847–1918), Canon of St. Paul's and later Regius Professor of Divinity at Oxford.

The music of the *English Hymnal* exhibits the same fine comprehensiveness as the words. On this side the book had the immense advantage of being under the editorship of the most distinguished of living English musicians, Dr. Ralph Vaughan Williams (b. 1872). He himself contributed a number of tunes, of which the now famous 'Sine Nomine' †641 and the beautiful 'Down Ampney' †152 stand in the first rank of modern hymn-tunes. His share was further increased when the music was revised in 1933 — notably by the stately 'King's Weston' †368, which had already appeared in *Songs of Praise*. Other important contributors were the brothers Martin Shaw (b. 1876) and Geoffrey Shaw (b. 1879). There was a splendid garnering of old tunes of all periods, many of which (it is only fair to say) had already made their appearance in the 1904 revision of *Hymns A. and M.* The Office Hymns were in each case accompanied by their plainsong melodies, with modern tunes as alternatives. The former were admirably reset in the 1933 revision by Mr. J. H. Arnold in accordance with the principles now generally commended by experts. In regard to tunes of later date the *English Hymnal* broke new ground in three directions in particular. First, in its inclusion of a number of the so-called "church melodies" which sprang up in France in the sixteenth and seventeenth centuries to provide settings in measured form in place of the unmeasured plainsong melodies. These tunes have often a fine sweeping quality that makes them attractive and popular, though some of them are liable to be obnoxious to purists as "debased" or "bastard" plainsong. The second class of new material consists of a number of the tunes produced in Methodist circles in Wales in the nineteenth century ; and the third of a larger collection of entirely new tunes based on English secular folk-songs. Both of these have been a good deal criticized. The Welsh tunes are often very dull : their form, in particular, is exceedingly monotonous, with its continual repetition of the same material (of four sections of each tune three are normally the same) and its incessant return to the "tonic". The English folk-tunes, too, though often beautiful in themselves, are not always appropriate to the atmosphere of a church and, reflecting as they do a "craze" of the period that converted them to new use, may not prove to wear very well. A further weakness of the *English Hymnal* on its musical side is its inability to resist the subtle temptation to present its German chorales in the elaborately harmonized versions of J. S. Bach. These are, of course, superb in themselves : but they were never intended, nor are they in the least suitable, for use in alliance with hymns containing a considerable number of verses. Nor is the exceedingly slow *tempo* adopted in Germany in singing chorales (under quite different conditions) consonant with modern English habit or preference. The arrangement, e.g., of 'Forty days and forty nights' †73 would weary any congregation to death. The compilers would have done well to heed Bridges's dictum already quoted (p. 101). If any German chorale is not suitable for use as an English hymn-tune, it should not be used for the purpose at all.

These, however, are but incidental blemishes in a hymnal which is for the most part admirable both in words and music. Its obvious excellences were certain to win for it enthusiastic approval in quarters which cared seriously about the quality of our Church song: and its use and popularity have steadily grown, especially in churches with congregations of the more educated type. In the early days of its existence, too, its claim to recognition as against the only current form of *Hymns A. and M.* was greatly enhanced by the fact that the latter was still in its unreformed "Victorian" state, owing to the complete failure of the 1904 revision. But the publication of the Second Supplement in 1916 has enormously strengthened the position of the older hymnal in this respect. We may add, further, that there are signs at present of a more critical attitude towards the *English Hymnal* among competent musicians than was apparent at first — a tendency to stress its defects as well as its qualities. This fact should be borne in mind by those who are zealous for hymnal reform, but are without much equipment for forming reliable artistic judgments for themselves. It is very doubtful, too, whether the musical revision undertaken in 1933 was in all respects an improvement.

In the enrichment of their book, particularly on its musical side, the compilers of the *English Hymnal* were able to draw not only on the admirable pioneer work of those responsible for the 1904 revision of *Hymns A. and M.*, but also on the extremely valuable collection published (also in 1904) by the Rev. G. R. Woodward with the title *Songs of Syon*. The music and the words were at first issued separately. The former was described by the editor as representing "an honest endeavour to raise the standard of English taste, by rescuing from oblivion some of the finest melodies of the sixteenth, seventeenth and eighteenth centuries". These were "presented in their primitive integrity and, where possible, with the original harmony". The accompanying words edition was described on the title page as "a collection of hymns and sacred poems mostly translated from ancient Greek, Latin and German sources". It was designed to furnish words to fit the melodies provided, most of which were in unusual metres, and so to make it possible to use them. It included some 50 examples from the accomplished hand of the editor himself — both translations (from all three languages) and original compositions. Woodward, like his greatly admired Neale, had a curiously mediaeval cast of mind, but with a lighter literary touch and a charming quaintness of language and fancy that borders at times on the fantastic — a quality even more evident in the carols that he translated or wrote for the *Cowley Carol Book* and other collections edited by him. "Compiled" (as its preface is careful to point out) "for the faithful", not for "the inquirers after truth", *Songs of Syon* was further "intended not to compete with existing hymnals but only to supplement them". It thus made no claim to be a complete hymn-book in itself: its importance lies in its value as a source-book. Four years later (in 1908) another collection of admirable literary and musical quality but with a similarly limited appeal was issued as the *Oxford Hymn Book* under the joint editorship of Dr. T. B. Strong, then Dean of Christ Church, and Dr. Basil Harwood. Its preface expressly disclaims any intention to provide a completely comprehensive hymn-book: the book seeks rather to "make a more restricted selection of those hymns which appear to satisfy a certain standard and to be content with a more approximate application of them to particular occasions".

The hymnals that have been spoken of hitherto were all definitely Church books intended for use by Churchpeople. The other Christian denominations had their own books, framed to meet their own needs and points of view.

Until recently this principle, "To every Christian body its own hymn-book," was taken for granted. But after the Great War the circumstances seemed propitious to the success of a book that should transcend denominational differences and appeal to all English-speaking Christians. The war had done much to familiarize men's minds with the idea of an undogmatic, unsectarian Christianity, which was already the theoretic basis of the religious instruction given in the State-provided schools, and which in the post-war years was to find expression in Brotherhoods, Guilds and similar gatherings. Moreover, hymnbooks were urgently needed for the schools, secondary and higher elementary, that were developing so rapidly all over the country : and these hymn-books, like the schools themselves, must be free from denominational bias. The tendency to transcend sectarian differences found an echo within the Church of England itself in an active and influential section which was "Modernist" in its outlook and, as such, inclined to sit lightly to the dogmatic affirmations of traditional Christianity. Christianity, it was urged, is not a body of theological beliefs, but an attitude of mind and heart that seeks to mould the life not only of the individual but of the nation and of human society as a whole in accordance with the spirit of Jesus Christ. In allegiance to that spirit all men of goodwill may be one, not only the members of all the Christian denominations but even those who are unable to accept *ex animo* the historic Creeds of the Church.

Such, roughly speaking, were the ideas that inspired the production of *Songs of Praise*, the most important addition to the long list of English hymn-books since the *English Hymnal*, and one that strikes out an entirely new line. It is not a Church hymn-book, but is designed for use by Christians of all denominations and even (at least in a great part of it) by those who would hesitate to call themselves Christians at all. Its preface expressly claims for it a "national" character and suitability not for public worship only but also "for schools, lecture meetings and other public gatherings".

Its editor, Dr. Percy Dearmer (1867–1936), had played a leading part in the compilation of the Anglo-Catholic *English Hymnal* some twenty years before. But in the interval his religious position had undergone a marked change. His Anglo-Catholicism had always been of the liberal and progressive sort, with a strong admixture of Christian Socialism. But now he had ceased to be an Anglo-Catholic altogether and ranked as a Modernist of an advanced type. A man of great ability and capacity for work, with a wide and cultivated knowledge of both literature and art, and at the same time singularly sensitive to every current of contemporary "progressive" thought, he was eminently fitted for editing a hymn-book on the lines which he proposed. Not only did he edit *Songs of Praise* but he also embarked on a campaign in its behalf which erred if at all on the side of excessive zeal. The book received a warm welcome from educational authorities in many parts of the country : and it was also taken up with enthusiasm by the authorities of the great new cathedral at Liverpool, who were entirely in sympathy with the ideals that inspired it.

Even those who do not share that sympathy will be forced to admit that *Songs of Praise* is a remarkable achievement and one likely to have a powerful influence on the English hymnody of the future. It has made available many fine specimens of English religious poetry of all periods that had not hitherto found a place in our hymn-books — with a special stress (as we might anticipate) on that element of "social service" which had already figured to some extent in the *English Hymnal* and had done much to commend that book to many who had little sympathy with it on its Anglo-Catholic side. In regard to many of these additions it may be doubted whether they are really suited for use as *hymns*. The editor has not always borne in mind the distinction between a hymn and a religious poem. Some of them, too, would seem to be pantheistic rather than Christian in outlook. But we must bear in mind the public for which the book is primarily intended — a public very different from the congregation of the ordinary parish church. Nor can it be denied that not a few of these poems do make admirable hymns, of which all future compilers of hymn-books will be forced to take notice. A number of these have been already mentioned in previous chapters of this book. On the musical side, too, *Songs of Praise* has introduced a good deal of valuable material retrieved from the past, in addition to much that had already figured in the *English Hymnal* and the Second Supplement of *Hymns A. and M.* Some, however, will be of opinion that, as in the case of the former of these books, an unduly large place has been given to Welsh Methodist tunes and to tunes adapted from English folk-songs, as well as to the often rather banal and vulgar products of English Methodism in the late eighteenth and early nineteenth centuries. On the other hand, the "Victorian" hymn-tune (in regard to which Dr. Dearmer entertained a prejudice which almost amounted to an obsession) is as far as possible eliminated altogether.

In addition to these "new-old" elements *Songs of Praise* also includes a large amount of entirely new material, both words and music, the work of contemporary writers and musicians. Among the former a prominent place is held by Dr. Dearmer himself, who, like other hymnal compilers before him, does not seem to have been always sufficiently on his guard against the very human prejudice of an author in favour of his own work. Some, too, of the classic hymns of Christendom are more or less recast in order to bring them into line with the "Modernist" standpoint. A noteworthy feature of the book is the "Proper of Saints" section, in which a gallant if not altogether successful attempt is made to solve a standing problem by providing a series of hymns which are mostly new compositions specially written by various writers. Among the composers of new tunes the two musical editors, Dr. Vaughan Williams and Dr. Martin Shaw, stand out conspicuous. It should be added that the book was enlarged and completely recast in 1931, when much new material was introduced and the total number of its contents was raised from 467 to 703.

The scope and purpose of *Songs of Praise* set it (strictly speaking) outside the limits of this book : but, as it has already achieved a fair currency in Anglican churches and is certain to have much influence in the future on Anglican hymnals proper, it has been thought necessary to say something about it. On the question of its merits and defects the present writer would prefer to add nothing to the little that he has already said. It is admittedly an experimental book, novel in its plan, challenging in its outlook and containing much entirely new and untried material. As to the value of this last for its purpose only posterity can judge : and no attempt is made here to don the prophet's mantle and anticipate the verdict. The book is as completely typical of the age which produced it as was the Victorian version of *Hymns A. and M.* : and no doubt in due course of time it will have to encounter precisely the same sharp fire of criticism to which its champions have subjected the older book. We may safely affirm, however, that both books contain much that will prove to be of permanent value ; and that each will be regarded a century hence as epoch-making in its own way.

PART II

PRACTICAL

CHAPTER XI

TOWARDS A POLICY

SO far as individual hymns are concerned, the account
given in the preceding chapters of Christian hymnody
throughout the ages has been mainly confined to
those permanently valuable products of every age which
have become available for the use of English Christians in
our own, either in their (more or less) original form or in
translations. A complete account of the whole output of
hymn-writing since the Church began is impossible : and
even if it were possible it would not be worth attempting.
Dr. Bridges has spoken of "thatt most depressing of all
books ever compiled by the groaning creatur, Julian's
hymn-dictionary".319 This judgment is not very
graciously expressed : for Julian's great work is a monument of learning and research and is indispensable to
every student. But it is certainly "depressing" in the sense
which Bridges, of course, intended — that it contains
notices of innumerable hymns which few students remember or want to remember, and more particularly of
hymns that had a transient currency in the less educated
religious circles of England and America in the second
half of the nineteenth century. Even so it only deals with
a fraction of what might have figured in its pages. Time,
on the whole, is a sound critic in hymnody as in other
matters : those hymns survive that deserve to survive. The
vogue of the moment is an extremely unsafe guide : but if
a hymn can still win love and admiration after several
centuries and can even surmount (as in many cases) the
serious handicap of translation, we may be fairly certain

that there is something about it worth keeping. Nor will a critical literary sense usually find much ground for serious quarrel with this verdict, if the limitations of what constitutes a hymn are borne in mind. It seems fair to say that at least the great majority of the hymns mentioned in the preceding pages can make a good claim to inclusion in any hymnal that purports to represent the best that Christian hymnody has bequeathed to us.

Starting from this basis and even applying a rigorous criticism to the material at our disposal, we should have a body of hymns of fairly imposing dimensions and one quite sufficient in itself to satisfy all reasonable requirements of the ordinary church. The only section inadequately provided for would be the "Proper of Saints" : but we do not really need hymns about such shadowy figures as St. Bartholomew or Saint Simon and Saint Jude, which even the most accomplished poet could hardly hope to make very inspiring. Is there, then, any real necessity to go beyond such a "classical" collection as would be forthcoming on these terms of entrance ?

The question raises issues of very practical importance. The average sort of congregation is mainly composed of the average sort of people, who have a very human objection to having things that they dislike thrust down their throats because somebody else thinks that they ought to like them. The dictum that "men must love the highest when they see it" does not, unfortunately, always hold good in practice. For instance, the *Yattendon Hymnal* is a casket of jewels : but there are good grounds for believing that Yattendon itself did not think very highly of it. Of the hymns in our suggested "classical" collection a considerable proportion have become established popular favourites : but many others appeal to the few rather than the many, and even the most determined efforts to popularize them seem hardly able to win for them anything more than toleration. On the other hand, congregations have a trying habit of manifesting a special liking for hymns that a refined literary or musical taste condemns. Take, for example, hymns of what is called the "mission" type. Such hymns have always been more popular among Nonconformists than in the Church of England: and the policy of the compilers of Church hymnals has usually been to include as few of them as possible. Yet if for any reason a hymn of this kind is introduced into the service of a church with a working-class congregation, the people will almost certainly "take to" it and demand its repetition. How far is this taste to be yielded to? It cannot be denied that to simple and uneducated minds such hymns make a great appeal: and the great revivalists of the past have had no hesitation in using them and have largely promoted the success of their work by doing so. The crude language and metaphors and floridly vulgar tunes of many early Methodist hymns, the sentimental catchiness of "Moody and Sankey", the adaptation to pious words of popular tunes of the moment by the Salvation Army — all these were an integral and deliberate part of the evangelism of those who adopted them. Nor can it be denied that all these movements did much good in a social *milieu* to which the 'standards of literary and musical criticism meant nothing at all. In the great work of saving souls questions of artistic taste are of secondary importance. The present writer remembers being struck by a remark made by the organist of a church famous for its exquisite musical services, to the effect that if he could fill an empty church and keep it full by using music that he knew to be artistically worthless he would not hesitate to do so.

The hymns of which we are speaking are, of course, an extreme case: but for that very reason they pose our problem in its most clear-cut and challenging form. The same problem, however, is raised less acutely by not a few hymns which (unlike these) figure prominently in our popular Church hymnals. In confronting it we may begin by setting down certain salient *facts* that need to be borne in mind.

1. The bulk of the public that we have to cater for judges much more by the tune than by the words. The vast crowd which sings 'Abide with me' before a Cup Final football match is not thinking at all about the words, which are as unsuitable as they could possibly be both to the occasion and to the sort of people who sing them. But they know and like the *tune*, which serves as an outlet to their pent-up excitement. In the same way, when a congregation sings a hymn in church with gusto it is the tune that bears them along. Many of them have only a vague general idea as to what their favourite hymns are about.

2. The explanation would appear to lie in the fact that for the ordinary man music has a wider range of expression than has language. The same phenomenon is visible in the case of the "theme-songs" that are heard at the cinema. The words of these are the most arrant rubbish : and no one pays heed to anything except their general sense. It is the tune that creates the required mood and atmosphere : and this is all that matters for the purpose in view.

3. In regard to words and music alike, only a small proportion of the public has enough of educated taste to judge whether a thing is good or bad. People will say that "they know what they like", but can give no better or clearer reason for their preference. Sometimes their judgment will coincide with that of the educated critic ; more often it is the exact opposite. We may add that, where hymns are concerned, the majority have often not enough of religious experience to enable them to enter into the emotion which prompted the author to write his hymn. The almost agonized sense of the dependence of the human soul upon God that inspired 'Abide with me' was very

real to Henry Francis Lyte : it means little to many who enjoy singing his hymn in church or elsewhere.

4. In the formation of popular judgments on hymns association is a much more powerful factor than intrinsic value. This applies not only to the uneducated but to the educated as well, if we may judge from the hymns sung at the funerals of famous and greatly gifted men as their "favourites". Here we face what is perhaps the most fundamental consideration of all. It is not so much what a hymn is or says that counts, as what it *means* to the individual who sings or hears it. Most of us will admit that there are some hymns and tunes which we are quite unable to look at from an external or objective point of view. Viewed through the golden mist of memory and association, even poor verse and undignified rhythm and melody may wear an entirely different look.

These, it must be repeated, are simple psychological *facts* : and in deciding what hymns we are to use we can only ignore them at the cost of alienating a large part of our congregations. The cultivated critic may rail as much as he likes against the preference of the ordinary worshipper in favour of the "Victorian" sentimental hymns and tunes : but he will neither be able to make him appreciate his own criteria of taste nor wipe out the associations that make such things dear. All he can do is to create new and better associations and to trust that the old associations will disappear with the lapse of time. Meanwhile, he may console himself by reflecting that, after all, the things which he dislikes so much are doing no great harm. It is sometimes alleged that the use of sentimental hymns and tunes is enervating, and calculated to sap the moral fibre of those who sing them. But this argument is hardly borne out by the facts. It is curious but undeniable that the most virile types of men — sailors, soldiers, miners and the like — show a special liking for just these sentimental hymns. Such men feel more deeply than they are usually willing to show : and, being for the most part simple, unsophisticated souls, they do not make a very clear distinction between sentiment and sentimentality. The present movement in favour of "stark" and "rugged" hymns proceeds from a cultivated artistic circle which is rather out of touch with the workaday world of the common man. The ordinary Englishman is decidedly a Philistine ; and seems likely to remain so in spite of all efforts to make him otherwise. In religion as in other matters he likes to express his emotions in ways that seem rather crude to a cultivated taste. We must take him as we find him : and if when he goes to church he prefers hymns like 'Abide with me' or 'Hark, hark my soul' to German chorales or a combination of Bridges and Bourgeois, we must not refuse him a measure of what he likes nor bolster up our refusal by pretending that such hymns make him "less of a man", when actually he is often more of a man than his better-educated critics. A church, after all, is a place to help the wayfaring man or woman along the rough road of life, not an academy of the fine arts. We are right to say that we must only offer our best to God : but we have no reason for supposing that God's idea of "the best" is purely or even primarily aesthetic. A poor hymn which *means* something, however dimly felt, to those who sing it is more acceptable to Him than the choicest poetry and music listened to with coldness and boredom. The reader may remember the poignant scene in a modern novel where a number of miners entombed in a pit sing 'Hold the fort,' and the author's comment : "Each and all realized that there are worse ways of going to one's death than singing a battle song by Moody and Sankey." [320]

Again, even in the matter of criteria of taste, it should not be forgotten that the literary and musical preferences of the cultivated minority at any given moment are far from representing a standard that is unalterably fixed. Fashions change : and the present taste for a stark and unsentimental directness is a natural reaction from the rhetoric and romanticism of the late nineteenth century. But we cannot be certain that the reaction will continue : and there is real danger lest, when we set to work to purge our hymnals, we "tip out the baby with the bath-water". The characteristic products of Victorian hymnody are probably neither as good as the Victorians thought them nor as bad as their critics of to-day think them. Time will winnow them out, as it has winnowed out the hymns of earlier ages. The great majority will become obsolete : but the best will remain and will be valued as typical of their age and style — and also as most characteristically *English*. Do not these hymns, after all, represent practically the only approach to a genuine "folk-song" that the present age can show ? Meanwhile we must be prepared for the "time-lag" which always dictates that the less worthy products of the preceding generation, which a critical judgment rightly rejects, shall retain their hold for the time being on the uncritical multitude. The inferior specimens among the "Georgian" hymns now being produced are likely to be just as much a nuisance to the musical reformers of fifty years hence as the bad "Victorian" hymns are to those of to-day.

What, then, is to be our practical line of action ? Certainly not to adopt a policy of drift and to abandon all efforts to improve the standard of our Church song. But it is no use to force the pace : we must proceed slowly. To begin with, we should remember that our attitude must be largely determined by the kind of church (and also the kind of service) for which provision has to be made. Much may be permitted in a mission church in a slum district that could not be tolerated for a moment in a church with an educated congregation. Then (bearing this distinction in mind) we must make it our business to put on our hymn lists as many good hymns as we dare ; and no more inferior hymns than we must in order to keep our congregations content. Above all, we must be careful to see that the new hymns which we introduce into our services are such as reach an adequate standard both in words and music, unless there be urgent *religious* reasons to the contrary. We may sometimes have to make concessions to popular taste : but we need not deliberately *encourage* it to be bad. Fortunately, a large number of popular hymns are also unexceptionable from the critic's standpoint : and this eases our problem considerably. A sound practical rule for those who have to choose hymns would seem to be this. In the case of hymns sung within the framework of the Divine Office itself (whether as "Office Hymn" before the Psalms or *Magnificat*, or as a substitute for the "Anthem" after the Third Collect) choose only hymns that are first-rate, with a special preference for hymns of the "objective" type, concerned with the glory and majesty of GOD and the great mysteries of the Faith rather than with the subjective moods and needs of the individual. The more "popular" and subjective hymns can be sung later, before or after the sermon, which is expected to deal largely with the more personal aspects of religion. At the Eucharist, too, the hymns chosen should be of the more objective and dignified type, in so far as they are not Eucharistic hymns. The latter will supply as much of the subjective element as is needful or desirable.

The same policy should be followed by those who have not simply to use hymnals but to compile or revise them ; unless, of course, they are in the lucky and exceptional position of having to provide (like the compilers of the *Oxford Hymn Book*) for an educated and critical *clientèle* only. Broadly speaking, we may say that hymns serve two purposes, and that a popular hymnal should be designed to meet them both. The first purpose may be described as "liturgical" — the adornment of the Church's worship with the best that is available and suitable in poetry and in art. The provision here should be confined to the classical products of every age, with a special preference for hymns that have stood the test of centuries. Such modern hymns as are included under this category should bear unmistakable signs of being of the highest order. In cases where the tunes to which the hymns in this class are usually sung are unworthy of the words, they should be reset to better tunes — here again preferably good old tunes, or, if modern tunes are used, those that are indubitably first-rate in the judgment of the musicians. The second purpose we may describe as "popular and missionary", aiming at the edification of the masses, not forgetting that the "masses" include many groups of individuals with special needs of their own. Here the compiler may allow himself more latitude, deliberately appealing to the taste of the age and remembering that each generation has its own way of envisaging religion and its own popular preferences in regard to its expression. Of course, there is a level below which even hymns in this class should not be allowed to sink : but the line must be drawn in such a way as to make a reasonable concession to the popular taste of the time. If hymns of a definitely "mission" type are used at all (and even the *English Hymnal* found it desirable to include such things as 'Hold the fort' and 'I hear Thy welcome voice'), they should be relegated to a separate section and not be mixed up with hymns less open to criticism.

All this means that a final and definitive hymnal is an impossibility. Hymnals are like most other human things— "they have their day and cease to be". For one thing, the "canon" of Christian hymnody is never closed. The output of hymns, good, bad and indifferent, goes on steadily : every age has its own contributions to make, and the best of them go in the end to swell the "classical" stock. The rest serve their turn for the time being, and then disappear. Many hymns will have a real value for the generation that produced them (and for the generation or two immediately following) which they will not retain for posterity. This, for example, has been the fate of the great majority of Charles Wesley's hymns. Written to serve an immediate need, they served it with acceptance : but the religious atmosphere which they reflect is different from that of our day, and they have lost their power to stir men's hearts. Thus every age has the task of scrapping a large amount of material that has gone out of date : and every hymnal must look forward to being supplanted in the end or at least to undergoing drastic revision.

Once again, in a comprehensive church like our own, different schools of thought have their particular preferences in hymns as elsewhere. The historic associations and the dogmatic content of the mediaeval Office Hymns and of many of the Tractarian hymns will make an appeal to the Anglo-Catholic which the Evangelical and still more the Modernist will be far from recognizing to the same extent. The Evangelical, on the other hand, has always shown a special preference for the "personal" type of hymn ; while the Modernist, with his distrust of doctrinal definition and desire to make the Church as comprehensive as possible, will be ready to admit into the hymnal he uses a number of religious lyrics which those who set more store by the traditional theology will regard as theistic rather than specifically Christian. These different schools of thought have all their recognized place within the corporate framework of Anglicanism : and as no single hymnal can give to all alike the hymns that each wants to use and no others, it is only natural that each should have a hymnal or hymnals of its own. This multiplication of hymnals has the further advantage of encouraging a wider range of research and experiment along different lines. For example, even those who do not entirely approve of *Songs of Praise* will admit that it is introducing and popularizing a considerable number of hymns that are likely to prove permanent additions to the "classical" hymnody of the future.

The desirability of this multiplication of hymn-books, with the confusion and competition that it inevitably brings in its train, has of course decidedly its limits. In the "experimental" period of the second half of the nineteenth century much practical inconvenience must have been caused by there being so many rival hymn-books in the field: and we can only rejoice that the range of choice has narrowed to-day. On the other hand, if the arguments adduced in this chapter hold good, it seems well to abstain from any attempts to stereotype our hymnody. A desire is sometimes expressed — though less frequently than a generation ago — that the Church of England might have an "official" hymn-book issued by authority for use in every church. But the case against this seems to be much stronger than the case in its favour. Such a book would be difficult to compile, more difficult to enforce in general use, and most difficult of all to change when once it was compiled and adopted. Yet there can be no life without change: and the Church must be ready to march with the times, in its hymnody as in other more important matters.

CHAPTER XII

SOME PRACTICAL COUNSELS

I. The Choice of Hymns

1. Who should choose the hymns to be sung in church ? The parson or the organist ? In practice it is sometimes the one and sometimes the other. But it is indubitably the parson's *right* to do so : and if the organist does so instead it can only be as the parson's deputy. Not only is it the parson's right but it is also his *duty*. It is he who is responsible for the services of which the hymns form a part : and it is for him to judge what is necessary to make these services as appropriate and as helpful as possible. Moreover, as he has the task of preaching as well, he will often have to choose hymns that may serve either to prepare his hearers for his discourse beforehand or to drive home its message afterwards. On the other hand, it can hardly be too much insisted on that the parson should take the organist into his confidence and assure himself of his co-operation and approval. If he is ignorant of music he should ask the organist's advice on the subject of tunes, supposing that the organist is competent to give it, which (of course) is by no means always the case. In the latter contingency he should seek the advice of those who *are* competent. In this connection both parson and organist will do well to lay to heart the findings of the admirable Report of the Archbishops' Committee on Church Music (revised edn. 1932), and especially the four criteria of a "good tune" laid down on pp. 7–9 and the remarks on hymn-singing on pp. 29 ff. In this way (granted a reasonable docility in both towards expert opinion) a common

ground may be achieved which will help to reconcile possible differences of view. In any case, the parson must take all possible pains to carry his organist with him. If he is an enthusiast for hymnal reform, he must learn to temper zeal with prudence, and remember that unless he can avoid alienating the organist — *and* the choir — his efforts are likely to do more harm than good. Tact and patience are nowhere more needed than in the difficult task of improving our Church music.

2. In choosing the hymns the parson must be willing to *take trouble*. In too many cases the job is done in a hurry. The vicar (or the curate) dashes into the vestry five minutes before the choir-practice, seizes a hymn-book, and rapidly turning over its pages chooses the first hymns catching his eye which "they know" and which have not been used (so far as his memory serves) on the last few Sundays. It is obviously impossible to do justice to the contents of any hymnal in this way. A certain number of hymns get worked to death ; while many other and better ones remain entirely unused, less by deliberate intent than from sheer forgetfulness that they exist. The duty of choosing hymns (surely not the most insignificant item in a parson's work) should be set about *in a systematic way*. On a day when he has a little time at his disposal, the parson should take down his hymn-book and make a list of all the hymns in it that are of a quality to make them worth singing on their merits, together with those hymns which, though he knows them to be poor stuff, must be sung at reasonable intervals because "the congregation likes them ". Using this first list as a basis he should make another list from time to time (say once a quarter), in which he should distribute over the coming Sundays (*a*) those hymns appropriate to the season which the congregation knows, (*b*) those which they don't know but would do well to learn, being careful to avoid repetitions unless he definitely feels them for any reason to be

desirable. Of course it is well not to put in more than a very few new hymns at a time, and also to allow the congregation to sing them at frequent intervals at first, so that it may get to know them. In compiling such a list he will do well to consult the list of suggested hymns for the different Sundays, etc., which some hymnals (e.g. *E.H.* and *S.P.*) provide, or the list issued periodically by the quarterly magazine of the School of English Church Music. The list which he has thus drawn up will serve as a basis for the lists that he makes for the several Sundays as they come, of course making such alterations as may be necessitated by the circumstances of the moment or by the subject of his sermon.

3. On the questions concerning (1) the extent to which the parson may give his people the hymns that they like, though he knows them to be intrinsically unworthy, and (2) the assignment of different kinds and qualities of hymns to different parts of the service, the reader is referred to what was said in the preceding chapter (p. 250 f.). Most congregations like plenty of hymns : and this preference where it exists may be freely indulged. From a liturgical point of view, however, the common practice of singing what are called "processional" and "recessional" hymns — i.e. hymns sung while the choir walks to the chancel and back again — is decidedly open to objection ; though where it rests on long-established usage it may be perilous to abolish it precipitately. In the case of the so-called "processional" hymn in particular it is obviously rather absurd for the priest to say "O Lord, open thou our lips" in the opening section of the service, when the choir and congregation have already joined lustily in a hymn. Up to that point the service should be kept as quiet and *sotto voce* as possible, all being *said* and not *sung*. If a "processional hymn" is sung, it should be on festal occasions (or in Rogationtide) and in the proper way, i.e. from the chancel and back to the chancel — at the

Eucharist before the service and at Evensong at the end of it before the final Blessing. Where an additional hymn is required besides those at the usual and obvious points, it may be inserted at the Eucharist between the Epistle and Gospel — the place occupied by the mediaeval Sequences — and at Evensong either before the Psalms or (the more usual place) before *Magnificat*, by analogy with the Breviary Office Hymns. The use of a "Vesper Hymn" at the end of evening service need not be too seriously opposed, if the congregation are accustomed to it and like it. It is rather sentimental in effect : but simple people often find it helpful. Care should be taken, however, in its selection ; as some of the most dreadful specimens of hymnody are to be found in this category. It should be sung, too, *before* the Blessing and not after it : and the same rule applies to the singing of the National Anthem. The Blessing is obviously the *end* of the service.

II. Congregational Hymn-Practices

[Inasmuch as the author has had no great experience of taking charge of these, he has invoked the help of his friend and colleague, Dr. Sydney H. Nicholson, who has kindly contributed the following :]

Congregational practices are certainly desirable; indeed without them it is almost impossible to effect improvement or to learn new music.

The best time for congregational practices will depend upon local conditions, but normally they should last about 20 to 30 minutes, either before or after a service.

It is a great advantage to have a more or less informal "congregational choir", which can be relied on to attend regularly and to make a habit of looking up the hymns before coming to church — to be, as it were, the responsible leaders. For this purpose the services of women singers will prove invaluable, as the main object is to get a clearly defined line of melody.

Theoretically it is best that the congregation should sing only the melody in unison, but in practice it is impossible to prevent those who will from "putting in a bit of tenor or bass" or "singing seconds". Curiously enough the effect of this "natural harmony" is not so bad as might be supposed: in any case it is inevitable, and must be accepted as such. It is indeed almost true to say that provided every one sings with enthusiasm it does not very much matter (apart from the tone-deaf) what he sings !

Thus only the broadest effects are within reach in most churches. Anything that requires a lot of instruction (like correct part-singing) is normally out of the question.

But there are certain things that can be done:

(1) The congregation can be taught to start with the choir, and not to be content to join in about the second line. Playing over the tune should be the signal for all to stand.

(2) They can be taught to take deep breaths, so that the voice will be under control and phrases need not be broken. A proper supply of breath is the first essential for singing. Most untutored singers do not take breath consciously at all — it is just left to instinct.

(3) They can be taught to give the natural speech-emphasis to the words. This means concentrating on the words uttered and defining the vowels and consonants: very often the words are taken as a mere vehicle to carry an attractive tune. It is most salutary to read the words aloud, pointing out (perhaps with a movement of the hand) where the main stresses fall. This may perhaps be illustrated by taking two stanzas of Bishop Ken's Evening Hymn.

More often than not a congregation will sing this either with equal emphasis on each note whether the syllable is strong or weak, or with a regular alternation of strong and weak notes in each line. But if the words are properly read it will be seen that this regular alternation of strong and weak really only fits one line (the fourth) in the first verse.

In line 1 the stress falls on the first syllable of "Glory", not the second.

In line 2 there are only three stressed syllables : "all", "bless(ings)" and "light".

In line 3 the stress is on the first syllable "Keep", not on "me".

So the verse should be accented thus :

> Glóry to Thée, my Gód, this níght
> For áll the bléssings of the líght :
> Kéep me, O kéep me, Kíng of kíngs,
> Benéath Thy ówn Almíghty wíngs.

In the third verse another simple point emerges :

Breath must not be taken at the end of lines 1 and 3, but they must be joined to lines 2 and 4 respectively. Thus :

> Téach me to líve,* that Í may dréad
> The gráve as líttle as my béd ;
> Téach me to díe,* that só I máy
> Rise glórious at the áwful dáy.

If a few simple principles like this can be explained to a congregation, it will make a wonderful difference in the vitality of the singing. For they cannot be carried out unless people are thinking of the words they are uttering : and that is the first necessity for interpretation and expression of meaning.

(4) Warning should be given about the importance of maintaining the rhythm or "swing" of a tune once it has become established. Much depends upon a suitable time being taken by the choir and organ, but no general rule can be laid down, for the "right pace" varies with different conditions.

(5) Variety can be secured by such simple means as the use of men's and women's voices in alternation, choir alone, congregation alone, unison with organ, or unison softly and without organ. This last is one of the most impressive in effect, yet is seldom used.

(6) In teaching new tunes it is best to take the melody line by line without the words, and if the conductor can give a pattern with his voice it will be better than relying on the organ. Indeed, much of a congregational practice should be taken without any instrument.

(7) It is useful if the choir can be present at a congregational practice, but it is wise, at any rate sometimes, to place them among the congregation — not in one block, but distributed. A very good plan is for the members of the choir to stand in the aisles, one at the end of each row of seats, just as though they were in procession. This will give great confidence to the congregation and at the same time place responsibility on the individual members of the choir.

The above are a few methods that have been found useful in practical experience.

III. CHILDREN'S HYMNS

1. It is only comparatively recently that sufficient attention has been paid to child-psychology to ensure that hymns written for children shall be also *suitable* for children. The seventeenth and eighteenth centuries expected children to be religious in the same way in which they were dressed — like little "grown-ups". The *Divine and Moral Songs for Children* of good Dr. Watts enjoy an unenviable notoriety for their failure to understand a child's mentality, their perpetual harping on the improving "moral" and their indifference to the possible effect on tender minds of their grim and threatening presentation of the religion of Jesus Christ. Dr. Dearmer

(who himself possessed a quite admirable gift for dealing with children) has given us some painful examples in his *Songs of Praise Discussed*.[321] The *Hymns for Children* of Charles Wesley reveal some of the same defects — indeed he seems to have deliberately avoided writing for children *as* children.[322] Even in the middle of the nineteenth century the gracious authoress of 'There is a green hill' and 'All things bright and beautiful' was also capable of perpetrating 'Within the churchyard, side by side'. Nowadays, however, all is changed: and the children of the present have small grounds in this respect for complaint concerning the hymns that they are normally expected to sing.

2. How far should the hymns given to children be confined to those that presuppose children as the singers? For various reasons it seems desirable that they should be encouraged to sing hymns written for general use as well, so long as these are suitable to their needs and simple enough for them to understand. The child looks forward to the day when he will be grown up: and it is good to encourage this feeling and not to harden him in a "childish" mentality. Again, the children's service and the Sunday School are designed as a training for the corporate worship of later life: and the children as they grow up will be more at home in this if they are familiar with the hymns. It may be added that even "children's hymns" should be to some extent "graded", just as the children themselves are graded. All children's hymns are not equally suitable for all children. It is unkind to ask big boys and girls of fourteen to describe themselves as "little children". Nor should hymns for the young insist only on the "meek and gentle" side of the Christian character, but on its high-spirited and heroic aspect as well. All these principles are well exemplified in the *Church and School Hymn Book* published by S.P.C.K., which is also excellent both in words and music. Such hymns as

267

Canon Crum's 'Let us sing to Him who gave us mirth and laughter' (288) and Mr. Erskine Clarke's 'O, David was a shepherd lad' (243) in this, and Dean Beeching's little poem, 'GOD who created me' (504), in *S.P.*, represent a type of hymn of which those who have to deal with growing boys will wish that there were more examples.

3. In choosing hymns for children we must be very careful about *quality*. Nothing is more fatally wrong than to say, "It is only for children : it doesn't matter whether the hymn is rubbish or not". Such an attitude is "poisoning the wells" with a vengeance ! The taste of the young is malleable as that of adults is not : it is "wax to receive", even as it is "marble to retain". Herein lies our chief hope for raising the standard of Christian hymnody, both by creating a liking for good things and, even more, by forming new "associations" for good hymns in place of the old associations for bad ones, which continually hamper us in dealing with older people. "Nothing is too good for the child." This principle is more and more inspiring our secular education : and the Church must see that it does not lag behind or choose a lower way.

On this note our book may fitly close. Its main purpose has been to show how Newman's dream for the Church of England almost exactly a century ago — of "a gradual drifting of precious things upon her shores, now one and now another, out of which she may complete her rosary and enrich her beads" [323] — has been in large measure fulfilled in that sphere of hymnody which he had in mind. True, these "precious things" are mingled with not a little that is inferior or even worthless. Yet they are ours, and they come to us from every age of the Christian past. It is for us to treasure them and to give them in our worship that place of honour which is their due. We cannot hope to keep them entirely free from admixture with baser elements : for there are many to whom it is not always given to appreciate their true worth, and the spiritual needs of these may require a different satisfaction. In striving, too, as we must, to make them more widely valued we shall have to contend with all the manifold influences that incessantly debauch the public taste. Yet that, after all, is only the handicap which besets the whole work of popular education. We must simply do the best we can.

NOTES

The following abbreviations are used :

JDH   Julian, Dictionary of Hymnology (revised ed.), 1907.
FHAM   Frere, Historical Edition of Hymns Ancient and Modern, 1909.
HDRE   Hastings' Dictionary of Religion and Ethics.
LDACL   *Dictionnaire de l'Archéologie chrétienne et de la Liturgie*, art. 'Hymne', by Dom Leclercq, in vol. vi (pt. 2), pp. 2826 ff.
PHEG   Pitra, *Hymnologie de l'Eglise grecque*, 1867.
NCH   Neale, Collected Hymns, Sequences and Carols, 1914.
WELH   Walpole, Early Latin Hymns, 1922.
AH   *Analecta Hymnica* (ed. Dreves and Blume), vols. I–LV.
RCLP   Raby, Christian Latin Poetry, 1927.
BAILH   Bernard and Atkinson, The Irish Liber Hymnorum (Henry Bradshaw Society), 1897–8.
OBMV   Oxford Book of Mediaeval Verse, 1928.
SH   Selborne, Hymns, 1892 (a reprint, with additions, of art. in Encyclopaedia Britannica, 9th ed., 1881).
BEH   Benson, The English Hymn, 1915.
DSPD   Dearmer, Songs of Praise Discussed, 1933.

[1] Hallam, Lord Tennyson, *Tennyson : a Memoir* ii. 401.
[2] Augustine, *En. in ps.* 148, 17 (P.L. xxxvii. 1947).
[3] Church, *Discipline of the Christian Character* 53.
[4] Introd. to *Hymns of the Eastern Church* (1862) in NCH, 219.
[5] FHAM ix.
[6] Procter and Frere, *Hist. of B.C.P.* 312.
[7] See Wagner, *Hist. of Plain Chant* (Eng. tr.) 14 ff.
[8] SH 6.
[9] Burn, art. 'Hymns' in Hastings, *Dict. of the Apostolic Church* i. 590.
[10] Art. 'Didache' in *Enc. Brit.*
[11] LDACL 2837.
[12] Justin M. I *Apol.* 67.
[13] LDACL 2832.
[14] Duchesne, *Christian Worship* (Eng. tr.) 50.
[15] LDACL 2835.

[16] PHEG 34 ff.
[17] Cabrol, *Liturgical Prayer, its History and Spirit* (Eng. tr.) 43.
[18] A. Baumstark, art. 'Hymns (Greek Christian)' in HDRE vii. 5.
[19] See Batiffol, *Histoire du bréviaire romain* 9 f.
[20] Tertullian, *Apol.* 39.
[21] Eusebius, *H.E.* v. 28.
[22] *Ib.* vii. 24.
[23] Pliny, *Epp.* x. 96.
[24] Duchesne, *Cuvette de fontaine et jambage d'autel* in De la Blanchère, Collection du musée Alaouï, fasc. I, pt. 49, n. I, quoted LDACL 2538. Cabrol, too, inclines to this view, *op. cit.* 102.
[25] Tertullian, *De carne Christi*, xvii. xx. (P.L. ii. 781, 786.)
[26] Irenaeus, *Adv. haer.* I. xv. 6.
[27] Eus. *H.E.* vii. 30.
[28] Rendell Harris, *Odes and Psalms of Solomon*, 1909, 2nd ed. 1911 : re-edited 1916–20.

[29] Bernard, *Odes of Solomon* 42.

[30] See Leclercq, art. 'Odes de Salomon' in DACL xii. 1903 ff.

[31] Basil, *De Spir. Sancto* xxix. 73 (P.G. xxxii. 205).

[32] *Ap. Con.* vii. 48, LDACL 2847.

[33] Cabrol, *op. cit.* 102.

[34] Procter and Frere, *op. cit.* 462.

[35] Duchesne, *op. cit.* 83.

[36] PHEG 37.

[37] Eng. tr. in *Ante-Nicene Christian Library* iv. 343. Another tr. 'Shepherd of tender youth' has found a place in various hymnals.

[38] LDACL 2853 f. Baumstark, HDRE vii. 6.

[39] LDACL 2850 f. Baumstark, HDRE vii. 6.

[40] The tradition in the *Liber Pontificalis* (i. 129) that it was introduced by Pope Telesphorus early in the second century, being said by the Pope on Christmas Eve, need not be taken seriously.

[41] JDH 1109 f.

[42] Wagner, *op. cit.* 39, with references to H. Gramme, *Der Strophenbau in den Gedichten Ephräms des Syrers*, and W. Meyer, *Anfang und Ursprung der Lat. und Griech. rythmischen Dichtung*.

[43] Duchesne, *Hist. of the Ancient Church* (Eng. tr.) ii. 137.

[44] Aug. *Conf.* ix. 7.

[45] Hefele-Leclercq, *Histoire des Conciles* vol. i. pt. 2, p. 1025.

[46] LDACL 2867.

[47] Socrates, *H.E.* vi. 8.

[48] See Elizabeth Barrett Browning's essay, "The Greek Christian Poets", in her *Collected Works* (1897) 597 ff.

[49] Gibbon, *Decline and Fall* (ed. Bury) ii. 324.

[50] E. B. Browning, *op. cit.* 602 ff. See also Glover, *Life and Letters in the fourth cent.* (ch. xiv.) 320 ff.

[51] PHEG 21.

[52] See Wagner, as above.

[53] S. Petrides, *Notes d'hymnographie byzantine* in Byzantinische Zeitschrift, 1904, xiii. 421–3, quoted LDACL 2874.

[54] PHEG 42 ff.

[55] JDH 460. Baumstark, HDRE vii. 9.

[56] JDH 460.

[57] Baumstark, HDRE vii. 8. See also LDACL 2879 f.

[58] PHEG 48, 51.

[59] *Analecta sacra* etc.

[60] Crist, *Anthologia graeca carminum christianorum* (1871) LI. f.

[61] LDACL 2882.

[62] NCH 220.

[63] PHEG 10 ff.

[64] LDACL 2878.

[65] PHEG 47 f.

[66] By Littledale, *Offices of the H.E. Church* 197—metrical form by W. C. Dix. JDH 976.

[67] First published in *Hymns of the Eastern Church* (1862), reprinted in NCH 223 ff.

[68] *Ib.* 222.

[69] Baumstark, HDRE vii. 10.

[70] On these see H. Leigh Bennett in JDH 464 f.

[71] FHAM 27.

[72] JDH 606 f.

[73] *Ib.* 465.

[74] NCH 219.

[75] Baumstark, HDRE vii. 11.

[76] By H. L. Bennett in JDH 465 f.

[77] Isidore, *De off. Eccl.* i. 6 (P.L. lxxxiii. 743).

[78] Printed in P.L. x. 551.

[79] Jerome, *De vir. illustr.* c.

[80] Aug. *Conf.* ix. 6, 7 (tr. Bigg).

[81] See Jerome's statement in *Praef. in Gal.* bk. ii., 'Gallos in hymnorum carmine indociles' (P.L. xxvi. 355).

[82] Mansi, *Concilia* ix. 778; viii. 330; ix. 803; x. 623: also Batiffol, *op. cit.* 208 f.

[83] See Burn, *The Hymn Te Deum and its author*, and the same writer's *Niceta of Remesiana*; W. Douglas, *Church Music in History and Practice*, 158 f.

[84] See Dr. A. J. Mason's art. 'The first Christian poet' in *J. of Theol. Studies*, April, 1904, and another by A. S. Walpole, 'Hymns attributed to Hilary of Poitiers', *ib.* July, 1905. See also art. 'Hilaire (saint)', by X. le Bachelet in Vacant, *Dictionnaire de Théologie catholique*, and Dreves in AH. L. 1–9.

[85] See WELH 1 ff. : also BAILH i. 36 ff., ii. 125 ff. and Warren, *Antiphonary of Bangor* (H.B.S.) ii. 36 ff. Gaselee in OBMV says : 'I query the ascription to St. Hilary only because the great name of William Meyer is against it,' 205.

[86] FHAM xii.

[87] JDH 442.

[88] Duchesne, *Christian Worship*, 32.

[89] Ambrose, *Sermo c. Auxentium* 34.

[90] Isidore, *De off. Eccl.* i. 6.

[91] Trench, *Sacred Latin Poetry* 86.

[92] The subject was first critically examined by Dr. L. Biraghi in *Inni sinceri e carmi di Sant' Ambrogio* (1862). His canons and conclusions have been accepted by Dreves, Blume and A. Steier, and in England by WELH 21 ff. and FHAM xii. f.

[93] Aug. *Retract.* i. 21. WELH 27 f.

[94] Aug. *De beata vita* 35, *Conf.* ix. 12, WELH 44 f.

[95] Aug. *De nat. et grat.* 63, WELH 39 f.

[96] See WELH 50 f.

[97] *Ib.* 35 f.

[98] *Ib.* 62 f.

[99] *Ib.* 104 f.

[100] Of these hymns WELH believes that Ambrose wrote (1), (2), (3) and "inclines to believe" that he wrote (4), 25 f, 108 f, 112.

[101] RCLP 34.

[102] Gastoué, *L' Eglise et la musique*, 125.

[103] Dreves, art. 'Hymns (Latin Christian)' in HDRE vii. 16.

[104] Trench, *op. cit.* 7 ff.

[105] *Ib.* 16 ff.

[106] *Ibid.* 26 ff.

[107] Guest, *History of English Rhythms* i. 116.

[108] Bigg, *Wayside Sketches in Eccl. History* 21.

[109] On this see Chesterton, *St. Francis*, 26, 37.

[110] Glover, *Life and Letters in the fourth cent.* (ch. xi.) 253, 275. On Prudentius see also Bigg, *op. cit.* 1 ff. ; Gaston Boissier, *La fin du paganisme* ii. 123 ff. : RCLP 44 ff. ; Dreves in HDRE vii. 17 ; and art.

by Dr. Nairne in *Ch. Quarterly R.*, July, 1928. The *Cathemerinon* was published in the "Temple Classics" series (1905) with a verse tr. and commentary by Dr. R. M. Pope.

[111] Glover, as above, 277.

[112] WELH 123 ff.

[113] *Ib.* 126.

[114] *Ib.* 130 f.

[115] *Ib.* 117 f.

[116] *Ib.* 119 f.

[117] *Ib.* 121 f.

[118] *Ib.* 139 ff.

[119] *Ib.* 149 ff.

[120] *Ib.* ix. He gives one example, *Iam Christus ascendit polum.*

[121] This seems to be much more than doubtful. But *an* Elpis may have written the hymn, WELH 395.

[122] Waddell, *Mediaeval Latin Lyrics*, 300 f. On Fortunatus see also RCLP 86 ff. and Tardi, *Fortunat.*

[123] Trench, *op. cit.* 129.

[124] RCLP 94.

[125] WELH 173 ff.

[126] Blount, *Compleat Office of the Holy Week* (1687) 224 f.

[127] WELH 165 ff.

[128] *Ib.* 178 f.

[129] This poem is the longest of several poetical epistles addressed to Felix, Bishop of Nantes. The first 54 lines are printed in WELH 182 ff. Complete text in AH. L. 76 f., with much information as to the use of various centos.

[130] See WELH 198 ff. and Dreves, *Hymnologischen Studien zu Ven. Fort.*, etc., 6 f: but also RCLP 92 n.

[131] Dreves in HDRE vii. 18.

[132] So N. J. D. White, *St. Patrick, His Writings and Life* 62, BAILH ii. 208. But Kuno Meyer in a note appended to his tr. of the Lorica ('The Deer's Cry') in *Ancient Irish Poetry* (25 ff.), says, "The hymn in the form in which it has come down to us cannot be earlier than the eighth century" (p. 112).

[133] Orig. text BAILH i. 133, tr. ii. 49 f. See also 208 f. The tr. in the text is from Whitley Stokes, *Tripartite Life of St. Patrick* (Rolls series) 381.

[134] Printed in Wright, *Writings of St. Patrick* (1889) 94.

[135] Ed. by F. L. Warren for Henry Bradshaw Soc. *Antiphonary of Bangor*, 2 vols. 1893–5.

[136] *Ib.* ii. 10 (text), 44 ff. (note). See also WELH 344.

[137] Tr. by Whitley Stokes, *op. cit.* ii. 397.

[138] Text in BAILH i. 66; OBMV 25 ff. 209.

[139] Adamnan, *Vita S. Columbae* ii. 9, iii. 23.

[140] FHAM xiii. ff.

[141] Blume's view with the evidence was first set out in *Der Cursus S. Benedicti, Nursini und die liturgischen Hymnen des 6–9 Jahrhunderts* . . . (Hymnologische Beiträge, 3er Band) Leipzig. He also summarized it in his introd. to AH. LI. The learned Belgian Benedictine Dom U. Berlière accepted it on its appearance (*Revue Bénédictine*, July, 1908): also A. S. Walpole (J.T.S. Oct. 1908 and introd. to WELH xi. ff.). Walpole says that "it is now generally accepted by scholars". See, however, RLCP 38 f. and 124 n.

[142] WELH 258 f.

[143] These hymns appear in 3 only of 5 MSS. and are therefore presumably later additions.

[144] WELH 349 f., 356 f.

[145] *Ib.* 298.

[146] *Ib.* 108 ff.

[147] See *ib.* 260–91.

[148] The Latin titles are *Martyr Dei, Rex gloriose* (384), *Aeterna Christi* (104), *Jesu corona* (112), *Sanctorum meritis, Virginis proles* and *Summe confessor* (Numbers in brackets indicate page on which hymn appears in WELH). The last is not in *E.H.*, as having failed to survive into Sarum Use.

[149] Orig. text in BAILH i. 62 f. (B), tr. ii. 23 f (B).

[150] WELH 264, 276.

[151] Cabrol, *op. cit.* 99.

[152] FHAM 120.

[153] WELH 316 ff.

[154] Walpole dates it VIth to VIIIth centuries, *ib.* 377.

[155] FHAM xxiv.

[156] Dreves in HDRE vii. 18. See also Batiffol, *op. cit.* 209 f.

[157] On Paul the Deacon see RLCP 163 f, Waddell *op. cit.* 311.

[158] On Hrabanus see RCLP 179 f, Waddell 314.

[159] Dreves in AH. L. 207.

[160] *Ib.* L. 193; also Dreves, *Hymnologischen Studien* 123 ff. But see RCLP 183 n.

[161] FHAM 259.

[162] RCLP 258 f.

[163] The "Benedictine abbess of the eleventh century" to whom it has been attributed is a mere myth. See art. by Reginald Vaux in *C. Q. R.* April, 1929: also OBMV 228.

[164] On Theodulph see RCLP 171 f.

[165] Warren, *The Sarum Missal in English* i. 224.

[166] On Abelard see RLCP 319 f.

[167] FHAM 512.

[168] Ed. H. C. Hoskier, 1929. Neale's tr. of the *Rhythm* is printed *in extenso* in NCH 203 ff.

[169] RCLP 437 f.

[170] FHAM 209.

[171] AH. XLVIII. 475.

[172] On what follows see FHAM xxviii. f. and Dr. Frere's more detailed treatment in his *Winchester Troper* (H.B.S.), introd. See also Wagner, *op. cit.* 243 ff., 219 ff.; RCLP 210 ff. and Blume and Bannister in AH. LIII. introd.

[173] Gastoué, *L'Eglise et la musique* 132.

[174] FHAM xxix.; also Frere in *Oxford History of Music*, introd. vol. 157 ff.; Hughes, *Anglo-French Sequelae*, introd.

[175] See Werner, *Notkers Sequenzen* (1901).

[176] On this see Chambers, *The Mediaeval Stage* ii. 29 ff.

[177] On Adam of St. Victor see RCLP 348 ff. and Blume and Bannister, AH. LIV. introd.

[178] *Les Proses d'Adam de Saint Victor*, Paris, 1900.

[179] See RCLP 343.

[180] *Ib.* 443 f.

[181] FHAM 417.

[182] See RCLP 405 f.

[183] JDH 1043 ff.

[184] FHAM xxix.

[185] See Leclercq's art. 'Liturgies néo-Gallicanes' in DACL ix. 1636 ff.

[186] FHAM xxvii.

[187] Ib. 545.

[188] See Moffatt, *Handbook to the Church Hymnary* (1927) 149.

[189] FHAM 59.

[190] Ib. 76, DSPD 53 f.

[191] Bridges in *Collected Essays* xxi–xxvi. 53.

[192] On German hymnody the English reader may consult Catherine Winkworth's charming book, *Christian Singers in Germany* (1869); the art. on 'Hymns (Modern Christian) 1. German', by J. G. Crippen in HDRE vii. 28 f.: and that on 'German Hymnody', by Dr. Philipp Schaff in JDH 412 ff. On the earlier period the chief authority is the monumental work by Wackernägel, *Das deutsche Kirchenlied von der ältesten Zeit bis zu Anfang des XVII Jahrhunderts*, 5 vols. 1864–77. On the tunes see J. Zahn, *Die Melodien der deutschen Evangelischen Kirchenlieder*, 6 vols. 1889–93 and W. Bäumker, *Das Katholische deutsche Kirchenlied in seinem Singweisen*, 4 vols. 1883–1911, for the Lutheran and Catholic sides respectively.

[193] Johannes Diaconus, *Vita Gregorii M.* ii. 7 (P.L. lxxv. 91).

[194] *Meyers - Lexikon* (Leipzig, 1928), art. 'Otfrid' ix. 191.

[195] Winkworth, *op. cit.* 28.

[196] DSPD 36.

[197] See art. 'Bohemian Brethren's Hymnody' in JDH 153 ff.

[198] Ib. 156, 1247.

[199] Letter 698 in Luther, *Briefwechsel*, bd. 3 (Weimar ed. 1933) p. 220.

[200] JDH 322 f.

[201] Crippen in HDRE vii. 29.

[202] FHAM lxxi. 165.

[203] JDH 963.

[204] Liddon, *Life of Pusey* i. 299.

[205] See JDH 454.

[206] Canon Crum's paraphrase of Isaiah lx. in the *Winchester Hymn Supplement* (4) is such an attempt and deserves wider use.

[207] Winkworth, *op. cit.* 202.

[208] DSPD 82.

[209] FHAM 175.

[210] Ib. lxxiv.

[211] See Spitta, *Life of Bach* iii. 109 ff.

[212] FHAM 445.

[213] Ib. lxxiv.

[214] Ib. 76 f.

[215] On the history of the French Psalter see art. 'Psalters (French)' in JDH 932 ff.

[216] See Douen, *Clément Marot et le Psautier huguenot* (1878) and articles on 'C. Marot and the Huguenot Psalms' in *Musical Times*, 1881.

[217] Prothero, *The Psalms in Human Life* 178 f.

[218] Ib.

[219] *Calvin's First Psalter*, ed. Terry, 1932.

[220] Quoted DSPD 391.

[221] FHAM xliii.

[222] For evidence see JDH 44.

[223] FHAM xlvi.

[224] Fuller, *Church History of Britain* (Oxford ed. 1845) iv. 73.

[225] Thomas Wilmot, Earl of Rochester, *Poems* (ed. 1926) 106.

[226] FHAM lviii.

[227] Ib. xl. See also an art. by Dr. Frere in *Music and Letters*, Jan. 1929.

[228] Nicholson, *Quires and Places where they sing* 132.

[229] Overton, *Life in the English Church*, 1660–1714, 186.

[230] DSPD xiv.

[231] Overton, *op. cit.* 186.

[232] FHAM lxxx.

[233] For examples see *ib.* lxxxi.

[234] See JDH 1022.

[235] FHAM lxv.

[236] Bede, *H. Eccl.* bk. iv. ch. 24.

[237] William of Malmesbury, *Gesta Pontificum*, bk. v. ch. 190 (Rolls Series ed.), 336.

[238] Comper, *Spiritual Songs from English MSS. of XIVth to XVIth centuries* 213, 223 f.

[239] Ib. xi.

[240] JDH 442 f.

[241] Cranmer, *Works* ii. 412.

[242] Gee and Hardy, *Documents* 435.

[243] JDH 580 ff.

[244] Walton, *Lives*, etc. (Libr. of Eng. Classics) 221.

[245] JDH 347, 1289, DSPD xv.

[246] SH 164.

[247] BEH 60.

[248] *Ib.* 63.

[249] Wood, *Athenae Oxonienses* (ed. Bliss, 1829) iv. 86.

[250] See JDH 617 ff., 1659.

[251] *Religio Medici*, pt. 2, § xii.

[252] Letter by R. E. Balfour in *Church Times*, Sept. 17, 1937.

[253] DSPD 271.

[254] *Ib.* 372.

[255] JDH 716 f.

[256] SH 172.

[257] See BEH ch. iii. 108 ff.

[258] *Ib.* 217.

[259] Quoted *ib.* 109.

[260] JDH 350.

[261] *Ib.* 1236 ff.

[262] DSPD xvi.

[263] *Ib.* 317.

[264] Gillman, *Evolution of the English Hymn* 209.

[265] T. Wright, *Life of Isaac Watts* 70.

[266] Moffatt, *op. cit.* 192.

[267] J. Wesley, *Letters* (Standard ed.) iii. 226 f.

[268] BEH 218.

[269] See articles on 'Methodist Hymns' and 'Wesley Family' in JDH 726 f, 1255 ff; also BEH ch. v. 219 ff.

[270] J. Wesley, *Journal* (Standard ed. by Curnock) i. 475 f.

[271] *Ib.* ii. 20.

[272] *Ib.* ii. 70.

[273] BEH 225.

[274] *Ib.* 231.

[275] JDH 681.

[276] See Grove's *Dict. of Music*, art. 'C. T. Carter' i. 571.

[277] FHAM lxxxix.

[278] DSPD 254.

[279] Chappell, *Popular Music of the Olden Time* ii. 669.

[280] DSPD 34.

[281] BEH 247.

[282] *Ib.* 257.

[283] *Ib.* 263 ff.

[284] Romaine, *An Essay in Psalmody* (1775) 105.

[285] FHAM 596.

[286] BEH 336 f.

[287] L. Stephen, art. 'Cowper' in DNB xii. 397.

[288] *Ib.* 396. See also David Cecil, *The Stricken Deer* 143.

[289] BEH 340.

[290] Johnson, *Works* (Oxford 1825) vol. ix. 221.

[291] In his *Directions to the Clergy* (1724).

[292] JDH 596 f.

[293] FHAM xc.

[294] *Foundling Hymns* (1809) 81.

[295] BEH 351 f.

[296] Quoted *ib.* 354.

[297] DSPD 48.

[298] BEH 438 f.

[299] *Ib.* 498.

[300] I. Williams, *Autobiography* 37 n.

[301] *Ib.* 36.

[302] Chandler, *Hymns of the Primitive Church*, preface, viii. f.

[303] Newman, *Apologia* 303 ff.

[304] In *Christian Remembrancer* vol. xviii. 302 ff.

[305] Neale, preface to *Mediaeval Hymns* (2nd ed. 1862), reprinted in NCH 5.

[306] *Ib.* 217 f.

[307] *Christian Remembrancer*, as above, 334 f.

[308] JDH 1287.

[309] Bumpus, *Eng. Cathedral Music* 513.

[310] FHAM ciii.

[311] *Remains of Rev. H. F. Lyte* (1850) li. f.

[312] Quoted DSPD 233 f.

[313] FHAM 30.

[314] The account that follows is based on FHAM cv. ff.

[315] BEH 510.

[316] W. Davies and H. Grace, *Music and Worship* 192 f.

[317] Bridges, *op. cit.* 66 n.

[318] FHAM cx.

[319] Bridges, *op. cit.* 52 n.

[320] Ian Hay, *A Safety Match*.

[321] DSPD 195 f.

[322] See J. Wesley's Preface (1790), quoted JDH 221.

[323] Newman, *Hymni Ecclesiae* (1838) xii.

PART III

APPENDICES

APPENDIX A

A BRIEF NOTE ON HYMN-METRES

1. *Iambic*. An *iambus* consists of a short syllable followed by a long, ⌣ —, e.g. ad-ore.

The majority of English hymns are in iambic metre, which is also that of the normal type of Latin Office Hymn. In the latter case the metre is known as *Iambic Dimeter* and consists of 4 iambic feet in each of the 4 lines of each stanza or verse:

E.g. Aet-er- | na Christ- | i mun- | er-a   etc.

This metre corresponds to the English *Long Measure* (L.M.), which consists of 4 iambic lines of 8 syllables each (8.8.8.8):

E.g. For why?	the LORD	our GOD	is good;
His mer-	cy is	for ev-	-er sure;
His truth	at all	times firm-	ly stood
And shall	from age	to age	en-dure.

When the quatrain is repeated twice in each verse we have *Double Long Measure* (D.L.M.) as in 'The spacious firmament on high.'

In *Common Measure* (C.M.) the number of syllables in line 1 and line 3 is again 8, but in line 2 and line 4 only 6 (8.6.8.6):

E.g. Through all	the chang-	ing scenes	of life,
In troub-	le and	in joy,	
The prais-	es of	my GOD	shall still
My heart	and tongue	em-ploy.	

When the quatrain is repeated we have *Double Common Measure* (D.C.M.), as in 'How shall I sing Thy majesty?'

In *Short Measure* (S.M.) the number of syllables in lines 1, 2, 4 is 6, and in line 3, 8 (6.6.8.6.):

The LORD	Who left	the heav'ns	
Our life	and peace	to bring,	
To dwell	in low-	li- ness	with men,
Their patt-	ern and	their King.	

When the quatrain is repeated we have *Double Short Measure* (D.S.M.), as in 'Crown Him with many crowns'.

N.B. In L.M., C.M. and S.M. alike a trochee (— ⌣) is frequently substituted for an iambus in the first foot of a line:

E.g. Glor-y | to Thee | my GOD | this night

2. *Trochaic.* A *trochee* is a long syllable followed by a short, — ⌣, e.g. mīght-y̆.

Some famous Latin hymns are written in the metre called *Trochaic Tetrameter*, consisting of 8 trochaic feet in each line :

E.g.

| Pān- gĕ | līng- ŭa | glōr-ĭ- | ō- sĭ | prōel-ĭ- | ūm cērt |
| Sing, my | tongue, the | glor-ious | bat-tle, | sing the | last, the |

| -ā- mĭn- | ĭs |
| dread af- | fray |

The characteristic later Sequence metre (see p. 90) is also trochaic :

E.g. Lāu-dă | Sī-ŏn | Sāl-vă- | tōr-ĕm

Many English hymns are in trochaic metre, the number of syllables in a line and the number of lines varying. E.g. 'Jesu, meek and lowly' (6.6.6.6), 'Rock of ages, cleft for me' (7.7.7.7.7.7) and 'Love Divine, all loves excelling' (8.7.8.7).

3. It is impossible here to give a detailed account of the less usual metres employed. We confine ourselves to illustrating some of the terms used in the text of this book.

(*a*) "*Feet.*" An anapaest is ⌣ ⌣ —, a dactyl — ⌣ ⌣, a spondee — —.

(*b*) *Metres.* The metre of a number of hymns is *anapaestic* :

E.g. Īm-mōr- | tăl, ĭn-vīs- | ĭ-blĕ, GŎD | ōn-lў wīse

In *Elegiacs* a hexameter is alternated with a pentameter, i.e. a line of 6 "feet" with a line of 5 "feet". These "feet" are either dactyls or spondees, in accordance with certain rules :

E.g. Strōng ĭn thy | fēr-tĭle ār- | rāy || Ō | trēe of | swēet-nĕss ānd | glo-ry,

Bēaring sŭch | nēw-found | fruit || mĭd thĕ grēen | wrēaths of Thy | boughs

In *Sapphics* 3 long lines are followed by a short :

E.g. Ah, holy Jesu || how hast Thou offended,
That man to judge Thee || hath in hate pretended ?
By foes derided, || by Thine own rejected,
O most afflicted.

APPENDIX B

A TABLE TO ILLUSTRATE THE DEVELOPMENT OF THE HYMNAL SCHEME OF THE ENGLISH MEDIAEVAL BREVIARIES

The abbreviation *id.* refers to the hymn indicated in the left-hand column or columns of the same line. * Indicates that the hymn is by St. Ambrose; P.M. that it appears in the Primitive Monastic Cycle. V. Vespers; M. Mattins; L. Lauds.

	Anglo-Irish Cycle (before IXth cent.)	Canterbury Hymnal (Xth cent.)	Sarum Breviary
A. COMMON OF SEASONS			
Prime	Jam lucis orto sidere	id.	id.
Terce	Nunc sancte nobis Spiritus	id.	id.
Sext	Rector potens verax Deus	id.	id.
None	Rerum Deus tenax vigor	id.	id.
Vespers	Lucis creator optime (*Sun.*)	id.	id.
	Immense caeli conditor (*Mon.*)	id.	id.
	Telluris ingens conditor (*Tu.*)	id.	id.
	Caeli Deus sanctissime (*Wed.*)	id.	id.
	Magnae Deus potentiae (*Th.*)	id.	id.
	Plasmator hominis Deus (*Fri.*)	id.	id.
	*Deus creator omnium (*Sat.*) P.M.	id.	id.
	O lux beata Trinitas (*Sat.*)	id.	id.

A. COMMON OF SEASONS—continued

	Anglo-Irish Cycle (before IXth cent.)	Canterbury Hymnal (Xth cent.)	Sarum Breviary
Nocturns (Mattins)	Primo dierum omnium (*Sun.*)	id.	id.
	Somno refectus artubus (*Mon.*)	id.	id.
	Consors paterni luminis (*Tu.*)	id.	id.
	Rerum creator optime (*Wed.*)	id.	id.
	Nox atra rerum contigit (*Th.*)	id.	id.
	Tu Trinitatis Unitas (*Fri.*)	id.	id.
	Summae Deus clementiae (*Sat.*)	id.	id.
		Nocte surgentes (daily in summer)	id.
Lauds	*Aeterne rerum conditor (*Sun.*) P.M.	id.	id.
	*Splendor paternae gloriae (*Mon.*) P.M.	id.	id.
	Ales diei nuntius (*Tu.*)	id.	id.
	Nox et tenebrae et nubila (*Wed.*)	id.	id.
	Lux ecce surgit aurea (*Th.*)	id.	id.
	Aeterna caeli gloria (*Fri.*)	id.	id.
	Aurora iam spargit polum (*Sat.*)		
Compline	Christe qui lux es et dies P.M.	Ecce iam noctis (daily in summer)	id.
	Te lucis ante terminum	id.	id. (Lent)
			id. (Ferial)
		Jesu redemptor saeculi	id. (Easter)
		Cultor Dei memento	id. (Passiontide)
			Jesu nostra redemptio (Ascension)
			Salvator mundi (Festivals)

282

B. PROPER OF SEASONS

Season		
Advent	Conditor alme siderum V.	id. V.
	Verbum supernum prodiens M.	id. M.
	Vox clara ecce intonat L.	id. L.
Christmas		*Veni redemptor gentium V.
	Christe redemptor omnium V.	id. M.
	Surgentes ad te Domine M.	
	Audi redemptor gentium L.	
	A solis ortus cardine V.	A solis ortus cardine L.V.
	Hostis Herodis impie L.	[Corde natus, *York*] *transferred to Christmas*
Epiphany		id. V.M.
		A patre unigenitus L.
Septuagesima	Alleluia dulce carmen V.	
	Alleluia piis edite laudibus M.	
	Almum sidereae L.	
Lent	Dei fide qua vivimus (Terce)	
	Meridie orandum est (Sext)	
	Perfecto trino numero (None)	
	Sic ter quaternis trahitur V.	
	Ex more docti mystico	
	Audi benigne conditor	
		Summi largitor praemii M. ⎫ 1st
		id. V. ⎬ fortnight
		id. L. ⎭
	Clarum decus ieiunii	Ecce tempus ieiunii V. ⎫ 2nd
	Jesu quadragenariae	id. M. ⎬ fortnight
		id. L. ⎭
Passiontide	Vexilla regis prodeunt V.	id. V.
	Auctor salutis L.	
Eastertide	*Jam surgit hora tertia (Terce)	Pange lingua M.L

	Anglo-Irish Cycle (before IXth cent.)	Canterbury Hymnal (Xth cent.)	Sarum Breviary
B. PROPER OF SEASONS—contd.			
Eastertide—contd.	Ad cenam Agni providi V.	id. V.	id. V.
Ascension	Aurora lucis rutilat L.	Jesu nostra redemptio M.	Chorus novae Hierusalem V. (Sat.) transferred to Ascension (Comp.)
		id. L.	id. M.I.
		Hymnum canamus domino V.	[id. York]
		Optatus votis omnium L.	
Whitsuntide		Jam Christus astra ascenderat (Terce)	Aeterne rex altissime V.M.
		Veni creator Spiritus V.	Tu Christe nostrum gaudium L. id. V.M.L.
		Beata nobis gaudia M.	
		Anni peractis mensibus L.	
Trinity Sunday		[Ave colenda Trinitas (not in Cant. Hl. but in later Anglo-Saxon Hymnals)]	id. (Terce)
			id. V.
C. COMMON OF SAINTS			
Apostles	Aeterna Christi munera	Exultet caelum laudibus	Adesto sancta Trinitas V.M.
	id. M.	id. M.	O pater sancte L.
		Annue Christe (with special verses for individual Apostles)	id. L.V.
			[id. M. York]
			id. (general verses only) V.M.
Martyrs	Martyr Dei qui unicum	id.	[In Eastertide pts. ii. or iii. of Aurora lucis]
	Rex gloriose martyrum	id.	id. V.M.
	Sanctorum meritis	id.	id. L.V.
			id. V.L.
			id. V.M.

Confessors Summe confessor sacer Iste confessor id. id. V.M.
Christe splendor gloriae id. L.V.
Jesu redemptor omnium id. M. id. L.V.
id. id. V.M.

Virgins Jesu corona virginum Quod chorus vatum
Virginis proles V.L.

D. PROPER OF SAINTS (most important only)

Purification Quod chorus vatum id V.
Annunciation Quem terra pontus aethera V. id. M.
Ave maris stella M. id. V.
Nativity of St. John Baptist Ut queant laxis id. pt. i. V., pt. ii. M.
SS. Peter and Paul Aurea luce et decore roseo id. V.M.L.
Visitation of B.V.M. Festum matris gloriosae V.M.L.
St. Mary Magdalene Collaudemus Magdalenae V.M.L.
Transfiguration Caelestis forma gloriae V.
O sator rerum M.
O nata lux de lumine L.
Exultet cor praecordiis V.
Jesu dulcis memoria M.L.

Holy Name Mysteriorum signifer id. V.M.
Tibi, Christe, splendor Patris M. id. L.
Michaelmas Christe sanctorum decus L.
All Saints Festiva saeclis colitur = Jesu salvator saeculi V.M.
Christe redemptor omnium M. id. L.
Omnium Christe pariter
tuorum L.

Dedication Urbs beata Hierusalem V.M.L.
Corpus Christi Sacris sollemniis V.
Pange lingua M.
Verbum supernum L.

APPENDIX C

OFFICE HYMNS FROM 'NEO-GALLICAN' BREVIARIES APPEARING IN ENGLISH VERSIONS IN *A.M.*, *E.H.* AND *P.H.B.*

[The Breviaries indicated are those in which the appended hymns *first* appeared.]

First line	Use	Author	English translation
PARIS BREVIARY, 1680			
Prome voce, mens, canoram	F. of five Wounds V[1,2]	C. de Santeuil	*103 †623
Templi sacratas pande	Purif. V[1]	J. B. de Santeuil	*407=**102
Patris aeterni suboles coaeva	Dedication L.	C. Guiet	*395 †171
CLUNIAC BREVIARY, 1686			
O qui tuo dux martyrum	St. Stephen M.	J. B. de Santeuil	*65
Quae dixit, egit, pertulit	St. John Ap. M.	Anon.	*66
Emergit undis et Deo	Oct. Epiph. L.V.	N. de Tourneaux	*487
Supreme rector caelitum	Whitsun Eve L.	Anon.	*151=†629
Quae gloriosum tanta . . .	Conv. of St. Paul L.	G. de la Brunetière	*405=(1904) 227=**99
Jussu tyranni pro fide	St. John ante P.L.L.	N. de Tourneaux	*458
Christe qui sedes Olympo	St. Michael V[1]	J. B. de Santeuil	*422
Supreme quales arbiter	C. of App. M.	,,	*431 †178
Caelestis aulae principes	,, L.	,,	*432 †177
Christi perennes nuntii	St. Mark, St. Luke V[1,2]	,,	*433
Ex quo salus mortalium	C. of a Mart. V[1,2]	,,	*443=757
Non parta solo sanguine	C. Justorum M.	,,	*451

Hymn	Occasion	Author	Ref
MEAUX BREVIARY, 1713			
Lapsus est annus	New Year's Eve C.	Anon.	*72
SENS BREVIARY, 1726			
Debilis cessent elementa . . .	Circumc. V¹	S. Besnault	*70
Felix dies quam proprio	,, M.	,,	*71 †36
BOURGES BREVIARY, 1734			
Pugnate, Christi milites	Vig. of All SS. M.	Anon.	*447 †480
PARIS BREVIARY, 1736			
Dies dierum principe	Sunday M.	C. Coffin	*33
O luce qui mortalibus	,, V.	,,	*479
O fons amoris, Spiritus	Terce	,,	*208 †453
Labente jam solis rota	None	,,	*13 †265
Dei canamus gloriam	Mon. M.	,,	*39
Jubes : et in praeceps aquis	Tu. M.	,,	*40
O quam juvat fratres, Deus	,, V.	,,	*273 = †398
Miramur, O Deus, tuae	Wed. M.	,,	*41
Iisdem creati fluctibus	Thur. M.	,,	*42
Jam sanctius moves opus	Fri. M.	,,	*43
Tandem peractis, O Deus	Sat. M.	,,	*44
Supreme motor cordium	,, V.	,,	*262
Instantis adventum Dei	Advent M.	,,	*48 †11
Jordanis oras praevia	,, L.	,,	*50 †9
In noctis umbra desides	,, C.	,,	*54
Jam desinant suspiria	Xmas D. M.	,,	*58 †27
Victis sibi cognomina	Circumc. V²	Anon.	*175 †37
Quae stella sole pulchrior	Epiph. V¹	C. Coffin	*77 †44
Divine crescebas puer	Sundays after Epiph. L.	J. B. de Santeuil	*78 †46
Christus tenebris obsitam	,, V.	,,	*(1904) 85
Te laeta mundi conditor	Septuag. V¹	C. Coffin	*83 = †64
Rebus creatis nil egens	,, L.	,,	*489

287

First line	Use	Author	English translation
PARIS BREVIARY, 1736—_continued_			
Solemne nos jejunii	Lent V.	Anon.	*84
Opprobriis, Jesu, satur	Passiontide M.	C. Coffin	*496
Opus peregisti tuum	Ascension V[1,2]	"	*146
Nunc suis tandem . . .	N. St. John B. L.	"	*414
CARCASSONNE BREVIARY, 1745			
En tempus acceptabile	Lent	Anon.	*492
LE MANS BREVIARY, 1748			
Die parente temporum	Sun. M. (summer)	Anon.	*34
PARIS BREVIARY, 1822			
Caelestis o Hierusalem	Vig. of All SS. L.	Anon.	*429 †251

ENGLISH HYMNS IN COMMON USE BASED ON THE PSALMS

Ps.	Title	Reference	Author
23	The GOD of love my shepherd is	†93 ‡653	G. Herbert
	The Lord my pasture shall prepare	†491 ‡656	J. Addison
	The King of love my shepherd is	*197 †490 ‡654	Sir H. W. Baker
34	Through all the changing scenes of life	*290 †502 ‡677	Tate and Brady
42	As pants the hart for cooling streams	*238 †367 ‡449	,, ,,
51	Have mercy, Lord, on me	*249	,, ,,
65	GOD of mercy, GOD of grace	*218 †395 ‡170	H. F. Lyte
84	How lovely are Thy dwellings fair	‡525	J. Milton
	O GOD of hosts, the mighty Lord	*237	Tate and Brady
	Pleasant are Thy courts above	*240 †469	H. F. Lyte
85–6	The Lord will come and not be slow	†492 ‡658	J. Milton
86	To my humble supplication	†90 ‡121	J. Bryan (c. 1620)
90	O GOD, our help in ages past	*165 †450 ‡598	I. Watts
100	All people that on earth do dwell	*166 †365 ‡443	W. Kethe
	Before Jehovah's awful throne	*516	I. Watts
103	Praise, my soul, the King of heaven	*298 †470 ‡623	H. F. Lyte
104	O worship the King	*167 †466 ‡618	Sir R. Grant (based on W. Kethe)
122	Pray that Jerusalem may have	†472 ‡628	Scottish Psalter (1650)
130	Out of the deep I call	*250	Sir H. W. Baker
136	Let us with a gladsome mind	†532 ‡12, cf. *381	J. Milton
139	O Lord, in me there lieth naught	‡605	Sir Philip Sidney
	Thou, Lord, by strictest search hast known	*658	Tate and Brady

Ps.	Title	Reference	Author
147	Hosanna ! music is divine	‡521	Christopher Smart (1722–71)
148	Praise the Lord, ye heavens adore Him	*292 †535 ‡624	Foundling Collection (c.1801)
	Praise the Lord of heaven	†534 ‡414	T. B. Browne (1805–74)
150	O praise ye the Lord	*308 ‡351	Sir H. W. Baker

INDEX OF SUBJECTS

Abelard, 84

Accentual versification, 26, 28, 32, 36, 54

Acclamations, 18, 25

Acrostic, 26, 36 f., 39, 45, 50

Adam of St. Victor, 90, 209

Addison, J., 165, 174

Adeste fideles, 98

Ahle, J. R., 115

Akathistos, 37

Alcuin, 79 f.

Aldhelm, 148

Alexander, C. F., 66, 224, 267

Alford, H., 219

Alfred, King, 148

Alleluia dulce carmen, 73

Allison's Psalter, 137

Altar Hymnal, 227

Ambrose, 50 ff., 69 ff., 166

Amherst papyrus, 25

Anatolius, 44

Andernach *Gesangbuch*, 122

Andrew of Crete, 41

Anglo-Genevan psalter, 133 f., 146

Anglo-Irish cycle, 70, 73

Antiphonary of Bangor, 66

Apocalypse, 15

Apostolic Constitutions, 23 f.

Arianism, 29

Arnold, J. H., 75, 238

" Association," 253, 268

Athanasius, 29

Attwood, T., 82

Auber, H., 220

Augustine, 2, 29, 47, 51, 155

Aurelian, 69

Austin, J., 161, 165, 174

Bach, J. S., 101, 104, 117, 215, 239

Baker, H. W., 221 ff.

Bardesanes, 28

Baring Gould, S., 226

Barley's Psalter, 136

Barnby, J., 225, 227

Barthélémon, F., 192

Barton, W., 159

Basil, 23

Baxter, R., 164

Bede, 78, 148

Benedict, 49, 51, 69

Benedictus, 13

Bernard of Morval (?), 85, 210

Besnault, S., 96

Beveridge, Bp., 142

Beza, T., 126

Bianco da Siena, 99

Bickersteth, E. H., 227

Blew, W. J., 220

Blount, W., 61

Blume, Fr., 69 ff.

Bohemian Brethren, 106, 118

Bonaventura, 86

Bourgeois, F., 127 f., 130 f., 232

Brady, N., 142 f.

Bray, Dr., 142

Breviary Hymn-cycles, 68 ff.

Bridges, M., 217

Bridges, R., 23, 81, 101, 128 f., 145, 230, 237, 249

Bright, W., 224

Bronte, E., 6

Browne, T., 157, 162

Bunyan, J., 163

Byrom, J., 194

Caedmon, 148

Caesarius, 51, 69

Calvin, 123 f., 127

Campbell, R., 213

Campion, T., 154

Canon, 39 ff.

Canterbury Hymnal, 71 f.; Psalter, 70

Carols, 86, 99, 104, 121, 150, 241

Caswall, E., 206

Cennick, J., 179, 185

Chandler, J., 201, 205

Charity-children, 192 f.

Charlemagne, 79 f., 102

Chatfield, A. W., 30 f., 214
Cherubic Hymn, 33
Chesterton, G. K., 238
Children's hymns, 167, 180, 195, 266
Choral Harmony, 215
Chorale Book, 215
Chrysostom, 29 f.
Church and School H. B., 267
" Church Tunes," 136 ff., 146 f.
Clarke, J., 145
Claudius, M., 120
Clausnitzer, T., 114
Clement of Alexandria, 25
Clement of Rome, 17
Cluniac Breviary, 94 f.
Coffin, C., 95
Collins, H., 217
Cologne *Gesangbuch*, 122
Columba, 67, 71
Contakia, 34 f.
Conyers, R., 187
Cooke, W., 220, 226
Copeland, W. J., 205
Corbeil, P. de, 96
Corpus Christi, 74, 91 f.
Cosin, J., 158
Cosmas, 41 f.
Cosyn's Psalter, 136
Cotterill, T., 112, 194 f.
Courteville, R., 144
Coverdale, Bp., 151
Cox, Bp. (R.), 132, 146
Cox, F. E., 214
Cranmer, Abp., 152
Croft, W., 144 f.
Crossman, S., 160
Crüger, J., 112, 115

Damon's Psalter, 136
Darwall, H., 164
De la Brunetière, G., 95
Dearmer, P., 168, 182, 212, 243 f., 266
Decius, N., 109 f.
Des Contes, J. B., 97
Didache, 16
Dies irae, 91 f.
Diognetus, Ep. to, 17
Divine Companion, 144
Doddridge, P., 170
Dodsworth, W., 205
Donne, J., 156
Dorotheus, 32
Douen, 127

Drese, A., 117
Dryden, J., 81
Dykes, J. B., 222 f.

Early Christian hymns, 14 ff.
Ellerton, J., 226
Elliott, C., 220
Elpis, 59
English Hymnal, 236 ff.
Ennodius, 59
Ephraem Syrus, 28
Ephymnion, 36
Este's Psalter, 136
Eucharistic Hymnal, 227
Eucharistic prayer, 16 f.
Euchologion, 39, 43
European Psalmist, 233
Eusebius, 20
Evangelical hymnody, 186 ff.

F.B.P., 155
Faber, F. W., 217
Filitz, F., 120
Fletcher, P., 157
Fortunatus, Venantius, 50, 59 ff., 125
Foundery Collection, 177
Foundling Hospital Collection, 192
Francis, 55, 85 f.
Franck, J., 114
French " Church-melodies," 239
Frere, W. H., 11, 50, 69 f., 92, 117, 129, 132 f., 137, 139, 180, 215, 232, 234
Freylinghausen, J. A., 117
Fulbert, 82
Fuller, 134

Gascoigne, T., 154
Gauntlett, H. J., 220
Geistreiches Gesangbuch, 117
Gellert, C. F., 120
Genevan Psalter, 125 ff.
Gerhardt, P., 101, 113 f.
German hymnody, 99 ff.
Germanus, 43
Gibbons, O., 157 f., 232
Gibson, Bp., 191
Gilding, E., 192
Gloria in excelsis, 21, 24, 27, 68, 110
Gnostic hymns, 21, 28
Goss, J., 215, 219

Goudimel, C., 129
Greek Christian hymns, 14 ff., 27 ff.
    Pagan hymns, 13
Gregory of Nazianzus, 30, 32
Gregory the Great, 64, 67, 71, 102
Guiet, C., 95

Hallel, 11
Harmonia Sacra, 178, 180
Hart, A., 146
Hassler, H. L., 114
Havergal, F. R., 225 ; W. H., 215
Haweis, T., 186
Haydn, F. J., 120 ; M., 120
Heber, R., 196 f.
Heermann, J., 112
Heilige Seelenlust, 122
Heirmos, 36 f., 39 f.
Herbert, G., 156, 165, 174
Heretical hymns, 21, 28 f.
Herrick, R., 157
Hilary, 47, 50
Hill, R., 195
Holland, H. S., 238
Holmes, O. W., 237
Hopkins, J., 130 f., 133, 144
Horologion, 39, 45
Hosmer, F. L., 237
Hour- services, 68
How, W. W., 225
Howard, S., 192
Hrabanus Maurus, 80
Huntingdon, Countess of, 183 ff.
Hupton, J., 210
Hymn, definition of, 2 ff.
Hymn-practices, 263 ff.
Hymnal Companion, 227
Hymnal Noted, 84, 97, 121, 208 f., 226
Hymnary, 226
Hymns, policy regarding, 249 ff. ; choice of, 260 ff.
Hymns Ancient and Modern, 221 ff., 229 ff.
Hypopsalma, 19

Iconoclasm, 34, 38, 40 ff.
Idiomela, 34, 43 f.
Irenaeus, 21
Irish hymnody (early), 65
Irons, W. J., 91, 213
Isidore of Seville, 47, 65

Jacopone da Todi, 86
Jerome, 47
Jesu dulcis memoria, 76, 82
John of Damascus, 31, 39 f., 41 f.
John the Deacon, 102
Johnson, S., 237
Joseph, G., 122
Joseph the Hymnographer, 44
Julian, *Dict. of Hymnology*, 92, 249
Justin Martyr, 17, 20

Keach, B., 166
Keble, J., 198, 216, 221
Kelly, T., 195
Ken, T., 30, 161 f.
Kendal H. B., 186
Kethe, W., 133 f., 146, 219
Kipling, R., 238
Knapp, W., 145
Knecht, J. H., 120
Knorr, C., 117
Kyrie eleison, 18, 27

La Feillée, 84
Lampe, J. F., 178
Langton, S., Abp., 91
Latin hymnody, 47 ff., 68 ff.
Lauda Sion, 91
Laudi Spirituali, 99
Laufenburg, H. von, 105
Lawes, H., 141
Le Tourneaux, N., 95
Leisen, 103
Leisentritt, 122
Leoni, 181
Liber Hymnorum, 66 f.
Litany, 18, 46
Littledale, R. F., 226
Lock Hospital Collection, 179, 187, 192
Loewen, A. von, 114
Logan, J., 170
Lorica, 65
Lowell, J. R., 237
Löwenstern, M. A. von, 112
Luther, M., 100, 107 f.
Lyra Davidica, 192
Lyte, H. F., 218, 253

Madan, M., 179, 187
Magnificat, 13
Maintzisch Gesangbuch, 97
Mant, R., 201

Marckant, J., 153, 165
Marot, C., 125 f., 130
Mason, A. J., 33, 63, 232 ; Jackson, 213 ; John, 164
Menaea, 38
Mercer, W., 215
Methodist hymnody, 171 ff., 184
Methodius, 19, 26, 35 ; 45
Metrical psalmody, tyranny of, 124, 153 f., 166 f., 191, 199
Metrophanes, 45
Milman, H. H., 196 f.
Milton, J., 157
Mission-hymns, 250
Monk, W. H., 219, 221 f.
Monogenes, 34
Montgomery, J., 185, 194, 215
Moody and Sankey, 251, 254
Moorsom, R. M., 214
Moravians, 118, 174 ff., 184 f.
More, H., 161
Murray, F. H., 220 f.

Neale, J. M., 5, 32, 35, 38 f., 41 ff., 76, 83, 121, 206 ff.
Neander, J., 115
Neo-Gallican breviaries, 93 ff.
Nepos, 20
New Version, 142 ff., 191 f., 212
Newman, J. H., 202 f., 217, 268
Newton, J., 1, 3 ff., 188 f.
Niceta of Remesiana, 49
Nicholson, S. H., 139, 178, 263 ff.
Nicolai, P., 111
Norton, T., 133
Notker, 88 f.
Nunc dimittis, 13, 23, 128, 132

Oakeley, F., 98, 205
Octoechus, 38, 42
Ode, 39
Odes of Solomon, 22
Old Church Harmony, 215
Old Version, 129 ff., 153, 191, 212
Olivers, T., 179, 181, 188
Olney Hymns, 1, 189 f., 217
Orton, J., 170
Otfrid, 102
Ouseley, F. A. G., 222
Oxford H. B., 241, 256
Oxford Movement, 198 ff.

Palmer, R., 237
Parakletike, 38

Paris Breviary, 94 f., 200 ff.
Parker, Abp., 140
Parry, C. H. H., 222, 230, 232
Paschal acclamations, 25, 27
Patrick, 65 f.
Paul, St., 3, 11, 13 ff., 19, 20
Paul of Samosata, 21
Paul the Deacon, 79
Paulinus, 58
Pentecostarion, 25, 39, 45
People's Hymnal, 226
Perronet, E., 186
Pestel, T., 157
Petri, Theodoricus, 121
Φῶς ἱλαρόν, 23
Piae cantiones, 121
Pietism, 116 ff.
Pitra, Cdl., 25, 33, 35 f., 45
Plainsong H. B., 234
Plainsong Hymn-Melodies and Sequences, 234
Playford, H., 144, 165 ; J., 138, 147, 158, 161
Pliny, 20
Praxis pietatis, 115
Prid, W., 155
Primers, 152, 159
Primitive Monastic Cycle, 69, 73
Προασμα, 37
Proses, 89
Prudentius, 56 f.
Prys's Psalter, 139
Psalm-tunes, method of performance, 139, 145, 171
Psalmi idiotici, 19 f., 23, 29
Psalms, Hebrew, 3, 11 f.
Psalmody, antiphonal, 12 ; responsorial, 12, 19
Psalters, Metrical : French-Swiss, 125 ff. ; English, 129 ff. ; Scottish, 146 f.
Pusey, P., 112

Ravenscroft's Psalter, 137, 146 f.
Refrain, 18 f., 26, 28, 30, 36 f.
Rhyme, 54
Richard de Caistre, 150
Riley, T., 192
Ringwaldt, B., 112
Rinkart, M., 111
Rochester, Lord, 134
Rolle, R., 149
Romaine, 186
Roman Breviary, 93, 202

Romanus, 35, 37 f.
Royal Injunctions (1559), 132, 153

St. Gall, 82, 88, 102
St. Sabas, 41 f.
Salisbury H. B., 216, 220
Sanctus, 24, 68, 121
Sandys, G., 141
Santeuil, de, C., 95 ; J. B., 95
Sarum Office-Hymns, 73 ff., 203, 232, 234, 236
Scheffler, J., 116, 122
Schenck, H., 117
Schmolck, B., 118
Schulz, J. A. P., 120
Schütz, J. J., 117
Sechnall, 66 f.
Sedulius, 59
Sequelae, 88
Sequence, 88 f.
Sergius, 37
Shakespeare, W., 154
Shaw, M., 238, 245 ; G., 238
Shirley, W., 186
Sidney, P., 154
Simphonia Sirenum, 97
" Sol-fa," origin of, 80
Songs of Praise, 161, 242 ff., 258
Songs of Syon, 240 f.
Sophronius, 38
Spanish hymnody, 48, 56, 65, 74, 84
Spener, P., 116 f.
Speratus, P., 109 f.
Stabat mater, 86, 92
Stanford, C. V., 178, 225, 230, 232
Sternhold, T., 129, 133, 144
Stichera, 34, 43 f.
Stone, S. J., 224
Strasburg Psalter, 127, 132
Strong, T. B., 241
Studium, 41, 43 f.
Sullivan, A., 226
Syllabic structure of Eastern hymns, 28, 36, 39
Synesius, 30 f.
Syriac hymnody, 28, 32

Tallis, T., 140 f.
Tate, N., 142 f.
Tauler, J., 104

Te decet laus, 24, 27
Te Deum, 48 f.
Tennyson, 1
Tersteegen, G., 118
Tertullian, 19, 21
Theoctistus, 44
Theodore, 43
Theodulph, 80, 83
Theotokion, 39
Thomas à Kempis, 87
Thomas Aquinas, 74, 82, 92
Thomas of Celano, 91
Thring, G., 226
Tisserand, J., 87 f.
Toplady, A. M., 187
Tractarian hymnody, 198 ff.
Translation of Latin hymns, 75 f.
Triodion, 38
Trisagion, 24, 27
Troparia, 32 ff., 39 ff.
Tropes, 87 f., 121
Tropologia, 34 ff.
Tunes Annext, 180
Tye, C., 136

Unitas fratrum, 106, 118

Vaughan, H., 157
Vaughan Williams, R., 64, 141, 163, 225, 238, 245
Veni Creator, 81 f., 152, 159
Veni sancte Spiritus, 91 f., 98
Veni, veni, Emmanuel, 97
Vexilla Regis, 60
Victimae paschali, 89, 92
Victorian hymn-tunes, 120, 223, 229 f., 244, 253 f.

Walther, J., 110
Watts, I., 1, 166 ff., 172, 184, 266
Webb, B., 208, 226
Webbe, S., 98
Weisse, M., 107, 110
Welsh tunes, 239
Wesley, C., 2, 173 ff., 225, 234, 258, 267
Wesley, J., 118, 161, 171 ff., 187
Wesley, S., sen., 143, 173 f. ; jun., 173 f.
Wesley, S. (musician), 114, 215

Wesley, S. S., 224, 233

White, G. C., 220 f.

Whitefield, G., 174, 183

Whittingham, W., 131, 135

Williams, I., 199 f.

Winkworth, C., 103, 113, 214 f.

Wipo, 89

Wither, G., 157

Woodford, J. R., 92, 213

Woodward, G. R., 104, 121, 240 f.

Wordsworth, C., 224 ; E., 108

Wotton, H., 154

Yattendon Hymnal, 231, 237, 250

Zinzendorf, N. L., Count, 117 f., 175

Zwingli, 123

INDEX OF HYMN-TITLES
[ENGLISH]

A great and mighty, 43
A living stream, 164
A safe stronghold, 108
Abide with me, 218, 252
Again the Lord's, 87
Ah, holy Jesu, 112
All creatures of, 86
All glory, laud, 83
All hail the power, 186
All my hope, 116
All people that, 133
All prophets hail, 81
All things bright, 224
Alleluia ! hearts, 224
Alleluia ! song, 73
Angels from, 185
And now, O Father, 224
Another year, 58
Around the throne, 210
Art thou weary, 45
As now the sun's, 96, 201
As pants the hart, 144
At the Cross, 86, 202
At the Lamb's, 213
Author of life, 178, 182
Ave Maria, 216
Awake, my soul, 162
Awake, our souls, 169

Be Thou my, 200
Before the ending, 70, 72
Behold, the Bridegroom, 45
Behold, the great, 157
Behold the sun, 158
Blessed are they, 96
Blessed city, 74
Blessed feasts, 92
Blessed Jesu, 118
Blest are the pure, 216
Blest Martyr, 58
Bread of the world, 129, 197
Bride of Christ, 96
Brief life is, 85

Bright the vision, 202
Brightest and, 197

Captains of the, 95
Children of the, 185
Christ hath a, 170
Christ is gone up, 210
Christ is our, 201
Christ, the fair, 81
Christ the Lord, 107, 215
Christ, whose glory, 115, 177
Christ will gather, 118
Christian, dost thou, 41
Christian, seek not, 220
Christians, awake, 194
Christians, to the Paschal, 89
City of GOD, 237
City of Peace, 155
Come down, O Love, 99
Come, Holy Ghost, 81
Come, Holy Ghost, Creator, 81
Come, Holy Ghost, Eternal, 81
Come, Holy Ghost, our souls, 81,
  159
Come, Holy Ghost, Who ever, 203
Come, let us join, 169
Come, my soul, 190
Come, my Way, 156
Come, O Thou Traveller, 180
Come, pure hearts, 91, 213
Come rejoicing, 89
Come, see the, 196
Come sing, ye, 91, 213
Come, thou bright, 117
Come, Thou Holy, 91
Come, Thou Redeemer, 52, 69
Come ye . . . anthem, 116, 210
Come ye . . . strain, 43
Come ye thankful, 220
Cometh sunshine, 114
Commit thou all, 114, 182
Conquering kings, 96, 201

Creator of the earth, 51, 69 f.
Creator of the world, 96
Creator Spirit, 81
Crown Him, 217

Dearest Jesu, 114
Deck thyself, 114
Disposer supreme, 95, 200
Draw nigh, 66
Drop, drop, 157

Earth hath many, 58

Father, most high, 58, 72
Father of spirits, 58
Fierce was the, 44
Firmly I believe, 204
For all the Saints, 225
For all Thy Saints, 202
For ever with, 185
For thee, O dear, 85
From east to west, 59
From glory to glory, 33
From Greenland's, 197
From highest heaven, 127

Gentle Jesus, 180
Give me the wings, 169
Glorious things, 120, 190
Glory and honour, 83
Glory to Thee, 162, 264
GOD from on high, 95
GOD moves in, 190
GOD of all grace, 46
GOD of mercy, 219
GOD of our fathers, 238
GOD that madest, 197
Great GOD, what, 109, 112
Great Shepherd, 190

Hail, festal, 63
Hail, gladdening, 23, 214
Hail, glorious, 161
Hail the day, 177
Hail thee, festival, 63
Hail to the Lord's, 115, 185
Hark ! a thrilling, 206
Hark ! hark, my, 217
Hark, my soul, how, 161
Hark, my soul, it is, 191
Hark the glad, 170
Hark ! the herald, 177

Hark, the sound, 224
Have mercy, Lord, 144
He that is down, 163
He wants not friends, 164
He Who would, 163
Hearts at Christmas, 114
How are Thy servants, 165
How bright those, 169
How brightly, 111
How shall I sing, 164
How sweet the name, 190
How vain the cruel, 59
How wonderful is, 90

I bind unto, 66
I could not do, 225
If there be, 87
In days of old, 43
In royal robes, 91, 213
In the hour, 157
In the Lord's atoning, 86

Jerusalem, my happy, 154
Jerusalem on high, 160
Jerusalem the golden, 85
Jesu, grant me this, 97
Jesu, Lover, 177
Jesu, meek and, 217
Jesu, my Lord, 217
Jesu ! name all, 44
Jesu, our hope, 72
Jesu, the very, 76, 82, 206
Jesu, the Virgins', 52, 71
Jesu, the world's, 72
Jesus Christ is risen, 192
Jesus lives, 120, 214
Jesus shall reign, 169
Jesus, still lead, 117, 118
Jesus, these eyes, 237
Jesus, where'er, 191
Joy and triumph, 91, 128
Judge eternal, 238
Just as I am, 220

Kindly spring, 190
King of glory, 115, 156

Lead, kindly, 204
Let all mortal, 33
Let all the world, 156
Let hearts awaken, 72
Let our choirs, 45
Let saints on, 179

Let the round world, 202
Let thine example, 80
Let us with, 157
Lift up thyself, 31
Lift up your heads, 185
Light's abode, 87
Light's glittering, 70, 122
Lo ! from the desert, 96
Lo ! GOD is here, 119, 182
Lo ! golden light, 58, 71
Lo ! He comes, 178
Lo ! round the, 195
Lo ! the blest, 62
Lord, in this Thy, 200
Lord, in Thy name, 216
Lord, it belongs, 164
Lord Jesus, think, 31, 214
Lord of all being, 237
Lord of our life, 112
Lord, Thy word, 222
Lord, to our humble, 46
Love Divine, 178

Martyr of GOD, 71
Most glorious Lord, 154
My GOD, and is, 170
My GOD, I love Thee, 97, 206
My GOD, how, 217
My Lord, my Life, 170
My song is love, 161
My soul, there is, 157

Never weather-beaten, 154
New every morning, 216
No coward soul, 6
Now GOD be, 107
Now, my soul, 95
Now, my tongue, 92
Now thank we, 111, 214
Now that the, 203

O Christ, Who art, 69 f., 206
O come, all ye, 98, 205
O come and mourn, 217
O come, O come, 97
O Faith of England, 127
O food of men, 97
O for a closer, 191
O for a thousand, 177
O gladsome Light, 23, 128
O glorious King, 71
O GOD of Bethel (Jacob), 170
O GOD of earth, 238

O GOD of hosts, 144
O GOD, our help, 5, 169
O GOD, our Maker, 149
O GOD, the joy, 96
O happy band, 45
O heavenly Jerusalem, 200
O help us, 197
O Holy Spirit, 96
O Jerusalem the, 84
O King enthroned, 45
O Lord, how joyful, 96
O Lord, in me, 154
O Lord, turn not, 153
O love, how deep, 87, 208
O Love, Who formedst, 116
O most merciful, 197
O Paradise, 217
O praise ye, 222
O sacred Head, 113
O Saviour, Lord, 72
O sinner, lift, 110
O sons and, 87, 88
O Spirit of the, 185
O Splendour of, 52, 69 ff.
O Thou, before, 178
O Thou from Whom, 186
O Thou in all, 237
O Unity of, 45
O what the[ir] joy, 84
O Word Immortal, 34
O Word of GOD, 95, 200
O worship the King, 219
Of the Father's, 57, 121
On Jordan's, 95, 201
Once in royal, 224
Once, only, 224
Once to every, 237
Our blest Redeemer, 220
Our Father's home, 87

Palms of glory, 185
Peace, perfect, 227
Pleasant are Thy, 219
Poor soul, the, 154
Praise, my soul, 219
Praise, O praise, 157
Praise, O Sion, 91
Praise the Lord ! ye, 192
Praise to the Holiest, 204
Praise to the Lord, 116, 215
Put thou thy, 114, 182

Receive, O Lord, 29
Rejoice ! The Lord, 178

Ride on, 197
Rock of ages, 187
Round me falls, 117

Safe home, 45
Saviour, again, 226
Saviour, and can it, 178
Saviour eternal, 89
See the destined, 202
Servant of GOD, 58, 72
Sing a song, 154
Sing Alleluia, 74
Sing, my tongue, 62
Sing praise to GOD, 117
Sing to GOD, 90
Sing we all, 82
Sing we triumphant, 78, 208
Sion's daughters, sons, 91
Soldiers who are, 96
Songs of praise, 185
Spring has now, 121
Stand up and, 185
Stars of the morning, 45
Sun of my soul, 216
Sweet flow'rets, 58
Sweet Saviour, in thy, 44
Sweet the moments, 186

Teach me, my GOD, 156
Ten thousand times, 220
The advent of our, 95
The Church's one, 224
The day is past, 44
The day of Resurrection, 39, 43
The day Thou gavest, 226
The duteous day, 105, 114
The earth, O Lord, 210
The eternal gifts, 52, 70, 71
The foe behind, 121
The GOD of Abraham, 181
The GOD of love my, 156
The GOD Whom earth, 64
The great forerunner, 79
The Head that, 196
The heavenly Child, 95, 201
The holy Son, 161
The hymn for, 79
The King of love, 222
The king, O GOD, 128
The Lamb's high, 70
The Lord and King, 44
The Lord is risen, 196
The Lord my pasture, 165
The Lord of heaven, 158

The Lord will come, 157
The merits of the, 71
The night is come, 157, 162
The Royal banners, 60
The Son of GOD goes, 197
The Son of Man from, 95
The spacious firmament, 165
The strain upraise, 89, 209
The strife is o'er, 97
The sun is sinking, 97
The voice that, 216
The winged herald, 58, 71
The Word of GOD, 92
The world is very, 85
Thee, O Christ, 81
Thee we adore, 92
Thee will I sing, 129
There is a book, 216
There is a fountain, 187, 191
There is a green hill, 224
There is a land, 169
This is the day, 169
They come, GOD's, 213
Thou hallowed, 43
Thou hidden Love, 119, 182
Thou, Lord, by, 144
Thou, Lord, hast, 45
Thou wast, O GOD, 164
Through all the changing, 144
Through the day, 196
Thy Kingdom come ! on, 237
Thy way, not mine, 6
To GOD, enthroned, 89
To GOD with heart, 158
Turn back, O man, 135

Victim Divine, 178
Virgin-born, we, 129, 197

Wake, O wake, 111
Welcome, morning, 63
We plough the, 120
We sing the praise, 196
What cause, 95
What star is this, 96
What sweet of life, 43
When at Thy footstool, 219
When all Thy mercies, 165
When GOD of old, 216
When I survey, 169
When our heads, 197
While shepherds, 143, 165
Who are these, like, 117, 214

INDEX OF HYMN-TITLES

Wilt Thou forgive, 156
With golden, 59
With solemn faith, 178

Ye choirs of new, 82, 213

Ye clouds and, 58, 71
Ye holy angels, 164
Ye servants of the, 170
Ye watchers and, 122
Yesterday with, 91
You that have spent, 154

PRINTED IN GREAT BRITAIN BY WILLIAM CLOWES AND SONS, LTD.,
LONDON AND BECCLES.